Music

IN THEORY AND PRACTICE

VOLUME I

Music

IN THEORY AND PRACTICE

VOLUME I

Eighth Edition

Bruce Benward
Late of the University of Wisconsin–Madison

Marilyn Saker
Eastern Michigan University

Boston   Burr Ridge, IL   Dubuque, IA   New York   San Francisco   St. Louis
Bangkok   Bogotá   Caracas   Kuala Lumpur   Lisbon   London   Madrid   Mexico City
Milan   Montreal   New Delhi   Santiago   Seoul   Singapore   Sydney   Taipei   Toronto

Published by McGraw-Hill, an imprint of The McGraw-Hill Companies, Inc., 1221 Avenue of the Americas, New York, NY 10020. Copyright © 2009, 2003, 1997, 1993, 1989, 1985, 1981, 1977. All rights reserved. No part of this publication may be reproduced or distributed in any form or by any means, or stored in a database or retrieval system, without the prior written consent of The McGraw-Hill Companies, Inc., including, but not limited to, in any network or other electronic storage or transmission, or broadcast for distance learning.

This book is printed on acid-free paper.

3 4 5 6 7 8 9 0 QPD/QPD 0 9

ISBN: 978-0-07-310187-3
MHID: 0-07-310187-7

Editor in Chief: *Mike Ryan*
Publisher: *William Glass*
Sponsoring Editor: *Christopher Freitag*
Marketing Manager: *Pamela Cooper*
Editorial Coordinator: *Marley Magaziner*
Production Editor: *Holly Paulsen*
Manuscript Editor: *Barbara Hacha*
Design Manager: *Cassandra Chu*
Text Designer: *Glenda King*
Cover Designer: *Ashley Bedell*
Photo Research: *Brian Pecko*
Media Project Manager: *Jessalyn Clark*
Supplements Producer: *Louis Swaim*
Production Supervisor: *Randy Hurst*
Composition: *10/12 Times Roman by Thompson Type*
Printing: *PMS 162, 45# New Era Matte Plus, Quebecor World*

Cover: Digital Vision/Getty Images

Credits: The credits section for this book begins on page 395 and is considered an extension of the copyright page.

Library of Congress Cataloging-in-Publication Data
Benward, Bruce.
    Music in theory and practice / Bruce Benward, Marilyn Saker.—8th ed.
        p. cm.
    ISBN-13: 978-0-07-310187-3
    ISBN-10: 0-07-310187-7
    1. Music theory. I. Saker, Marilyn Nadine. II. Title.
MT6.B34 M9 2008
781—dc21

www.mhhe.com

Contents

Contents

Preface

TO THE STUDENT

Before you begin your study of music theory, we would like to discuss the subject in general and explain what you may expect to gain from its study. You have probably had little previous experience in music theory, and you may be wondering why you should occupy your time with it.

If you are typical of most young musicians beginning a serious study of your art, you already play an instrument or sing well, but you are interested in acquiring further technical skills and interpretive insights. You probably have been a performer for some years and have had success in public concerts either as a soloist or as part of a group (band, orchestra, or chorus). From these experiences you have developed a keen musical intuition and want to strengthen it further. Your musical intuition includes a vast storehouse of familiar sounds, established patterns of melody, harmony, and rhythm, and an artistic consciousness that you draw upon thousands of times in the performance of a single composition, without conscious remembering or reasoning. You make split-second decisions about the phrasing of a melody, the application of dynamics (indications of loud and soft), and the tempo of the music you play. Your musical intuition has become a part of you through your experience and, indeed, is one of the most valuable gifts in your possession.

The study of music theory interacts with intuition—honing, sharpening, and enhancing it with further insights and perceptions. Much of what you learn from this book will at first seem to be simply surface information, but that information will eventually amplify and broaden your musical intuition.

This book is essentially a study of patterns in music. It looks at music literature as highly organized tonal designs. With few exceptions, the terms we employ are in common use, and many of the procedures we use in analysis and composition are standard practice. The conclusions we reach, however, may differ at times from your judgments or from those of your professor. As long as your analysis is backed by logical reasoning and is a true assessment of the sounds you hear, such differences of opinion are healthy and are positive indications that you are developing your own convictions—certainly one of the objectives of the course.

Included in the book are a large number of musical examples. Each one illustrates a point we make in the text, so it is critical that you study the musical examples and, if possible, play them on the piano. Descriptions and definitions are often explained better through music illustrations than by long, involved written explanations, so our narrative material is rather short and to the point. It is vital that you experience musically the materials in this course. It does not suffice simply to know terms—you must go one step further and make these terms and ideas a familiar and practical part of your entire approach to music.

There are three types of assignments, and each has its specific purpose:

1. *Concentrated drill on a particular musical pattern or patterns.* Many patterns do not occur in sufficient quantity in a single composition to give you enough practice in identifying them, so these drills contain patterns extracted from their musical setting to let you work on a large variety in a shorter space of time.
2. *A search for patterns and relationships in a music composition.* This exploration inspects multiple aspects of a work and seeks those components that create musical style. You will gain skill in analysis, of critical importance to all musicians.
3. *Composition.* Learning to manipulate musical devices successfully in a composition is the most important goal of this text.

Summary

1. Your musical intuition is a valuable asset. Use it often.
2. A study of musical theory makes you think consciously about the patterns in music.
3. The study of music theory will enhance and reinforce your musical intuition.
4. Although terms and procedures are objective, conclusions in the analysis of music are often subjective, and thus differing viewpoints should be expected and accepted.
5. The music illustrations are even more important than textual material. Study the illustrations at least as diligently as the written material.
6. Application of terms and concepts to actual musical situations is of the utmost importance. The memorizing of definitions is in itself of little significance.
7. In the world of music the highest premiums go to those with the most perceptive, imaginative, and creative minds. Creativity combined with a thorough knowledge of music is the best guarantee for a successful career in music.

TO THE INSTRUCTOR

In the words of the composer George Crumb, "Music might be defined as a system of proportions in the service of a spiritual impulse." In the same vein, music theory might be defined as the study of the artful designs, ingenious proportions, and inventive patterns in music that are transformed by the mind into aesthetic experience. The purpose of this two-volume text is to present the basic ingredients of the art of music so that structure, design, and language are made clear and accessible to the student examining the array of tonal configurations found in music literature. The text provides a basis for the integration of the following skills and knowledge, which are important in any undergraduate theory program:

Analysis Skills	The ability to discern the design, proportions, and patterns of music.
Historical Perspective	An understanding of the rich heritage of the past and the styles of music that evolved during the different periods of musical writing.
Compositional Skills	Insight into the ways in which music is put together and into the forms, elements, and resolutions required of the composer.
A "Seeing" Ear	The ability to hear music and determine the nature of the musical devices, the melody, the harmony, the rhythm, and the form. Although this book does not address itself specifically to the topic, the professor may utilize materials from it for this purpose. (Additional material may be found in *Ear Training: A Technique for Listening* by Bruce Benward and J. Timothy Kolosick.)
A "Hearing" Eye	The ability to look at music and determine from sight alone how it will sound. (Additional material to develop this skill may be found in *Sight Singing Complete* by Maureen Carr and Bruce Benward.)
Performance	This book does not address itself specifically to performance; however, it provides ample opportunity for the developing musician to improve performance skills while gaining analytical, historical, and compositional perspectives.

Although this text is written from a traditional point of view, the following features distinguish it from some other books in music theory:

1. No previous knowledge of music theory is required; however, the ability to read music and play an instrument or sing is assumed.
2. The fundamentals of music are thoroughly presented.
3. Two-part and four-part voice leading and harmonization are considered important priorities.
4. A thorough study of melody, rhythm, and texture is included. In this way, the authors hope to present a more balanced view of the structure of music than those books that concentrate only on harmony and voice leading.

5. The text offers a historical perspective. Each chapter includes a short section labeled "History" which relates the topic at hand to the history of music. A brief overview of music history and its relation to European and American history is included in Appendix D.

6. Music from the Renaissance to the contemporary period is examined in both volumes.

7. The text integrates a study of jazz and popular music, which is indigenous to American culture, into the traditional study of European art music.

8. Specific compositions are studied. The text continually directs attention to the musical examples and encourages class discussion of them.

9. The in-class composition and performance of music is encouraged. Many of the assignments are designed to promote student interest in developing composition skills.

10. The two volumes provide a complete basis for the study of music theory. Volume 1 is usually completed in the first year of instruction and volume 2 in later courses.

11. The chapters may be studied in the order preferred by the instructor. Some recommendations for reorganization are listed in the instructor's manuals that accompany the two volumes.

12. An outline format is maintained throughout the two volumes. This format ensures conciseness, efficiency, and ease in locating specific topics.

13. This textbook is a part of a carefully integrated package. An instructor's manual accompanies each volume. It offers helpful hints in presenting class material and answers to objective text assignments. Two workbook/anthologies for students and solutions manuals for those workbook/anthologies are also available.

NEW TO THIS EDITION

The eighth edition of *Music in Theory and Practice*, volume 1, incorporates the following significant changes:

1. The assignment sections of this text have been expanded to provide additional practice materials for students. The new course-tested assignments are appropriate for both in-class study and homework.

2. All of the musical examples have been newly engraved and designed with the student in mind. The revised notation includes ample workspace and staff-size adjustments to facilitate student work.

3. The chapter on voice leading in two voices has been expanded to include all five species of modal counterpoint. This change was made in response to numerous requests for an in-text presentation of all five species.

4. Another change recommended by reviewers and reflected in this edition is the organization of the chapters. The modulation chapter now appears after, instead of before, the chapter on secondary dominants and leading-tone chords. Nevertheless, the two chapters have been written so that either topic can be presented in the instructor's order of preference.

5. The appendix section includes a summary of four-part voice-leading practices, in addition to updated listings of macro analysis and popular music symbols.

6. The macro analysis descriptions have been enhanced throughout this volume, and a large number of the musical examples include both Roman numeral and macro analysis.

7. Online support for this edition has been expanded. Resources available from the McGraw-Hill Online Learning Center include assignment templates compatible with Finale™ music notation software, supplementary drill assignments, testing materials, and additional recordings. Visit www.mhhe.com/mtp8 for these items.

8. Recordings are available for both the textbook and the workbook of this edition of *Music in Theory and Practice*. The CD that accompanies this text includes recordings for several of the assignment scores. The following graphic identifies these text recordings:

Recordings for compositions presented in the workbook anthology are included at the Online Learning Center.

Acknowledgments

I am profoundly grateful to Bruce Benward, my inspirational teacher and respected mentor, for allowing me the chance-of-a-lifetime opportunity to join him in working on *Music in Theory and Practice*. His supportive guidance and intelligent advice proved to be astoundingly accurate over the years, and I will never forget the significant influence he has had on my life. It is a genuine honor to be a recipient of Bruce Benward's legacy to the world of music theory instruction.

I would also like to thank those colleagues whose scholarly expertise contributed to the preparation of the eighth edition. I am ever indebted to Nancy Redfern of Northern Michigan University and Garik Pedersen of Eastern Michigan University for creating new recordings to accompany both volumes of the textbook and the workbook. I am also grateful for the generous support provided by Mark Pappas of Eastern Michigan University—particularly with regard to the newly updated jazz and popular music symbols. The thoughtful care with which these three musicians approach their scholarship has significantly benefited *Music in Theory and Practice,* and I am grateful for their contributions.

Grateful acknowledgement is extended to the following individuals, whose suggestions and reviews were extremely helpful:

Marc Aust, *Eastern Michigan University*
Bill Carmody, *Sierra College*
Thomas M. Couvillon, Jr., *Sam Houston State University*
James L. Denman, *Seattle Pacific University*
Warren Gooch, *Truman State University*
G. Fredrick Guzasky, *Bridgewater State College*
Paul Halversen, *Spokane Falls Community College*
Jason Haney, *James Madison University*
Robert Howard, *McKendree College*
Darleen Mitchell, *University of Nebraska at Kearney*
Kathy Morgan, *Collin County Community College*
Roy Nitzberg, *Queens College*
Terry A. Oxley, *Bloomsburg University*
Rosângela Yazbec Sebba, *Mississippi State University*
Edward W. West, *Oral Roberts University*

My acknowledgements would not be complete without mentioning the highly professional staff at McGraw-Hill. The expert guidance provided by Chris Freitag, Melody Marcus, Barbara Curialle, Beth Ebenstein, Marley Magaziner, and Jeff Neel has been invaluable, and I am indebted to Holly Paulsen, Barbara Hacha, Jerome O'Mara, and the entire production staff for their attentive assistance. Appreciation is also extended to John Pierce and Gary Karsten of Thompson Type for their generous help with the new art files. I cannot imagine a better team of colleagues and am grateful for their continuing support of *Music in Theory and Practice.*

Marilyn Saker

The Materials of Music: Sound and Time

TOPICS

Sound	Tone	Beat
Vibration	Intensity	Rhythm
Compression	Acoustics	Timbre
Rarefaction	Decibels	Harmonic Series
Frequency	Duration	Partials
Pitch	Meter	Fundamental

The basic materials of music are sound and time. When you play an instrument or sing, you are producing sounds, so it is important that you thoroughly understand these basic materials. Sounds are used to structure time in music. Time occurs in the duration of the sounds and the silences between sounds. This book is devoted to a study of the complex relationship between these two basic materials.

SOUND

Sound is the sensation perceived by the organs of hearing when vibrations (sound waves) reach the ear.

Vibration

Vibration is the periodic motion of a substance. When you play an instrument, parts of the instrument (the strings, sounding board, etc.) and the air inside and around the instrument vibrate.

Compression and Rarefaction

These terms refer to the alternation of increased (*compression*) and decreased (*rarefaction*) pressure in the air caused by an activated (vibrating) surface or air column. One complete cycle of compression and rarefaction produces a vibration, or sound wave.

Sound Waves

Compression
(increased air pressure)   +

Elastic Surface at Rest

Rarefaction
(decreased air pressure)   −

Compressions

Rarefactions

Frequency	*Frequency* refers to the number of compression–rarefaction cycles that occur per unit of time, usually one second. Audible sounds for the human ear range from 20 to 20,000 cycles per second.

THE FOUR PROPERTIES OF SOUND

Sound has four identifiable characteristics or properties: *pitch, intensity, duration,* and *timbre.* Despite how complicated a composition may be, these four are the only variables with which composers and performers have to work.

Pitch

Pitch is the highness or lowness of a sound. Variations in frequency are what we hear as variations in pitch: The greater the number of sound waves produced per second of an elastic body, the higher the sound we hear; the fewer sound waves per second, the lower the sound.

Tone

A *tone* is a musical sound of definite pitch.

Intensity

Intensity (amplitude) is heard as the loudness or softness of a pitch. In *acoustics* (the science of sound), intensity is the amount of energy affecting the vibrating body, and the physicist measures intensity on a scale from 0 to 130 in units called *decibels.* In musical notation, gradations of intensity are indicated with the following Italian words and their abbreviations:

Italian Word	Symbol	Translation	Average Decibels
Pianissimo	*pp*	Very soft	40
Piano	*p*	Soft	50
Mezzo piano	*mp*	Moderately soft	60
Mezzo forte	*mf*	Moderately loud	70
Forte	*f*	Loud	80
Fortissimo	*ff*	Very loud	100

Duration

Duration is the length of time a pitch, or tone, is sounded. For patterns of duration, the following terms are used: *meter* and *rhythm.*

Meter

Meter describes regularly recurring pulses of equal duration, generally grouped into patterns of two, three, four, or more with one of the pulses in each group accented. These patterns of strong (>) and weak (⌣) pulses are called *beats.* For example:

Duple (two-beat) meter and triple (three-beat) meter are the two basic meters. All other meters result from some combination of these two.

Rhythm

Operating in conjunction with the meter, *rhythm* is a pattern of uneven durations. While the steady beats of the meter combine to form measures, a rhythm may be a pattern of almost any length.

Meter   Rhythm

Meter   Rhythm

Timbre

Timbre is the tone quality or color of a sound. It is the property of sound that permits us, for instance, to distinguish the difference between the sound of a clarinet and an oboe.

This sound quality is determined by the shape of the vibrating body, its material (metal, wood, human tissue), and the method used to put it in motion (striking, bowing, blowing, plucking). It is also the result of the human ear's perception of a series of tones called the harmonic series, which is produced by all instruments.

Harmonic Series

A *harmonic series* includes the various pitches produced simultaneously by a vibrating body. This physical phenomenon results because the body vibrates in sections as well as in a single unit. A string, for example, vibrates along its entire length as well as in halves, thirds, quarters, and so on.

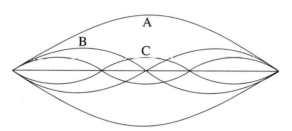

A—String Vibrating as a Unit
B—String Vibrating in Halves
C—String Vibrating in Thirds

Partials

The pitches produced simultaneously by the vibrating sections are called *partials* or *harmonics.* The first partial, often called the *fundamental,* and the series of partials constitute a musical tone. Since the fundamental is the lowest frequency and is also perceived as the loudest, the ear identifies it as the specific pitch of the musical tone.

Although the harmonic series theoretically goes to infinity, there are practical limits; the human ear is insensitive to frequencies above 20,000 Hz. (Hz is the abbreviation for hertz, a standard measurement of frequency expressed in cycles per second.) The following illustration carries the harmonic series of an A fundamental to the sixteenth partial:

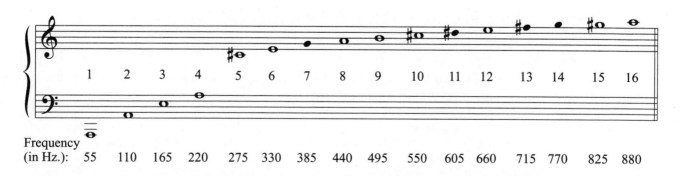

	1	2	3	4	5	6	7	8	9	10	11	12	13	14	15	16
Frequency (in Hz.):	55	110	165	220	275	330	385	440	495	550	605	660	715	770	825	880

The individual partials that make up a musical tone are not distinguished separately but are heard by the human ear as a blend that characterizes timbre.

You may notice that the harmonic series looks very similar to the "open" tones on brass instruments. The brass instruments and some other instruments, such as the woodwinds, are capable of playing various pitches in the harmonic series.

SUMMARY

Music is an art of sound and time, and the basic characteristics of musical tone—pitch, duration, intensity, and timbre—are the fundamental elements. The principal concern in this book will be to determine how musical tones interact with each other to produce music.

The Fundamentals of Music

Before you begin your study of the structure of music, you must first understand the notation and basic elements of music: the fundamentals of music. As an experienced musician, you have probably learned many of these concepts in your previous studies. Our purpose here is to present these basic musical facts in a systematic way to aid you in gaining fluency and filling any gaps in your knowledge. Even if you know the materials presented here, we urge you to take this opportunity to practice until you can recall the fundamentals without a moment of hesitation. Your success in understanding the structure of music will depend on this ability.

Our goal in this and the following book is to show you how music is put together. We will deal with a wide variety of music from very early to the most recent, from art music to folk and popular music. As a prelude to this adventure, you must understand in broad terms the history of Western music and see the relationships among the various styles. For this reason we have included a brief overview of music history in Appendix D. We wish you success in your work and hope that you find here the beginning of a lifetime of exciting and serious study of the art of music.

CHAPTER 1

Notation

TOPICS

Pitch
Staff
Letter Names
Clefs
Treble Clef
Bass Clef
Grand Staff
Middle C
Ledger Lines
C Clef
Alto Clef
Tenor Clef
Soprano Clef
Mezzo Soprano Clef
Baritone Clef
Octave Identification
Accidentals
Sharp
Flat
Natural
Double Sharp
Double Flat
Interval
Enharmonic Equivalents
Half-Step Motion
Duration
Breve and Rest
Whole Note and Rest
Half Note and Rest
Quarter Note and Rest
Eighth Note and Rest
Sixteenth Note and Rest
Thirty-Second Note and Rest
Sixty-Fourth Note and Rest
Tie
Dot
Second Dot
Irregular Divisions and Subdivisions
Rhythm
Pulse or Beat
Meter
Meter Signatures
Simple Meter
Compound Meter
Duple, Triple, and Quadruple Meters
Asymmetrical Meter
Syncopation
Dynamic Markings

IMPORTANT CONCEPTS

Music notation is much more precise and complicated than written language. When we notate music, we use symbols that show three of the four properties of sound described in the introduction: pitch and duration are given accurately, and relative intensity is indicated. Furthermore, pitch and duration are shown simultaneously.

Notation of Pitch

The term *pitch* describes the highness or lowness (the frequency) of a tone. In music notation, pitches are represented by symbols positioned on a staff and identified with letter names.

The Staff

The *staff* consists of five equally spaced horizontal lines.

Figure 1.1

Five Lines 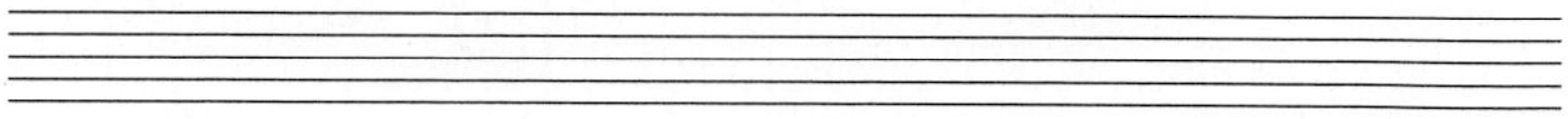

Letter Names

The various pitches are referred to by the first seven letters of the alphabet (A B C D E F G), as shown on the piano keyboard in Figure 1.2.

Figure 1.2

The Clefs

A *clef* is a symbol placed at the beginning of a line of music that establishes the letter names of the lines and spaces of the staff.

Treble Clef (G)

The *treble clef* or *G clef* is an ornate letter G. The curved line terminates at the second line of the staff, thus designating the letter name of a note on that line as G.

Figure 1.3

Staff with Treble or G Clef

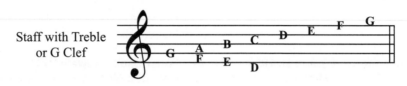

Bass Clef (F)

The *bass clef* is called the *F clef* because it was derived from the letter F. The dots are placed above and below the fourth line of the staff, designating that line as F.

Figure 1.4

Staff with Bass or F Clef

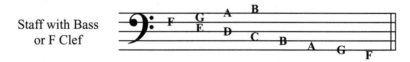

Grand Staff

Together, the treble and bass staves make up a *grand staff.* Figure 1.5 shows the point at which both clefs converge. The two Cs are the same pitch: *middle C.*

Figure 1.5

Grand Staff

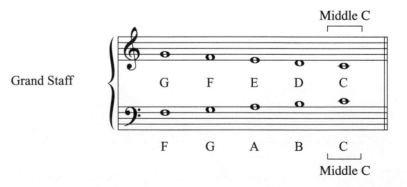

PART A   The Fundamentals of Music

The grand staff is associated most often with keyboard music. Figure 1.6 shows the relationship between the grand staff, the standard 88-key piano keyboard, and middle C.

Figure 1.6

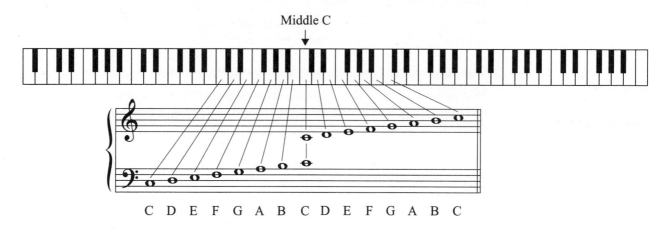

Middle C

C D E F G A B C D E F G A B C

Ledger Lines

Pitches that go beyond the limits of the staff are written by adding *ledger lines* above or below the staff. Ledger lines, which parallel the staff, accommodate only one note (see Figure 1.7).

Figure 1.7

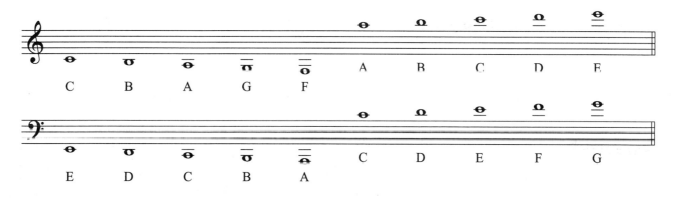

C Clef

A *C clef* may be positioned on any line of the staff to designate middle C. This clef is coupled with a set of secondary names that identify each of the possible positions (see Figure 1.8).

Figure 1.8

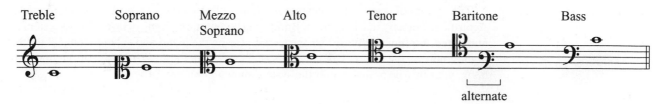

Alto Clef

The *alto clef* is a C clef that designates the third line of the staff as middle C. It is the standard clef used in music for viola.

Tenor Clef

The *tenor clef* is a C clef that designates the fourth line of the staff as middle C. The tenor clef is occasionally found in music written for cello, bassoon, or trombone.

Soprano, Mezzo Soprano, and Baritone Clefs

The *soprano, mezzo soprano,* and *baritone clefs* are C clefs used less often than the alto and tenor clefs. In each case the line indicated by the notch of the clef is designated as middle C.

Do Ex 1.1, 1.2

Octave Identification

Since the pitch spectrum is so wide, it is often necessary to identify a specific note by the *octave* in which it appears. Thus, middle C is distinguished from any other C in the pitch spectrum by the written designation C4 (see Figure 1.9).

Figure 1.9

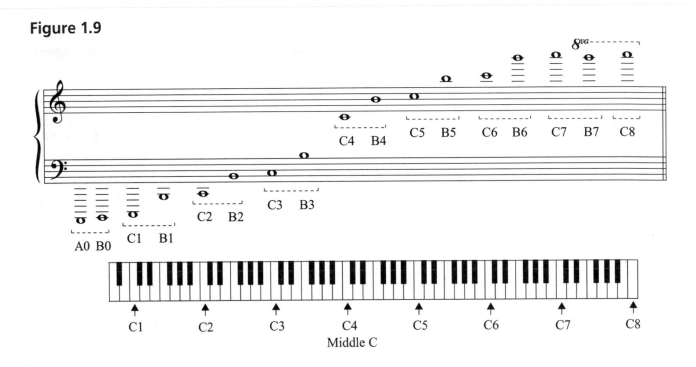

The *8va* above the right portion of the treble staff in Figure 1.9 means that the pitch sounds an octave above the written note. This symbol is used when a large number of ledger lines make note reading difficult. A related symbol, *8vb,* is used to indicate when a pitch sounds an octave below the written note.

The system of octave identification in Figure 1.9 is recommended by the International Acoustical Society and is used in Braille music notation. Each octave of this system is numbered, beginning with A0 for the lowest note on the piano and extending to C8 for the highest note on the piano. Although the system shown in Figure 1.9 is used throughout this book, your instructor may prefer the system shown in Figure 1.10.

Figure 1.10

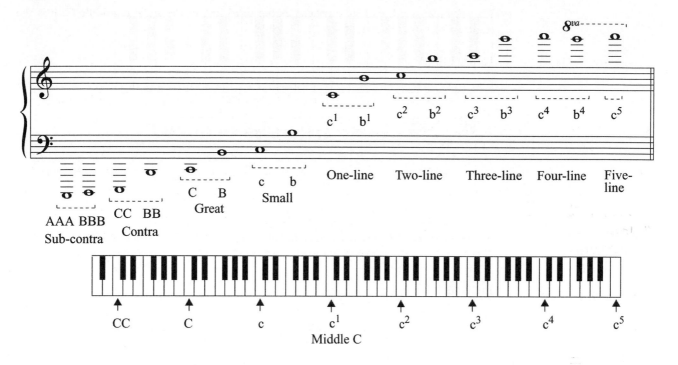

The octave identification system in Figure 1.10 is often referred to as the Helmholtz system after the German acoustician who made the system popular. This widely used designation method has been prevalent since the nineteenth century.

Accidentals

Accidentals are symbols that are placed to the left of the noteheads to indicate the raising or lowering of a pitch.

Sharp (♯)—raises the pitch a half step.

Flat (♭)—lowers the pitch a half step.

Natural (♮)—cancels any previous sharp or flat and returns to the natural, or unaltered, pitch.

Double Sharp (✕)—raises the pitch two half steps.

Double Flat (♭♭)—lowers the pitch two half steps.

Figure 1.11

G Sharp   G Flat   G Natural   G Double-Sharp   G Double-Flat

Interval

An *interval* is the relationship between two tones. In Western music, the half step is the smallest interval used. It is the interval between any two adjacent keys—black or white—on the keyboard.

Figure 1.12

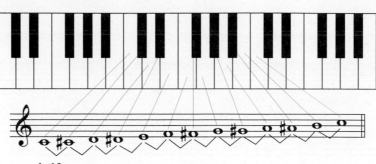

half steps

Do Ex: 1.3

Enharmonic Equivalents

Enharmonic equivalents are tones that have the same pitch but different letter names.

Figure 1.13

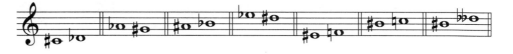

Do Ex 1.4

Half-Step Motion

In passages of music involving *half-step motion,* a flatted note is followed most often by a note with a different letter name a half step lower.

Figure 1.14

A sharped note is followed most often by a note with a different letter name a half step higher in passages involving half-step motion.

Figure 1.15

The notation of *duration* is illustrated in the following chart:

Notation of Duration

PART A   The Fundamentals of Music

Figure 1.16

Name	Note	Rest	Equivalents	
Breve (Double Whole Note)	⊟ or ‖o‖		Two Whole Notes	
Whole Note	o		Two Half Notes	
Half Note			Two Quarter Notes	
Quarter Note			Two Eighth Notes	
Eighth Note			Two Sixteenth Notes	
Sixteenth Note			Two Thirty-second Notes	
Thirty-second Note			Two Sixty-fourth Notes	
Sixty-fourth Note			Two One Hundred Twenty-eighth Notes	

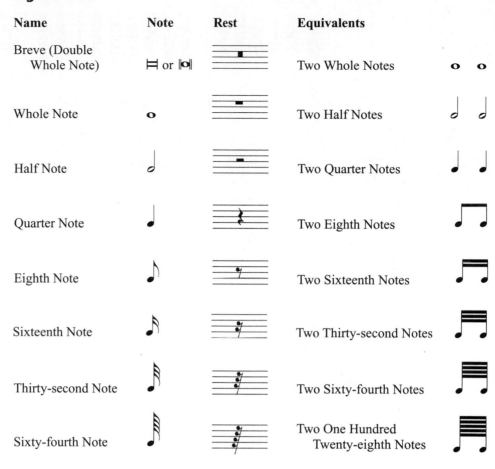

The Tie

The *tie* is a curved line that connects two adjacent notes of the same pitch into a single sound with a duration equal to the sum of both note values.

Figure 1.17

The Dot

Placed to the right of a note head, the *dot* lengthens the value of the note by half again its value. A *second dot* lengthens the dotted note value by half the length of the first dot.

Figure 1.18

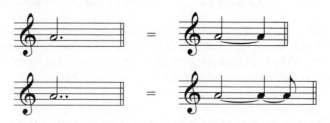

Dots may also be used with rests and affect them in the same way.

Figure 1.19

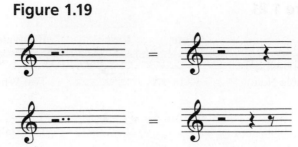

Irregular Division of Notes

A note value may be divided or subdivided into any number of equal parts, as shown in the chart in Figure 1.20. Those divisions and subdivisions that require added numbers are called *irregular divisions and subdivisions*.

Figure 1.20

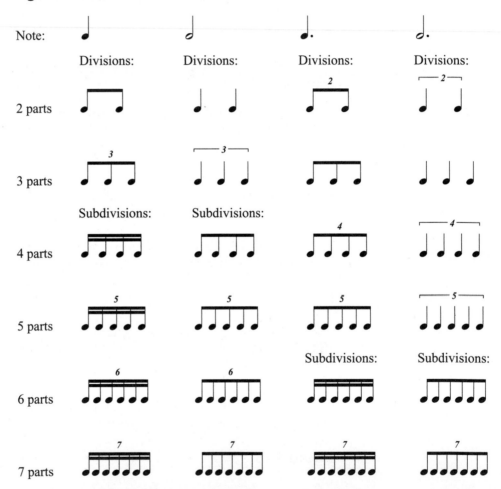

Rhythm

Rhythm is a general term used to describe the motion of music in time. The fundamental unit of rhythm is the *pulse* or *beat*. Even persons untrained in music generally sense the pulse and may respond by tapping a foot or clapping.

Meter Signatures

Meter can be defined as a regular, recurring pattern of strong and weak beats. This recurring pattern of durations is identified at the beginning of a composition by a *meter signature* (time signature).

Figure 1.21

The upper digit indicates the number of basic note values per measure. It may or may not indicate the number of pulses per measure (as we will be see later in compound meters).

The lower digit indicates a basic note value: **2** signifies a half note, **4** refers to a quarter note, **8** to an eighth note, and so forth.

Figure 1.22

Although meter is generally indicated by time signatures, it is important to realize that meter is not simply a matter of notation.

Simple Meter

In *simple meter,* each beat is divided in two parts (simple division). The upper numbers in simple meter signatures are usually **2**, **3**, or **4** indicating two, three, or four basic pulses. Some simple meters showing the division of the beat are shown in Figure 1.23.

Figure 1.23

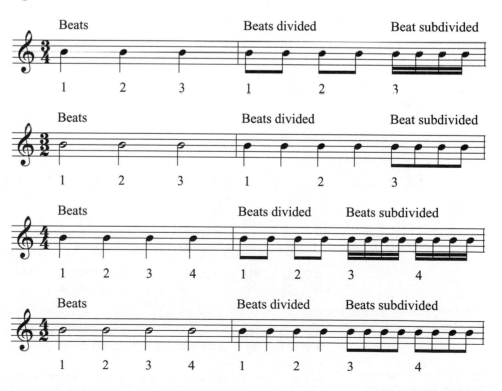

The basic pulse in simple meter will be some kind of a note value that is *not* dotted:

Figure 1.24

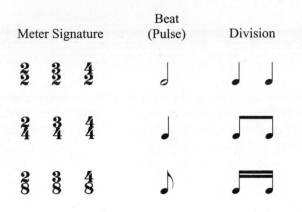

In compound meter, each pulse is a dotted note, which is divided into groups of three parts (compound division). The upper numbers in compound meter signatures are usually **6**, **9**, and **12**. In compound meter signatures, the lower number refers to the division of the beat, whereas the upper number indicates the number of these divisions per measure.

Compound Meter

Figure 1.25

Note that the basic pulse in compound meter will be some kind of dotted note value:

Figure 1.26

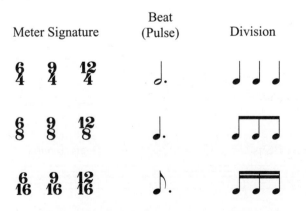

In $\frac{6}{8}$ meter there are only two basic pulses, in $\frac{9}{8}$ meter there are three, and in $\frac{12}{8}$ meter there are four.

Figure 1.27

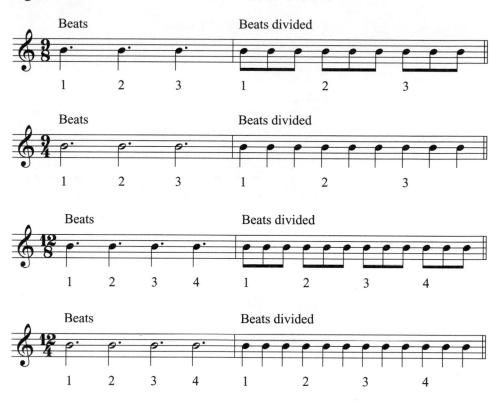

Duple, Triple, and Quadruple Meters

Both simple and compound meters will have two, three, or four recurring pulses. Meters are identified as *duple* if there are two basic pulses, *triple* if there are three, or *quadruple* if there are four. These designations are often combined with the division names to describe a meter. For example, $\frac{2}{4}$ is a "simple duple" meter and $\frac{6}{8}$ is a "compound duple" meter.

Figure 1.28

	Simple Meters			Compound Meters		
Duple Meters	$\frac{2}{4}$	$\frac{2}{2}$	$\frac{2}{8}$	$\frac{6}{8}$	$\frac{6}{4}$	$\frac{6}{16}$
Triple Meters	$\frac{3}{4}$	$\frac{3}{2}$	$\frac{3}{8}$	$\frac{9}{8}$	$\frac{9}{4}$	$\frac{9}{16}$
Quadruple Meters	$\frac{4}{4}$	$\frac{4}{2}$	$\frac{4}{8}$	$\frac{12}{8}$	$\frac{12}{4}$	$\frac{12}{16}$

Asymmetrical Meters

The term *asymmetrical* means "not symmetrical" and applies to those meter signatures that indicate the pulse cannot be divided into equal groups of 2, 3, or 4 beats. The upper numbers in asymmetrical meters are usually 5 or 7.

Figure 1.29

Asymmetrical Meter Signatures:

| **Syncopation** | If a part of the measure that is usually unstressed is accented, the rhythm is considered to be *syncopated*. |

Figure 1.30

Beethoven: String Quartet in C-sharp Minor, op. 131, IV, mm. 1–4.

Parker: *Au Privave*, mm. 1–4.

Beethoven: String Quartet in A Major, op. 18, no. 5, III, Variation I, mm. 7–8.

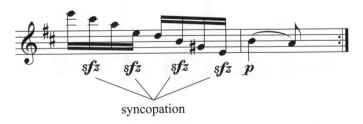

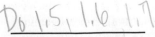

Dynamic Markings

Dynamic markings indicate the general volume (amplitude) of sound. Although imprecise, such marks denote approximate levels of intensity. The following words, abbreviations, and signs are common:

Symbol	Term	Definition
pp	Pianissimo	Very soft
p	Piano	Soft
mp	Mezzo piano	Moderately soft
mf	Mezzo forte	Moderately loud
f	Forte	Loud
ff	Fortissimo	Very loud
<	Crescendo (cresc.)	Gradually become louder
>	Decrescendo (decresc.), or diminuendo (dim.)	Gradually become softer
sfz, sf	Sforzando, sforzato	Sudden accent on a single note or chord
sfp	Sforzando piano	Sudden accent followed immediately by soft
fp	Fortepiano	Loud followed immediately by soft

History

The notation of both pitch and duration has evolved over the centuries. It has been a gradual process of transformation that continues yet today.

Neumatic Notation

From about 650 to 1200, music notation consisted of a set of symbols called *neumes* (pronounced "newms"). These symbols took their name from the Greek word *forgesture*. Written above the Latin texts associated with the liturgy of the Christian church, neumes could not convey pitch or duration, but rather served as a memory aid in recalling previously learned melodic lines. Figure 1.31 is an example of neumatic notation from a twelfth-century manuscript.

Figure 1.31

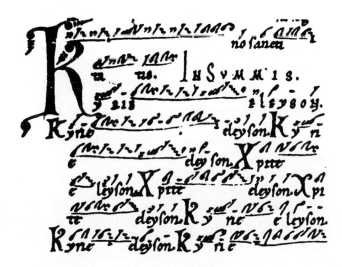

Horizontal lines were gradually added to indicate the locations of F and C. In the eleventh century, a four-line staff appeared that included the F line, the C line, and two additional lines. Later, neumes were square or diamond-shaped, as shown in Figure 1.32. Combined with the staff, neumes could now indicate specific pitches. The four-line staff is still used to notate Gregorian chant.

Figure 1.32

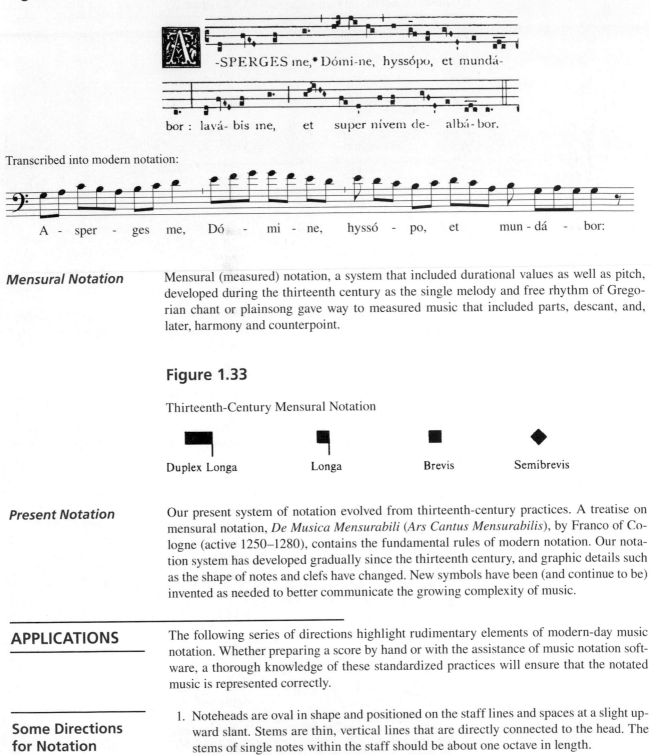

Transcribed into modern notation:

Mensural (measured) notation, a system that included durational values as well as pitch, developed during the thirteenth century as the single melody and free rhythm of Gregorian chant or plainsong gave way to measured music that included parts, descant, and, later, harmony and counterpoint.

Mensural Notation

Figure 1.33

Thirteenth-Century Mensural Notation

| Duplex Longa | Longa | Brevis | Semibrevis |

Present Notation

Our present system of notation evolved from thirteenth-century practices. A treatise on mensural notation, *De Musica Mensurabili* (*Ars Cantus Mensurabilis*), by Franco of Cologne (active 1250–1280), contains the fundamental rules of modern notation. Our notation system has developed gradually since the thirteenth century, and graphic details such as the shape of notes and clefs have changed. New symbols have been (and continue to be) invented as needed to better communicate the growing complexity of music.

APPLICATIONS

The following series of directions highlight rudimentary elements of modern-day music notation. Whether preparing a score by hand or with the assistance of music notation software, a thorough knowledge of these standardized practices will ensure that the notated music is represented correctly.

Some Directions for Notation

1. Noteheads are oval in shape and positioned on the staff lines and spaces at a slight upward slant. Stems are thin, vertical lines that are directly connected to the head. The stems of single notes within the staff should be about one octave in length.

Figure 1.34

Stems one octave long

2. When a staff contains only a single melody, stems go down on those notes above the middle line and up on those notes below the middle line. When a note is on the middle line, the stem is usually down, except when the stems of adjacent notes are in the opposite direction.

Figure 1.35

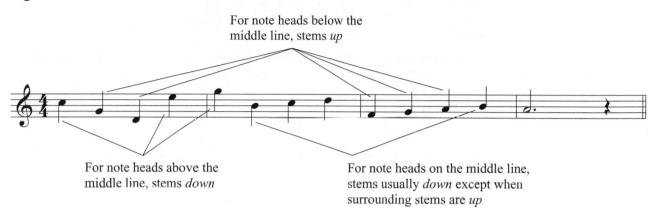

For note heads below the middle line, stems *up*

For note heads above the middle line, stems *down*

For note heads on the middle line, stems usually *down* except when surrounding stems are *up*

3. When stemmed notes are placed on ledger lines, the stems should extend to the middle line of the staff.

Figure 1.36

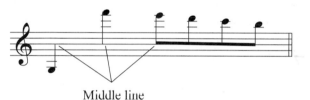

Middle line

4. When connected by beams, stemmed notes should be modified so that the beams are slanted to cross no more than one line of the staff for each group of notes. Beams are slightly thicker than note stems.

Figure 1.37

Beam does not pass more than one staff line per two notes

5. When two melodies occupy the same staff, the stems for one melody are up, and the stems for the other melody are down. This makes it possible to distinguish the melodies.

Figure 1.38

Wrong   Right

6. Beam groups of eighth notes (and smaller values) according to the beats in the measure.

Figure 1.39

7. In compound meter, it is important to show the basic pulse structure of the measure and the division (of three) as clearly as possible.

Figure 1.40

8. Use flags for eighth or shorter-value notes that are not grouped within a beat.

Figure 1.41

9. Connect no more than six notes by beams unless all are part of one beat.
10. Flagged and beamed notes are generally not mixed, except when notating vocal music. In vocal music, flagged notes have traditionally been used when the text–music relationship involves one note for each syllable. However, modern practice has moved toward the use of "instrumental" notation for vocal music.

Figure 1.42

PART A   The Fundamentals of Music

11. Irregular divisions of a beat or measure are indicated by showing the number of notes in the resulting group by means of an Arabic numeral. The note values of the irregular group are notated the same way as the regular group, provided the number of notes in the irregular group is less than twice that of the regular. For example, a triplet retains the same note values as a regular duplet.

Figure 1.43

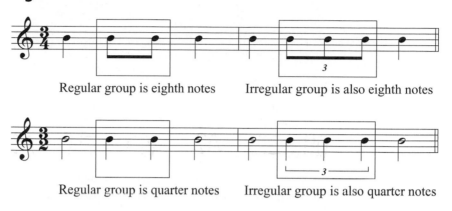

Regular group is eighth notes   Irregular group is also eighth notes

Regular group is quarter notes   Irregular group is also quarter notes

When the number of notes in the irregular group is more than twice the number of the regular, then the next smaller note value is used; for example, a quintuplet would employ the next smaller note value.

Figure 1.44

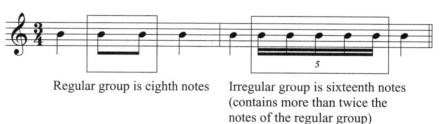

Regular group is eighth notes   Irregular group is sixteenth notes
(contains more than twice the
notes of the regular group)

12. The whole rest can be used to indicate a full measure of rest in any meter.
13. Use two quarter rests rather than a half rest in $\frac{3}{4}$ meter.

Figure 1.45

Wrong   Right

14. When notes of a chord are on an adjacent line and space, the higher of the two is always to the right, regardless of the direction of the stem.

Figure 1.46

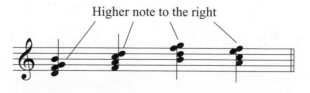

Higher note to the right

15. When a dotted note is on a line, the dot is usually placed slightly above the line. When two separate voices are placed on a single staff, the dots are below the line on the notes with stems down.

Figure 1.47

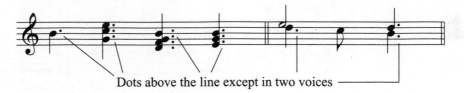

Dots above the line except in two voices

16. Dynamic markings should be added above, between, or below staves according to the nature of the music or score:

Instrumental Music

The markings in *instrumental music* are usually placed beneath the staff to which they refer. Sometimes, because of inadequate space, it is necessary to place markings above the staff.

Vocal Music

Vocal music markings are usually placed above the staff to which they refer. This is done to avoid confusion with the words of the text.

Piano Scores

The markings in *piano scores* are placed between the staves if the markings are to apply to both staves. If markings are needed for each staff individually, the markings should go just above or below the staff to which they refer.

Markings should not be placed on the staff, although the crescendo and diminuendo will protrude into the staff on occasion.

Figure 1.48

11/02/10

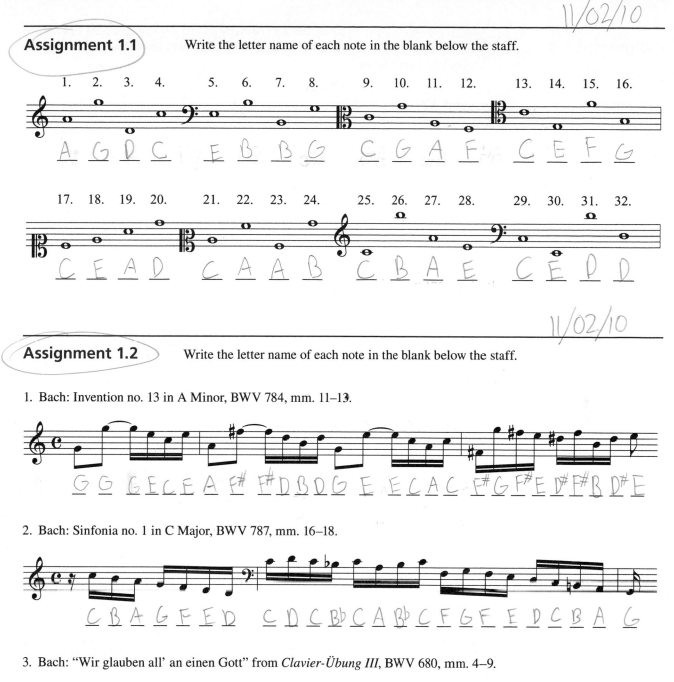

Assignment 1.1   Write the letter name of each note in the blank below the staff.

11/02/10

Assignment 1.2   Write the letter name of each note in the blank below the staff.

1. Bach: Invention no. 13 in A Minor, BWV 784, mm. 11–13.

2. Bach: Sinfonia no. 1 in C Major, BWV 787, mm. 16–18.

3. Bach: "Wir glauben all' an einen Gott" from *Clavier-Übung III*, BWV 680, mm. 4–9.

4. Bach: Prelude in C Major ("Leipzig"), BWV 547, mm. 68–72.

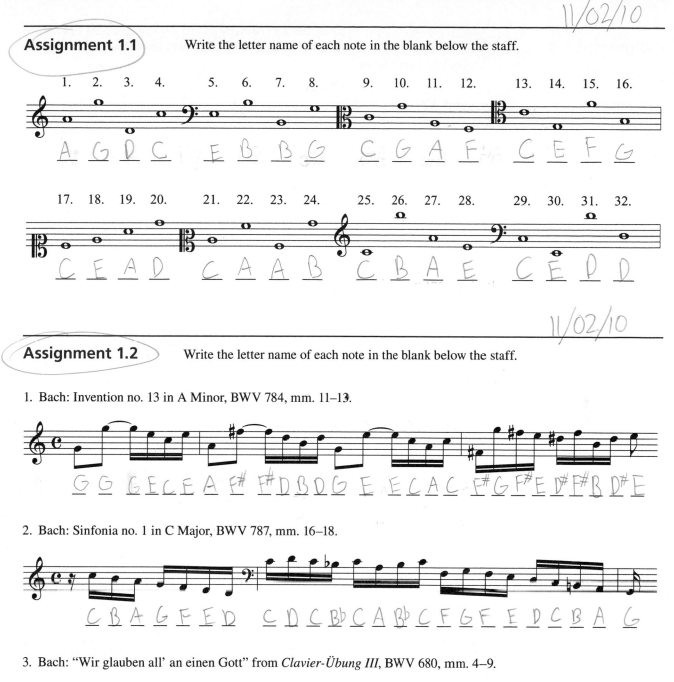

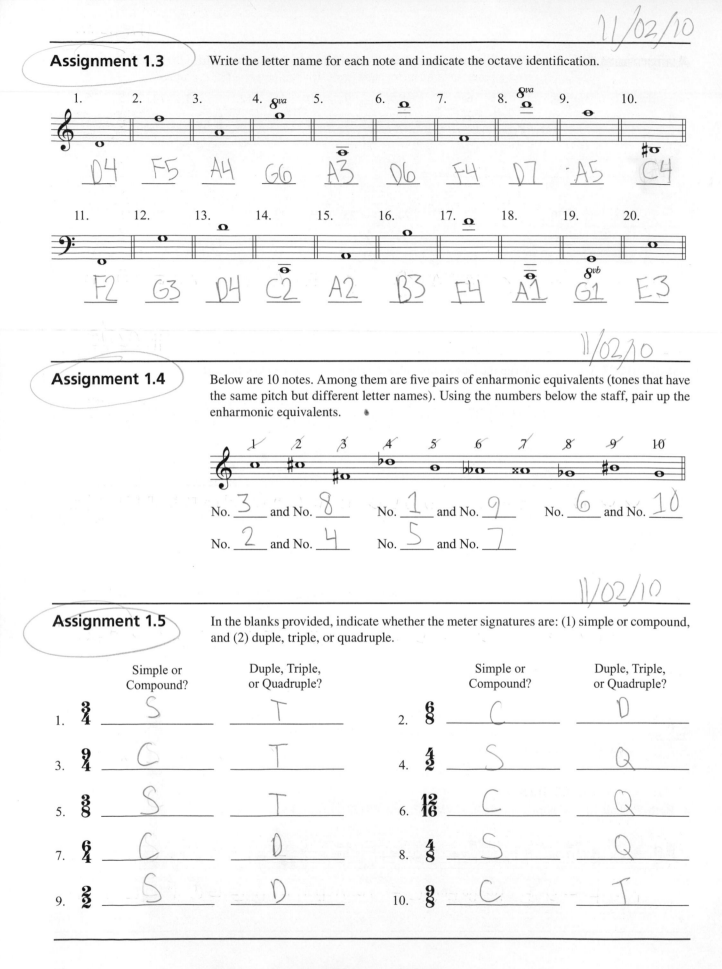

11/02/10

Assignment 1.3

Write the letter name for each note and indicate the octave identification.

1. D4 2. F5 3. A4 4. G6 5. A3 6. D6 7. F4 8. D7 9. A5 10. C4

11. F2 12. G3 13. D4 14. C2 15. A2 16. B3 17. F4 18. A1 19. G1 20. E3

11/02/10

Assignment 1.4

Below are 10 notes. Among them are five pairs of enharmonic equivalents (tones that have the same pitch but different letter names). Using the numbers below the staff, pair up the enharmonic equivalents.

No. 3 and No. 8   No. 1 and No. 9   No. 6 and No. 10

No. 2 and No. 4   No. 5 and No. 7

11/02/10

Assignment 1.5

In the blanks provided, indicate whether the meter signatures are: (1) simple or compound, and (2) duple, triple, or quadruple.

	Simple or Compound?	Duple, Triple, or Quadruple?		Simple or Compound?	Duple, Triple, or Quadruple?
1. $\frac{3}{4}$	S	T	2. $\frac{6}{8}$	C	D
3. $\frac{9}{4}$	C	T	4. $\frac{4}{2}$	S	Q
5. $\frac{3}{8}$	S	T	6. $\frac{12}{16}$	C	Q
7. $\frac{6}{4}$	C	D	8. $\frac{4}{8}$	S	Q
9. $\frac{2}{2}$	S	D	10. $\frac{9}{8}$	C	T

Assignment 1.6

Following are five melodies without meter signatures. Indicate the meter signature or, in some cases, the two meter signatures that render the notation correct.

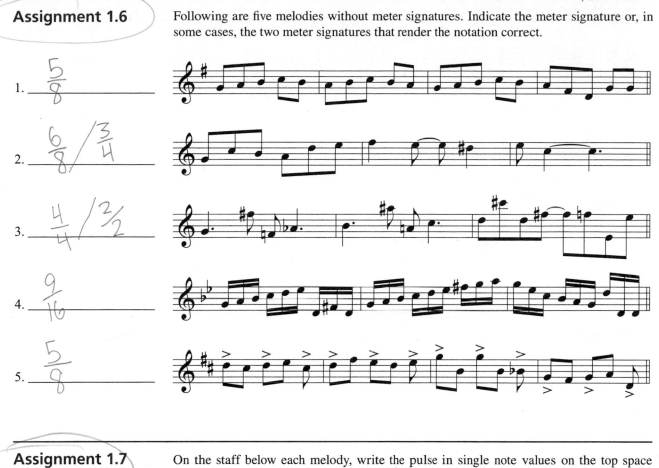

1. $\frac{5}{8}$ _____

2. $\frac{6}{8}$ / $\frac{3}{4}$ _____

3. $\frac{4}{4}$ / $\frac{2}{2}$ _____

4. $\frac{9}{16}$ _____

5. $\frac{5}{8}$ _____

Assignment 1.7

On the staff below each melody, write the pulse in single note values on the top space and the division of the pulse on the bottom space of the staff (see example). Consider the tempo in making your decision. Play or sing each melody. The neutral clef at the beginning of each bottom staff means that no specific pitch is designated.

1. (Ex.) Ives: *Three Places in New England,* II: Putnam's Camp, Redding, Connecticut, mm. 107–108, CD Track 1

2. French Folk Song. CD Track 2

3. French Hymn Tune. **CD Track 3**

4. Bartók: "Bulgarian Rhythm" from *Mikrokosmos,* vol. IV, no. 115, mm. 25–28. **CD Track 4**

5. Dutch Folk Song. **CD Track 5**

6. Chorale Tune: "All Creatures of Our God and King." **CD Track 6**

7. Finnish Folk Song. **CD Track 7**

Below are 18 measures of music. In each case, the notation is either confusing or incorrect. Rewrite each measure on the staff provided and clarify or correct the notation.

Assignment 1.9

Each of the following rhythms lacks beams. Rewrite each rhythm and add beams to reflect the given meter signature.

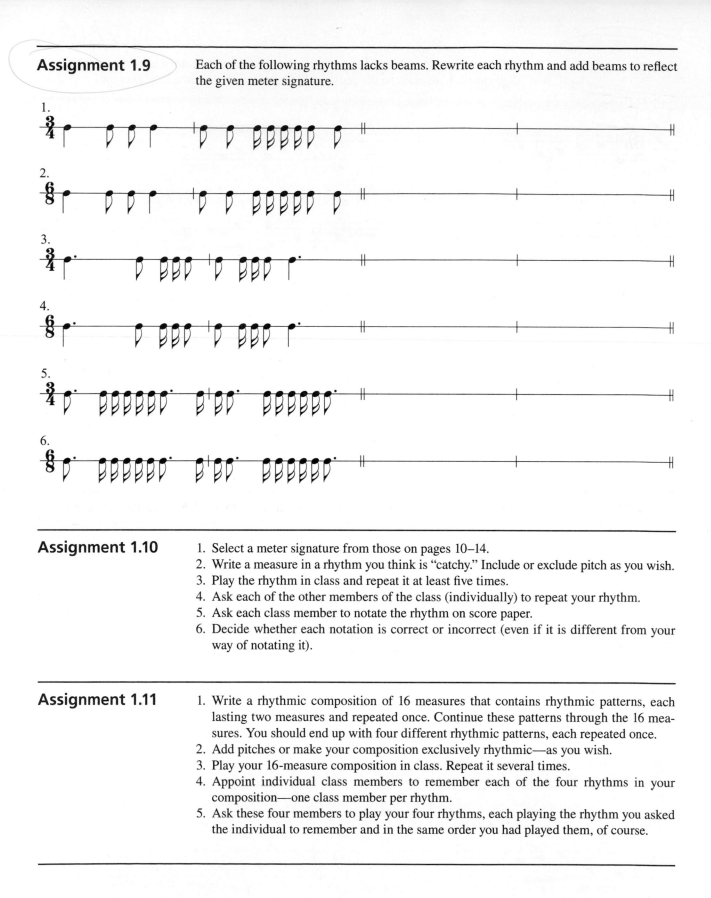

Assignment 1.10

1. Select a meter signature from those on pages 10–14.
2. Write a measure in a rhythm you think is "catchy." Include or exclude pitch as you wish.
3. Play the rhythm in class and repeat it at least five times.
4. Ask each of the other members of the class (individually) to repeat your rhythm.
5. Ask each class member to notate the rhythm on score paper.
6. Decide whether each notation is correct or incorrect (even if it is different from your way of notating it).

Assignment 1.11

1. Write a rhythmic composition of 16 measures that contains rhythmic patterns, each lasting two measures and repeated once. Continue these patterns through the 16 measures. You should end up with four different rhythmic patterns, each repeated once.
2. Add pitches or make your composition exclusively rhythmic—as you wish.
3. Play your 16-measure composition in class. Repeat it several times.
4. Appoint individual class members to remember each of the four rhythms in your composition—one class member per rhythm.
5. Ask these four members to play your four rhythms, each playing the rhythm you asked the individual to remember and in the same order you had played them, of course.

CHAPTER 2

Scales, Tonality, Key, Modes

TOPICS

Scale	Natural Minor Scale	Pentatonic Scale
Pitch Class	Harmonic Minor Scale	Nondiatonic Scales
Diatonic Scales	Melodic Minor Scale	Chromatic Scale
Tonic	Relative Minor	Whole-Tone Scale
Scale Degree Names	Relative Major	Blues Scale
Major Scale	Circle of Fifths	Octatonic or Diminished Scale
Tetrachord	Parallel Relationship	Mode
Transposition	Tonality	Solfeggio
Key Signature	Key	Pitch Inventory

IMPORTANT CONCEPTS

Performers often practice scales to develop their technique. The collections of pitches and recurring patterns performers use to focus attention on technical aspects are the same building blocks of musical composition.

Scale

A *scale* is a collection of pitches in ascending and descending order. Musicians use a scale as a convenient way of displaying the notes used in a melody or harmony. In Figure 2.1, the melody consists of 24 notes but only seven different letter names.

Pitch Class

A *pitch class* contains all notes of the same name regardless of octave. The pitch classes for the melody in the second part of Figure 2.1 on page 28 are arranged in ascending order to form a scale. The caret (^) above each number indicates that the number represents a scale degree.

Figure 2.1

Haydn: Symphony no. 94 in G Major ("Surprise"), III: Menuetto, mm. 1–8.

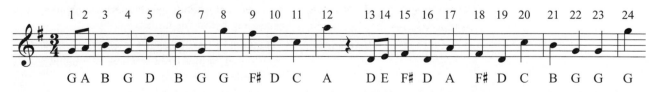

Notes of the melody arranged as a scale:

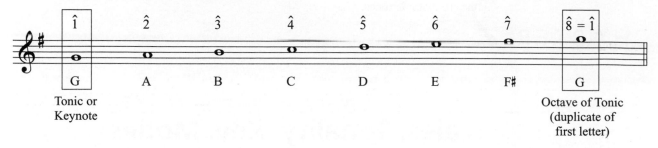

Although an infinite variety of pitch combinations is available, the following scales represent those in most common use during the past 200 years.

Diatonic Scales

Diatonic (literally "across the tones") defines a scale of mixed half and whole steps (and an occasional step and a half) in which each individual tone plays a role. The first tone of a scale, the *tonic,* is a point of rest and is considered to be the most stable. Other tones lead toward or away from it, creating varying degrees of tension or relaxation.

Since the tonic is the focal point of the scale, the most stable note, and the point of greatest relaxation, diatonic melodies frequently end on the tonic note. At times the word diatonic is used to indicate a tone that is part of a particular scale pattern—as distinguished from a nondiatonic tone that does not belong to the scale pattern.

Scale Degree Names

Each degree of the seven-tone diatonic scale has a name that relates to its function.

Scale Degree	Name	Meaning
1st	Tonic	Tonal center—the final resolution tone.
2nd	Supertonic	One step above the tonic.
3rd	Mediant	Midway between tonic and dominant.
4th	Subdominant	The lower dominant—the fifth tone down from the tonic (also the fourth tone up from the tonic).
5th	Dominant	So called because its function is next in importance to the tonic.
6th	Submediant	The lower mediant—halfway between tonic and lower dominant (subdominant). The third tone down from the tonic (also the sixth tone up from the tonic).
7th	Leading Tone	Strong affinity for and leads melodically to the tonic. Used when the seventh tone appears a half step below the tonic.
7th	Subtonic	Used only to designate the seventh degree of the natural minor scale (a whole step below the tonic).

Two different scales are shown in Figure 2.2 to illustrate the application of scale degree names to diatonic tones.

Figure 2.2

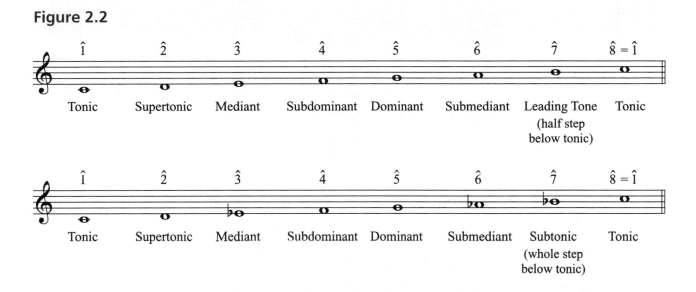

The *major scale* is a scale of seven different pitch classes with whole steps separating adjacent tones, except for half steps between the third and fourth degrees and between the seventh and eighth (or first) degrees. The eighth pitch has the same letter name as the first and thus is treated as a duplication.

All adjacent keys on the piano are a half step apart. Figure 2.3 shows that by beginning on C and playing in order only the white keys to the next C, you build a *C major* scale.

Major Scale

Figure 2.3

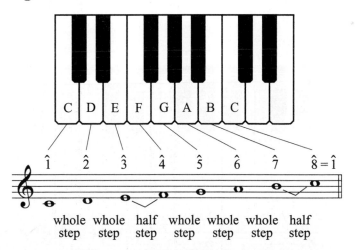

The major scale includes two *tetrachords* (groups of four pitches) constructed with the same arrangement of intervals—two whole steps followed by a half step. The two tetrachords of the major scale are separated by a single whole step.

Tetrachord

Figure 2.4

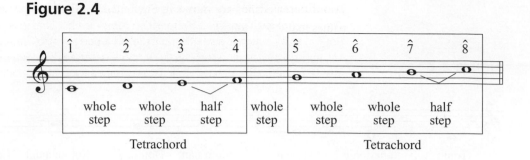

The melody in Figure 2.5 utilizes the notes of the C major scale.

Figure 2.5

Hatton: "Duke Street."

Transposition

This same major scale pattern of half and whole steps can be duplicated at any pitch. Such rewriting is called *transposition*. In Figure 2.6, the major scale is transposed so that its first tone is G. This is the G major scale.

Figure 2.6

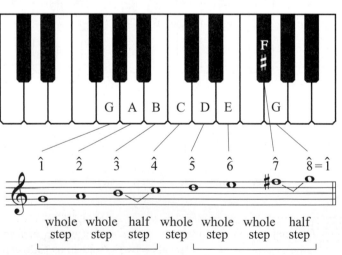

Key Signature

From Figure 2.6, it can be seen that a sharp is necessary if the major scale pattern of whole and half steps is to be carried out in the transposition. Figure 2.7 provides a convenient way to memorize the sharps or the flats needed when the scale begins on various pitches. The arrangement of the necessary sharps or flats is called a *key signature* and appears at the beginning of each staff in a composition after the clef. Notice that each successive tonic, or beginning note, is five scale degrees (called a perfect fifth) above or four scale degrees below the previous tonic. A new sharp is added to the key signature for each ascending perfect fifth (P5); in the flat signatures, a flat is dropped for each ascending P5 (see Figure 2.19).

Figure 2.7

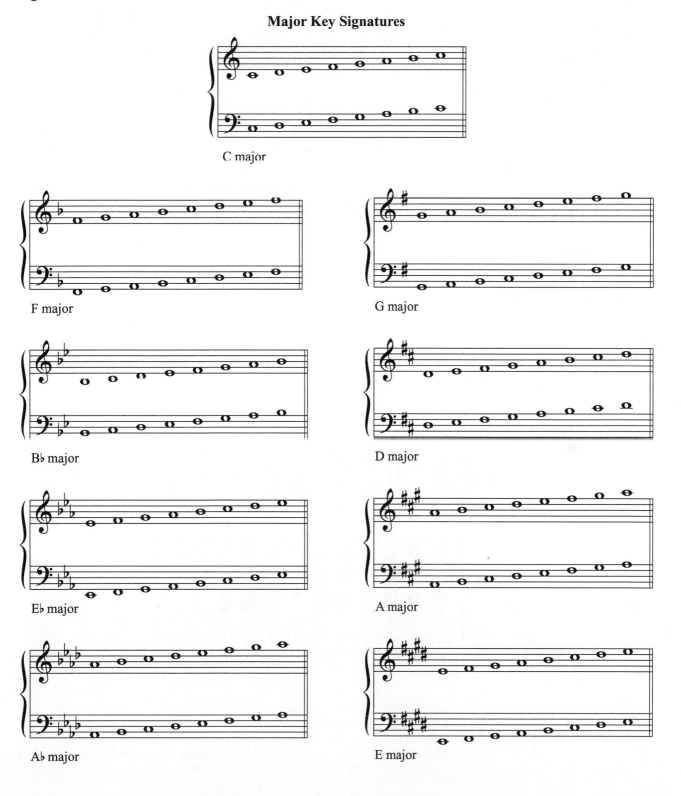

Major Key Signatures

C major

F major

G major

B♭ major

D major

E♭ major

A major

A♭ major

E major

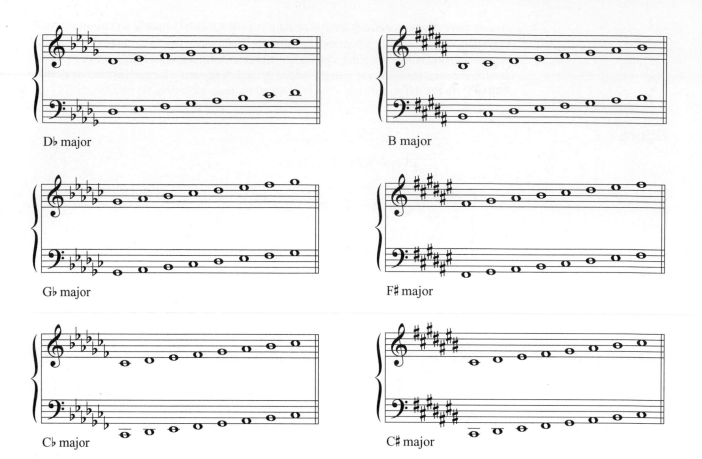

D♭ major

B major

G♭ major

F♯ major

C♭ major

C♯ major

Minor Scale

The *minor scale* is another common diatonic scale. It is more varied in pitch material because there are two different versions of both the sixth and seventh scale degrees. Traditionally, the minor scales have been described as having three distinct forms, but in practice, composers use all the scale resources of the minor scale within a single composition. The three traditional forms of the minor scale are called natural, harmonic, and melodic.

Natural Minor Scale

The *natural minor scale* contains seven different pitches with whole steps separating adjacent tones, except for half steps between the second and third degrees and between the fifth and sixth degrees. Its pitches are those of the white keys of the piano from A to A:

Figure 2.8

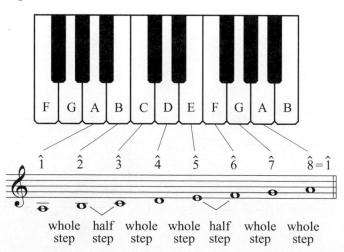

whole step	half step	whole step	whole step	half step	whole step	whole step

PART A   The Fundamentals of Music

The natural minor scale can be thought of as a major scale from the sixth to the sixth degree.

Figure 2.9

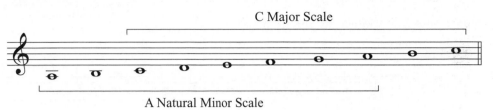

The excerpt from a familiar carol in Figure 2.10 employs the natural minor scale.

Figure 2.10

Carol: "God Rest Ye Merry, Gentlemen" (Refrain).

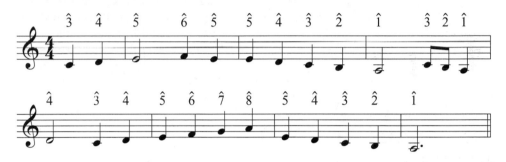

Harmonic Minor Scale

The *harmonic minor scale* has a raised seventh degree. The added impetus of a raised seventh degree gives more melodic thrust toward the tonic. Raising the seventh degree creates a step and a half between the sixth and seventh degrees, and a half step between the seventh and eighth degrees. Accidentals used to raise the seventh degree do not appear in the key signature. The pattern of half steps ($\hat{2}$–$\hat{3}$, $\hat{5}$–$\hat{6}$, $\hat{7}$–$\hat{8}$) is shown in Figure 2.11.

Figure 2.11

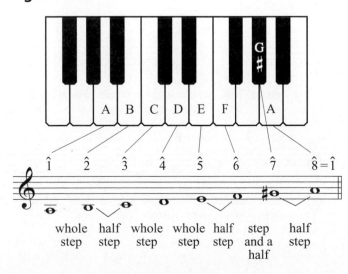

The Mozart excerpt in Figure 2.12 utilizes the harmonic minor scale. Notice the presence of G-sharps in every measure except 5 and 6.

Figure 2.12

Mozart: Sonata in A Minor, K. 310, III, mm. 1–8.

Melodic Minor Scale

The *melodic minor scale* appears in both ascending and descending form. Besides the half step between the second and third degrees, the ascending form includes raised sixth and seventh scale degrees, producing a half step between the seventh and eighth degrees. The descending form is the same as the natural minor.

The melodic minor scale developed because composers liked the urgency of the raised seventh, but found the step-and-a-half interval between the sixth and seventh degrees of the harmonic minor scale too harsh, especially for smooth vocal writing. In descending melodic passages, no need exists for the raised seventh, so composers most often used the natural minor with the lowered seventh and sixth degrees.

Figure 2.13

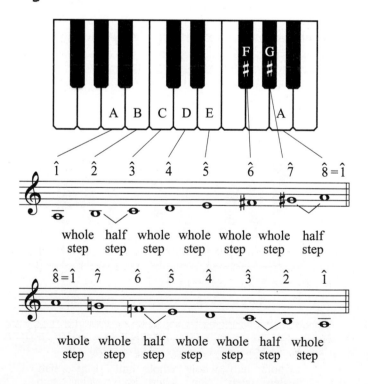

The excerpt in Figure 2.14 includes the ascending and descending forms of the melodic minor scale.

Figure 2.14

Chorale Melody: "Schwing' dich auf zu deinem Gott," ("Soar Upward to Thy God"), mm. 5–12 (transposed).

An examination of music literature, especially vocal and choral, reveals that composers consider the natural, harmonic, and melodic minors as arrangements of the same scale, with each form to be used according to need. This excerpt by Bach utilizes the various forms of the A minor scale in a single phrase of music:

Figure 2.15

Bach: "Herr Jesu Christ, du höchstes Gut" ("Lord Jesus Christ, Thou Highest Good"), BWV 113, mm. 1–2 (transposed).

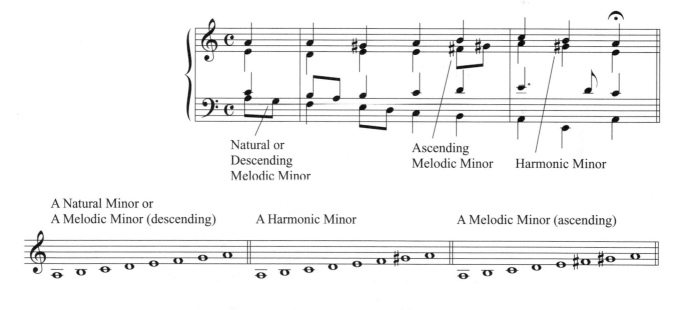

Scale Relationships

It is important to associate and compare the patterns present in major and minor scales. Two significant associations are byproducts of the overall organizational scheme: the relative and parallel relationships.

Relative Relationship

A major and a minor scale that have the same key signature are said to be in a relative relationship. To find the *relative minor* of any major scale, proceed to the sixth degree of that scale. This tone is the tonic of the relative minor.

Figure 2.16

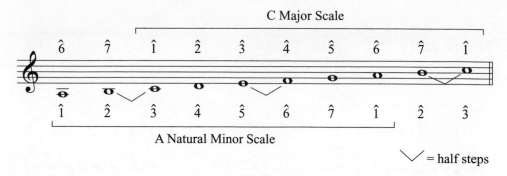

C Major Scale

A Natural Minor Scale

$\vee$ = half steps

To find the *relative major* of a minor key, proceed to the third degree of the minor scale. This tone is the tonic of the relative major key.

Figure 2.17

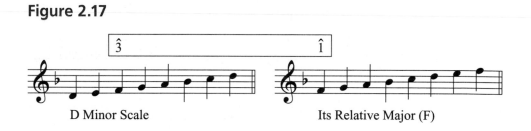

D Minor Scale   Its Relative Major (F)

Figure 2.18 summarizes the relative relationships between all of the major and minor scales. The organizational pattern perpetuating the major scale key signatures is also present in minor scales. Each minor key tonic is five scale degrees above (or four scale degrees below) the previous tonic.

Figure 2.18

Relative Major and Minor Relationships

Major	Relative Minor	Number of Sharps or Flats	Letter Names	Key Signatures and Key Notes
C	a	None		
G	e	1 Sharp	F♯	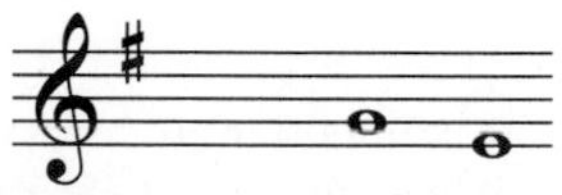
D	b	2 Sharps	F♯, C♯	

Relative Major and Minor Relationships

Major	Relative Minor	Number of Sharps or Flats	Letter Names	Key Signatures and Key Notes
A	f♯	3 Sharps	F♯, C♯, G♯	
E	c♯	4 Sharps	F♯, C♯, G♯, D♯	
B = C♭	g♯ = a♭	5 Sharps / 7 Flats	F♯, C♯, G♯, D♯, A♯ / B♭, E♭, A♭, D♭, G♭, C♭, F♭	
F♯ = G♭	d♯ = e♭	6 Sharps / 6 Flats	F♯, C♯, G♯, D♯, A♯, E♯ / B♭, E♭, A♭, D♭, G♭, C♭	
C♯ = D♭	a♯ = b♭	7 Sharps / 5 Flats	F♯, C♯, G♯, D♯, A♯, E♯, B♯ / B♭, E♭, A♭, D♭, G♭	
A♭	f	4 Flats	B♭, E♭, A♭, D♭	
E♭	c	3 Flats	B♭, E♭, A♭	
B♭	g	2 Flats	B♭, E♭	
F	d	1 Flat	B♭	

Circle of Fifths

Another way to visualize the relationship between the major scales and their relative minors is with the *circle of fifths* (Figure 2.19). All of the key signatures are given within the circle. The major scale tonics are listed outside the perimeter of the circle. The relative minors appear within the inner circle.

Figure 2.19

Circle of Fifths

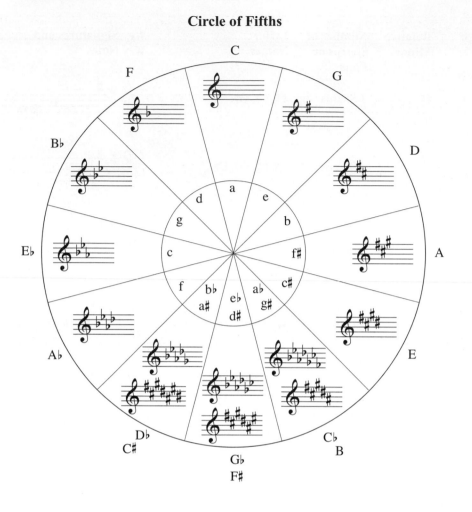

Parallel Relationship   A major and a minor scale that begin on the same tonic note are said to be in *parallel rela-tionship*. Figure 2.20 shows the major scales and their parallel minors.

Figure 2.20

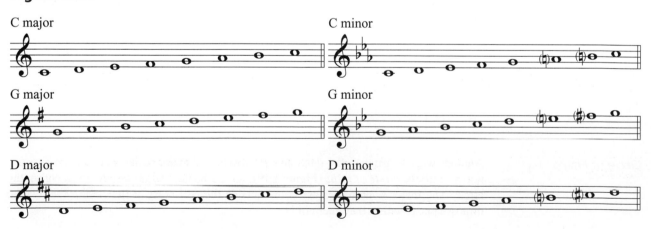

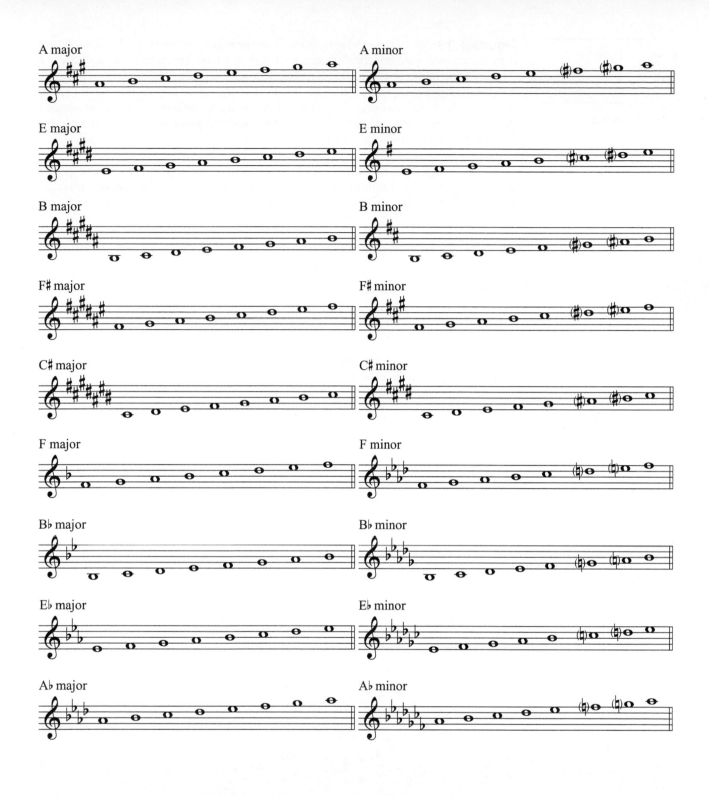

Tonality

Tonality refers to an organized system of tones (e.g., the tones of a major or minor scale) in which one tone (the tonic) becomes the central point to which the remaining tones are related. In tonality, the tonic (tonal center) is the tone of complete relaxation, the target toward which other tones lead.

Key

The term *key* refers to the tonal system based on the major and minor scales. This system is by far the most common tonal system, but tonality can be present in music not based on the major and minor scales (see the later chapters of volume 2).

Other Scales

Although the great majority of western European music written from the seventeenth through the nineteenth centuries is based on the major and minor scales, a number of other scales are found occasionally. The following descriptions are some of these scales.

Pentatonic Scale

As its name suggests, the *pentatonic scale* is a five-tone scale. It is an example of a gapped scale, one that contains intervals of more than a step between adjacent pitches. It is convenient to think of the common pentatonic scale as an incomplete major scale.

Figure 2.21

Other arrangements of the gaps are also found in music. The pentatonic scale in Figure 2.22 is based on the natural minor scale.

Figure 2.22

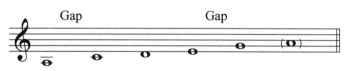

The sequence of black keys on the keyboard coincides with the interval relationships of the pentatonic scale. A brilliant use of the pentatonic scale occurs at the end of Chopin's Etude in G-flat Major, op. 10, no. 5, the popular "Black Key" Etude.

Figure 2.23

Chopin: Etude in G-flat Major ("Black Key"), op. 10, no. 5, mm. 83–85.

Ravel also used pentatonic material in his *Ma mère l'Oye* (Mother Goose) suite. The pitches in Figure 2.24 also correlate with the piano black keys.

Figure 2.24

Ravel: "Laideronnette, Imperatrice des Pagodes" from *Ma mère l'Oye* (Mother Goose), mm. 9–13.

The first two phrases of the following familiar tune are based on a pentatonic scale.

Figure 2.25

Foster: "Oh, Susanna," mm. 1–8.

Although all the preceding examples illustrate gapped scales typical of Western music, nongapped pentatonic scales (all adjacent intervals of the same size) occur in the music of other cultures. One such culture is Java, where a pentatonic scale consisting of five nearly equal intervals (whole plus a quarter step) forms the basis for a large body of music literature.

Nondiatonic Scales

A scale that does not observe the interval sequence of the diatonic or pentatonic scales is called a *nondiatonic scale*. Many nondiatonic scales have no identifiable tonic.

Chromatic Scale

A *chromatic scale* is a nondiatonic scale consisting entirely of half-step intervals. Since each tone of the scale is equidistant from the next, it has no tonic.

Figure 2.26

Ascending Chromatic Scale

Descending Chromatic Scale

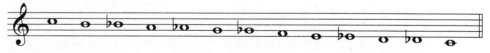

Chromaticism in Diatonic Music

Sometimes, however, a melody based on a regular diatonic scale (major or minor) is laced with many accidentals, and although all 12 tones of the chromatic scale may appear, the tonal characteristics of the diatonic scale are maintained. The following excerpt from

Purcell's *Dido and Aeneas* demonstrates this use of chromatic half steps by including 11 of the 12 tones in its gradual descent.

Figure 2.27

Purcell: "Thy Hand, Belinda" from *Dido and Aeneas,* Z. 626, mm. 1–10.

*Note the chromatic descent.

Whole-Tone Scale

A *whole-tone scale* is a six-tone scale made up entirely of whole steps between adjacent scale degrees.

Figure 2.28

Whole-Tone Scale

Examples of whole-tone material are found in music from the late romantic and impressionistic periods:

Figure 2.29

Debussy: *Voiles* (Sails) from Preludes, Book I, no. 2, mm. 1–2.

Blues Scale

The *blues scale* is a chromatic variant of the major scale with flat third and flat seventh. These notes, alternating with the normal third and seventh scale degrees, create the blues inflection. These "blue notes" represent the influence of African scales on this music. [See Gunther Schuller's *Early Jazz: Its Roots and Musical Development* (New York: Oxford University Press, 1968), pp. 46–52, for a complete discussion of the blue notes.]

Figure 2.30

Blues Scale in C

Non-Western Scales

Other cultures have many scales that are not diatonic. Figure 2.31 shows one of the *thaats*, or seven-note scales, of northern Indian music.

Figure 2.31

Todi (a northern Indian mode)

Octatonic or Diminished Scale

The *octatonic scale* is an eight-note scale composed of alternating whole steps and half steps. Jazz musicians refer to this scale as *diminished* because the chords resulting from this scale's pitches are diminished.

Figure 2.32

Octatonic or Diminished Scale

Nontraditional Scales

A number of nontraditional scales occur occasionally in the music of the late nineteenth and twentieth centuries. Most of these scales are made of a symmetrical pattern of intervals.

Figure 2.33

Augmented Scale

History

The scales used in music have developed and changed over the various historical periods. For additional information concerning the historical periods of music, see Appendix D.

Modal Scales

A *mode* is a series of pitches within the octave that make up the basic material of a composition. On first investigation it would seem that the terms mode and scale are entirely synonymous, but in certain instances, especially in medieval church music, the modes transcend mere scale formations and are regulated by idiomatic melodic expressions.

Church Modes

From roughly 800 to 1500, the church modes formed the basis for nearly all Western music. Notice in Figure 2.34 that modal scales are divided by range and that the beginning tone is called the *final* rather than the tonic as in the other diatonic scales. Modes I, III, V, and VII are called *authentic* because the final is at the bottom of the range. Modes II, IV, VI, and VIII are called *plagal* and contain the same pattern of half and whole steps as the authentic forms, except that their range surrounds the final. The prefix *hypo-* indicates that the plagal modes begin a fourth lower than the authentic forms.

Figure 2.34

Authentic Name	Number	Range	Final	Half Steps Between	Tonal Scale Comparison
Dorian	I			$\hat{2}$–$\hat{3}$, $\hat{6}$–$\hat{7}$	Natural minor scale with raised sixth degree
Phrygian	III			$\hat{1}$–$\hat{2}$, $\hat{5}$–$\hat{6}$	Natural minor scale with lowered second degree
Lydian	V			$\hat{4}$–$\hat{5}$, $\hat{7}$–$\hat{8}$	Major scale with raised fourth degree
Mixolydian	VII			$\hat{3}$–$\hat{4}$, $\hat{6}$–$\hat{7}$	Major scale with lowered seventh degree

Plagal Name	Number	Range	Final	Half Steps Between	Tonal Scale Comparison
Hypodorian	II			$\hat{2}$–$\hat{3}$, $\hat{6}$–$\hat{7}$	Natural minor scale with raised sixth degree
Hypophrygian	IV	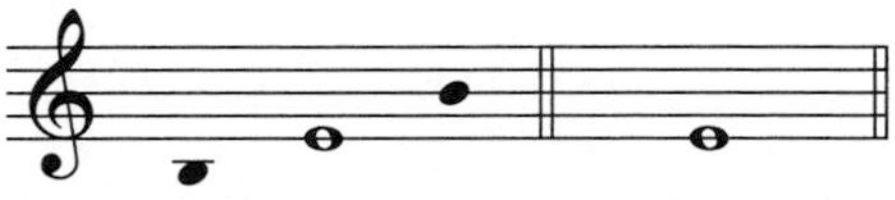		$\hat{1}$–$\hat{2}$, $\hat{5}$–$\hat{6}$	Natural minor scale with lowered second degree
Hypolydian	VI			$\hat{4}$–$\hat{5}$, $\hat{7}$–$\hat{8}$	Major scale with raised fourth degree
Hypomixolydian	VIII			$\hat{3}$–$\hat{4}$, $\hat{6}$–$\hat{7}$	Major scale with lowered seventh degree

Early in the Renaissance period (1450–1600), other modes were recognized. The Aeolian is the same as the natural minor scale, and the Ionian is the same as the major scale.

Figure 2.35

Authentic Name	Number	Range	Final	Half Steps Between	Tonal Scale Comparison
Aeolian	IX	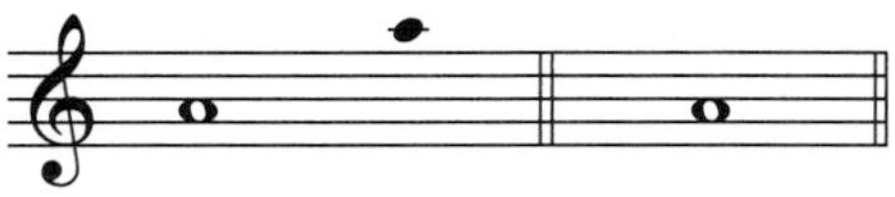		$\hat{2}$–$\hat{3}$, $\hat{5}$–$\hat{6}$	Same as natural minor scale
Ionian	XI			$\hat{3}$–$\hat{4}$, $\hat{7}$–$\hat{8}$	Same as major scale

Plagal Name	Number	Range	Final	Half Steps Between	Tonal Scale Comparison
Hypoaeolian	X			$\hat{2}$–$\hat{3}$, $\hat{5}$–$\hat{6}$	Same as natural minor scale
Hypoionian	XII	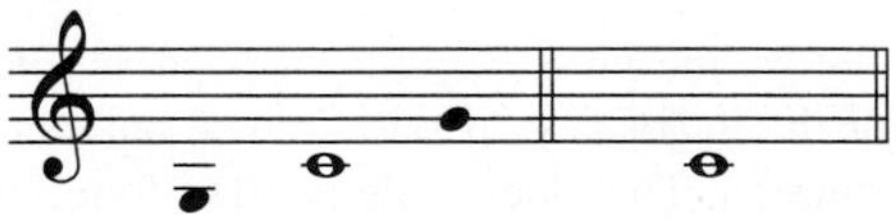		$\hat{3}$–$\hat{4}$, $\hat{7}$–$\hat{8}$	Same as major scale

For a more complete explanation of the modal scales, see Chapter 8 of this volume.

Solfeggio Syllables

Certain systems of *solfeggio* (vocal exercises sung to a vowel, syllables, or words) use the syllables *do, re, mi, fa, sol, la, ti* to indicate scale degrees. The present-day movable-*do* and fixed-*do* systems are derived from Guido d'Arezzo, an eleventh-century monk who sought to teach sight singing through the use of a well-known hymn to Saint John, *Ut queant laxis* (Figure 2.36). The beginning notes of the first six phrases of Guido's melody form the first six notes of the scale: C, D, E, F, G, A. The syllables beginning these phrases are *ut, re, mi, fa, sol, la*.

Scale degree:	C	D	E	F	G	A
Syllable:	*ut*	*re*	*mi*	*fa*	*sol*	*la*

Figure 2.36

Hymn to Saint John (*Ut queant laxis*).

Tonal Scales

The tonal system of major and minor scales developed during the early part of the baroque period. This coincided with the emergence of key consciousness in music. By the end of the baroque period, the church modes had generally ceased to have any influence in music.

The major and minor keys were the basis of music in the classical period. Chromaticism was decorative for the most part, and shifts from one key to another (see Chapter 15) were used to create formal divisions (see Chapters 16 and 17).

During the romantic period, chromaticism increased to the point that the major-minor key system began to be threatened. By the end of the period, composers often shifted keys so rapidly over the course of a composition that tonality itself began to break down.

Expanded Scale Use

With the breakdown of the major-minor key system, impressionist composers began to experiment with other scales. They were particularly fond of pentatonic, modal, and whole-tone scales.

Twentieth-century composers have continued to expand the scale basis of their music. The chromatic scale has predominated in much of the music of our period, but a number of composers have experimented with nontraditional scales and microtonal scales (scales with intervals smaller than a half step).

Twentieth-century popular music has remained the last bastion of the major-minor key system. Until the 1960s, the great majority of popular songs were written in major keys. This preference for the major keys persists today, but songs in minor keys have become somewhat more common. The blues scale is often found in jazz and popular music with blues influence, and the modes are an integral part of jazz composition and improvisation.

APPLICATIONS

As a first step in understanding the structure of a composition, determining its scale basis is important. You can do this by forming a pitch inventory.

Pitch Inventory

A *pitch inventory* is a scalewise list of the tones used in a composition or section thereof. For purposes of organization, the pitch inventories in this text always begin with the pitch A. Many students will have no need to prepare a pitch inventory, but for those students who have yet to develop a "hearing eye" that would allow instantaneous recognition of keys and tonal centers, a pitch inventory may be a necessity. A pitch inventory permits quick assessment of the selected pitches without prejudice to key or tonality. From there you can make a fairly accurate determination of key by observing the location of half and whole steps, accidentals such as raised sevenths, etc., and particular notes of the melody that are emphasized.

With practice, the need for a pitch inventory will diminish and the calculations will become automatic. The following illustration provides a melody, its pitch inventory, and finally its scale.

Figure 2.37

Dvořák: Symphony no. 9 in E Minor, op. 95 ("From the New World"), I, mm. 149–156.

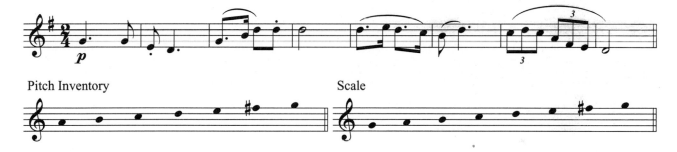

Assignment 2.1

1. Write the scales requested in the ascending form.
2. When the melodic minor scale is requested, add the first three notes of the descending form.
3. Write the accidentals to the left of the notes as they occur in the scale, not as a key signature.

1. F major

2. C minor (natural)

3. G minor (harmonic)

4. E minor (melodic)

5. B♭ major

6. D minor (harmonic)

7. B major

8. E♭ minor (natural)

9. A major

10. F♯ minor (melodic)

11. C♯ minor (harmonic)

12. A♭ major

Assignment 2.2

Write the key signature for each of the following major and minor scales.

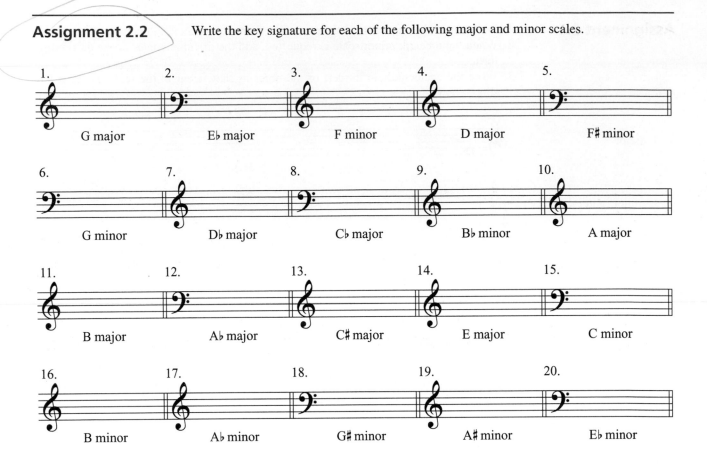

1. G major
2. Eb major
3. F minor
4. D major
5. F# minor
6. G minor
7. Db major
8. Cb major
9. Bb minor
10. A major
11. B major
12. Ab major
13. C# major
14. E major
15. C minor
16. B minor
17. Ab minor
18. G# minor
19. A# minor
20. Eb minor

Assignment 2.3

Following are groups of four successive notes of major scales. Most of these tetrachords are part of two major scales, but three examples are part of only one major scale. Name the scales of which each example is a part. (See the example for the pattern.)

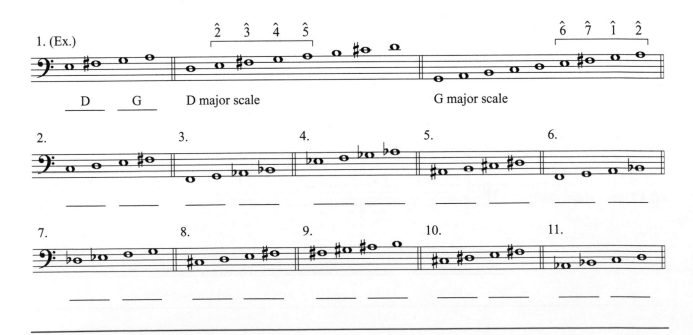

1. (Ex.)   D   G   D major scale   G major scale

2.   3.   4.   5.   6.

7.   8.   9.   10.   11.

Assignment 2.4

Each of the following groups of four tones is part of a harmonic minor scale. Name the harmonic minor scale of which it is a part.

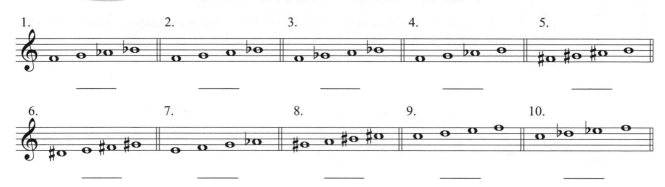

1. _____ 2. _____ 3. _____ 4. _____ 5. _____

6. _____ 7. _____ 8. _____ 9. _____ 10. _____

Assignment 2.5

The scale and scale degree are given, but the letter name of the note is missing. Fill in the letter name. Be sure to consider both ascending and descending forms of the melodic minor scales.

Scale	Scale Degree	Letter Name	Scale	Scale Degree	Letter Name
1. G minor (harmonic)	Submediant	_____	6. C♯ minor (harmonic)	Dominant	_____
2. B major	Supertonic	_____	7. G♯ minor (melodic)	Submediant	_____
3. B♭ minor (natural)	Subdominant	_____	8. D major	Mediant	_____
4. F♯ minor (melodic)	Submediant	_____	9. F minor (natural)	Subtonic	_____
5. E♭ major	Leading tone	_____	10. D♯ minor (harmonic)	Subdominant	_____

Assignment 2.6

1. Match the column at right with the column at left. The left column refers to key signatures.
2. Number 1 is completed correctly as an example.

Key Signature

_____H_____ 1. 1 sharp

_____ 2. 4 sharps

_____ 3. 2 flats

_____ 4. 5 sharps

_____ 5. 1 flat

_____ 6. 2 sharps

_____ 7. 6 flats

_____ 8. 3 sharps

_____ 9. 5 flats

_____ 10. 4 flats

Key

A. Relative major of D minor

B. Relative major of B-flat minor

C. Parallel minor of C-sharp major

D. Parallel minor of F major

E. Relative major of E-flat minor

F. Parallel major of A minor

G. Relative minor of B-flat major

H. Relative minor of G major

I. Parallel major of B minor

J. Parallel minor of B major

Assignment 2.7

1. Each of the following seven melodies is based on one of the following scales:

   pentatonic   chromatic   whole tone   minor

2. Determine the scale upon which each melody is based and place the name in the blank provided.
3. For melodies in minor, indicate the form that predominates.

1. _____

2. _____

3. _____

4. _____

5. _____

6. _____

7. _____

Assignment 2.8

On the blank staff under each of the following melodies, write:

1. The pitch inventory beginning on A (or A-flat or A-sharp).
2. The scale with the tonic as the first note. (Indicate scale degrees with carets.)
3. The key. (For melodies in minor keys, indicate the form that predominates.)

Suggested procedure:

1. Sing each melody enough times to be familiar with it.
2. Look carefully at the pitch inventory to determine the number of sharps or flats.
3. Reconstruct the key signature if possible. Remember that the raised seventh degree in the harmonic minor might mislead you.
4. When you think you have the correct key signature, you should then try to determine whether the melody is major or minor.
5. Go back to the melody itself and sing it again. Your ear can be a great help. Sometimes the first and last note will be a clue as to the tonic note. If this fails, try to find outlined triads in the melody line—such outlined triads are often either tonic or dominant.
6. When you have decided the key signature and the tonality (whether major or minor), write the scale on the blank staff.

1. Haydn: Symphony no. 28, IV: Presto assai, mm. 1–4. CD Track 8

2. D. Scarlatti: Sonata, K. 53, L. 261, mm. 1–5. CD Track 9

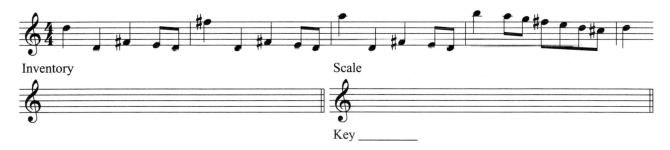

3. Mozart: *Eine kleine Nachtmusik,* K. 525, II: Menuetto, mm. 1–5. CD Track 10

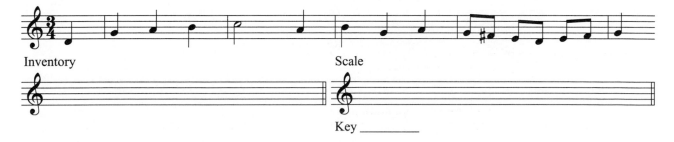

4. Franck: Quintet for Piano and Strings, mm. 7–10. **CD Track 11**

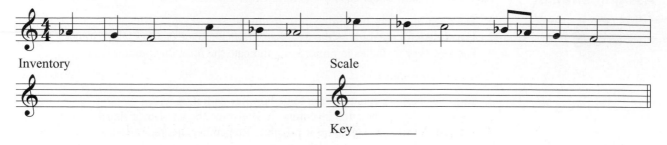

Inventory

Scale

Key _____

5. Bach: Little Prelude, BWV 943, mm. 1–5. **CD Track 12**

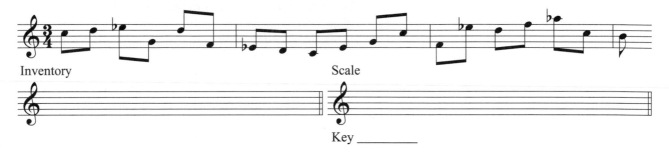

Inventory

Scale

Key _____

6. Kirnberger: *Les Carillons* (The Bells), mm. 21–25. **CD Track 13**

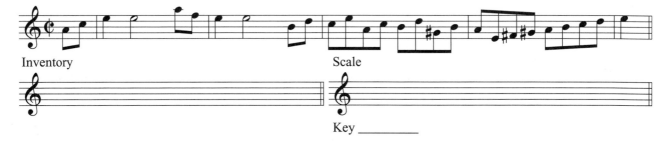

Inventory

Scale

Key _____

7. Couperin: *Concerts Royaux*, no. 8. **CD Track 14**

Number 7 is slightly more difficult than the first six. Your best clue is the contour of the melody notes and the notes on the accented beats.

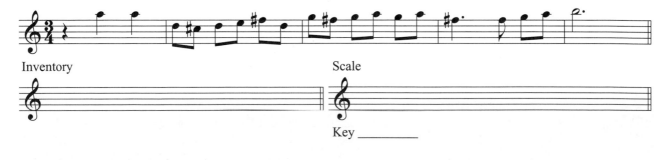

Inventory

Scale

Key _____

CHAPTER 3

Intervals and Transposition

TOPICS

Interval
Octave
Unison
Perfect, Major, and Minor
   Intervals
Consonance and Dissonance

Augmented and
   Diminished Intervals
Enharmonic Intervals
Tritone
Inversion of Intervals
Compound Intervals

Simple Intervals
Tuning Systems
Melodic Intervals
Harmonic Intervals
Transposition

**IMPORTANT
CONCEPTS**

Tone combinations are classified in music with names that identify the pitch relationships. Learning to recognize these combinations by both eye and ear is a skill fundamental to basic musicianship. Although many different tone combinations occur in music, the most basic pairing of pitches is the interval.

Intervals

An *interval* is the relationship in pitch between two tones. Intervals are named by the number of diatonic notes (notes with different letter names) that can be contained within them. For example, the whole step G to A contains only two diatonic notes (G and A) and is called a second.

Figure 3.1

    Second   1 – 2

The following figure shows all the numbers within an octave used to identify intervals:

Figure 3.2

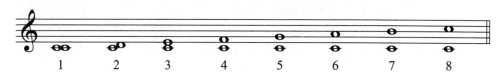

  1   2   3   4   5   6   7   8

Notice that the interval numbers shown in Figure 3.2 correspond to the scale degree numbers for the major scale.

The term *octave* refers to the number 8, its interval number.

Figure 3.3

Octave = 1   2   3   4   5   6   7   8   =   8

The interval numbered "1" (two notes of the same pitch) is called a *unison*.

Figure 3.4

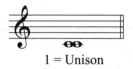

1 = Unison

Perfect, Major, and Minor Intervals

The intervals that include the tonic (keynote) and the fourth and fifth scale degrees of a major scale are called *perfect*.

Figure 3.5

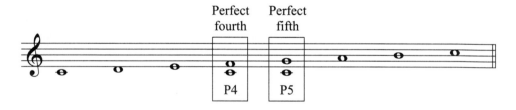

In addition, the unison and the octave are called *perfect*.

Figure 3.6

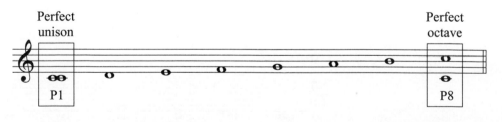

The intervals from the tonic (keynote) in an upward direction to the second, to the third, to the sixth, and to the seventh scale degrees of a major scale are called *major*.

Figure 3.7

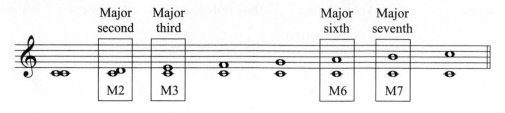

Notice the standard abbreviations for intervals in Figures 3.5, 3.6, and 3.7. For example, P1 = perfect unison, M2 = major second.

When a major interval is made one half step smaller, it becomes *minor*. This can be done either by raising the bottom note or lowering the top note.

Figure 3.8

Notice the standard abbreviation for minor intervals: a lower case "m" followed by an interval number.

Major, minor, and perfect intervals are illustrated in Figure 3.9.

Figure 3.9

Name	Abbreviation	Illustration	Number of Half Steps	Convenient Example
Perfect Unison (also Prime)	P1		0	
Minor 2nd	m2		1	$\hat{7}-\hat{8}$ of Major Scale
Major 2nd	M2		2	$\hat{1}-\hat{2}$ of Major Scale
Minor 3rd	m3	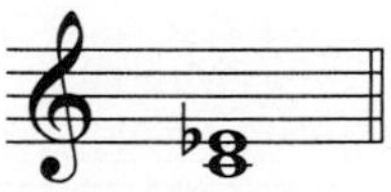	3	$\hat{1}-\hat{3}$ of Minor Scale
Major 3rd	M3		4	$\hat{1}-\hat{3}$ of Major Scale

Name	Abbreviation	Illustration	Number of Half Steps	Convenient Example
Perfect 4th	P4		5	$\hat{1}-\hat{4}$ of Major or Minor Scale
Perfect 5th	P5		7	$\hat{1}-\hat{5}$ of Major or Minor Scale
Minor 6th	m6		8	$\hat{1}-\hat{6}$ of Harmonic Minor Scale
Major 6th	M6		9	$\hat{1}-\hat{6}$ of Major Scale
Minor 7th	m7		10	$\hat{1}-\hat{7}$ of Natural Minor Scale
Major 7th	M7		11	$\hat{1}-\hat{7}$ of Major Scale
Perfect Octave	P8		12	$\hat{1}-\hat{8}$ of Major or Minor Scale

Consonance and Dissonance

The terms *consonance* and *dissonance* are defined in a variety of ways, depending on the context. In acoustics, the consonances are those intervals that are found as the lower members of the harmonic series (see page xv). We will define the term consonance in a musical sense as intervals that are treated as stable and not requiring resolution. The consonant intervals are the P1, m3, M3, P5, m6, M6, and P8. All other intervals within the octave are considered dissonant.

Augmented and Diminished Intervals

If a perfect or major interval is made one half step larger (without changing its interval number) it becomes *augmented*. If a perfect or minor interval is made one half step smaller (without changing its interval number) it becomes *diminished*.

Figure 3.10

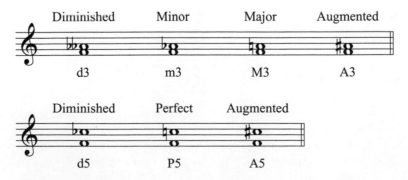

Notice the standard abbreviations for augmented and diminished intervals. For example, d3 = diminished third and A3 = augmented third.

Enharmonic Intervals

Enharmonic intervals are intervals with the same sound that are spelled differently. Such intervals result, of course, from enharmonic tones (see "Enharmonic Equivalents," page 8). All of the following intervals sound identical but are spelled differently.

Figure 3.11

You must take care in spelling intervals. If a specific interval is requested, the enharmonic equivalent spelling is not correct. Thus, if a major third above E is called for, A-flat is not correct, even though it sounds the same as G-sharp. If a perfect fifth above F is called for, B-sharp is not correct, even though it sounds the same as C.

Figure 3.12

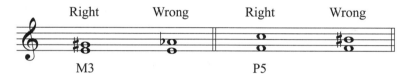

The Tritone

The most common enharmonic intervals are the augmented fourth and the diminished fifth, which divide the octave into two equal parts.

Figure 3.13

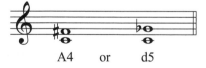

These intervals are usually referred to as the *tritone,* since they contain three whole steps.

Figure 3.14

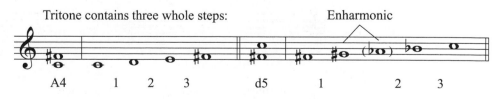

Inversion of Intervals

The *inversion of an interval* means that the lower tone of an interval becomes the higher tone, or the higher tone becomes the lower tone.

Figure 3.15

The following table shows various intervals and their inversions:

Interval Name	When Inverted Becomes
Perfect	Perfect
Major	Minor
Minor	Major
Diminished	Augmented
Augmented	Diminished
Unison	Octave
2nd	7th
3rd	6th
4th	5th
5th	4th
6th	3rd
7th	2nd
Octave	Unison

Figure 3.16 shows some typical intervals and their inversions.

Figure 3.16

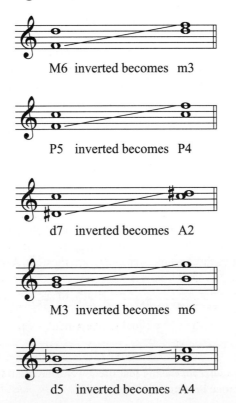

M6 inverted becomes m3

P5 inverted becomes P4

d7 inverted becomes A2

M3 inverted becomes m6

d5 inverted becomes A4

Compound Intervals and Simple Intervals

Intervals greater than an octave are called *compound intervals*. These intervals are named in a similar manner to the intervals within an octave (*simple intervals*).

Figure 3.17

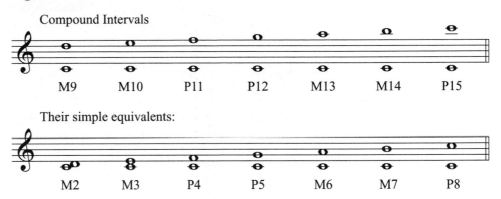

Compound Intervals

M9 M10 P11 P12 M13 M14 P15

Their simple equivalents:

M2 M3 P4 P5 M6 M7 P8

Compound intervals are often labeled as their simple equivalents—as if an octave were removed from the interval. The compound names are used only if it is important to stress the exact interval size.

History

Not all intervals are exactly the same size today as they were in earlier times, and in fact, the size differences in many cases are audible. Various *tuning systems* throughout the centuries have dictated specific distances between interval pitches.

Tuning Systems

In modern times the equal temperament system of tuning has been accepted as the standard for nearly all music written in the Western world. Nevertheless, the history of music reveals a variety of methods that preceded equal temperament. Many are still in use throughout the world.

Pythagorean Tuning

Attributed to the sixth-century B.C. philosopher Pythagoras, Pythagorean tuning is a system of tuning that uses only the pure fifth found in the harmonic series. The Pythagorean system would appear to be ideal because of the purity of the fifths, but other intervals, particularly the seconds and thirds, are compromised. Major seconds and thirds in Pythagorean tuning are larger than their equal-temperament counterparts, whereas minor seconds and thirds are smaller.

Just Intonation

Just intonation, which flourished in the fifteenth century, solved the problem of out-of-tune major chords by tuning a few major thirds according to the harmonic series. The result of this method was that the majority of thirds and some of the fifths were pure, but the remaining fifths were smaller.

Unequal Temperaments

By 1650, musicians had found a number of unequal temperaments that met their needs for playing in a variety of keys. These temperaments gave up the purity of the thirds and fifths, but distributed the error over enough intervals that most chords were acceptable. Many systems were used, but the best known are those of Andreas Werckmeister (1645–1706), whose treatise *Musikalische Temperatur* (1691) gave a number of unequal temperaments that are still in use today, particularly in pipe organs. It is certain that Bach's *Well-Tempered Clavier* (1722–1742) was composed for an instrument tuned to one of the unequal temperaments rather than equal temperament, as has sometimes been supposed.

Equal Temperament

Equal temperament divides the octave into 12 equal half steps, thus further compromising both pure fifths and pure thirds. Fretted string instruments were responsible for much of the early interest in equal temperament, since the frets passed under all the strings, and this required that all the half steps be as equal as possible. During the later nineteenth and twentieth centuries, equal temperament became the standard system of tuning, and most modern instruments approximate this system as nearly as possible.

Despite the standardization of equal temperament as the prevailing tuning system, the interest in historically accurate performance has led to the construction of instruments employing various historical tunings. New applications of the tuning systems continue to be developed. A number of twentieth-century composers have experimented with tuning systems as the basis for new musical styles.

APPLICATIONS

Fluency with Intervals

It is vital that you develop speed and accuracy in the identification and spelling of intervals. Much of your future work in music theory will require this ability. Many musicians use the following method to help them identify intervals more quickly.

1. Notice in writing thirds, fifths, and sevenths that the two notes are either on lines or on spaces.

Figure 3.18

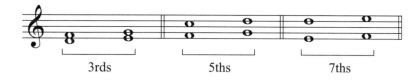

3rds   5ths   7ths

2. Seconds, fourths, sixths, and octaves involve a note on a line and a note on a space.

Figure 3.19

2nds   4ths   6ths   Octaves

3. Fourths, fifths, and octaves are perfect if the accidentals are the same, except for the fourth and fifth involving B and F.

Figure 3.20

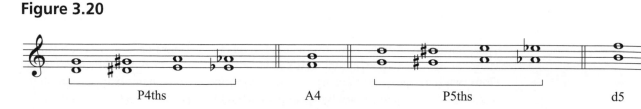

P4ths   A4   P5ths   d5

4. Seconds are major and sevenths are minor if the accidentals are the same, except for those involving E–F and B–C.

Figure 3.21

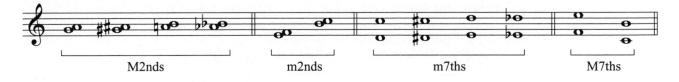

M2nds   m2nds   m7ths   M7ths

5. Thirds built on C, F, and G are major if the accidentals are the same. Thirds built on the remaining notes are minor if the accidentals are the same.

Figure 3.22

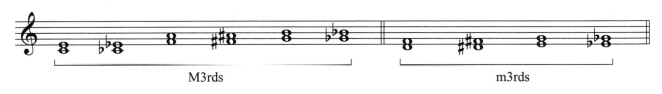

M3rds   m3rds

6. Sixths whose upper tones are C, F, or G are minor if the accidentals are the same. Sixths whose upper tones are any of the remaining notes are major if the accidentals are the same.

Figure 3.23

m6ths   M6ths

7. You can quickly determine other interval qualities by reducing the interval to the "same accidental" form and then noting the effect on interval size when the accidental(s) are replaced.

Figure 3.24

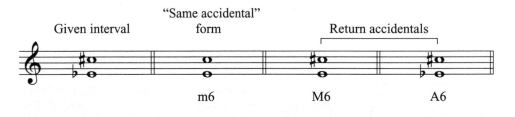

Given interval   "Same accidental" form   Return accidentals

m6   M6   A6

With sufficient practice, determining the size of intervals will become automatic. In the assignments for this chapter, work first for accuracy and then try to develop speed.

Melodic and Harmonic Intervals

The two pitches of an interval will occur either in succession or simultaneously. If two tones are positioned adjacently and sound one after the other, the resulting interval is considered to be *melodic*.

Figure 3.25

D. Scarlatti: Sonata in C Major, K. 159, L. 104, mm. 1–2.

If two tones sound at the same time, the resulting interval is said to be *harmonic*. Figure 3.26 demonstrates a series of harmonic intervals occurring between the left-hand and right-hand parts of a keyboard composition.

Figure 3.26

D. Scarlatti: Sonata in C Major, K. 159, L. 104, mm. 1–2.

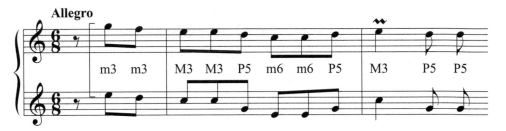

Figure 3.27 illustrates the notation of both types of intervals. Although most harmonic intervals are aligned vertically, unisons and seconds require offset positioning. Notice that the noteheads of harmonic unisons and seconds touch, but never overlap.

Figure 3.27

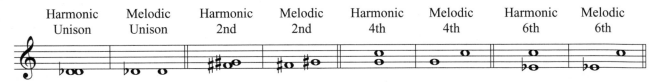

| Harmonic Unison | Melodic Unison | Harmonic 2nd | Melodic 2nd | Harmonic 4th | Melodic 4th | Harmonic 6th | Melodic 6th |

Transposition

Transposition is the process of rewriting a piece of music or a scale so that it sounds higher or lower in pitch. This involves raising or lowering each pitch by the same interval.

Methods of Transposition

The ability to transpose rapidly and accurately is a fundamental skill that all musicians need. Singers often transpose songs to fit their particular voice ranges, and anyone writing for instrumentalists will often need to transpose parts for them. Many musicians are expected to be able to transpose while they perform. This is particularly true of certain wind instrumentalists, but pianists and organists are also called on to transpose at sight. There are several methods of transposition; the choice of method is an individual matter. We will examine two methods here.

Method 1: Interval Transposition

One common technique for transposition is by interval. In this method an interval of transposition is established, and all pitches are moved up or down by that interval.

Figure 3.28

Interval Transposition

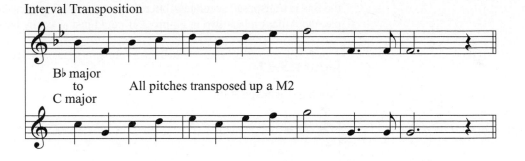

Bb major
to
C major

All pitches transposed up a M2

Method 2:
Clef Transposition

Some musicians prefer to transpose by clef. In this method a clef is chosen that would put the part on the correct transposed pitch, and any key signatures are changed. For example, a baritone saxophone player can take music written in the bass clef and transpose it by imagining that it is written in the treble clef with a key signature that has three fewer flats or three more sharps. (Accidentals within the part will have to be converted also.)

Figure 3.28 will now be transposed from B-flat major to C major by substituting the alto clef and changing the key signature. Notice that it is sometimes necessary to change the octave of the clef in making a clef transposition.

Figure 3.29

Clef Transposition

Substitute alto clef and new key signature

If a particular transposition is often required, particularly when you are transposing at sight, clef transposition may be the easiest method.

Tonal and Nontonal
Transposition

If the music is tonal and written with a key signature (including C major), the transposition includes transposing the key signature.

Figure 3.30

Tonal Transposition

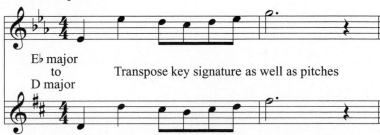

Eb major
to
D major

Transpose key signature as well as pitches

If the music is written without key signatures and is chromatic, the transposed parts will also appear without key signature. In this case, you must take particular care to ensure that the line is transposed accurately, but enharmonic notations may be freely written. For example, the A-flat on beat two in Figure 3.31 could just as easily have been written as G-sharp.

Figure 3.31

Nontonal Transposition

Assignment 3.1

Write the name of each interval on the blank provided.

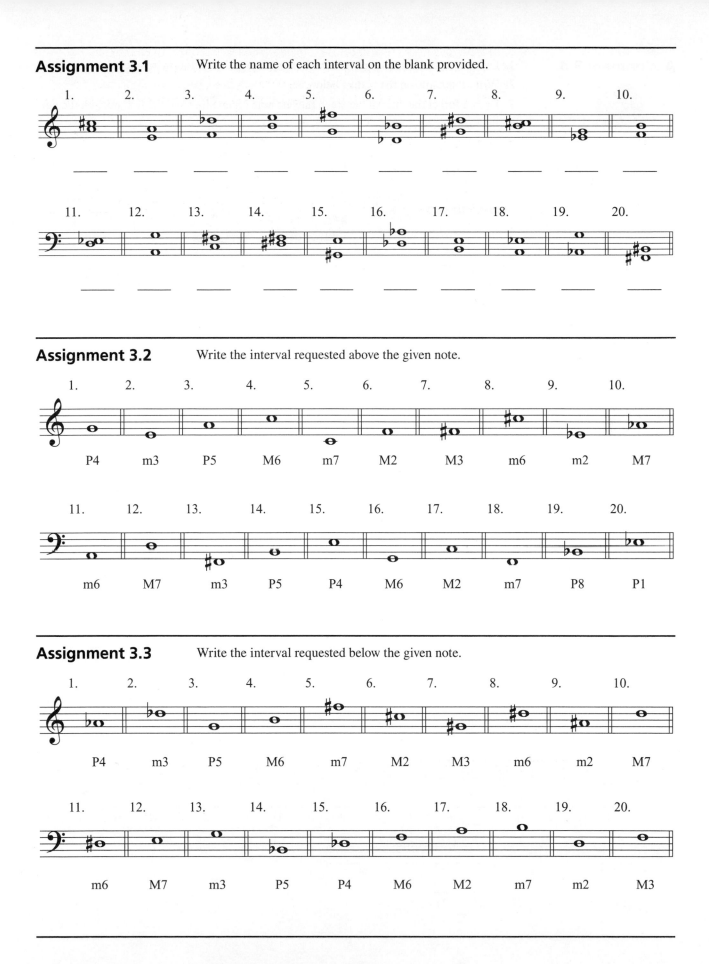

CHAPTER 3   Intervals and Transposition

67

1. Determine the interval between each pair of notes in the following melodies.
2. Write the name on the blanks below.
3. Do not forget the interval between the last note on one line and the first note on the next line.

1. Bach: Fugue in G Minor, BWV 542, mm. 29–32. CD Track 15

2. Bach: Fugue in G Minor, BWV 542, mm. 71–75. CD Track 16

3. Bach: Prelude in C Major ("Leipzig"), BWV 547, mm. 68–72. CD Track 17

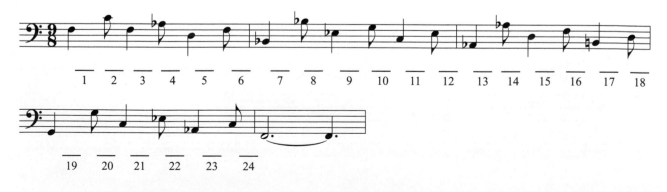

Assignment 3.5

1. Write the interval requested above the given note.
2. Determine the inversion of the interval and write the name in the blank provided.
3. On the staff, write the inversion of the original interval.

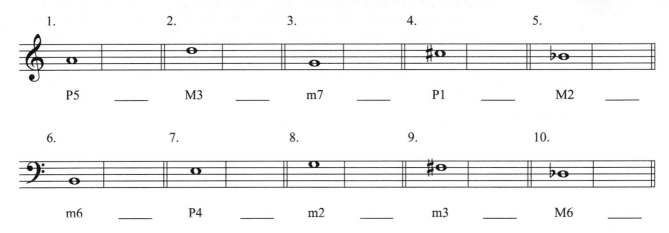

Assignment 3.6
(Keyboard)

1. Play all major, minor, and perfect intervals (m2, M2, m3, M3, P4, P5, m6, M6, m7, M7, P8) above and below any given note.
2. Name the inversion of each interval you play and play the inversion.

Assignment 3.7

1. Indicate the intervals between the two voices on the blanks provided.
2. Predict (by interval inversion) the intervals that will be produced if the upper voice is placed an octave lower (inversion at the octave).
3. Write out the two voices in inversion to show the intervals as inverted.
4. Play both versions on the piano or join another student in singing both versions.

Handel: *Te Deum* (Chandos). CD Track 18

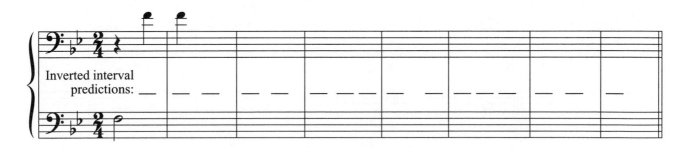

Assignment 3.8

1. Indicate the intervals between the two voices of this canon. (A canon is a contrapuntal composition in two or more parts, each part consisting of the same melodic line, but starting at different times and frequently at different pitches.)

2. Predict (by interval inversion) the intervals that will be produced if the upper voice is placed an octave lower and the lower voice placed an octave higher (inversion at the double octave). You may indicate compound intervals with their simple equivalents.

3. Write out the canon in inversion to show the intervals as inverted.

4. Play both versions on the piano or join another student in singing both versions.

Strict canon, invertible at the double octave. CD Track 19

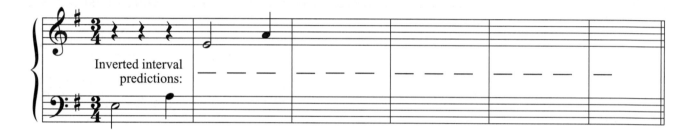

Assignment 3.9

1. Write the interval requested above the given note.

2. Determine the simple equivalent of the interval and write the name in the blank provided.

3. On the staff, write the simple equivalent of the original interval.

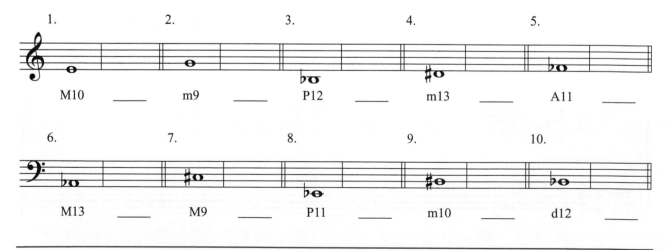

| 1. M10 _____ | 2. m9 _____ | 3. P12 _____ | 4. m13 _____ | 5. A11 _____ |
| 6. M13 _____ | 7. M9 _____ | 8. P11 _____ | 9. m10 _____ | 10. d12 _____ |

Assignment 3.10

Write the name of each interval on the blank provided.

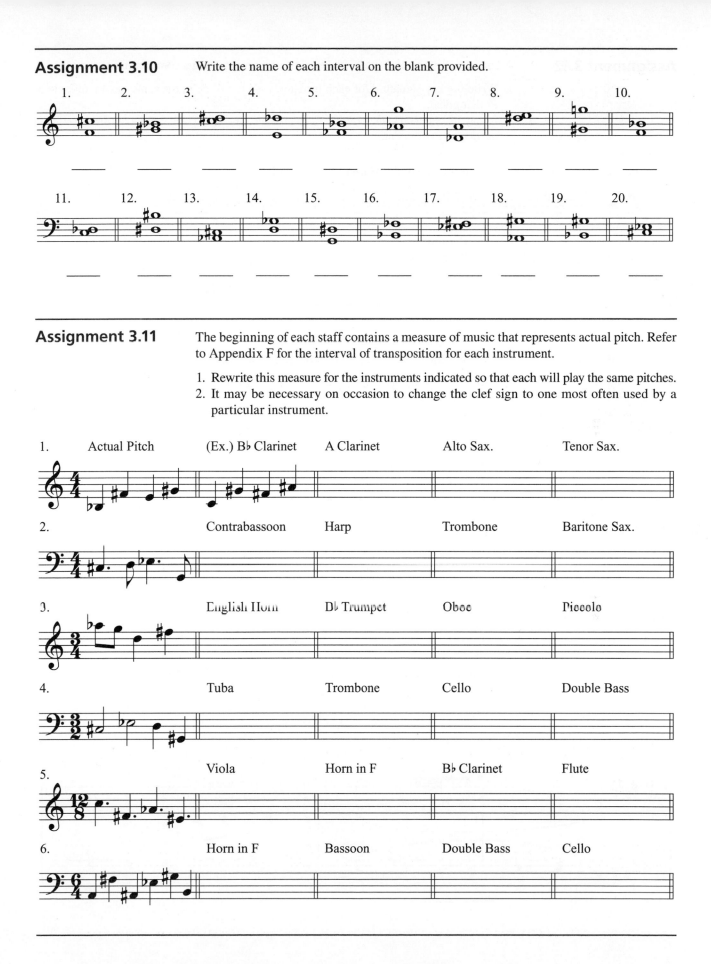

Assignment 3.12   At the beginning of each staff is a key signature representing a composition at actual pitch.

1. Write the key signature for each instrument so it will be in the same key (actual pitch) as that given.
2. It may be necessary on occasion to change the clef sign to the one most often used by a particular instrument.

1.   Actual Pitch   Alto Sax.   English Horn   Horn in F   B♭ Trumpet   Flute   Piccolo

2.   Actual Pitch   Trombone   Baritone (treble clef)   Viola   Double Bass   Baritone Sax.   Tuba

Assignment 3.13   Following is an excerpt from a string quartet by Mozart.

1. On a separate sheet of score paper, arrange the eight measures for one or more of the following groups of instruments:
   a. 2 alto saxophones   b. 1 flute   c. 1 B-flat trumpet
      1 tenor saxophone   2 clarinets   2 horns in F
      1 baritone saxophone   1 bassoon   1 tuba

   If needed transpositions prove difficult in the original key of E major, choose a more appropriate key that will make transpositions less awkward.
2. Write a separate staff for each instrument.
3. Perform the arrangement in class.
4. If none of the above combinations of instruments is available in your class, write for four instruments that are available.

Mozart: String Quartet in A Major, K. 464, II: Menuetto, mm. 73–80. CD Track 20

CHAPTER **4**

Chords

IMPORTANT CONCEPTS

In the previous chapter, pairs of pitches were assigned specific names for identification purposes. The phenomenon of tones sounding simultaneously frequently includes groupings of three, four, or more pitches. As with intervals, identification names are assigned to larger tone groupings with specific symbols.

Harmony

Harmony is the musical result of tones sounding together. Whereas melody implies the linear or horizontal aspect of music, harmony refers to the vertical dimension of music.

Chord

A *chord* is a harmonic unit with at least three different tones sounding simultaneously. The term includes all possible such sonorities.

Figure 4.1

Triad

Strictly speaking, a *triad* is any three-tone chord. However, since western European music of the seventeenth through the nineteenth centuries is *tertian* (chords containing a superposition of harmonic thirds), the term has come to be limited to a three-note chord built in superposed thirds.

Triad Root

The term *root* refers to the note on which a triad is built. "C major triad" refers to a major triad whose root is C. The root is the pitch from which a triad is generated.

Four types of triads are in common use. They are identified by the quality names major, minor, diminished, and augmented.

Major Triad

A *major triad* consists of a major third and a perfect fifth.

Figure 4.2

M3 + P5 = Major Triad   M3 + P5 = Major Triad

Minor Triad

A *minor triad* consists of a minor third and a perfect fifth.

Figure 4.3

m3 + P5 = Minor Triad   m3 + P5 = Minor Triad

Diminished Triad

A *diminished triad* consists of a minor third and a diminished fifth.

Figure 4.4

m3 + d5 = Diminished Triad   m3 + d5 = Diminished Triad

Augmented Triad

An *augmented triad* consists of a major third and an augmented fifth.

Figure 4.5

M3 + A5 = Augmented Triad   M3 + A5 = Augmented Triad

Figure 4.6 demonstrates how each of the four types of triads can be constructed. Each triad includes a root, a third, and a fifth.

Figure 4.6

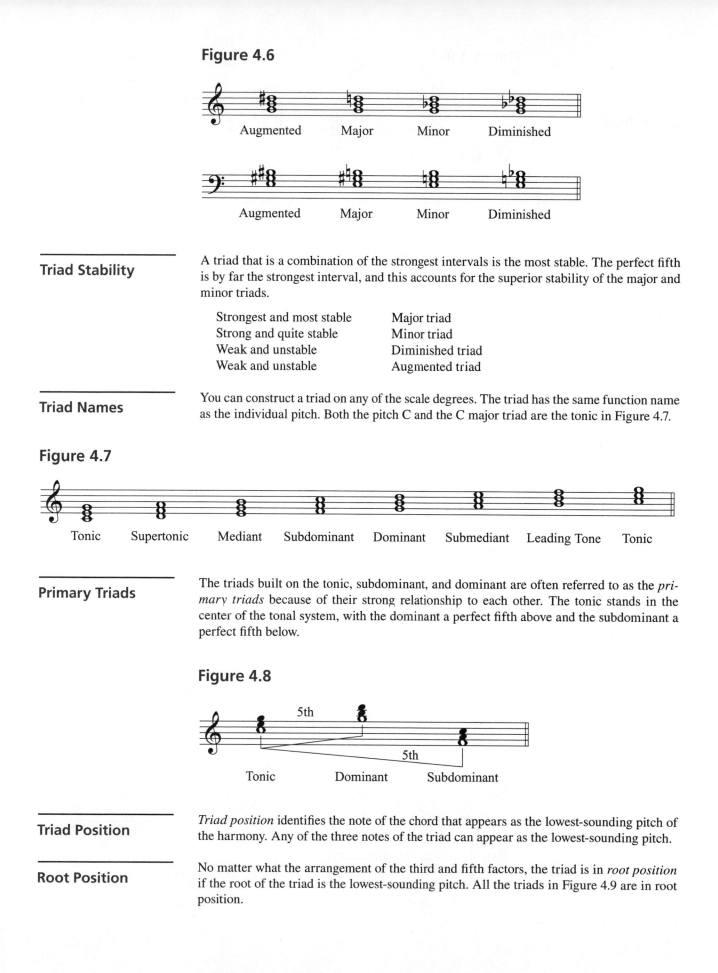

| Augmented | Major | Minor | Diminished |

| Augmented | Major | Minor | Diminished |

Triad Stability

A triad that is a combination of the strongest intervals is the most stable. The perfect fifth is by far the strongest interval, and this accounts for the superior stability of the major and minor triads.

Strongest and most stable	Major triad
Strong and quite stable	Minor triad
Weak and unstable	Diminished triad
Weak and unstable	Augmented triad

Triad Names

You can construct a triad on any of the scale degrees. The triad has the same function name as the individual pitch. Both the pitch C and the C major triad are the tonic in Figure 4.7.

Figure 4.7

| Tonic | Supertonic | Mediant | Subdominant | Dominant | Submediant | Leading Tone | Tonic |

Primary Triads

The triads built on the tonic, subdominant, and dominant are often referred to as the *primary triads* because of their strong relationship to each other. The tonic stands in the center of the tonal system, with the dominant a perfect fifth above and the subdominant a perfect fifth below.

Figure 4.8

5th

5th

| Tonic | Dominant | Subdominant |

Triad Position

Triad position identifies the note of the chord that appears as the lowest-sounding pitch of the harmony. Any of the three notes of the triad can appear as the lowest-sounding pitch.

Root Position

No matter what the arrangement of the third and fifth factors, the triad is in *root position* if the root of the triad is the lowest-sounding pitch. All the triads in Figure 4.9 are in root position.

Figure 4.9

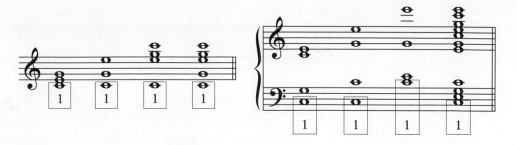

Triad Inversion

An *inversion* of a triad occurs when the root is not the lowest-sounding pitch.

Figure 4.10

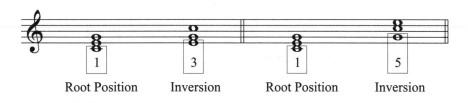

Root Position   Inversion   Root Position   Inversion

First Inversion

No matter what the arrangement of the root and fifth factors, the triad is in *first inversion* if the third factor is the lowest-sounding pitch.

Figure 4.11

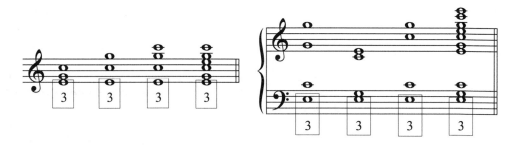

Second Inversion

No matter what the arrangement of the root and third factors, the triad is in *second inversion* if the fifth factor is the lowest-sounding pitch.

Figure 4.12

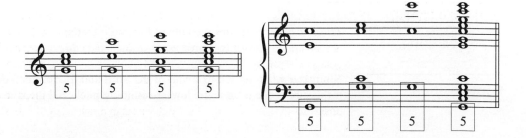

Other Tertian Chords

Triads by no means exhaust the possible tertian sonorities. We can continue adding thirds to tertian chords, resulting in seventh chords, ninth chords, eleventh chords, and thirteenth chords (discussed in detail in the latter chapters of this volume and in volume 2).

Figure 4.13

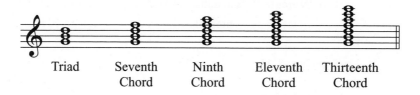

Triad Seventh Chord Ninth Chord Eleventh Chord Thirteenth Chord

Seventh Chords

Although triads are the focus of this chapter, you will also encounter seventh chords when analyzing music. A *seventh chord* is formed by adding another third above the fifth of a triad. The seventh chord built on the dominant is the most common seventh chord in tonal music (see Figure 4.14).

Figure 4.14

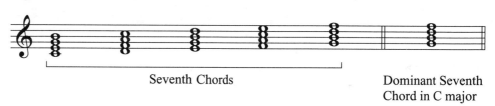

Seventh Chords   Dominant Seventh Chord in C major

History

Emerging during the thirteenth century from a composition type known as *organum,* harmony developed gradually during the medieval and Renaissance periods. In the Renaissance period (1450–1600) harmony was the result of the combination of melodic lines, and the study of harmony was a study of the consonant and dissonant relationships between melodic lines.

During the baroque period (1600–1750) the concept of accompanying a melody with chords was developed. The keyboard performer was expected to improvise the accompaniment from a given bass line and a set of symbols used to indicate in a general way the chords to be used. The bass line with its accompanying symbols is called a *figured bass,* and the instruments that play from this part are called the *continuo.* Musicians employed the figured-bass system throughout the baroque period for keyboard accompaniments and keyboard parts for solo songs, solo instrumental compositions, and small and large ensembles.

In 1722 Jean-Phillipe Rameau wrote the *Traité de l'harmonie* (*Treatise on Harmony*), which described a theory of harmony. In Book One of this treatise, Rameau discusses the inversion of chords, a concept that profoundly influenced later theoretical writing. Many of the principles presented in this book are direct outgrowths of Rameau's ideas.

APPLICATIONS

Musicians analyze harmonic elements in music using sets of symbols to identify chord types, function, and relationships. A chord's connection to a key center, or perceived forward motion in a composition, can often be explained through harmonic analysis. Two analytical methods, Roman numeral analysis and macro analysis, are presented throughout this volume as tools for categorizing tonal harmonies and chord relationships.

Symbols are not limited to analysis. Composers and arrangers use both the baroque figured-bass system and modern-day popular music symbols as shorthand systems to reveal harmonic vocabulary to performers.

Roman Numeral Analysis

In analysis, *Roman numerals* are used to distinguish triads based on scale degrees (Arabic numerals with carets are used for scale degrees themselves). Memorize the type of triads that appear on each tone of the major scale and the three forms of the minor scale.

Capital Roman numerals	= Major triads	Examples: I, IV, V
Lowercase Roman numerals	= Minor triads	Examples: ii, iii, vi
Lowercase Roman numerals with °	= Diminished triads	Examples: ii°, vii°
Capital Roman numerals with +	= Augmented triads	Example: III+

Figure 4.15

In the major scale:

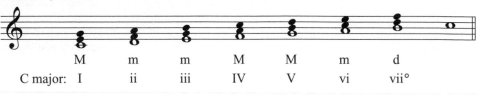

```
         M    m    m    M    M    m    d
C major: I    ii   iii  IV   V    vi   vii°
```

In the natural minor scale:

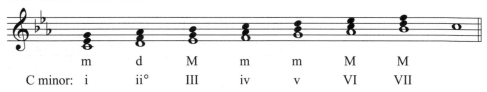

```
         m    d    M    m    m    M    M
C minor: i    ii°  III  iv   v    VI   VII
```

In the harmonic minor scale:

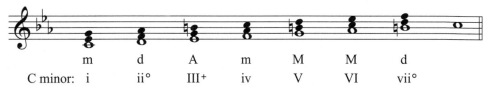

```
         m    d    A     m    M    M    d
C minor: i    ii°  III+  iv   V    VI   vii°
```

In the melodic minor scale:

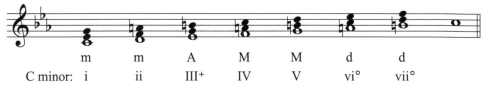

```
         m    m    A     M    M    d    d
C minor: i    ii   III+  IV   V    vi°  vii°
```

The following chart is a summary of triad types in the diatonic scales:

Scale	Major Triads on	Minor Triads on	Diminished Triads on	Augmented Triads on
Major	I, IV, V	ii, iii, vi	vii°	None
Natural Minor	III, VI, VII	i, iv, v	ii°	None
Harmonic Minor	V, VI	i, iv	ii°, vii°	III+
Melodic Minor	IV, V	i, ii	vi°, vii°	III+

Root-position triads are indicated with Roman numerals without additional symbols. First-inversion triads are indicated with a superscript ^{6} to the right of the Roman numeral. Second-inversion triads are indicated with a superscript $^6_4$ to the right of the Roman numeral.

When triads are reduced to three notes spaced as close together as possible, we say they are in *simple position*.

Figure 4.16

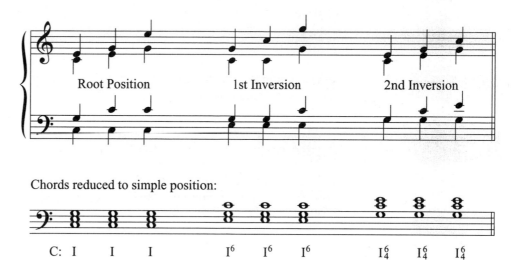

Chords reduced to simple position:

Although ^{6} and $^6_4$ accompany Roman numerals to indicate inversions, they are short-hand symbols to represent intervals above the lowest sounding note. Figure 4.17 illustrates the complete interval figures for triads, along with the abbreviated symbols.

Figure 4.17

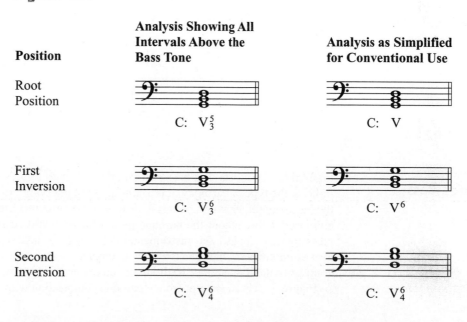

We indicate root-position seventh chords by adding a small superscript ^{7} to the right of the Roman numeral.

Figure 4.18

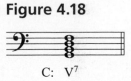

C: V^7

The dominant seventh chord can appear in various inversions, including *third inversion,* as shown in Figure 4.19.

Figure 4.19

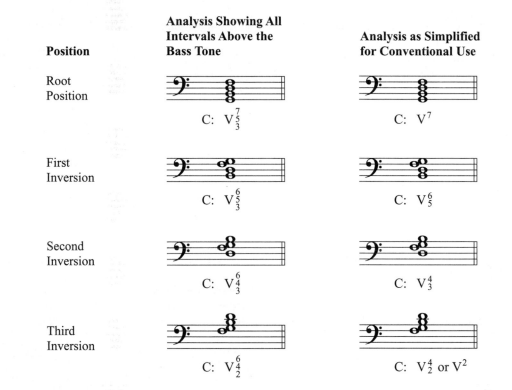

Position	Analysis Showing All Intervals Above the Bass Tone	Analysis as Simplified for Conventional Use
Root Position	C: $V^7_5_3$	C: V^7
First Inversion	C: $V^6_5_3$	C: V^6_5
Second Inversion	C: $V^6_4_3$	C: V^4_3
Third Inversion	C: $V^6_4_2$	C: V^4_2 or V^2

Figured bass consists of a bass part (single line) with figures (mostly numbers) below to indicate the type of harmony. It is a contrapuntal, intervallic shorthand method of showing the harmony (along with nonharmonic tones). Because this method saved time, musicians employed it throughout the baroque period for keyboard accompaniments and keyboard parts for solo songs, solo instrumental compositions, and small and large ensembles. It also exemplifies the baroque tendency to emphasize the outer voices (soprano and bass) in contrast to the Renaissance tradition of equal voices (soprano, alto, tenor, and bass).

Figure 4.20 is an excerpt from a baroque composition with figured bass.

Figure 4.20

Cesti: *Bella Clori* (Beautiful Chloris), mm. 185–188.

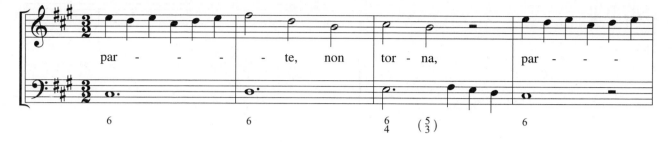

Modern editions of music are often printed with the figured bass *realized*. This means that the harmony is filled in according to the figures. Figure 4.21 shows the previous excerpt with a *realization* of the figured bass.

Figure 4.21

Cesti: *Bella Clori* (Beautiful Chloris), mm. 185–188, with figured bass realized.

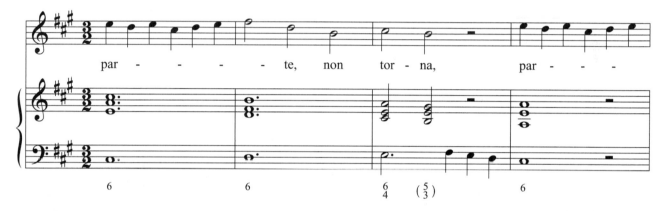

Figured-Bass Symbols

As we have seen, the numbers ^{6} and $^6_4$ refer to intervals above the bass note, but they imply others such as 3, 8, or an additional 6 or 4 to fill out the four voices. Figured-bass numbers do not denote specific arrangements; they do not indicate what note should be placed in a particular voice (soprano, alto, or tenor). Composers of the baroque period could have indicated all intended notes above the bass note—including octaves, thirds, and doublings where they occur—but this would have proven burdensome. In actual practice they chose only figures that would specifically define a position (root, first inversion, or second inversion). Thus, ^{6} clearly distinguishes first inversion from root position (no numbers) and second inversion ($^6_4$).

Some standard figured-bass symbols along with their realizations are shown in the following table and in Figure 4.22.

Symbol	Meaning	Realizations
None	Triad in Root Position	Short for: $\frac{5}{3}$, $\frac{3}{3}$, $\frac{8}{5}$, $\frac{5}{5}$, $\frac{5}{3}$, or $\frac{8}{8}$.
^{6}	Triad in First Inversion	Short for: $\frac{6}{3}$, $\frac{6}{6}$, $\frac{8}{6}$, $\frac{6}{3}$, or $\frac{6}{3}$.
$^6_4$	Triad in Second Inversion	Short for: $\frac{8}{6}$, $\frac{6}{6}$, or $\frac{6}{4}$.

Figure 4.22

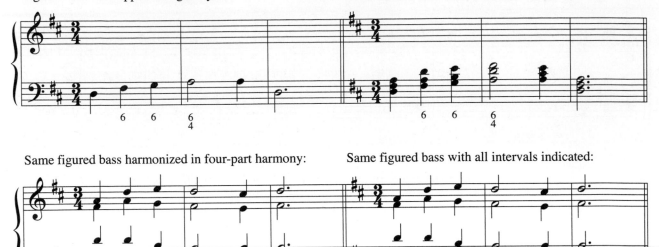

Figured bass as it appears originally:

Same figured bass harmonized in simple position:

Same figured bass harmonized in four-part harmony:

Same figured bass with all intervals indicated:

When you are considering triads, note that any figured bass that contains a 6 but *not* a 4 means first inversion. Any figured bass that contains a 6 *and* a 4 means second inversion.

Sometimes it is necessary to indicate sharps, flats, or naturals above the bass note. These are shown in the following manner:

Symbol	Meaning
♯, ♭, or ♮	A sharp, flat, or natural alone beneath a bass note indicates a triad in root position with the third interval above the bass note sharped, flatted, or naturaled.
$^6_♯$, $^6_♭$, or $^6_♮$	A sharp, flat, or natural below a 6 indicates a first-inversion triad with the third interval above the bass note sharped, flatted, or naturaled.
♯6, ♭6, ♮6, $^{♯6}_4$, $^6_{♭4}$	Any sharp, flat, or natural sign on either side of a number indicates that this interval above the bass note should be sharped, flatted, or naturaled depending on the symbol. Remember that accidentals beside numbers do not change the original intent of the numbers themselves.
8̸, 6̸, 4̸, 4, 2̸	A slash mark through a number indicates that this interval above the bass note should be raised a half step. It means the same as a sharp sign beside the number. The plus sign (4) also has the same meaning.

If none of these symbols are present, assume that you should follow the key signature in realizing figured-bass symbols.

Figure 4.23

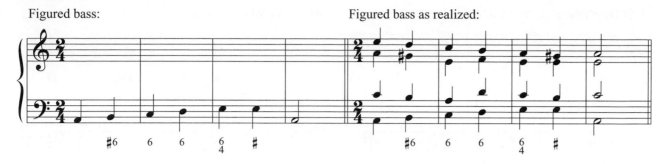

Figured bass: Figured bass as realized:

Macro Analysis

Macro analysis is an analytical procedure that you can employ along with, or instead of, more conventional methods of analysis. The system's name *macro* (meaning large) defines the technique's fundamental purpose—to reveal large harmonic gestures in music. Patterns that are not easily seen in music become more visible through the use of macro analysis. Although Roman numeral analysis monitors chord-by-chord harmonic details, macro analysis provides a panoramic view of a composition's harmonic landscape.

The excerpt in Figure 4.24 has been analyzed using the two techniques. Note the relationship between the macro analysis symbols in the top layer and the Roman numeral analysis below. Both share a similar use of capital and lowercase letter symbols to identify chord qualities, but macro analysis identifies chord roots with letters instead of Roman numerals. The macro symbols should not be confused with other letter-based symbols (such as popular-music symbols). Instead, think of them as a shorthand analysis system.

Macro analysis exposes the harmonic durations and forward motion (with slur symbols), whereas the Roman numeral analysis draws attention to smaller details such as chord position.

Figure 4.24

Rinck: "St. Lucian," mm. 1–4

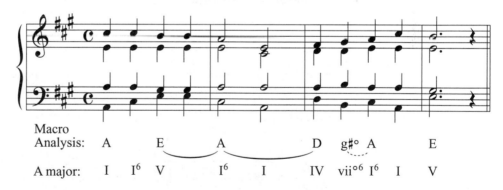

Macro Analysis:	A		E		A		D	g#°	A		E
A major:	I	I⁶	V		I⁶	I	IV	vii°⁶	I⁶	I	V

The system employs letters to indicate the roots of chords, accompanied by specific symbols to depict chord quality. The letter symbol will correspond with the pitch name of the root of the triad. Macro analysis symbols for triads are written as follows:

1. Major triads are represented by capital letter names.
2. Minor triads are represented by lowercase letter names.
3. Diminished triads are represented by lowercase letter names followed by the ° symbol.
4. Augmented triads are represented by capital letter names followed by the + symbol.

Figure 4.25

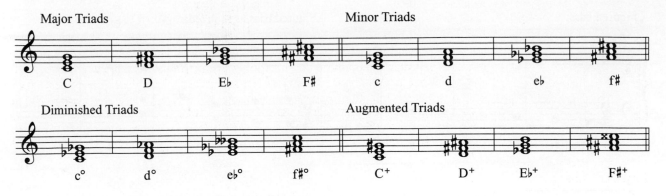

Major Triads   Minor Triads

C   D   E♭   F♯   c   d   e♭   f♯

Diminished Triads   Augmented Triads

c°   d°   e♭°   f♯°   C⁺   D⁺   E♭⁺   F♯⁺

The dominant seventh chord is represented by a capital letter followed by the superscript ^{7} symbol.

Figure 4.26

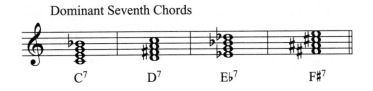

Dominant Seventh Chords

C^7 D^7 $E\flat^7$ $F\sharp^7$

Slur symbols are used in macro analysis to label forward motion in music. Two types of slurs are added to the letter-based symbols:

1. The solid slur is attached to adjacent letter symbols whose roots are either an ascending fourth or a descending fifth apart. In macro analysis, this type of progression is known as a *circle progression*.
2. The dotted slur is connected to leading-tone chords whose roots resolve up a half step. Since the leading tone is functioning as a substitute for the dominant in this type of progression, the dotted slur indicates the use of a related chord as a substitute. In macro analysis, this type of progression is known as a *leading-tone progression*.

Refer to Chapter 10 for additional information about types of harmonic progressions.

Figure 4.27

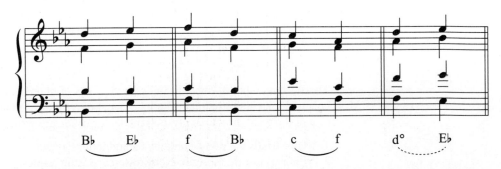

B♭   E♭   f   B♭   c   f   d°   E♭

Macro analysis symbols are traditionally positioned below the score. If used in conjunction with Roman numerals, the macro analysis will occupy the upper level with the Roman numerals positioned below. A summary of macro analysis symbols can be found in Appendix B.

Popular-Music Symbols

Just as figured bass was the shorthand of the eighteenth century, popular-music symbols are the shorthand of the twentieth century—a system for notating chords when the performer is expected to improvise the specific details. Instead of writing out the exact notes on score paper, popular music composers and arrangers indicate the chords to be used for accompaniment with chord symbols written above the melody line of the composition. Such a score, with the melody and the popular-music symbols, is called a *lead sheet* or *fake sheet*.

Figure 4.28

Coltrane: *Mr. P.C.*

Popular-music symbols, like figured-bass symbols, give the performer information about the chords required, but popular-music symbols usually give no information about the bass line. The performer is expected to improvise that part.

The chord indications are simple to master and generally refer to root-position chords. Guitar players and keyboard players alike can read and interpret them. The addition of rhythmic patterns and arrangements of the chord factors is left to the performers, most of whom are well trained in the art of improvisation. Although chord indications are given in root position, most performers will voice the chords—that is, arrange them for the best voice leading, which may mean placing some chords in inversion. In some recent popular music, the bass position is indicated with a slash followed by the bass note: C/G means a C major chord with G in the bass.

The following examples illustrate popular-music chord symbols for triads, as well as some of the chords with added sixths and sevenths that are common in jazz and popular music. These symbols are presented in *The New Real Book* series (Sher Music Co.) and are adaptations of the recommendations made by Carl Brandt and Clinton Roemer in *Standardized Chord Symbol Notation* (Roevick Music Co., 1976). Other symbols that are sometimes seen in popular music and jazz are shown in Appendix C.

Popular music symbols for triads are written as follows:

1. A major triad is shown by a capital letter designating the root.
2. A minor triad is shown by a capital letter with MI added.
3. A diminished triad is shown by a capital letter with ^{dim.} added.
4. An augmented triad is shown by a capital letter with ⁺ added.

Figure 4.29

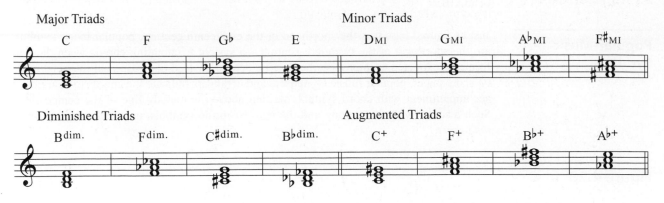

Major Triads   Minor Triads

C   F   G♭   E   Dᴍɪ   Gᴍɪ   A♭ᴍɪ   F♯ᴍɪ

Diminished Triads   Augmented Triads

Bdim.   Fdim.   C♯dim.   B♭dim.   C⁺   F⁺   B♭⁺   A♭⁺

A triad with an added tone a major sixth above the triad root (common in popular music) is indicated by adding a superscript ^{6} after the letter designating the triad (C^6).

Figure 4.30

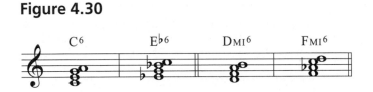

C^6 E♭^{6} Dᴍɪ^6 Fᴍɪ^6

Seventh chords appear regularly in popular music. Figure 4.31 provides an example of some of the more common seventh chords.

Figure 4.31

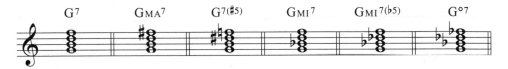

G^7 Gᴍᴀ^7 G$^{7(♯5)}$ Gᴍɪ^7 Gᴍɪ$^{7(♭5)}$ G$^{°7}$

Summary

Four methods for labeling chords have been presented in this chapter: Roman numerals, figured bass, macro analysis symbols, and popular-music symbols. Each system has advantages and disadvantages. The Roman numeral system has the advantage that it shows both the quality of the chord and its relationship to a diatonic scale. This relationship is vital to your understanding of the structure of harmony, and for this reason the Roman numeral system will be the primary system for labeling chords in this book. The figured-bass system is useful in learning voice leading since it shows some details of melodic motion; you will see it in many assignments. The macro analysis system excels at identifying both the root and quality of a chord while highlighting important harmonic motion within a composition. The popular-music symbols are universally used in jazz and popular music, and an understanding of these symbols is vital for studying this music.

Assignment 4.1

Indicate the type of triad shown using the following abbreviations: M = major, m = minor, d = diminished, and A = augmented.

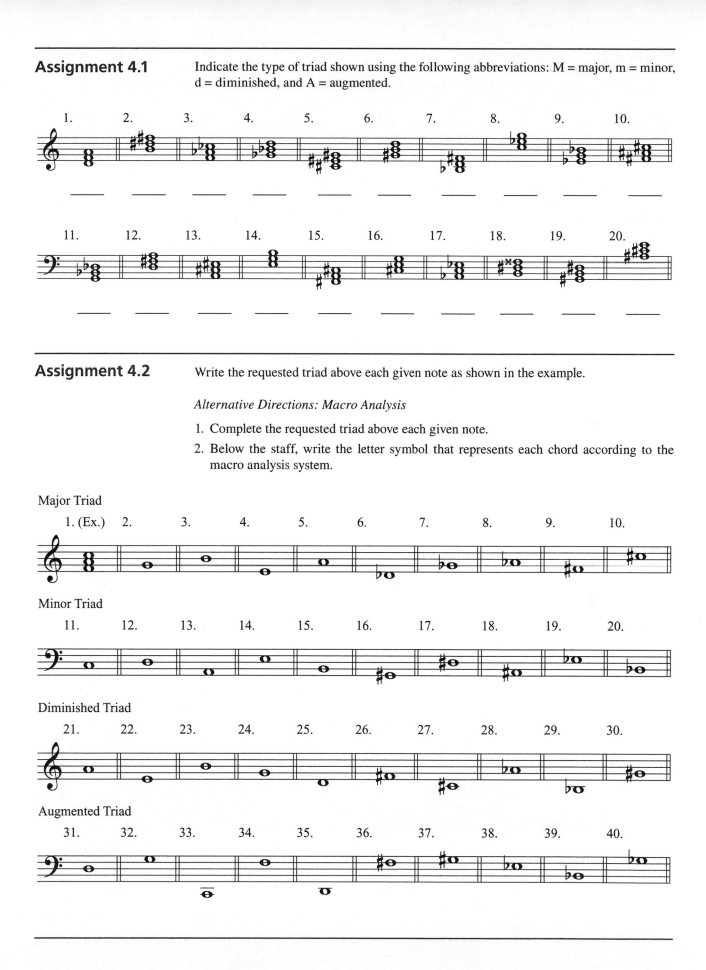

Assignment 4.2

Write the requested triad above each given note as shown in the example.

Alternative Directions: Macro Analysis

1. Complete the requested triad above each given note.
2. Below the staff, write the letter symbol that represents each chord according to the macro analysis system.

Major Triad

Minor Triad

Diminished Triad

Augmented Triad

Assignment 4.3

1. Write the requested triads as shown by the Roman numerals.
2. Be sure to write the correct accidentals to the left of the appropriate notes.

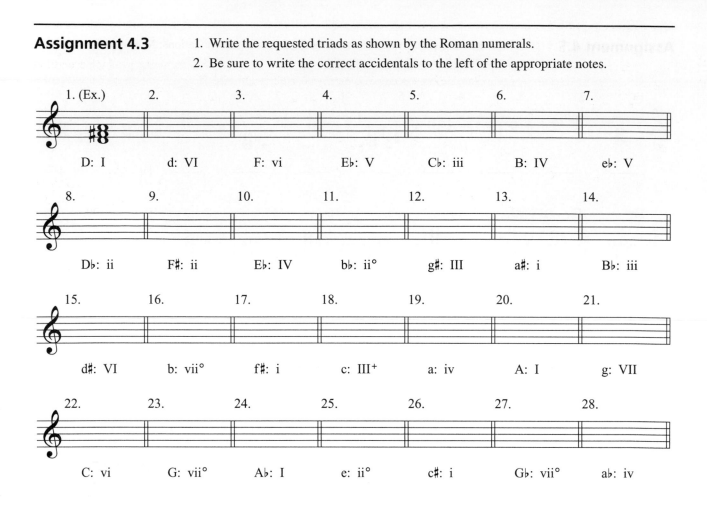

Assignment 4.4

1. Following is a series of major triads.
2. Write the three major keys and the two minor keys (harmonic form) in which each triad is diatonic. The example is worked correctly for you.

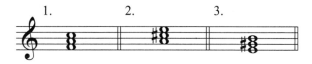

Chord	Key	Chord	Key	Chord	Key
1. (Ex.) I in F major		2. _____ in _____		3. _____ in _____	
IV in C major		_____ in _____		_____ in _____	
V in Bb major		_____ in _____		_____ in _____	
V in Bb minor		_____ in _____		_____ in _____	
VI in A minor		_____ in _____		_____ in _____	

Assignment 4.5

1. Following is a series of minor triads.
2. Write the three major keys and the two minor keys (harmonic form) in which each triad is diatonic. The example is worked correctly for you.

	Chord		Key		Chord		Key			Chord		Key
1. (Ex.)	ii	in	F major	2.	_____	in	_____	3.		_____	in	_____
	iii	in	E♭ major		_____	in	_____			_____	in	_____
	vi	in	B♭ major		_____	in	_____			_____	in	_____
	i	in	G minor		_____	in	_____			_____	in	_____
	iv	in	D minor		_____	in	_____			_____	in	_____

Assignment 4.6

1. Following is a series of diminished triads.
2. Write the one major key and the four minor keys (two harmonic form and two melodic form) in which each triad is diatonic. The example is worked correctly for you.

	Chord		Key		Chord		Key			Chord		Key
1. (Ex.)	vii°	in	E♭ major	2.	_____	in	_____	3.		_____	in	_____
	ii°	in	C minor (harmonic)		_____	in	_____			_____	in	_____
	vii°	in	E♭ minor (harmonic)		_____	in	_____			_____	in	_____
	vi°	in	F minor (melodic)		_____	in	_____			_____	in	_____
	vii°	in	E♭ minor (melodic)		_____	in	_____			_____	in	_____

Assignment 4.7

1. Following are 10 triads, in various positions and of various types, arranged in four-part harmony (soprano, alto, tenor, and bass).

2. Complete the blanks as requested. The example is worked correctly for you.

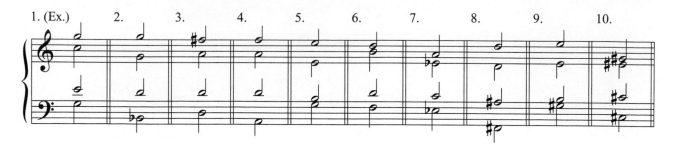

	Root	Position	Type		Analysis Symbol
Chord No. 1:	C	2nd Inversion	Major	in G major:	IV$_4^6$
Chord No. 2:	_____	_____	_____	in F major:	_____
Chord No. 3:	_____	_____	_____	in A major:	_____
Chord No. 4:	_____	_____	_____	in F major:	_____
Chord No. 5:	_____	_____	_____	in B minor (harmonic):	_____
Chord No. 6:	_____	_____	_____	in A minor (natural):	_____
Chord No. 7:	_____	_____	_____	in B♭ minor (harmonic):	_____
Chord No. 8:	_____	_____	_____	in B minor (harmonic):	_____
Chord No. 9:	_____	_____	_____	in G♯ minor (harmonic):	_____
Chord No. 10:	_____	_____	_____	in F♯ major:	_____

Assignment 4.8

The following are excerpts from music literature.

1. Identify the triads in each excerpt. Certain notes have been circled. These are not considered part of the triads. Brackets have been added to numbers 3, 4, and 5 to identify the triads more clearly.

2. Write the Roman numeral analysis of each chord and indicate the position: ^{6} if in first inversion, $^6_4$ if in second inversion, and no numbers if in root position.

3. Each chord is numbered for convenience in class discussions.

Alternative Directions: Macro Analysis

Provide the correct letter symbol for each chord and add slur symbols according to the information on pages 83–84.

1. Tallis: "God Grant We Grace" ("Tallis's Canon"), mm. 5–8. **CD Track 21**

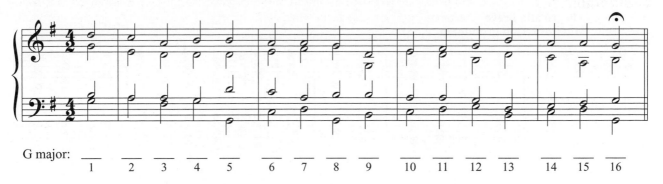

G major: ‾1‾ ‾2‾ ‾3‾ ‾4‾ ‾5‾ ‾6‾ ‾7‾ ‾8‾ ‾9‾ ‾10‾ ‾11‾ ‾12‾ ‾13‾ ‾14‾ ‾15‾ ‾16‾

2. Crüger: "Herr, ich habe missgehandelt" ("Lord, I have transgressed"), mm. 1–9. **CD Track 22**

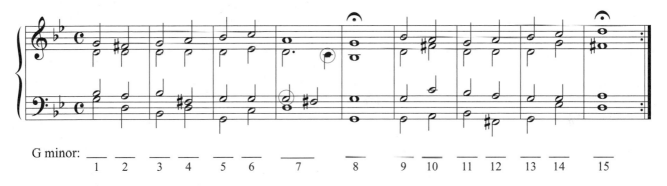

G minor: ‾1‾ ‾2‾ ‾3‾ ‾4‾ ‾5‾ ‾6‾ ‾7‾ ‾8‾ ‾9‾ ‾10‾ ‾11‾ ‾12‾ ‾13‾ ‾14‾ ‾15‾

3. Mozart: Sonata in C Major, K. 545, I, mm. 63–66. **CD Track 23**

C major: ‾1‾ ‾2‾ ‾3‾ ‾4‾

‾5‾ ‾6‾ ‾7‾ ‾8‾

4. Mussorgsky: "The Great Gate of Kiev" from *Pictures at an Exhibition*, mm. 1–8. CD Track 24

5. Mendelssohn: *Songs Without Words* op. 53, no. 3, mm. 95–103. CD Track 25

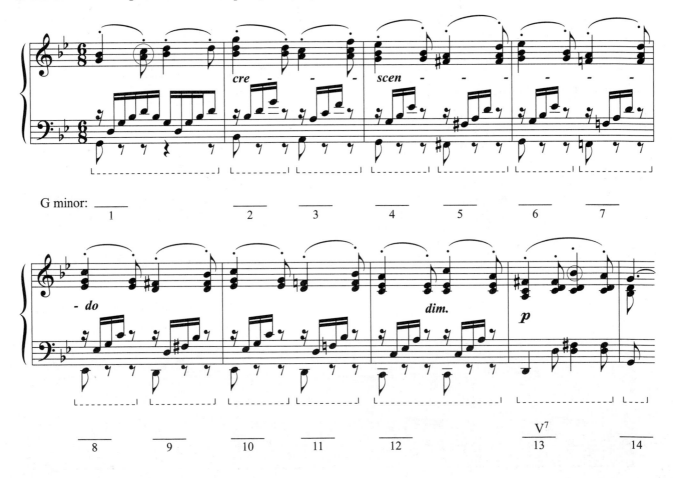

Assignment 4.9

Following are several four-part chorale phrases harmonized by J. S. Bach. (Certain embellishing tones have been omitted.)

1. Under the staves, indicate the figured-bass symbols that would be used to obtain the chords written by Bach.
2. This assignment is designed to help you learn figured-bass symbols. In selecting chords that require a variety of symbols, some chords have been included that are not intended for analysis at this time, so you are asked to supply only figured-bass symbols and not Roman numerals. The example illustrates the correct procedure.
3. One figured-bass symbol (in no. 2) has been supplied for you.

1. (Ex.) Bach: "Von Gott will ich nicht lassen" ("I Will Not Leave God"), BWV 418, mm. 5–6. CD Track 26

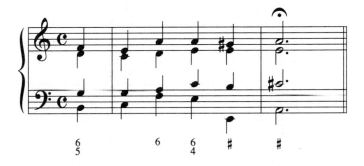

2. Bach: "Das neugeborne Kindelein" ("The Newborn Child"), BWV 122, mm. 13–16. CD Track 27

3. Bach: "Seelen-Bräutigam," ("Bridegroom of the Soul"), BWV 409, mm. 1–2. CD Track 28

4. Bach: "Schwing' dich auf zu deinem Gott" ("Soar Upward to Thy God"), BWV 40, mm. 1–2. CD Track 29

5. Bach: "O Lamm Gottes, unschuldig" ("O Lamb of God, Most Stainless"), BWV 401, mm. 3–4. CD Track 30

Assignment 4.10

Fill in the macro analysis symbol below each of the given chords.

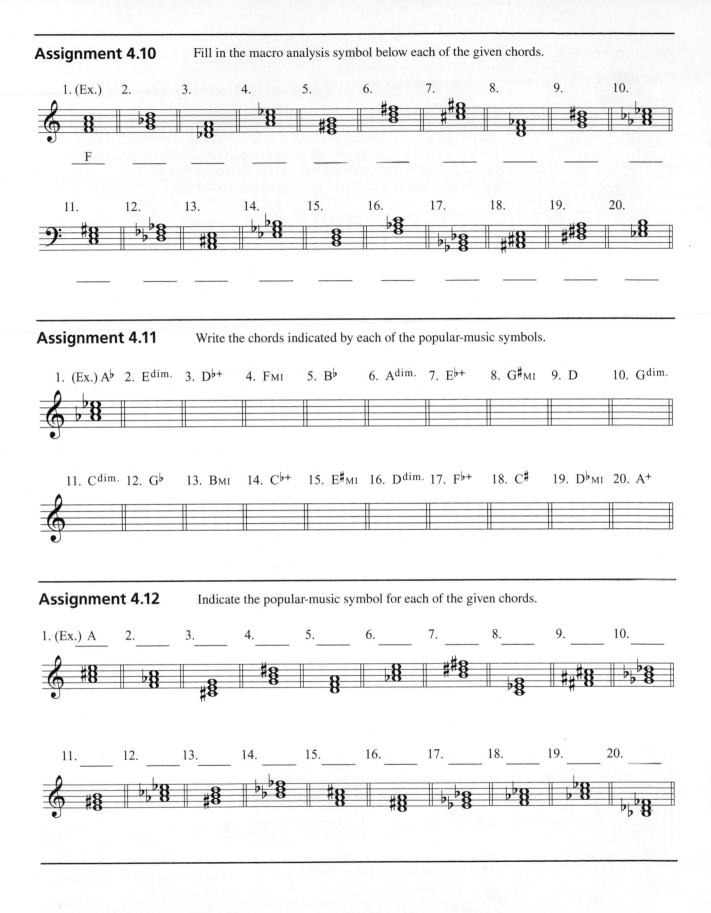

1. (Ex.)   2.   3.   4.   5.   6.   7.   8.   9.   10.

F

11.   12.   13.   14.   15.   16.   17.   18.   19.   20.

Assignment 4.11

Write the chords indicated by each of the popular-music symbols.

1. (Ex.) A♭   2. E^dim.   3. D♭+   4. F^MI   5. B♭   6. A^dim.   7. E♭+   8. G♯^MI   9. D   10. G^dim.

11. C^dim.   12. G♭   13. B^MI   14. C♭+   15. E♯^MI   16. D^dim.   17. F♭+   18. C♯   19. D♭^MI   20. A+

Assignment 4.12

Indicate the popular-music symbol for each of the given chords.

1. (Ex.) A   2. ___   3. ___   4. ___   5. ___   6. ___   7. ___   8. ___   9. ___   10. ___

11. ___   12. ___   13. ___   14. ___   15. ___   16. ___   17. ___   18. ___   19. ___   20. ___

The Structural Elements of Music

The study of the structure of music begins with the classification of all aspects of music into five basic categories: sound, harmony, melody, rhythm, and form—the *structural elements*.

The *sound* of the music is the result of the voices and/or instruments used, the texture of the music, and the effects of dynamics. In music, *texture* refers to the way the melodic, rhythmic, and harmonic materials of a composition are woven together.

The study of the *harmony* of a composition includes the harmonic patterns and progressions, the tonal implications of the harmony, and how the harmony is sustained and elaborated.

The study of the *melody* of a composition includes the prominent melodic lines and their repetition and variation, the range and contour of melodic material, the phrase structure of the melodic lines, the scale basis for melodic materials, and the relationship and relative prominence of the various melodic ideas that appear together in a work.

The study of the *rhythm* in a composition includes the nature of rhythmic activity, the tempo and tempo changes, the density of rhythmic activity, and the harmonic rhythm or rate of harmonic change throughout a composition.

Form refers to the larger shape of the composition. Form in music is the result of the interaction of the four structural elements previously described. Certain formal patterns recur often enough in Western music to be given names (see Chapters 16–17).

We will consider each of the basic structural elements in isolation so that you can focus your attention on each in turn. However, you must always bear in mind that these structural elements seldom function in isolation in a piece of music.

Cadences and Nonharmonic Tones

**IMPORTANT
CONCEPTS**

Composers organize chords in specific combinations to signal the conclusion of musical passages. These points of repose are known as *cadences*. Furthermore, composers frequently embellish chords with nonchord pitches known as nonharmonic tones. This chapter is devoted to these two fundamental elements of musical composition.

Phrase

A *phrase* is a substantial musical thought, which ends with a musical punctuation called a cadence. Phrases are created in music through an interaction of melody, harmony, and rhythm. The first part of this chapter concentrates on the harmonic and rhythmic aspects of phrases; in Chapter 6 we will take up the melodic aspects.

Harmonic Cadence

A *harmonic cadence* is musical punctuation that closes a phrase or section of music. Cadences differ considerably in musical strength. Some signify the end of a complete musical thought and can be compared to the period (.). Others bring an incomplete idea to a close but suggest something else to come. These can be compared to a comma (,) or a semicolon (;). Most cadences conclude with either the V or I chord. The dominant frequently appears as a seventh chord (V^7).

Figure 5.1

A. Scarlatti: "O cessate di piagarmi," from *Pompeo*, mm. 5–8.

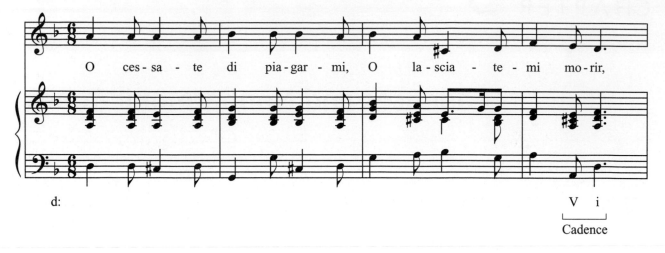

Perfect Authentic Cadence

The *perfect authentic cadence* is a progression from V to I in major keys and V to i in minor keys. Both chords must be in root position. In this cadence the tonic note must also be the highest sounding pitch in the tonic triad. From the standpoint of finality, the perfect authentic cadence is the strongest cadence of all.

Imperfect Authentic Cadence

The *imperfect authentic cadence* is slightly weaker than the perfect authentic cadence. A perfect authentic cadence becomes imperfect when:

1. The highest-sounding tone in the tonic triad is a tone other than the tonic note.
2. The vii° triad is substituted for the V, making the cadence vii°⁶ to I or vii°⁶ to i.
3. One or both of the chords (V or I) is inverted. Examples are: V⁶ to I or V to i⁶.

Figure 5.2 illustrates both perfect and imperfect authentic cadences.

Figure 5.2

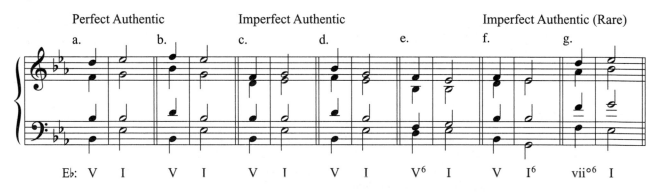

Half Cadence

If the second chord of a cadence is V, it is a *half cadence*. This permits a large number of possibilities, but composers actually employ only a few. I to V, IV to V, or ii to V account for the vast majority of half cadences. A half cadence from iv⁶ to V in a minor key is sometimes called a *Phrygian half cadence* (see Figure 5.3d).

Figure 5.3

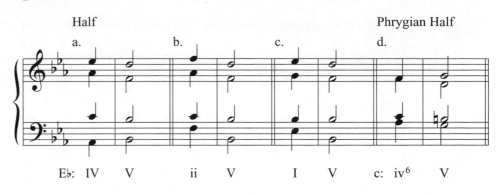

Half

Phrygian Half

Eb: IV V   ii V   I V   c: iv⁶ V

Plagal Cadence

The *plagal cadence* is nearly always one progression: IV to I in major keys, or its equivalent, iv to i in minor keys. Infrequently, the progression ii⁶ to I occurs as a plagal cadence.

Figure 5.4

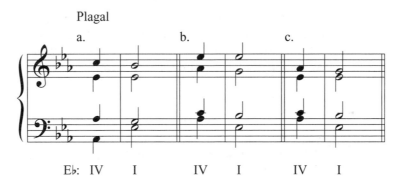

Plagal

Eb: IV I   IV I   IV I

Deceptive Cadence

If the first chord is V and the second is not I, the cadence is *deceptive*. Although there arc a large number of possibilities, composers most often select vi (VI in minor). Figure 5.5 illustrates deceptive cadences.

Figure 5.5

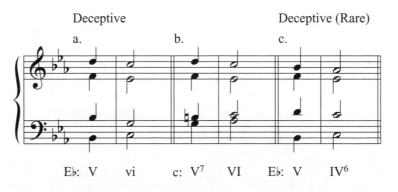

Deceptive

Deceptive (Rare)

Eb: V vi   c: V⁷ VI   Eb: V IV⁶

Rhythmic Cadence

Phrase endings often contain characteristic rhythmic patterns that create a *rhythmic cadence*. Notice in Figure 5.6 that the phrase ending can be sensed by tapping the rhythm alone.

Figure 5.6

Bach: Brandenburg Concerto no. 3 in G Major, BWV 1048, I, mm. 1–2 (modified).

Rhythmic cadence: └────────┘

Rhythmic cadences often end with a longer note than the prevailing note values or are followed by a rest, which, in effect, lengthens the final note. A rhythmic cadence pattern may recur several times throughout a given composition (see Figure 5.7).

Figure 5.7

Polish Folk Song.

Rhythmic cadence: └──────┘   Rhythmic cadence: └──────┘

Rhythmic cadence: └──────┘   Rhythmic cadence: └──────┘

Phrases can exist at the rhythmic level alone, independent of harmony and melody. Drum cadences, for example, are clear examples of rhythmic phrases.

History

The history of harmonic cadences is interesting because so many early cadence types now sound quaint and unfulfilling. Prior to the baroque period and the establishment of functional harmony, cadences were considered simply a manipulation of melodic lines that converged or diverged to a point of rest, usually the final (the first degree of a mode). The following are typical of early cadences.

Figure 5.8

Firenze (c. 1375)   **Machaut (1300–77)**   **Binchois (1400–67)**   **Palestrina (1525–94)**

Double Leading-tone
Cadence: Landini Cadence: Plagal Cadence:

The advent of the baroque period with its tonality and functional harmony brought about the familiar cadence types.

Figure 5.9

The standard cadences (authentic, half, plagal, and deceptive) continued with little change from the baroque period throughout the classical period.

Figure 5.10

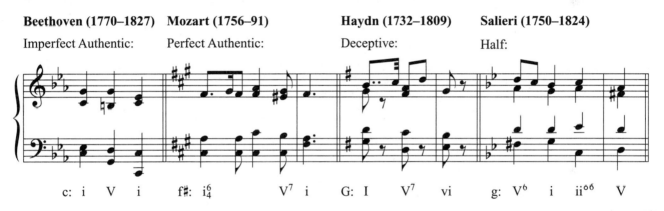

Cadence types remained virtually unchanged during the romantic period, but composers sometimes decorated their cadences in a more florid manner. In the post-romantic and impressionistic period, some cadences were simply highly decorated (and often camouflaged) traditional cadences. Others resembled a return to the linear cadences of the pre-baroque.

During the contemporary period, the idea of cadence formulae (distinct types such as authentic, half, etc.) became nearly extinct. Some composers of atonal (no tonal center) music employed interpretation markings (crescendo, loud dynamics, etc.) effectively to bring their compositions to a close. Others, in an effort to avoid stereotyped cadences, chose to allow their compositions to come to a halt without any hint of cadence.

Jazz and popular music frequently include traditional cadences similar to those studied in this text, but often disguised with substitutions and decorations. During the third quarter of the twentieth century, some creative jazz artists adapted free-tonal and atonal techniques to suit their improvisational styles. Free-tonal style permits free use of all 12 tones of the octave but maintains a tonal center. Atonal music contains no tonal center whatsoever. Figure 5.11 shows some traditional cadences that have been decorated.

Figure 5.11

Decorated Authentic:

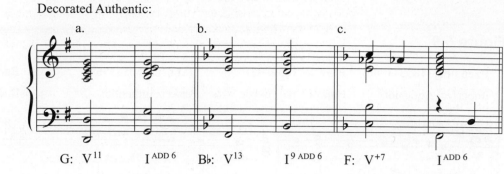

G: V^{11} I$^{\text{ADD 6}}$ B♭: V^{13} I$^{9\,\text{ADD 6}}$ F: V^{+7} I$^{\text{ADD 6}}$

In Figure 5.11a the dominant (V) is decorated with an eleventh and the tonic contains an added interval of a sixth above the bass note. In Figure 5.11b the tonic chord contains the intervals of a sixth and a ninth above the bass note. In Figure 5.11c the tonic chord contains a thirteenth (an octave plus a sixth) above the root.

Nonharmonic Tones

Harmonic tones should be familiar to you by now. They are the chord tones: root, third, or fifth. *Nonharmonic tones* (nonchord tones) are pitches that sound along with a chord but are not chord pitches. Most nonharmonic tones are dissonant and create intervals of a second, fourth, or seventh. Diminished or augmented intervals are also considered dissonant. The dissonance created by nonharmonic tones is calculated against the lowest-sounding tone of a chord, no matter how many other voices are present. An exception occurs when the nonharmonic tone is positioned in the lowest-sounding voice itself (usually bass). Nonharmonic tones generally occur in a pattern of three pitches:

1	2	3
Preceding tone (chord tone)	Nonharmonic tone (not a chord tone)	Following tone (chord tone)

A few nonharmonic tones involve patterns of more than three pitches and will be discussed later in the chapter.

The various nonharmonic tones are named by the intervals between the preceding tone, the nonharmonic tone, and the following tone. Figure 5.12 shows the common three-tone patterns. The nonharmonic tone is circled in each case.

Figure 5.12

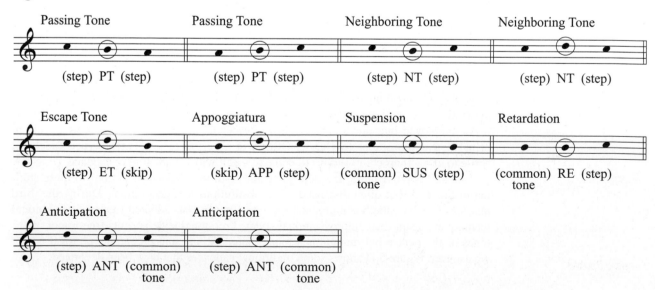

Passing Tone   Passing Tone   Neighboring Tone   Neighboring Tone

(step) PT (step)   (step) PT (step)   (step) NT (step)   (step) NT (step)

Escape Tone   Appoggiatura   Suspension   Retardation

(step) ET (skip)   (skip) APP (step)   (common) SUS (step)   (common) RE (step)
                                                  tone   tone

Anticipation   Anticipation

(step) ANT (common)   (step) ANT (common)
                 tone   tone

The most important distinction among the various nonharmonic tones is whether the dissonance occurs on the beat (accented) or off the beat (unaccented). Dissonances placed on the beat are much stronger and often create a powerful emotional impact, whereas those placed off the beat generally pass almost unnoticed smoothing out melodic lines. Some nonharmonic tones occur in both accented and unaccented contexts; others appear only as accented or as unaccented dissonances.

Unaccented Nonharmonic Tones

The common *unaccented nonharmonic tones* are the unaccented passing tone, unaccented neighboring tone, escape tone, and anticipation.

Unaccented Passing Tone

Figure 5.13 shows various *unaccented passing tones* in a four-voice texture. Figures 5.13a and 5.13b show single unaccented passing tones in descending and ascending patterns. Figures 5.13c–e show double unaccented passing tones in a variety of patterns.

Figure 5.13

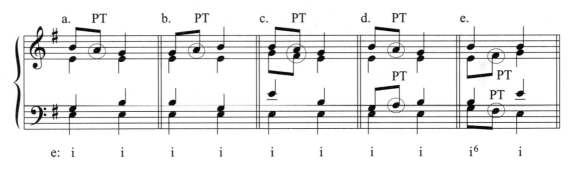

Unaccented Neighboring Tones

Figure 5.14 shows various *unaccented neighboring tones* in a four-voice texture. Figures 5.14a and 5.14b show single unaccented neighboring tones. Figures 5.14c and 5.14d show double unaccented neighboring tones.

Figure 5.14

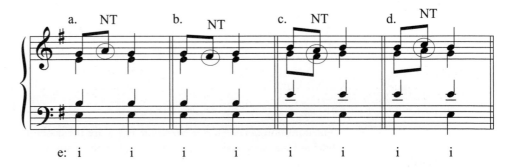

Escape Tones

Escape tones occur only as unaccented nonharmonic tones. Figure 5.15 shows the most common pattern, in which a step upward is followed by a skip downward by a third.

Figure 5.15

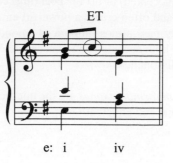

e: i   iv

Anticipation

Anticipations occur only as unaccented nonharmonic tones. Figure 5.16 shows two common patterns.

Figure 5.16

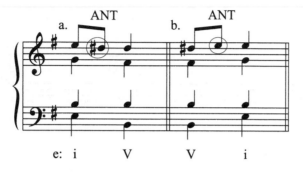

e: i   V   V   i

All four of the unaccented nonharmonic tones (passing tone, neighboring tone, escape tone, and anticipation) appear in the Handel minuet excerpt shown in Figure 5.17.

Figure 5.17

Handel: Minuet in G Minor, G. 242, mm. 13–16.

g: iv⁶   V⁷   i   V   i

Accented Nonharmonic Tones

The common *accented nonharmonic tones* are the accented passing tone, accented neighboring tone, suspension, retardation, and appoggiatura.

Accented Passing Tone

Figure 5.18 shows some *accented passing tones* in a four-voice texture. Compare the musical effect of these accented passing tones with the unaccented passing tones shown in Figure 5.13.

Figure 5.18

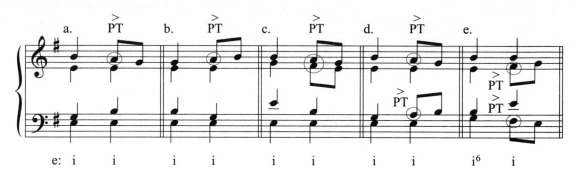

Accented Neighboring Tone

Figure 5.19 shows some *accented neighboring tones* in a four-voice texture. Compare them with the unaccented neighboring tones shown in Figure 5.14.

Figure 5.19

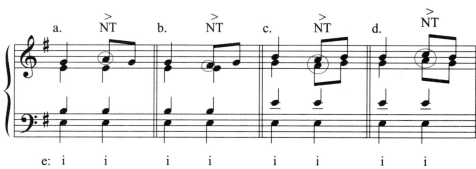

The excerpt by Verdi in Figure 5.20 includes both accented passing tones and accented neighboring tones.

Figure 5.20

Verdi: "Tu vedrai che amore" from *Il Trovatore*, mm. 1–5.

Suspension

The *suspension* occurs only as an accented nonharmonic tone. The melodic pattern of the suspension figure is always as follows: the preparation, the suspension, and the resolution (Figure 5.21).

Figure 5.21

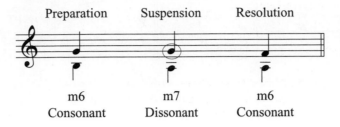

The suspended tone (the middle tone of the figure) is always dissonant. Suspensions are designated by the interval forming the suspended tone and resolution with the lowest sounding voice. Three common suspension types are shown in Figure 5.22.

Figure 5.22

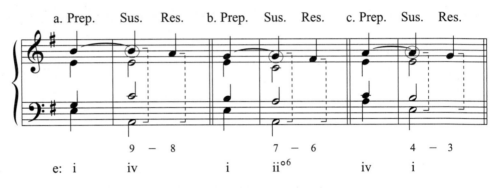

In determining the interval of suspension, the octave is usually removed. Thus 4–3 is used instead of 11–10. The exception is the 9–8 suspension.

Another common suspension is the 2–3 suspension. Whereas the suspension figure is in one of the upper voices in the three suspensions shown in Figure 5.22, in the 2–3 suspension the suspended tone is in the lower voice.

Figure 5.23

2–3 suspension showing suspension figure in lower voice.

The other voice (not containing the suspension figure) may move in almost any way as long as it provides the necessary preparation, suspension, and resolution phases for the suspension figure.

Figure 5.24

Suspending Voice:

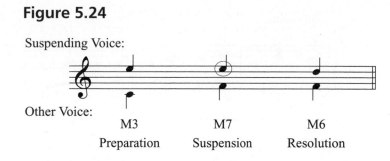

Other Voice:

M3	M7	M6
Preparation	Suspension	Resolution

Remember that suspensions occur only between two voices—even in four-voice writing. You may ignore the other voices when considering the preparation, suspension, and resolution. The following are suspensions found in a four-voice setting.

Figure 5.25

a. Bach: "Freu' dich sehr, o meine Seele" ("Rejoice Greatly, O My Soul"), BWV 25, mm. 12–13.

b. Bach: "Was Gott tut, das ist wohlgetan" ("What God Does Is Well Done), BWV 69a, mm. 3–4 (modified).

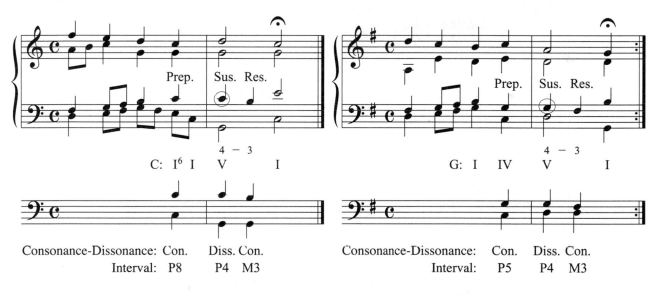

Suspensions can occur simultaneously in pairs, have decorated resolutions, occur in chains, or be accompanied by a changing bass line.

Figure 5.26

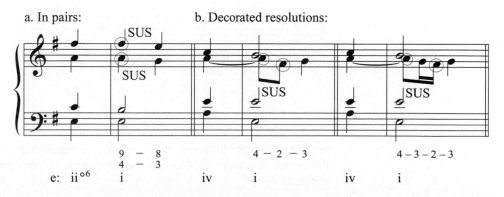

a. In pairs:

b. Decorated resolutions:

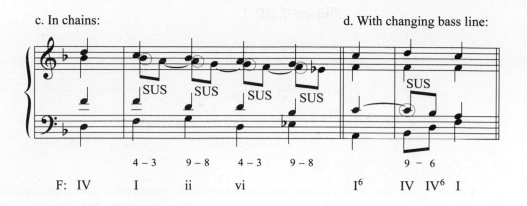

c. In chains: **d. With changing bass line:**

4 – 3   9 – 8   4 – 3   9 – 8   9 – 6

F: IV   I   ii   vi   I⁶   IV IV⁶ I

Retardation

A *retardation* is a nonharmonic tone similar to a suspension, except that the resolution is upward instead of downward.

Figure 5.27

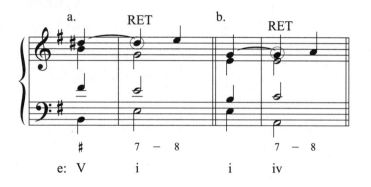

e: V   i   i   iv

Appoggiatura

The *appoggiatura* is a nonharmonic tone that is approached by skip and resolved by step in the opposite direction. It generally occurs as an accented nonharmonic tone.

Figure 5.28

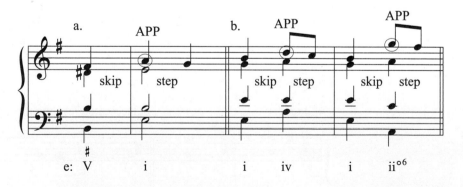

e: V   i   i   iv   i   ii°⁶

The Haydn piano sonata excerpt that follows includes a suspension, an appoggiatura, and a retardation. Although the retardation in Figure 5.29 looks similar to a grace note, performance practice dictates that the retardation be performed on beat one—not before the beat.

Figure 5.29

Haydn: Sonata in A Major, Hob. XVI:30, II: Var. 1, mm. 14–16.

Accented versus Unaccented Nonharmonic Tones

Compare the two phrases from Bach chorales shown in Figure 5.30. Figure 5.30a contains only unaccented nonharmonic tones, whereas 5.30b has three accented nonharmonic tones. The nonharmonic tones in 5.30a add rhythmic interest and make the voice leading smoother, but the dissonances in 5.30b are much more dramatic in effect and add considerable tension to the musical setting.

Figure 5.30

a. Bach: "Valet will ich dir geben" ("Farewell I Gladly Bid Thee"), BWV 415, mm. 1–2.

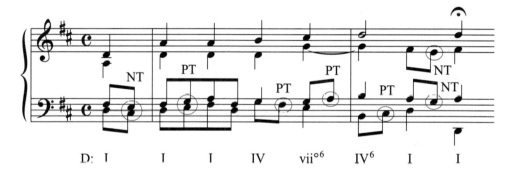

b. Bach: "Liebster Jesu, wir sind hier" ("Blessed Jesu, At Thy Word"), BWV 373, mm. 1–2.

Nonharmonic Tones Involving More Than Three Pitches

A few nonharmonic tones occur in patterns of four or more pitches. The most common are *successive passing tones, changing tones,* and the *pedal tone.*

Successive Passing Tones

Two passing tones occasionally fill an interval of a fourth. In such cases both the passing tones may be unaccented (Figure 5.31a) or they may be a combination of accented and unaccented passing tones (Figure 5.31b).

Figure 5.31

e: i   i   G: I   V

Changing Tones

Changing tones consist of two successive nonharmonic tones. The first leads by step from a chord tone, skips to another nonharmonic tone, and then leads by step to a chord tone (often the same chord tone). Other terms often used instead of changing tones are *double neighboring tones* or *neighbor group*. In many ways the two changing tones resemble neighboring tones with a missing (or perhaps implied) middle tone.

Figure 5.32

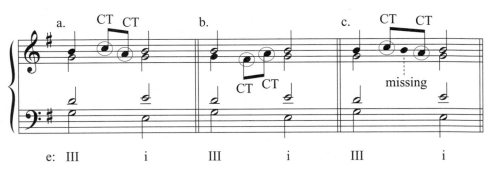

e: III   i   III   i   III   i

Pedal Tone

A *pedal tone* (also called a pedal point) is a held or repeated note, usually in the lowest voice, that alternates between consonance and dissonance with the chord structures above it. Thus, the dissonances are created by the moving chords above rather than the pedal tone itself. When a pedal tone occurs above other voices, it is called an *inverted pedal tone*.

Figure 5.33

Con. Diss. Con.   Diss. Diss. Diss.   Diss. Con. Diss.   Con. Con. Con.

Observe the successive passing tones, changing tones, and pedal tone in the concluding measures of an organ chorale prelude by Walther.

Figure 5.34

Walther: Chorale Prelude on "Lobt Gott, ihr Christen, allzugleich" ("Praise God, Ye Christians, All Together"), mm. 10–13.

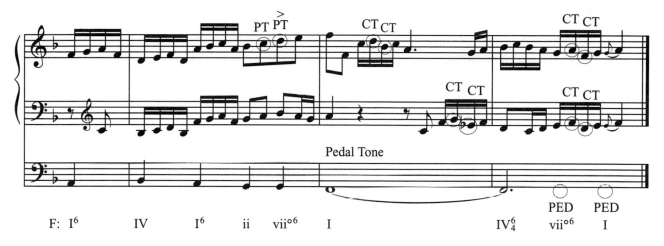

Summary of Nonharmonic Tones

The following chart is a summary of nonharmonic tones studied in this chapter.

PT	= Passing Tone	NT	= Neighboring Tone	ET	= Escape Tone
ANT	= Anticipation	SUS	= Suspension	RE	= Retardation
APP	= Appoggiatura	CT	= Changing Tones	PED	= Pedal Tone

Type	Approach	Departure	Voice	Accented or Unaccented
PT	Step	Step	Any	May be either
NT	Step	Step	Any	May be either
ET	Step	Skip	Soprano	Unaccented
ANT	Prefer step	Same tone	Usually soprano	Unaccented
SUS	Same pitch	Step down	Any	Accented
RE	Same pitch	Step up	Usually soprano	Accented
APP	Skip	Step	Usually soprano	Accented
CT	NA		Any	Usually neither note accented
PED	NA		Usually bass	Both

Assignment 5.1

The second and third chords of each exercise form a cadence.

1. Analyze each chord in the blanks provided.
2. Write the name of the cadence type in the blank above the exercise.

1. _____ 2. _____ 3. _____ 4. _____ 5. _____

G: ___ ___ ___   e: ___ ___ ___   C: ___ ___ ___   Eb: ___ ___ ___   F: ___ ___ ___

6. _____ 7. _____ 8. _____ 9. _____ 10. _____

Eb: ___ ___ ___   D: ___ ___ ___   A: ___ ___ ___   b: ___ ___ ___   Ab: ___ ___ ___

Assignment 5.2

Following are nonharmonic tones excerpted from music literature.

1. Circle the nonharmonic tone or tones.
2. Write the name of the type of nonharmonic tone in the blank provided.

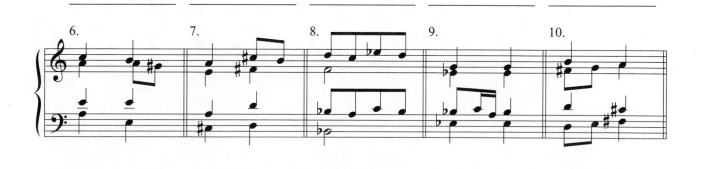

_____ _____ _____ _____ _____

Assignment 5.3

The following is an example from music literature.

1. Write the Roman numeral analysis of each chord and indicate the position as follows: ^{6} if in first inversion, $^6_4$ if in second inversion, and no numbers if in root position.

2. All the nonharmonic tones in this composition are unaccented passing tones. Circle the passing tones and write the abbreviation PT nearby.

3. Indicate the type of cadence at each fermata.

Alternative Directions: Macro Analysis

1. Write the macro letter symbol that represents each chord.

2. Include slurs wherever appropriate to identify circle progressions.

3. Indicate the type of cadence at each fermata.

Bourgeois: "Old Hundredth" from the *Genevan Psalter.* CD Track 31

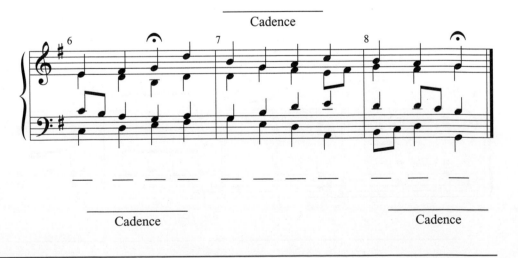

Assignment 5.4

The following are examples from Bach chorales.

1. Write the Roman numeral analysis of each chord and indicate the position as follows: ^{6} if in first inversion, $^6_4$ if in second inversion, and no numbers if in root position.

2. Circle all nonharmonic tones and write the abbreviations representing the name nearby. For convenience use the following abbreviations:

   Unaccented passing tone = PT

   4–3 suspension = 4–3 SUS

   Unaccented neighboring tone = NT

3. The first chord of each example is analyzed correctly for you.

4. Indicate the type of cadence at each fermata.

1. "Allein Gott in der Höh' sei Ehr'" ("Only to God on High Be Glory!"), BWV 104, mm. 1–2. **CD Track 32**

Cadence

2. "Mach's mit mir, Gott, nach deiner Güt'" ("Do with Me as Thy Goodness Prompts Thee"), BWV 377, mm. 1–2. **CD Track 33**

Cadence

3. "Christus, der ist mein Leben" ("Christ Is My Life"), BWV 282, mm. 1–4.
   CD Track 34

G: I   ___   ___   ___   ___   ___   ___

                                        _____
                                              Cadence

4. "Ermuntre dich, mein schwacher Geist" ("Rouse Thyself, My Weak Spirit"),
   BWV 43, mm. 20–22. CD Track 35

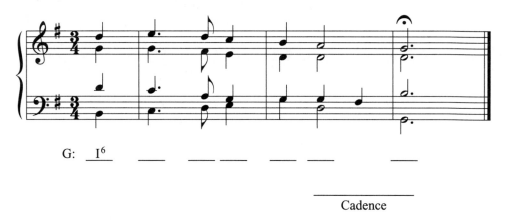

G: I⁶   ___   ___   ___   ___   ___

                                   _____
                                        Cadence

5. "Nun danket alle Gott" ("Now Let Us All Thank God"), BWV 386, mm. 1–2.
   CD Track 36

A: I   ___   ___   ___   ___

                              _____
                                   Cadence

Assignment 5.5

Following are four excerpts from music literature.

1. Analyze each chord with Roman numerals, also indicating its position. Some chords are provided to help you understand the procedure.

2. Circle and indicate the type of each nonharmonic tone next to the circle. For convenience use the following abbreviations:

> PT = Unaccented passing tone
>
> $\overset{>}{PT}$ = Accented passing tone
>
> NT = Unaccented neighboring tone
>
> $\overset{>}{NT}$ = Accented neighboring tone
>
> ET = Escape tone
>
> SUS = Suspension and type (9–8, 7–6, 4–3, 2–3)

3. Indicate the type of cadence used at each phrase ending.

4. In numbers 1 and 2, the chords change every quarter note. In numbers 3 and 4, the chords are bracketed—one chord per bracket.

1. Bach: "Als Jesus Christus in der Nacht" ("When Jesus Christ in the Night"), BWV 265, mm. 1–2. CD Track 37

F: vi   ii$^6_5$*

_____
Cadence

*Not explained in the text yet. Ignore for the moment.

2. Bach: "Ach bleib bei uns, Herr Jesu Christ" ("Ah, Stay With Us, Lord Jesus Christ"), BWV 253, mm. 8–10. CD Track 38

A: vi

_____
Cadence

CHAPTER 5 Cadences and Nonharmonic Tones   **117**

3. Caldara: "Alma del core" from *La constanza in amor vince l'inganno*, mm. 23–26. CD Track 39

Al - ma del co - - - re, spir - to __ dell' al - ma,

A: I

Cadence

The following hints will help you complete the analysis of the excerpt by Corelli.

1. The analysis for three of the chords is provided. The chord at number 1 is given to help you get started. The analysis at numbers 9 and 12 is also given.

2. The chords at numbers 6 and 7 are incomplete. Each requires another note to complete the triad. These are called implied harmonies, meaning that the missing note is suggested but not stated.

   Hint for chord 6: the missing triad note is suggested in chord 5. Which note of chord 5 would fill out the triad in chord 6?

   Hint for chord 7: the missing triad tone is suggested in chord 8. Which note of chord 8 would fill out the triad in chord 7?

3. The answer to the analysis of the C in chord 7 is found on pages 107–108.

4. Corelli: Sonata for Two Violins and Violone/Archlute in F Major, op. 3, no. 1, II: Allegro, mm. 34–37. CD Track 40

1   2   3   4   5   6   7   8   9   10 11 12

F: vi   V⁷   I

Cadence

Melodic Organization

IMPORTANT CONCEPTS

This chapter discusses the organization of melodic thought and the ways in which musical units are combined into larger and larger sections. In much the same way as written language is made meaningful through the grouping of sentences and paragraphs, melody is grouped into convenient and meaningful units or sections.

The Motive

A *motive* (or *motif*) is a short, recurring figure that appears throughout a composition or section of music. It is considered to be the germinating cell or organic unit that unifies a larger expanse of music. Distinctive melodic and/or rhythmic patterns form the underlying structure of a motive.

Melodic Motive

A *melodic motive* is a repeated pitch pattern. It usually recurs accompanied by the same or a similar rhythmic pattern.

Figure 6.1

Rimsky-Korsakoff: *Scheherazade,* op. 35, II, mm. 26–30.

Rameau: "Guerriers, suivez l'Amour" from *Dardanus,* act I, scene III, mm. 1–5.

Lalo: *Concerto Russe,* op. 29, I, mm. 74–79.

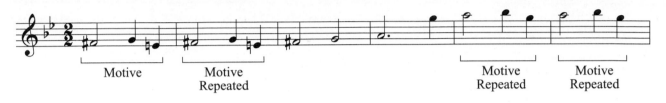

Rhythmic Motive

A recurring rhythmic pattern in a piece of music is called a *rhythmic motive.* Although melodic motives typically contain rhythmic motives, in many cases rhythmic motives function independently of melodic patterns, as the examples in Figure 6.2 illustrate.

Figure 6.2

British Folk Song.

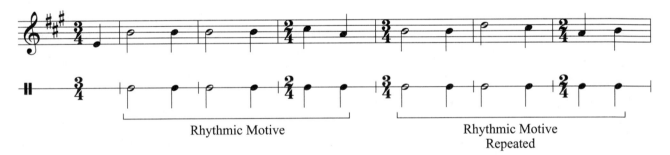

J. Revaux and C. François: "My Way," mm. 55–58.

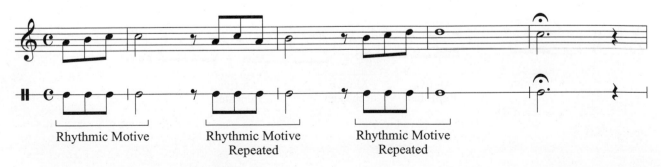

Copland: *Appalachian Spring*, mm. 80–82.

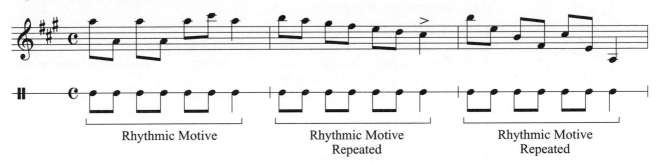

Rhythmic Motive   Rhythmic Motive   Rhythmic Motive
                            Repeated   Repeated

Rhythmic motives not associated with melodic motives also commonly appear as the motives in accompaniment figures. Accompaniments typically include a limited number of rhythmic motives that are repeated with only slight variation. This lack of rhythmic variety helps subordinate the accompaniment to the melody.

Figure 6.3

Mendelssohn: *Songs Without Words* op. 62, no. 1, mm. 1–2.

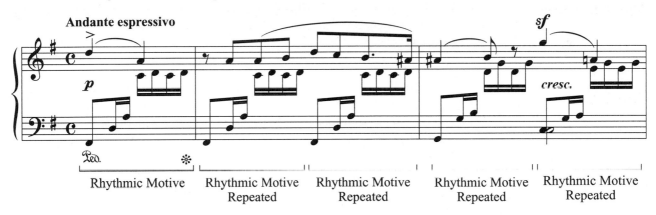

Rhythmic Motive   Rhythmic Motive   Rhythmic Motive   Rhythmic Motive   Rhythmic Motive
                     Repeated   Repeated   Repeated   Repeated

Chopin: Mazurka in G Minor, op. 67, no. 2, mm. 1–4.

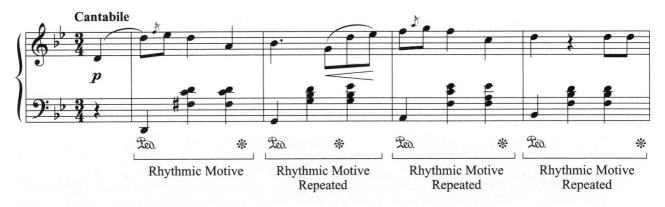

Rhythmic Motive   Rhythmic Motive   Rhythmic Motive   Rhythmic Motive
                         Repeated   Repeated   Repeated

Sequence

A *sequence* is the immediate restatement of a melodic motive or longer figure in the same instrumental or vocal part at a higher or lower pitch. Each separate unit of the sequence forms a segment. The sequence is one of the most common basic methods of melodic elaboration found in the eighteenth and nineteenth centuries. The following list describes some characteristics of sequences:

1. A sequence requires at least two segments.
2. Most sequences contain no more than three or four segments.
3. Sequences usually have only one direction—the segments succeed each other at continuingly higher pitches or continuingly lower pitches.
4. Sequence segments usually continue by the same interval distance. As an example, if the first segment begins on C and the next starts with E, then the remainder of the segments will continue in thirds.

Real Sequence

A *real sequence* contains continuing segments that are exact transpositions of the first segment. Every tone is transposed at exactly the same intervallic distance.

Figure 6.4

Beethoven: Symphony no. 9 in D Minor, op. 125, IV: Prestissimo, mm. 1–4.

Tonal Sequence

A *tonal sequence* accommodates the diatonic scale, so that only diatonic notes of the scale are used. This means that the transposition of the segments may not be exact. In Figure 6.5, note that in some segments, the half-step and whole-step patterns of the first segment are not reproduced exactly.

Figure 6.5

Sibelius: Symphony no. 5 in E-flat Major, op. 82, I, mm. 114–119.

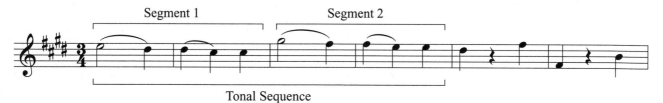

Tchaikovsky: Symphony no. 5 in E Minor, op. 64, I, mm. 1–6.

Modified Sequence

In a *modified sequence* some of the segments may be decorated or embellished in a way that does not destroy their original character.

Figure 6.6

C. P. E. Bach: Sonata for Violin and Piano.

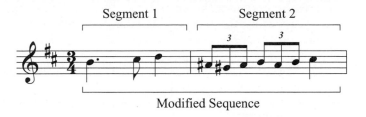

Modified Sequence

False Sequence

A *false sequence* repeats part of a figure and states the remainder in sequence—a mixture of sequence and repetition.

Figure 6.7

Beethoven: Trio in B-flat Major for Piano, Clarinet or Violin, and Cello, op. 11, II: Adagio, mm. 1–4.

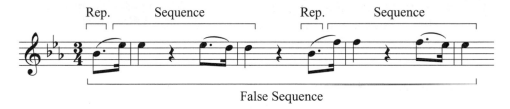

False Sequence

Schubert: Symphony no. 5 in B-flat Major, D. 485, I, mm. 5–8.

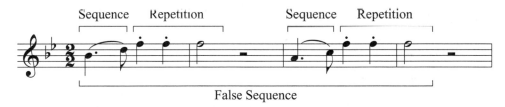

False Sequence

Phrase

A *phrase* is a substantial musical thought usually ending with a harmonic, melodic, and rhythmic cadence. The presence of a cadence distinguishes a phrase from a motive. Phrases are frequently four measures long, but may be longer or shorter. A phrase presents a complete (though sometimes dependent) musical thought.

Figure 6.8

Haydn: Symphony no. 102 in B-flat Major, IV: Finale, mm. 1–4.

Phrase Member   Phrases frequently contain slight melodic interruptions and thus divide into two *phrase members*. Phrase members are sufficiently separated, usually by a longer note value or rest, to distinguish them as individual units. Sometimes the second phrase member is either a repetition or a sequence of the first; however, it is just as often contrasting.

Figure 6.9

Angerer: *Berchtoldsgaden Musick,* "Kindersinfonie" ("Children's Symphony"), I, mm. 22–25.

Haydn: Trio no. 1 in G Major for Piano, Violin, and Cello, Hob. XV:25, III, mm. 1–4.

Mozart: Sonata in D Major, K. 284, I, mm. 1–4.

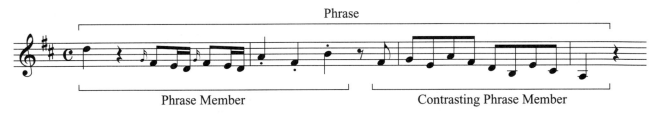

Under certain conditions, phrase members may be nearly indistinguishable from phrases themselves, with only the tempo serving as the deciding factor. We might interpret Figure 6.10 as two phrases at a slow tempo because of the clear rhythmic cadence, but because there is no harmonic cadence in measure 2, we hear the passage as a four-measure phrase.

Figure 6.10

Mozart: Sonata in C Major, K. 309, II, mm. 1–4.

Period

Two adjacent phrases may combine to form a *period* if:

1. The second phrase ends with a strong cadence—usually perfect authentic. Closure (finality) must be achieved at the end of the second phrase.

2. The first phrase ends with a weaker cadence than the second. A half cadence is common at the end of the first phrase.

3. The two phrases bear some musical relationship to each other. Often, they will create a "question–answer" effect called *antecedent–consequent*. The first phrase acts as the antecedent (question) and the second phrase as the consequent (answer).

Parallel Period

Two adjacent phrases form a *parallel period* if they both begin in the same manner. The two phrases may be nearly identical except for the cadences, or they may only be similar for a measure or two.

Figure 6.11

Foster: "Camptown Races," mm. 1–8.

Folk Song: "Cockles and Mussels."

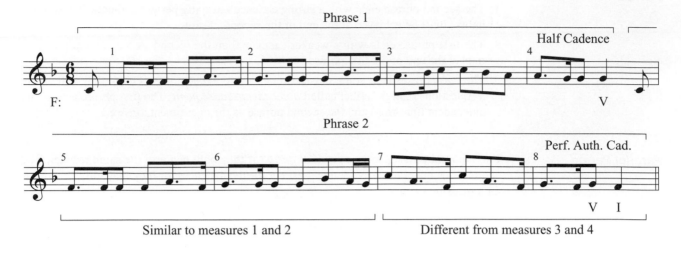

In Figure 6.12, only the three final notes of the second phrase are different from the first. The three differing pitches of the second phrase are necessary to accommodate the stronger perfect authentic cadence.

Figure 6.12

Schubert: Impromptu op. 90, no. 1, D. 899, mm. 2–9.

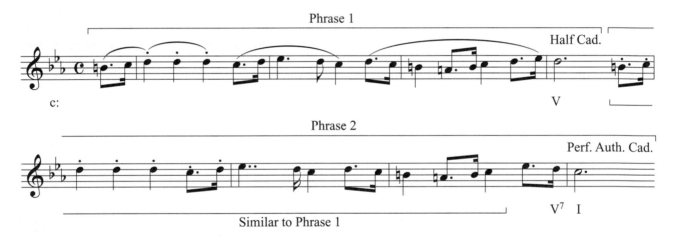

Contrasting Period

A *contrasting period* results when the two phrases are not similar in melodic content. The second (consequent) phrase may be different because of a change in the melodic contour or the inclusion of a dissimilar rhythmic figure, or it may simply differ in the lack of reference to material contained in the first phrase.

Figure 6.13

Folk Song: "The Ash Grove," mm. 1–8.

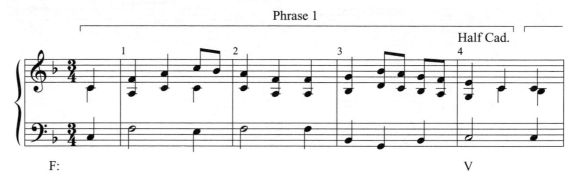

Phrase 1

Half Cad.

F: V

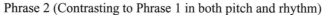

Phrase 2 (Contrasting to Phrase 1 in both pitch and rhythm)

Perfect Authentic Cad.

V   I

Three-Phase Period   Although most periods are composed of just two phrases, those of three and more do occur. The *three-phrase period* may be organized as A A B (antecedent, antecedent, consequent) or A B B (antecedent, consequent, consequent). Whatever the relationship, the third phrase must end with a stronger cadence than either of the first two.

Figure 6.14

Haydn: Sonata in E-flat Major, Hob. XVI:49, I, mm. 1–12.

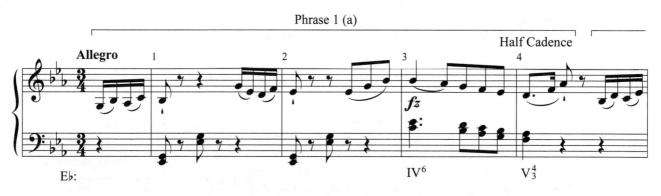

Phrase 1 (a)

Half Cadence

E♭:   IV⁶   V₃⁴

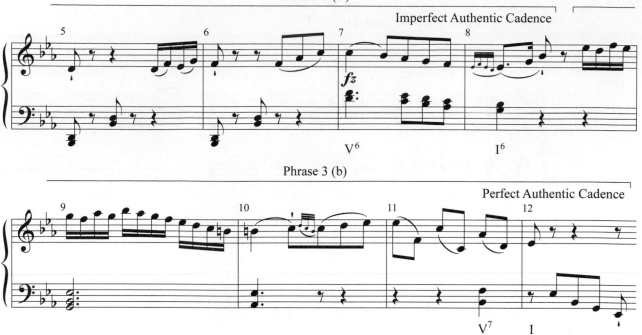

Double Period
(Four-Phrase Period)

Sometimes known as the *four-phrase period,* the *double period* allows for a variety of phrase relationships. However, the same principle that governs two-phrase periods applies here as well: the fourth phrase must bring the period to closure and should be at least as strong as any of the other three.

Figure 6.15

Mozart: Sonata in C Major, K. 309, II, mm. 1–16.

Phrase 3 (a′)

Imperfect Authentic Cad.

V^7 I

Phrase 4 (b′)

Perfect Authentic Cad.

V^7 I

Repeated Phrases

Repeated phrases, whether identical or modified, are not typically regarded as period structures because the second phrase is not dependent on the first. Thus the antecedent–consequent concept does not apply. Figure 6.16 illustrates a modified repeated second phrase and a perfect authentic cadence as the completion of both phrases.

Figure 6.16

Herbert: "Gypsy Love Song" from *The Fortune Teller,* mm. 20–27.

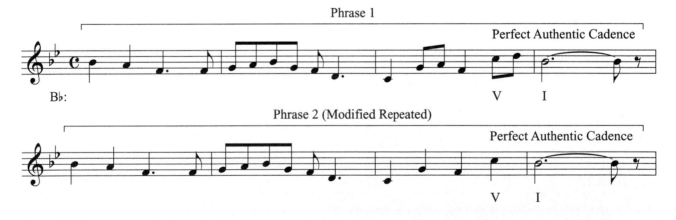

Phrase 1

Perfect Authentic Cadence

B♭:   V   I

Phrase 2 (Modified Repeated)

Perfect Authentic Cadence

V   I

Nonperiod Construction

Sometimes a series of phrases, some of which may be unrelated or lacking closure, do not arrange themselves conveniently into periods. Terms for such groupings range from "phrase groups" or "phrase chains" to "dissimilar phrases" or "dissolved periods." For purposes of analysis here, these nonperiod combinations can be called *dissimilar phrases.*

Modification of the Phrase

Composers often seek to modify a phrase in one way or another, sometimes to lengthen it and sometimes to provide other forms of variety.

Phrase Extension

An *extended phrase* is one whose length has been increased through the elongation of some part of it. Figures 6.17 through 6.20 illustrate both sequence and repetition as devices to extend a phrase. Phrases may be extended by a few beats or up to twice their normal length. The extensions may be near the beginning, in the middle, or near the cadence.

Beginning Extension

Phrases may be extended near the beginning by repeating or sequencing a few opening tones. Note that the following phrase would be complete without the bracketed section.

Figure 6.17

Haydn: Symphony no. 104 in D Major, III, mm. 53–58.

Internal Extension

A small melodic group may be repeated in the middle of the phrase to extend its length. The following phrase would be shorter, but nonetheless complete, without the extension.

Figure 6.18

Haydn: Symphony no. 101 in D Major ("Clock"), I, mm. 24–28.

Cadential Extension

Elaborating or repeating a cadence, a cadence figure, or individual cadence chords is an effective way in which to extend a phrase. The following phrase would be complete without the cadential extension.

Figure 6.19

Mendelssohn: *Songs Without Words* op. 85, no. 6, mm. 64–69.

Although extending a phrase adds to the overall length, some phrases are longer than others simply by design and not by extension:

Figure 6.20

Haydn: Symphony no. 95 in C Minor, III, mm. 13–18.

Change of Mode

Phrases are sometimes modified by a *change of mode* from major to parallel minor or vice versa.

Figure 6.21

Smetana: "The Moldau" from *My Country,* mm. 40–43 and 333–336.

Measures 40–43 (E minor)

e:

Measures 333–336 (E major)

E:

Melodic Structure

Up to this point, the discussion has centered on the organization of melody into units such as motives, phrases, and periods. The following section focuses on the nature of melody itself.

We do not yet clearly understand many aspects of melody. For example, why is the first movement of Beethoven's "Moonlight Sonata" (op. 27, no. 2) so well known when the sonatas preceding and following it are relatively unfamiliar to large audiences? Despite our inability to fully explain the nature of melody, we can gain much information by investigating a number of melodies to see what they have in common.

If you examine a large number of tonal melodies, a number of similarities emerge.

General Characteristics

1. Most tonal melodies contain a climax tone. A *climax tone* is the highest stressed pitch of a phrase or other unit. Usually the climax tone is reached only once, but it can appear with reiterations of the pitch and with embellishments. In Figure 6.22, the climax tone is D-flat and occurs only once.

Figure 6.22

Mahler: "Urlicht" from *Des Knaben Wunderhorn,* mm. 3–7.

Db:

2. Most phrases contain an *ascent* to and *descent* from the climax tone. Although fluctuations in the prevailing direction are a common occurrence, you should consider the overall direction when assessing the ascent and descent.

Figure 6.23

Beethoven: Symphony no. 3 in E-flat Major ("Eroica"), op. 55, IV: Finale, mm. 76–83.

3. Many melodic phrases contain significantly placed pitches of the tonic triad (scale degrees $\hat{1}$, $\hat{3}$, and $\hat{5}$) that are important in shaping the entire phrase. Tonic triad pitches are circled in Figure 6.24.

Figure 6.24

Corelli: Concerto Grosso in G Minor, op. 6, no. 8, II: Allegro, mm. 1–7.

4. Scale pitches $\hat{3}$–$\hat{2}$–$\hat{1}$ often conclude those phrases that end with the tonic pitch. The chorale melody in Figure 6.25 is a simple example of scale degrees $\hat{3}$–$\hat{2}$–$\hat{1}$ completing a phrase.

Figure 6.25

"Christ lag in Todesbanden" ("Christ Lay in the Bonds of Death"), mm. 1–2.

Figure 6.26 does not end with scale degrees $\hat{3}$–$\hat{2}$–$\hat{1}$ because the phrase concludes with a half cadence—the final pitch, F, is a part of the V chord but not a part of the I chord that would be necessary for a perfect authentic cadence.

Figure 6.26

Beethoven: Symphony no. 3 in E-flat Major ("Eroica"), op. 55, IV: Finale, mm. 76–83.

In Figure 6.27 the $\hat{3}$–$\hat{2}$–$\hat{1}$ progression is distributed over two phrases, a fairly common event. The first phrase ends before it reaches the tonic, then the second phrase repeats the $\hat{3}$–$\hat{2}$–$\hat{1}$ progression before concluding on the tonic.

Figure 6.27

Bach: "Aus meines Herzens Grunde" ("From the Depths of My Heart"), BWV 269, mm. 1–7.

History

The idea of the four-bar phrase, so common in the mid- to late-seventeenth century, developed gradually during the late Renaissance period. Although examples of fairly strict phrasing can be found, Figure 6.28 is representative of the period. The phrase endings occur in measures 2, 6, and 8—far from the balanced and regular phrase structure of later periods.

Figure 6.28

Morley: "Nancie" from *The Fitzwilliam Virginal Book,* mm. 1–8.

The development of phrase and period construction advanced rapidly during the years 1600 to 1675, and by the latter half of the baroque period, phrase structure was quite regular. Figure 6.29 illustrates contrasting period construction.

Figure 6.29

Purcell: "Chaconne" from *King Arthur,* Z. 628, mm. 81–88.

The classical period, represented by the works of Haydn, Mozart, and Beethoven, is perhaps the culmination of formal phrase construction. Many of the examples in this chapter were drawn from music of this period.

Although the highly formal style of the classical period began to fade from 1800 to about 1830, the romantic period maintained the basic elements of phrase and period construction.

As functional harmony and strict key-oriented tonality gradually diminished in importance with the onset of post-romanticism and impressionism, so did the earlier ideas concerning phrase relationships. Nevertheless, we can still detect phrase and period construction in the works of composers of this period.

In the wide range of new musical styles of the twentieth and twenty-first centuries, the musical phrase, although stylistically much changed from its progenitors of the baroque period, is still a dominant influence in music.

Phrase construction in American popular music is influenced by the phrase lengths and organizational traditions established centuries ago. Note the strict four-bar phrases in Figure 6.30, a song from the 1950s that has remained popular for decades.

Figure 6.30

John R. Cash: "I Walk the Line," Verse 1.

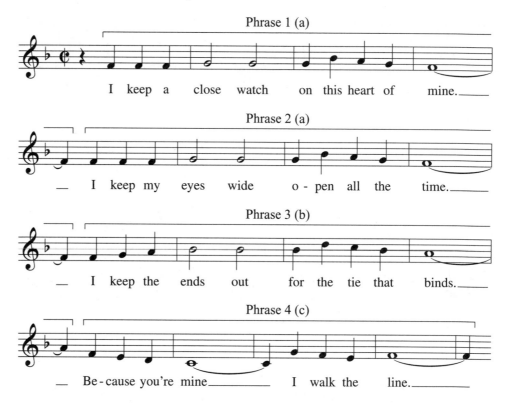

Jazz, up to about 1945, had regular phrase structures, but with the rise of Charlie Parker and other noted improvisers of that period, irregular and unbalanced phrases become more fashionable.

Assignment 6.1

Each melodic excerpt consists of two phrases.

1. Determine if the two phrases form a period.
2. If a period is formed, indicate the type—either parallel or contrasting.
3. If the phrases do not form a period, indicate the reason.

1.

Is a period formed? _____ If so, name the type. If not, explain why. _____

2.

Is a period formed? _____ If so, name the type. If not, explain why. _____

3.

Is a period formed? _____ If so, name the type. If not, explain why. _____

4.

Is a period formed? _____ If so, name the type. If not, explain why. _____

5.

Is a period formed? _____ If so, name the type. If not, explain why. _____

6.

Is a period formed? _____ If so, name the type. If not, explain why. _____

7.

Is a period formed? _____ If so, name the type. If not, explain why. _____

8.

Is a period formed? _____ If so, name the type. If not, explain why. _____

9.

Is a period formed? _____ If so, name the type. If not, explain why. _____

10.

Is a period formed? _____ If so, name the type. If not, explain why. _____

Assignment 6.2

Use the following phrases from music literature as a basis for period construction. On a separate sheet of score paper:

1. Write an additional phrase for each in parallel construction.
2. Write an additional phrase for each in contrasting construction.
3. Select two of the melodies and write two additional phrases to make a three-phrase period.
4. Discuss the analysis of each phrase.

1. Haydn: Sonata in G Major, Hob. XVI:40, I: Allegretto e innocente, mm. 1–4. CD Track 41

G:

2. Bizet: "La fleur que tu m'avais jetée" from *Carmen*, act II, mm. 1–4. CD Track 42

Db:

3. Sullivan: "When Britain Really Ruled the Waves" from *Iolanthe*, mm. 5–8. CD Track 43

A:

4. Couperin: *La Bandoline* from the *Fifth Ordre,* mm. 1–4. CD Track 44

a:

5. Brahms: Waltz in E Major, op. 39, no. 2, mm. 1–4. CD Track 45

E:

6. Weber: *Concertstück,* op. 79, mm. 1–4. CD Track 46

f:

7. Schubert: Sonata in G Major, op. 78, D. 894, III: Menuetto, mm. 1–4. CD Track 47

b:

8. Diabelli: Sonatina in F Major, op. 151, no. 3, II, mm. 1–4. CD Track 48

B♭:

9. Tchaikovsky: *Italian Song,* op. 39, no. 15, mm. 1–8. CD Track 49

D:

10. Chopin: Mazurka in F Major, op. 68, no. 3, mm. 1–8. CD Track 50

F:

Analyze the following Mozart sonata excerpt by answering the questions below. For the purpose of these questions, be concerned only with the melody (highest sounding tones):

1. A period made up of parallel phrases occurs at _____ (measure numbers).

2. A sequence occurs at _____ (measure numbers).

3. Including the repeat marks, a repeated period occurs at _____ (measure numbers).

4. A phrase extension occurs at _____ (measure numbers).

5. The phrase (see no. 4 above) is extended in _____ (part of the phrase).

6. A phrase that is contrasting to all other phrases occurs at _____ (measure numbers).

Mozart: Sonata in A Major, K. 331, I, mm. 1–18. **CD Track 51**

Assignment 6.4

1. An excerpt from Schubert's Impromptu op. 142 follows.
2. The following chart analyzes the structure of the first sixteen measures.
3. On a separate piece of paper, chart the remainder of the composition.
4. For the purpose of this chart, be concerned only with the melody (highest sounding tones).

Measures	Phrase Number	Phrase Relationship	Period Number	Period Relationship
1–4	1	Phrase 1 (a)	1	Period 1
5–8	2	Contrasting to Phrase 1 (b)		
9–12	3	Phrase 1 modified (a′)	2	Period 1 modified
13–16	4	Phrase 2 modified (b′)		

Schubert: Impromptu op. 142, no. 4, D. 935. mm. 1–36. CD Track 52

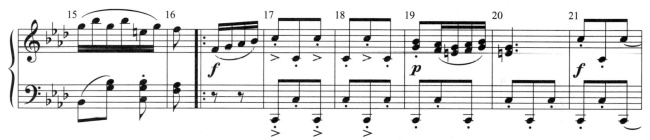

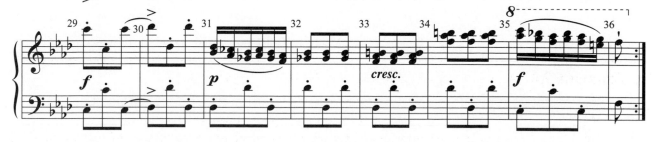

Assignment 6.5

1. Write a four-measure melody in A major and include a tonal sequence of two segments.

2. Write a four-measure melody in B minor, using the harmonic form of the minor scale, and include a tonal sequence of three segments.

3. Write a four-measure melody starting in D major and include a real sequence of two segments.

4. Write a four-measure melody starting in E minor, using the harmonic form of the minor scale, and include a real sequence of three segments.

5. Write a four-measure melody in E-flat major and include a modified tonal sequence of two segments.

6. Write a four-measure melody in D minor, using the harmonic form of the minor scale, and include a modified tonal sequence of three segments.

7. Write a four-measure melody in B-flat major and include a false sequence of two segments.

Assignment 6.6

1. Write a four-measure phrase of music in G minor using the harmonic form of the minor scale. Then rewrite it with an extension at the beginning.

2. Write a four-measure phrase of music in A-flat major. Then rewrite it with an extension in the interior of the phrase.

3. Write a four-measure phrase of music in F major. Then rewrite it with an extension at the end of the phrase.

4. Write a four-measure phrase in F-sharp minor using the harmonic form of the minor scale. Follow it with a modified repeated phrase that includes a change of mode.

Assignment 6.7

Each exercise consists of a phrase or more of melody from music literature. Analyze each melody by adding the following symbols.

Climax tone   □

Ascent

Descent

Tonic triad   ○

Concluding scale degrees $\hat{3}$–$\hat{2}$–$\hat{1}$

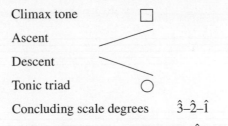

Remember that scale degrees $\hat{3}$ and $\hat{2}$ must occur in that order but may be scattered throughout the excerpt, whereas $\hat{1}$ is always the final pitch of the phrase or period.

1. (Ex.) Haydn: Sonata in C Major, Hob. XVI:3, III, mm. 31–34.

2. "The Star Spangled Banner," last phrase.

3. Folk Song: "I've Been Working on the Railroad," mm. 13–16.

4. Folk Song: "Row, Row, Row Your Boat."

5. Folk Song: "Long, Long Ago," last seven measures.

6. Folk Song: "The Wearing of the Green," last four measures.

7. Annie Harrison: "In the Gloaming," mm. 9–16.

8. Mozart: Sonata in D Major, K. 284, III, mm. 14–17.

9. Mozart: Sonata in E-flat Major, K. 282, II: Menuetto I, mm. 29–32.

10. Haydn: Sonata in E Major, Hob. XVI:13, III, mm. 48–52.

11. Haydn: Sonata in D Major, Hob. XVI:4, II, mm. 19–22.

12. Haydn: Sonata in F Major, Hob. XVI:9, III, mm. 21–24.

CHAPTER 7

Texture and Textural Reduction

TOPICS	

Texture	Homorhythmic Texture	Harmonic and Rhythmic
Density	Primary Melody (PM)	Support (HRS)
Range	Secondary Melody (SM)	Harmonic Support (HS)
Monophonic Texture	Parallel Supporting	Rhythmic Support (RS)
Polyphonic Texture	Melody (PSM)	Textural Reduction
Homophonic Texture	Static Support (SS)	

IMPORTANT CONCEPTS

The sound of music is the direct result of the instruments and voices the composer employs and the way they are combined. Instruments and voices are like primary colors blended together to create the many hues that give music its beautiful surface. Although a detailed study of the characteristics and properties of instruments goes beyond the scope of this book, it is important for you to understand certain fundamental facts about sound and texture.

Texture

The term *texture* refers to the way the melodic, rhythmic, and harmonic materials are woven together in a composition. It is a general term that is often used rather loosely to describe the vertical aspects of music. Since changes of texture often mark formal divisions in music and textural matters often complicate harmonic analysis, it is important that we deal with texture in a more specific way. Texture is often described in terms of density and range. Although these are good descriptive terms, they are less useful analytically than the more precise description of texture types that you will learn in this chapter.

Density

The *density* of texture is often described as "thick," consisting of many voices or parts, and "thin," consisting of few voices. An example of thin texture is shown in Figure 7.1, and you will find an example of thick texture in Figure 7.2.

Figure 7.1

Haydn: Sonata in G Major, Hob. XVI:11, III, mm. 25–29.

Figure 7.2

Billy Taylor: *Taylor Made Piano,* p. 158, Example B.

Range

The *range* of a texture is often described as "wide" or "narrow," depending on the interval between the lowest and highest tones. Wide range is shown in Figure 7.3. Narrow range is shown in Figure 7.4.

Figure 7.3

Berlioz: Agnus Dei from *Grande messe des morts* (Requiem), op. 5, no. 10, mm. 69–76.

Figure 7.4

Elliott Carter: Eight Etudes and a Fantasy for Woodwind Quartet, III, mm. 1–4.

Texture Types

Although density and range are usually described in relative terms, the description of texture type is much more precise. A number of texture types occur from time to time, but the most common are monophonic, polyphonic, homophonic, and homorhythmic.

Monophonic Texture

Monophonic texture is the simplest texture type in music, consisting of a single melodic line, as shown in Figure 7.5.

Figure 7.5

Sequence: "Dies Irae."

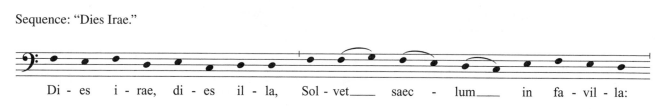

Monophonic textures can be expanded by doubling in octaves or at other intervals. Octave doubling occurs in Figure 7.6, and doubling at other intervals, also called parallelism, is shown in Figure 7.7.

Figure 7.6

Sousa: *Washington Post March,* mm. 1–5.

Figure 7.7

Debussy: Sarabande from *Pour le Piano* (For the Piano), mm. 1–2.

Polyphonic Texture

Polyphonic textures consist of two or more lines moving independently or in imitation with each other. Figure 7.8 shows two independent lines. Figure 7.9 shows two lines in imitation.

Figure 7.8

Bach: Invention no. 5 in E-flat Major, BWV 776, mm. 1–2.

Figure 7.9

Bach: Invention no. 4 in D Minor, BWV 775, mm. 1–4.

The various lines may be similar or contrasting in character. Lines with similar rhythmic values and contour appear in Figure 7.10. Lines with contrasting rhythmic values and contour appear in Figure 7.11.

Figure 7.10

Josquin des Prez: *Tu Solus Qui Facis Mirabilia* (You Alone Perform Such Wonders), mm. 35–38.

Figure 7.11

Bach: *Fuga Canonica* from *The Musical Offering,* BWV 1079, mm. 1–3.

Homophonic Texture

The most common texture in Western music is *homophonic texture,* which is made up of a melody and an accompaniment. The accompaniment provides rhythmic and harmonic support for the melody.

Figure 7.12

Mendelssohn: *Songs Without Words* op. 30, no. 6, mm. 7–10.

The rhythmic and harmonic supporting functions may be combined in the same material, or separate parts may be assigned to each function. Rhythmic and harmonic support are combined in Figure 7.13. Separate harmonic support is shown in Figure 7.14.

Figure 7.13

Schumann: "Ich Grolle Nicht" ("I Bear No Grudge") from *Dichterliebe,* op. 48, no. 7, mm. 1–4.

Figure 7.14

Mozart: Symphony no. 40 in G Minor, K. 550, I: Molto Allegro, mm. 221–225.

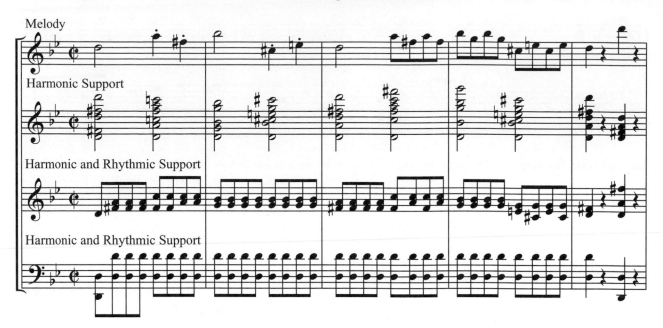

Homorhythmic Texture

Homorhythmic texture is a texture with similar rhythmic material in all parts. This texture is often referred to as "hymn style," "chordal homophony," or "chordal texture," depending on the presence or absence of melodic material (Figure 7.15).

Figure 7.15

Owens: "Freely, Freely," mm. 26–32.

History

During each period in the history of music, composers employed distinctive textural features. We can generally state that a distinguishing texture type predominates each era.

The characteristic texture type of the Renaissance period is polyphonic texture. Since harmony was largely described in terms of the relationship of voices, it is natural that a texture of multiple voices would be the result. Renaissance composers placed great value on the independence of lines, although they used imitation at the beginning of most phrases. The textures were of moderate range and seldom very dense (see Josquin des Prez: *Tu Solus Qui Facis Mirabilia,* page 148).

The rise of the figured-bass concept, which is basically an accompaniment technique, signaled the beginning of interest in homophonic texture in the baroque period. Both polyphonic and homophonic textures were used, but seldom in the same composition or movement. Textures in the baroque period were generally denser than those of the Renaissance period, and the rise of instrumental music allowed for wider ranges (see Bach: Invention no. 4 and Invention no. 5, page 148).

During the classical period, homophony became the standard texture, and composers engaged in much greater contrast of range and density than in the baroque period (see Mozart: Symphony in G minor, page 150).

The romantic period maintained the predominance of homophonic texture, but with increased range and density (see Schumann: "Ich grolle nicht" from *Dichterliebe,* page 149). Textures in the romantic period became more complex and often shifted suddenly for emotional effect (see Berlioz: "Agnus Dei," from *Grande messe des morts,* page 146).

Composers of the post-romantic period generally maintained the textures that the romantic period composers used, but with the impressionists, texture took on new significance. Many impressionist works depended heavily on texture for their effect (see Debussy: Sarabande from *Pour le Piano,* page 147). Typical texture types of the impressionistic period are expanded monophonic texture (parallelism) and homophonic texture.

In the twentieth century, no "typical" texture type has prevailed. Constant texture change characterizes many styles. Composers who choose to imitate the styles of previous periods (in neoclassicism, for example) typically imitate the textures as well. In other styles, the fabric of music explodes into small fragments and textural continuity breaks down.

Popular music is nearly all homophonic texture. Much of jazz is also homophonic (see Billy Taylor: *Taylor Made Piano,* page 146). However, the simultaneous improvisations of some jazz musicians creates true polyphony, with considerable independence of line.

APPLICATIONS

You can use both aural and visual assessments to identify texture types. The analysis and reduction of individual elements provide the means for evaluating textures accurately.

Analysis of Texture

The analysis of texture involves a process of recognizing and labeling the primary elements of the texture, as well as the identification of texture type. The textural elements are primary melody (PM), secondary melody (SM), parallel supporting melody (PSM), static support (SS), harmonic support (HS), rhythmic support (RS), and harmonic and rhythmic support (HRS).

Primary Melody (PM)

Primary melodies (PM) are the most important lines in a musical texture. In homophonic textures, there is usually only one primary melody (Figure 7.16), but in polyphonic textures, where the lines are of equal importance, there may be several primary melodies (Figure 7.17).

Figure 7.16

Mendelssohn: *Songs Without Words* op. 30, no. 6, mm. 7–10.

Figure 7.17

Mozart: *Recordare* from Requiem in D Minor, K. 626, mm. 54–57.

Although the primary melody frequently occurs as the highest part in a composition, it can reside in other positions. The primary melody in Figure 7.18 appears as the lowest-sounding voice.

Figure 7.18

Chopin: Prelude no. 6 in B Minor, op. 28, mm. 1–4.

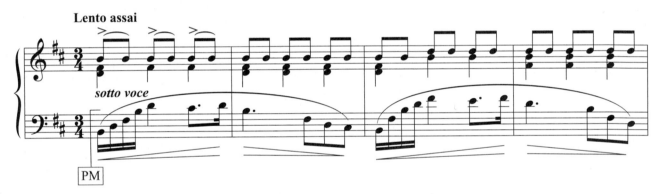

Secondary Melody (SM)

Other melodic lines that are not equal in significance to the primary melody are called *secondary melodies (SM)*.

Figure 7.19

Bach: *Fuga Canonica* from *The Musical Offering,* BWV 1079, mm. 1–3.

The process of deciding whether a melody is primary or secondary requires musical judgment, and there are differences of opinion. Performers indicate their understanding of the relative importance of melodies by how they choose to balance the parts or by the lines they choose to bring out. Thus the decision about primary and secondary melody is crucial to music interpretation.

Parallel Supporting Melody (PSM)

Parallel supporting melodies (PSM) are melodies that are similar in contour to a primary melody (Figure 7.20) or secondary melody (Figure 7.21). They often maintain a constant interval relationship with the melody they support.

Figure 7.20

Debussy: Sarabande from *Pour le Piano* (For the Piano), mm. 1–2.

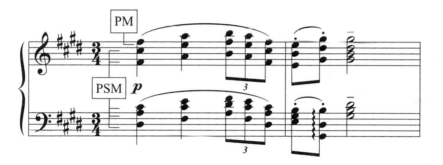

Figure 7.21

Bach: Chorale Prelude on "Erschienen ist der herrliche Tag" from *Orgelbüchlein,* BWV 629, mm. 1–4.

Static Support (SS)

Static supporting (SS) parts are of two types: (1) sustained tones or chords, which are often pedal tones (Figure 7.22), and (2) repeated melodic and rhythmic figures or ostinati (Figure 7.23).

Figure 7.22

Bach: Fugue no. 2 in C Minor from *The Well-Tempered Clavier*, Book I, BWV 847, mm. 29–31.

Figure 7.23

Borodin: *Serenade* from *Petite Suite,* mm. 7–10.

Harmonic and Rhythmic Support (HRS)

As we discussed in the definition of homophonic texture, harmonic and rhythmic elements are often combined in the same textural elements. Such elements are labeled as *harmonic and rhythmic support (HRS)*. If these support functions are separated, they are labeled as *harmonic support (HS)* or *rhythmic support (RS)* as follows.

Figure 7.24

Mendelssohn: *Songs Without Words* op. 30, no. 6, mm. 7–10.

Figure 7.25

Mozart: Symphony no. 40 in G Minor, K. 550, I: Molto Allegro, mm. 221–225.

Textural Reduction

When harmonic and rhythmic support functions are combined, it is often difficult to gain a clear understanding of the harmony. However, you can resolve the problem by removing the rhythmic materials from the texture and writing the result as block chords. The following example has been reduced to clarify the harmony and embedded voice leading (see Chapter 9).

Figure 7.26

Bach: Prelude no. 1 in C Major from *The Well-Tempered Clavier,* Book I, BWV 846, mm. 1–2.

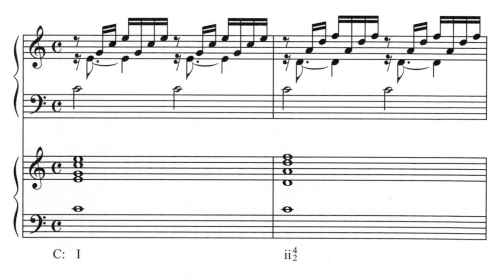

C: I   ii$^4_2$

With practice you will be able to see the chords in accompaniment textures without writing reductions, but this skill can be developed and improved by practice in writing block chords. To write a reduction, first determine the duration of each chord by playing or listening to the example in Figure 7.27. Since nonharmonic tones may appear within accompaniment figures, you will need to be alert for tones that do not seem to be part of the surrounding harmony.

Figure 7.27

Chopin: Nocturne in C-sharp Minor, op. post., mm. 9–12.

Now write the pitches of the chords in the order they appear using note values to show the duration of each chord. Maintain the original register of the chord pitches even though the rhythmic elements may have changed to reflect the harmonic rhythm.

Figure 7.28

Chopin: Nocturne in C-sharp Minor, op. post., mm. 9–12.

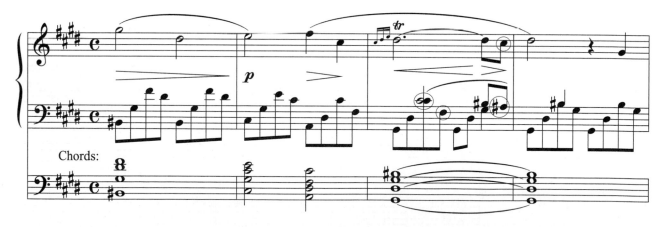

Assignment 7.1

1. Identify the following textures by texture type (monophonic, polyphonic, homophonic, or homorhythmic).
2. Label the elements of each texture using the labels PM, SM, PSM, SS, HS, RS, and HRS (see pages 151–155).

1. Palestrina: *In Festo Transfigurationis Domini.* CD Track 53

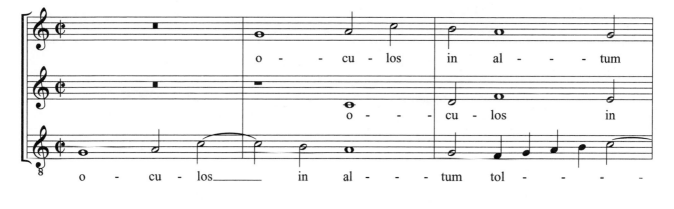

Texture type_____.

2. Schumann: "Soldatenmarsch" ("Soldiers' March") from *Album for the Young,* op. 68, mm. 1–8. CD Track 54

Texture type_____.

3. Schubert: "Wohin?" ("Where to?") from *Die schöne Müllerin,* op. 25, no. 2, mm. 3–4. CD Track 55

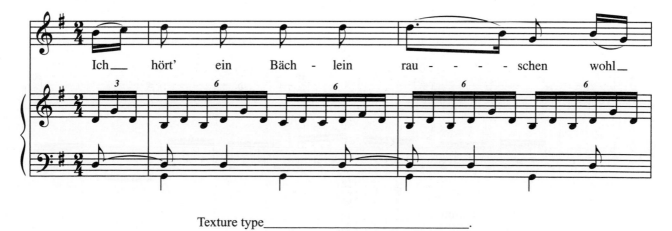

Texture type_____.

4. Bach: Courante from Suite no. 1 in G Major for Violoncello Solo, BWV 1007, mm. 1–3. **CD Track 56**

Texture type_____.

5. Bach: Sinfonia no. 4 in D Minor, BWV 790, mm. 1–2. **CD Track 57**

Texture type_____.

6. Chopin: Mazurka in B-flat Major, op. 17, no. 1, mm. 1–4. **CD Track 58**

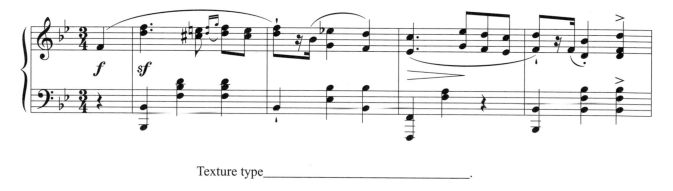

Texture type_____.

7. Haydn: String Quartet in E-flat Major, op. 76, no. 6, Hob. III:80, I, mm. 45–48. **CD Track 59**

Texture type_____.

8. Beethoven: Minuet no. 3 from Six Minuets, WoO 10, mm. 9–12. CD Track 60

Texture type_____.

9. Debussy: *La cathédrale engloutie* (The Engulfed Cathedral) from Preludes, Book I, no. 10, mm. 28–32. CD Track 61

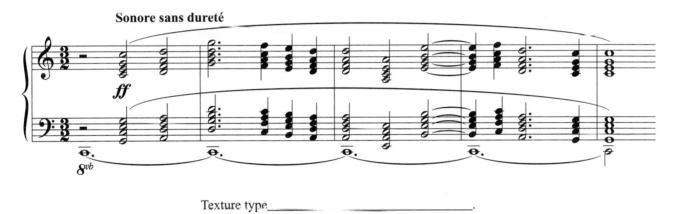

Texture type_____.

10. Jones and Schmidt: "Try to Remember" from *The Fantasticks,* mm. 9–13. CD Track 62

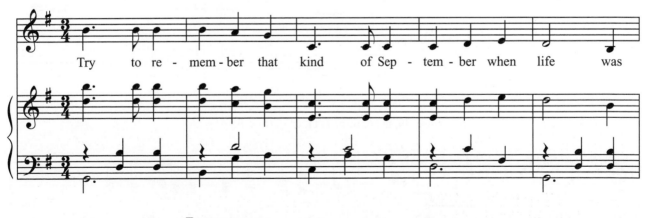

Texture type_____.

Assignment 7.2

Write harmonic reductions for the following excerpts:

1. Determine the harmonic rhythm.
2. Circle any nonharmonic tones.
3. Write the chords using the rhythmic values of the harmonic rhythm. Preserve the original pitch register of each chord (see pages 155–156).
4. Label the elements of each texture as PM, SM, PSM, SS, HS, RS, or HRS.

1. Beethoven: Sonata in G Major, op. 79, III: Vivace, mm. 72–75. **CD Track 63**

2. Liszt: *Au lac de Wallenstadt* (At Wallenstadt Lake), no. 2 from *Années de pèlerinage, première année, Suisse,* mm. 35–38. **CD Track 64**

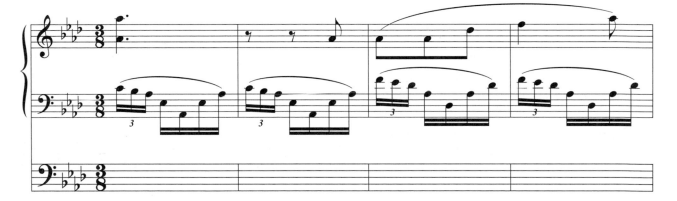

3. Mendelssohn: *Songs Without Words* op. 19, no. 6, mm. 7–11. **CD Track 65**

4. Mendelssohn: *Songs Without Words* op. 53, no. 3, mm. 9–12. CD Track 66

5. Bach: Prelude no. 2 in C Minor from *The Well-Tempered Clavier,* Book I, BWV 847, mm. 1–2. CD Track 67

6. Mozart: *Bastien und Bastienne,* K. 50, no. 1, mm. 11–14. CD Track 68

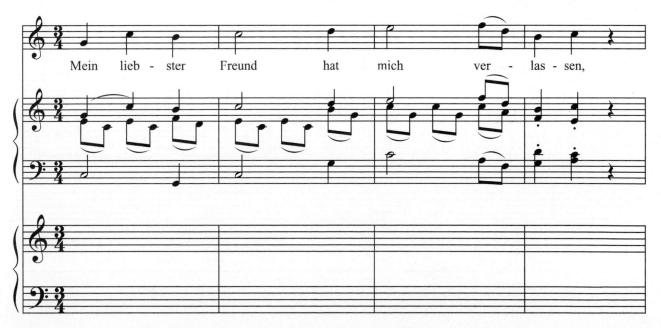

Mein lieb - ster Freund hat mich ver - las - sen,

7. Schubert: Sonatina for Violin and Piano in G Minor, op. 137, no. 3, D. 408, III, mm. 39–42. CD Track 69

8. Beethoven: Sonata in C Minor, op. 10, no. 1, I: Allegro molto e con brio, mm. 56–63. CD Track 70

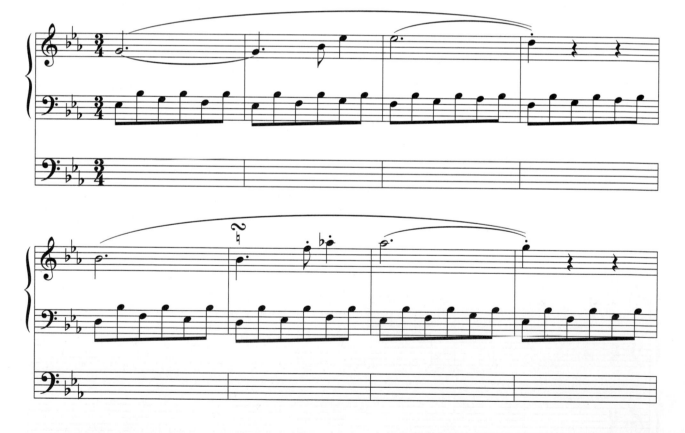

CHAPTER 8

Species Counterpoint

TOPICS

Voice Leading
Species Counterpoint
Cantus Firmus
Counterpoint
First Species
Second Species
Third Species
Fourth Species
Fifth Species
Modal Scales
Final
Musica Ficta
Nota Cambiata

IMPORTANT CONCEPTS

Voice leading is the term used to describe the linear aspect of musical writing. The individual melodic lines (called voices) that make up a composition interact to create harmony. The vertical aspect (chords) and the horizontal aspect (voices) are equally important in western European art music. This chapter will focus on the melodic aspects of voice leading using a modal two-voice approach. Chapter 9 will deal with the interaction of melody and harmony in a tonal four-voice context.

Species Counterpoint

Species counterpoint is an approach to counterpoint through the addition of contrapuntal voices to a given melody called the *cantus firmus*. Species counterpoint begins with simple note-against-note counterpoint and progresses to complex counterpoint in five stages, called the *five species*.

The Cantus Firmus

A cantus firmus is a fixed melody, one phrase in length, that terminates in a melodic cadence. It serves as the basis for other independent, but related, melodies.

Figure 8.1

A Cantus Firmus.

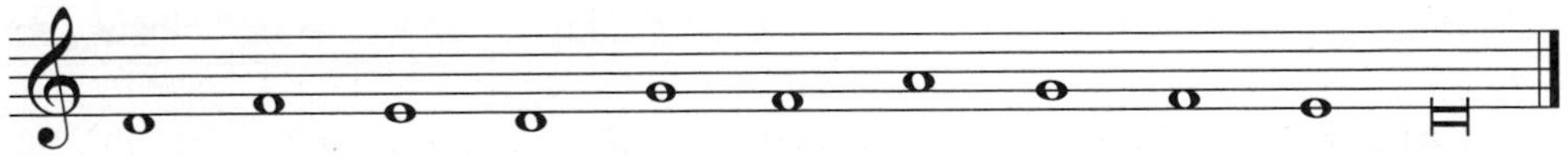

The Counterpoint

The *counterpoint* is a second voice, created according to specific principles, that accompanies the cantus firmus. For each note in the cantus firmus (c.f.), the counterpoint (cpt.) will have one or more notes.

First Species Counterpoint

First species counterpoint consists of one note in the counterpoint for each note in the cantus firmus.

Figure 8.2

Fux: Example of First Species Counterpoint.

Second Species Counterpoint

In *second species* there are two tones in the counterpoint for each tone in the cantus firmus.

Figure 8.3

Fux: Example of Second Species Counterpoint.

Third Species Counterpoint

Third species counterpoint has four tones for each tone in the cantus firmus.

Figure 8.4

Fux: Example of Third Species Counterpoint.

Fourth Species Counterpoint

The *fourth species,* often called *syncopation* or *ligature,* consists of tied notes over nearly every bar in the counterpoint, creating a syncopated effect with the cantus firmus. Many of the tied notes are suspensions.

Figure 8.5

Fux: Example of Fourth Species Counterpoint.

Fifth Species Counterpoint

The *fifth species* is called *florid counterpoint* and combines elements of all the other species. This species introduces rhythmic variety into the counterpoint.

Figure 8.6

Fux: Example of Fifth Species Counterpoint.

History

Johann Joseph Fux (1660–1741) was Kapellmeister to the court in Vienna when he wrote *Gradus ad Parnassum* in 1725. In his preface to the work, Fux says that he intended to invent "a simple method by which the novice can progress gradually, ascending step by step to attain mastery in this art." He was well aware that in 1725 musical styles had changed fairly drastically from those of the Renaissance. In fact, he laments that he cannot "call back composers from the unrestrained insanity of their writing to normal standards." Fux's work greatly influenced the Viennese classical composers. Haydn worked through all the exercises and it is likely that Mozart studied the work and used it as a text with his students. Beethoven studied *Gradus,* first with Haydn and later with Johann Schenk and Johann Georg Albrechtsberger.

The text, originally in Latin, was translated into German in 1742 and to Italian in 1761. A paraphrased French version appeared in 1773 and an English paraphrase in 1791. Thus *Gradus ad Parnassum* came to be the standard approach to counterpoint throughout Europe. A complete English translation by Alfred Mann appeared in 1943.

The book consists of a dialog between a master and his willing pupil. Fux tells us that the master, Aloysius, is none other than Giovanni Pierluigi da Palestrina (c. 1525–1594), the most famous Renaissance composer. The pupil, Josephus, is a brilliant student who remembers everything his teacher tells him and yet manages to time his mistakes perfectly to allow the master to introduce the principles in a logical manner. The book is interesting reading quite aside from its pedagogical value.

APPLICATIONS					

This section presents the five species of two-voice writing in order. Although it is important that you achieve some mastery of each species before progressing to the next, you must first be thoroughly familiar with the modal scales and the basic elements of writing a melody.

Modal Scales

The *cantus firmi* and contrapuntal melodies of species counterpoint are composed using *modal scales* (see Chapter 2, Figures 2.34 and 2.35). Each mode is identified by its beginning tone, called the *final,* and consists of a specific arrangement of whole and half steps.

Figure 8.7

Mode Name	Range	Final	Half Steps Between	Tonal Scale Comparison
Dorian			$\hat{2}$–$\hat{3}$, $\hat{6}$–$\hat{7}$	Natural minor scale with raised sixth degree
Phrygian			$\hat{1}$–$\hat{2}$, $\hat{5}$–$\hat{6}$	Natural minor scale with lowered second degree
Lydian			$\hat{4}$–$\hat{5}$, $\hat{7}$–$\hat{8}$	Major scale with raised fourth degree
Mixolydian			$\hat{3}$–$\hat{4}$, $\hat{6}$–$\hat{7}$	Major scale with lowered seventh degree
Aeolian			$\hat{2}$–$\hat{3}$, $\hat{5}$–$\hat{6}$	Same as natural minor scale
Ionian			$\hat{3}$–$\hat{4}$, $\hat{7}$–$\hat{8}$	Same as major scale

Like the major and minor scales, the modes may begin on any tone as long as the arrangements of whole and half steps remain the same. Since the final of each transposed mode lies in the same relationship to the tonic of the major scale with the same key signature, the identity of a transposed mode can be quickly determined.

1. The final of the Dorian mode is always the second degree of a major scale.
2. The final of the Phrygian mode is always the third degree of a major scale.
3. The final of the Lydian mode is always the fourth degree of a major scale.
4. The final of the Mixolydian mode is always the fifth degree of a major scale.
5. The final of the Aeolian mode is always the sixth degree of a major scale.
6. The final of the Ionian mode is always the first degree of a major scale.

To illustrate, the final of nontransposed Dorian is the second degree of a C major scale.

Figure 8.8

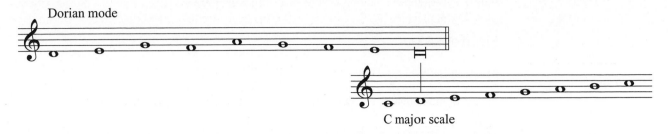

Dorian mode

C major scale

The final of Dorian transposed to G is the second degree of an F major scale.

Figure 8.9

Dorian mode (same melody)

F major scale

Melodic Characteristics

Melodies in species counterpoint (both the cantus firmus and the contrapuntal melody) consist primarily of conjunct motion with an occasional leap. For example, the cantus firmus presented in Figure 8.10 contains seven steps and only three leaps. The best general contour is a rise to a single climax tone followed by a descent.

Figure 8.10

Example of a Good Melody.

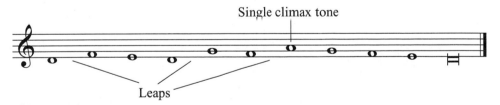

Single climax tone

Leaps

Two successive leaps in the same direction are usually not a part of the style, unless they outline a triad.

Figure 8.11

Successive Leaps.

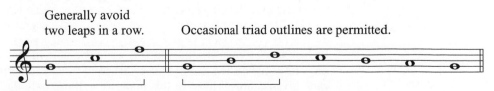

Generally avoid two leaps in a row.   Occasional triad outlines are permitted.

Melodies should never leap by diminished or augmented intervals or by a seventh. The octave is the largest leap that should appear in a melody.

Figure 8.12

Leaps to Be Avoided.

Augmented 4ths   Diminished 5ths   Major and Minor 7ths

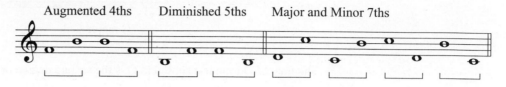

You can avoid the tritone (A4 or d5) occurring between the pitches F and B by flatting the B. In species counterpoint, descending scale motion often includes B♭ to avoid exposing the B to F tritone. As a general rule, avoid using B♭ too closely to B♮ by separating them by three or more measures.

Figure 8.13

Use B♭ to avoid tritones: Add B♭ to descending scales outlining B–F:

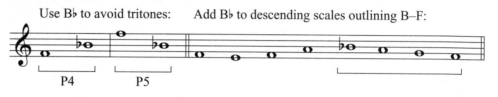

Avoid repeated figures, sequences, and melody segments that outline a tritone (A4 or d5).

Figure 8.14

Avoid repeated   Avoid sequences.   Avoid melodic segments that outline
figures.   a tritone.

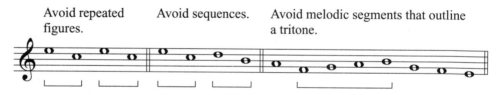

The total range of a melody should rarely exceed an octave and should never exceed a tenth.

Figure 8.15

Good melodic range (P5th)   Range too large (P11th)

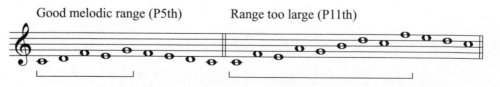

Writing First Species Counterpoint

In first species counterpoint you will write one note in the counterpoint for each note in the cantus firmus (c.f.). You will be asked to write counterpoints both above and below each given cantus firmus. In this book we will use only the treble and bass clefs, but in *Gradus ad Parnassum* Fux employed soprano, alto, tenor, and bass clefs.

Beginning the Counterpoint

If the counterpoint is above the cantus firmus, the first note of the counterpoint should be a P1, a P5, or a P8. If the counterpoint is below the cantus firmus, the first note of the counterpoint should be a P1 or a P8.

Figure 8.16

Correct Intervals at the Beginning of a Counterpoint.

For counterpoint above:

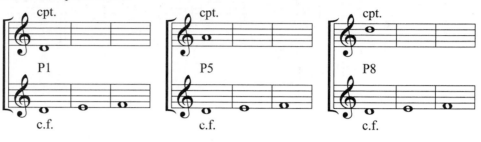

For counterpoint below:

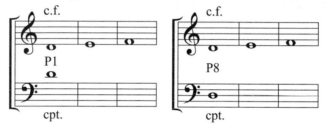

Ending the Counterpoint

The cantus firmi of species counterpoint are in Dorian, Phrygian, Lydian, Mixolydian, Aeolian, or Ionian modes. In every case the cantus firmus will end with a descent by step to the final of the mode. There is a fixed formula for ending the counterpoint in each mode, as shown in Figure 8.17.

Figure 8.17

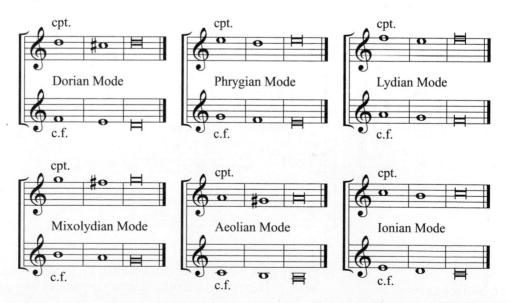

Notice that a raised leading tone is required in the Dorian, Mixolydian, and Aeolian modes. The raised leading tone (sometimes called *musica ficta*) is used only at the end of the exercise, and it is best to avoid using the natural form of the seventh scale degree in near proximity to the raised form. A good principle is to avoid the seventh scale degree in the last four tones before the raised leading tone.

Figure 8.18

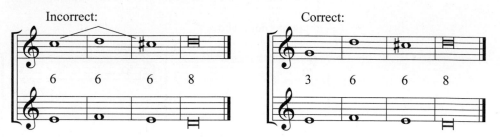

Filling in the Remaining Notes

With the beginning and the end of the exercise completed, it is time to fill in the remaining notes. In first species counterpoint, the only intervals allowed between the two voices are M3, m3, P5, M6, m6, P8, M10, and m10. The unison is not acceptable in any place other than the first and final measure of the exercise.

Figure 8.19

Allowable Intervals in First Species Counterpoint.

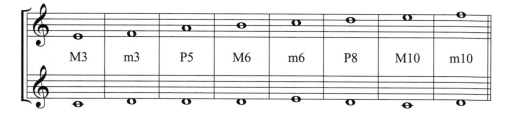

As stated by Fux, the four basic principles for voice leading in first species counterpoint are:

1. From one perfect consonance (P1, P5, P8) to another perfect consonance, proceed in contrary or oblique motion.

Figure 8.20

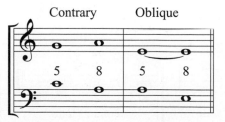

2. From a perfect consonance (P1, P5, P8) to an imperfect consonance (M3, m3, M6, m6, M10, m10), proceed by similar, contrary, or oblique motion.

Figure 8.21

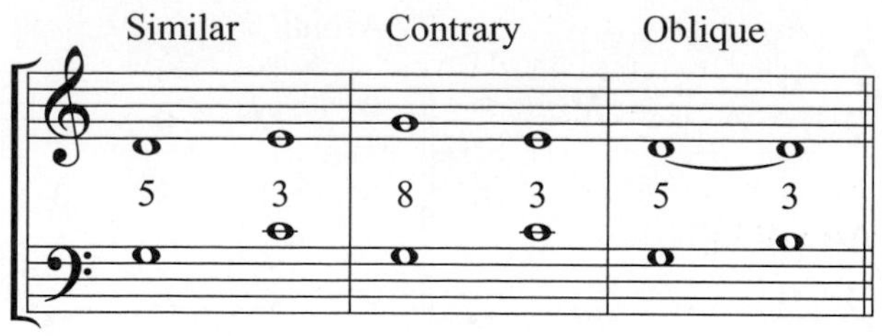

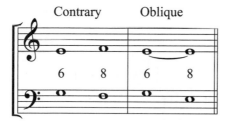

3. From an imperfect consonance to a perfect consonance, proceed in contrary or oblique motion.

Figure 8.22

Contrary   Oblique

4. From one imperfect consonance to another imperfect consonance, proceed in contrary, parallel, similar, or oblique motion.

Figure 8.23

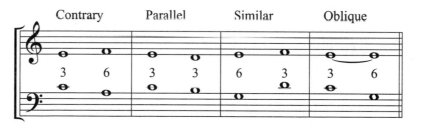

In general, there should be no more than two tied (or repeated) notes in a single exercise. Therefore, you should use oblique motion sparingly.

Figure 8.24

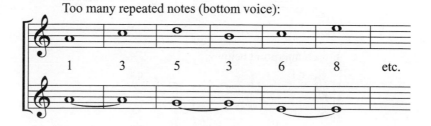

Avoid extended passages in parallel motion. For the most part, there should be no more than three successive parallel thirds or sixths.

Figure 8.25

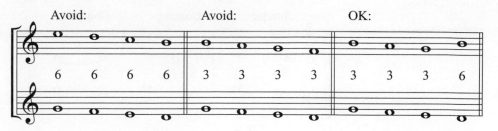

In second species counterpoint you will write two notes for each note of the cantus firmus except for the final note, which will be a single note (see Figure 8.3). The basic principles presented in the previous sections on melodic writing and first species counterpoint still apply here.

At the beginning of the exercise, the first measure may contain two half notes or a half rest and a single half note.

Writing Second Species Counterpoint

Beginning the Counterpoint

Figure 8.26

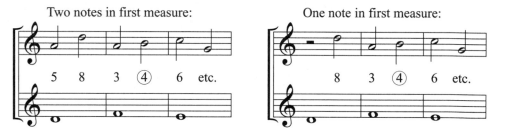

The first note in the counterpoint must form a perfect consonance with the cantus firmus whether it is on the first beat or after a half rest. The allowable consonances are the same as for first species counterpoint.

Figure 8.27

Ending the Counterpoint

The cadence pattern (2–1 in the cantus firmus and 7–8 in the counterpoint) established in first species is maintained in the second species. The second half note in the next to last measure of the counterpoint must be the leading tone. The cadence patterns in the counterpoint for second species are shown in Figure 8.28. As you can see, it is possible to revert to first species in the cadence.

Figure 8.28

For counterpoint above:

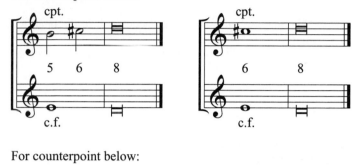

For counterpoint below:

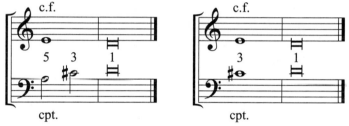

Filling in the Remaining Notes

1. The first half note in each measure must be a consonance (perfect or imperfect).
2. The second half note in each measure may be a consonance or a dissonant passing tone. Leaps to or from a dissonance are not allowed. Allowable dissonances are M2, m2, P4, A4, d5, M7, m7, M9, and m9. The only allowable dissonance in second species is the passing tone.

Figure 8.29

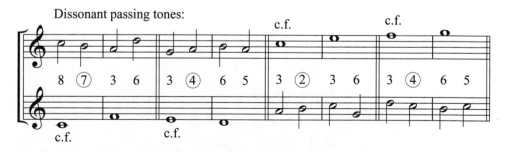

3. If two successive measures have the same perfect consonance (P1, P5, P8) on the first beat, the ear will hear them as if the intervening note was not present. The result is unacceptable parallel perfect consonances.

Figure 8.30

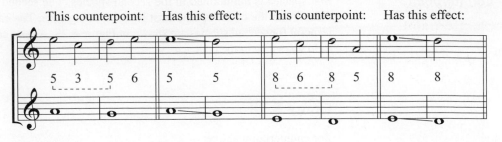

This counterpoint: Has this effect: This counterpoint: Has this effect:

4. You may use a unison on the second half of the beat in second species but never on the first beat.

Figure 8.31

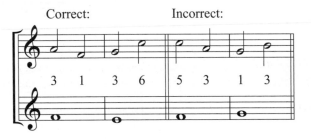

Correct: Incorrect:

5. It is best to approach and depart from leaps greater than a third in contrary motion. Stepwise motion is preferred because it usually results in a better melodic line.

Figure 8.32

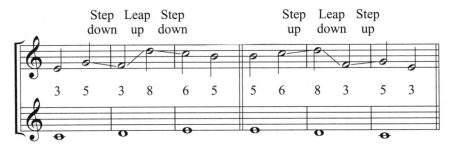

Step Leap Step   Step Leap Step
down   up   down   up   down   up

6. Repeated notes, tied notes, sequences, and repeated melodic figures are not allowed in second species counterpoint.

Figure 8.33

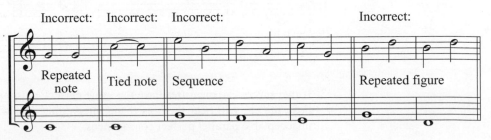

Incorrect: Incorrect: Incorrect: Incorrect:

In third species counterpoint you will write four notes for each note of the cantus firmus. You may wonder why there is no species with three notes in the counterpoint. This is because species counterpoint is based entirely on common time and three-against-one counterpoint would require triplets.

Beginning the Counterpoint

The first measure of the exercise may contain four quarter notes or a quarter rest and three quarter notes.

Figure 8.34

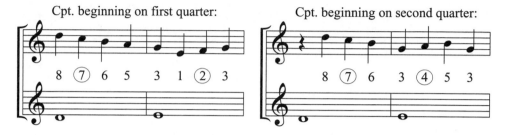

The first note in the counterpoint must form a perfect consonance with the cantus firmus whether it is on the first or second beat (see Figure 8.34). The allowable consonances are the same as for the first notes in first and second species counterpoint.

Ending the Counterpoint

The next to last note of the counterpoint must be the leading tone, just as in first and second species counterpoint. Fux suggests the following standard patterns for the next to last measure. Feel free to use these patterns or make up your own. (The dissonance in Figure 8.35b will be explained in item 3 of the next section.)

Figure 8.35

Filling in the Remaining Notes

1. The first note in each measure must be a consonance (perfect or imperfect).
2. The remaining three notes may be dissonant or consonant, but one of the last two notes in each measure must be a consonance.

Figure 8.36

Acceptable practice: first quarter and one of the last two quarters are consonant.

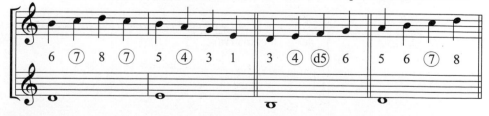

3. Allowable dissonances include the accented and unaccented passing tones, the upper and lower neighboring tones, and a figure called the *nota cambiata*. The nota cambiata occurred primarily in Renaissance music. It is the only dissonance in species counterpoint in which there is a leap away from a dissonance.

Figure 8.37

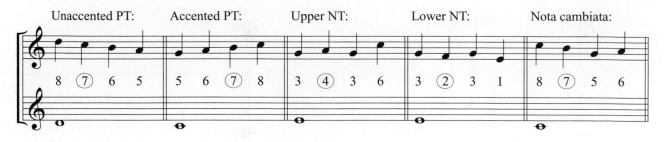

The nota cambiata always has the same interval pattern: a step down, a third down, and a step up. The first and third notes in the pattern must be consonant, but the second and fourth may be dissonant. (Note that in Figure 8.35b you see the nota cambiata as part of a cadence formula.)

Figure 8.38

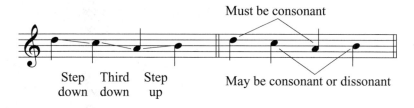

The nota cambiata must begin on the first or third quarter of the measure.

Figure 8.39

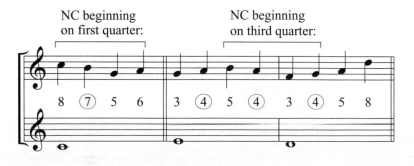

4. Allow at least two notes between perfect fifths and octaves to avoid the effect of parallel perfect intervals.

Figure 8.40

5ths OK with two notes between: 5ths not OK with one note between:

5. Watch out for melodic designs of four to six notes that are repeated or transposed elsewhere in the exercise. Avoid repeated melodic motives.

Figure 8.41

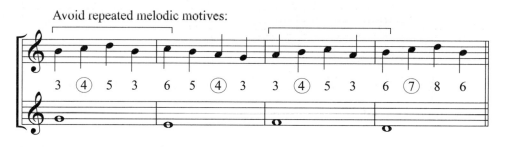

Avoid repeated melodic motives:

6. Do not write melodic motives that are simple arpeggios. Remember to use leaps sparingly in species counterpoint.

Figure 8.42

Avoid obvious arpeggiations:

Writing Fourth Species Counterpoint

Fourth species counterpoint is a study in suspensions, and the goal is to include as many of these devices as possible. The fourth species is the first that allows, and even encourages, dissonance on the first beat of the measure. Figure 8.43 shows a typical fourth species example.

Figure 8.43

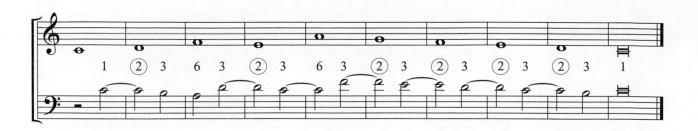

Beginning the Counterpoint

Begin the counterpoint with a half rest and a half note. The first note must be one of the consonances allowed at the beginning in the other species.

Figure 8.44

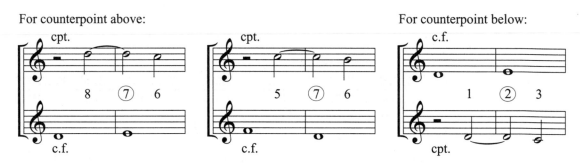

For counterpoint above:

For counterpoint below:

Ending the Counterpoint

The cadence patterns in fourth species are similar to those of previous species in that the counterpoint must arrive on the leading tone. Figure 8.45 shows typical cadence formulas in fourth species, with a suspension as a part of the pattern. Feel free to reproduce these formulas as cadence patterns for your counterpoints.

Figure 8.45

For counterpoint above:

For counterpoint below:

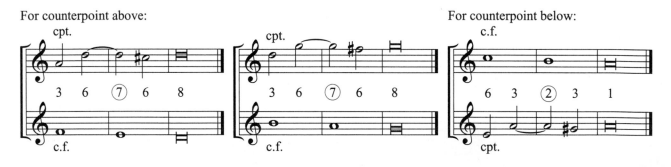

Filling in the Remaining Notes

Writing fourth species counterpoint requires you to look ahead to see what interval will be created in the following measure since the second half note in most measures will be tied over.

1. The second half note in every measure must be a consonance.
2. The first half note in the measure may be consonant or dissonant. The only dissonance allowed is the suspension. The three allowable suspension patterns are shown in Figure 8.46. Use these suspension patterns as often as possible since suspensions are the goal in fourth species counterpoint.

Figure 8.46

3. If you cannot arrange a suspension on the first beat of a measure, write tied consonant notes, if possible.

Figure 8.47

4. If neither a suspension nor a tied consonance is possible, it is permissible to break the fourth species pattern and write untied half notes. Notice that the examples of fourth species counterpoint presented in Figure 8.5 and in Figure 8.43 have one instance where the ties are broken. Try to limit the number of such exceptions to one or two per exercise.
5. In fourth species it is sometimes possible to write sequences where successive fifths have only one note between. These patterns are not considered incorrect if no leaps are involved. Leaps tend to place undue emphasis on the fifths and are unacceptable.

Figure 8.48

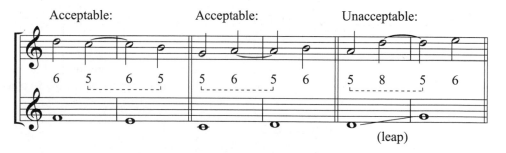

Writing Fifth Species Counterpoint

Fifth species counterpoint combines the basic elements of the other four species, accompanied by several requisites to accommodate the shift from one species type to the next. Fifth species also introduces the rhythmic value of the eighth note.

Beginning the Counterpoint

The exercise should begin with either second or fourth species (see Figures 8.26–8.27 for second species and Figure 8.44 for fourth species). Although it is permissible in these two species to begin with a half note, fifth species most often begins with a half rest.

It is recommended that you use fourth species to conclude the counterpoint (see Figure 8.45). Although any of the standard cadential patterns presented thus far may appear in concluding measures, fifth species examples frequently end with a suspension. As we will see later, you can decorate these concluding suspensions with embellishments.

Use second, third, and fourth species to fill in the remaining notes. It is important not to exploit one species type over the others. The counterpoint should be characterized by rhythmic variety, but within the context of good melodic contour and rhythmic flow. As a general rule, do not use one species type for longer than two and a half measures.

The note values associated with species one, two, three, and four receive very specific application in fifth species counterpoint.

1. The whole-note value observed in first species will appear only in the last measure. Do not use whole notes to complete any other part of the counterpoint.
2. The individual half note from second species should emerge most often at the beginning of the measure (on the first quarter). Avoid positioning half notes on the second quarter because it will create syncopation—a rhythmic effect considered to be unstylistic. Half notes can begin in the second half of the measure (on the third quarter) but should be tied to a half note or quarter note at the beginning of the next measure.

Figure 8.49

It is important to remember that if two notes are tied, the first note is required to be a half note. The second note may be a half or quarter note. No other note values may be tied together in fifth species writing.

Figure 8.50

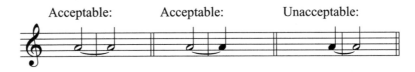

3. Third species is frequently used to create forward momentum within a counterpoint. Quarter notes should never appear in isolated pairs in place of a half note.

Figure 8.51

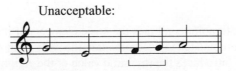

4. The tied half notes and suspensions of fourth species maintain their original rhythmic placement when appearing in fifth species. The two half notes must be tied over the barline and should never be tied within the same measure together.

Figure 8.52

5. In addition to the duration values presented in the first four species, eighth notes may be included—but sparingly and as pairs. In general, no more than one eighth-note pair should occur every two measures. Eighth notes must be approached and left by step, and occur on the second or fourth quarters.
6. Eighth notes can appear as lower neighboring tones, but not as upper neighboring tones. The lower neighbor can occur as either the first or second note of an eighth-note pair.

Figure 8.53

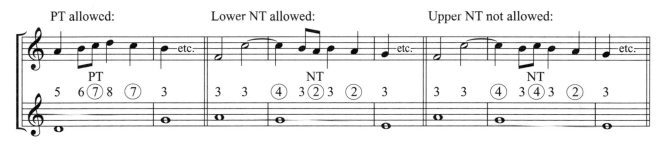

7. Suspensions are often decorated in fifth species. These embellishments are typically achieved through the use of a single quarter note or a pair of eighth notes.
   a. The resolution pitch of a suspension may be anticipated by a quarter note.
   b. The dissonant pitch of the suspension may be embellished with a quarter-note escape-tone type figure.
   c. A quarter-note consonant leap to a consonant interval may follow the dissonant pitch.
   d. Double eighth notes may be used to anticipate the resolution if the second eighth is a lower neighboring tone.

As you can see in Figure 8.54, the application of these ornaments requires you to alter the value of the dissonant pitch to accommodate the embellishment.

Figure 8.54

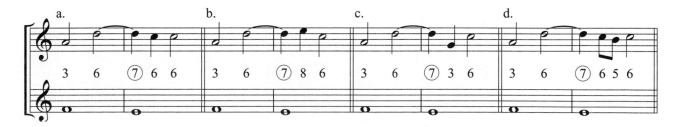

Assignment 8.1

Following are six cantus firmi composed by Fux based on the modal scales. Write the name of each mode in the blank provided.

1. _____

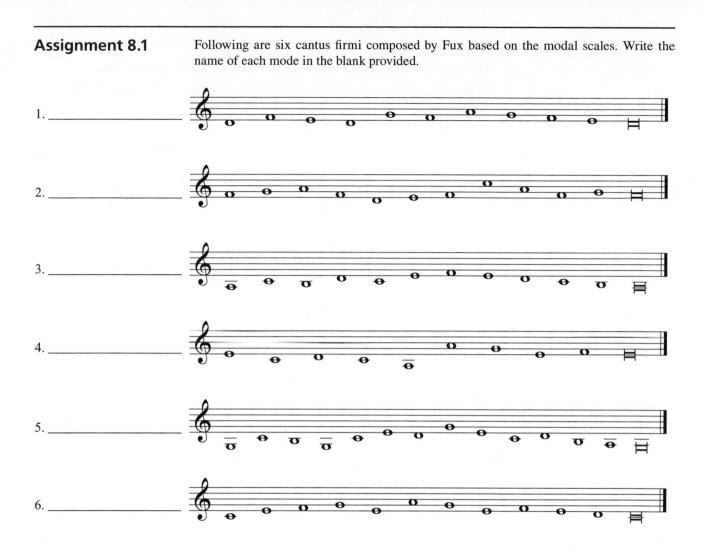

2. _____

3. _____

4. _____

5. _____

6. _____

Assignment 8.2

Following are six modal scales that have been transposed. Write the name of each mode in the blank provided.

1. _____   2. _____

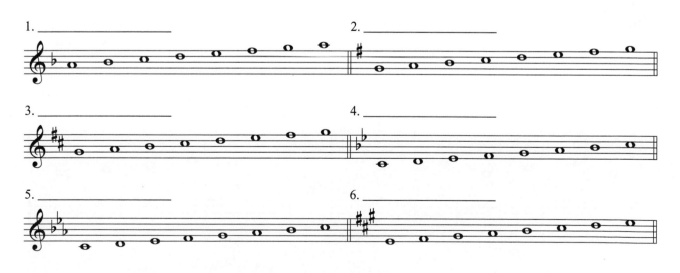

3. _____   4. _____

5. _____   6. _____

Assignment 8.3

Compose a counterpoint in first species for each cantus firmus that follows.

1. Make sure your counterpoint observes the principles for first species writing.
2. Pay particular attention to the proper beginnings and endings for each example.
3. Analyze all harmonic intervals using numbers.

1. Schenker

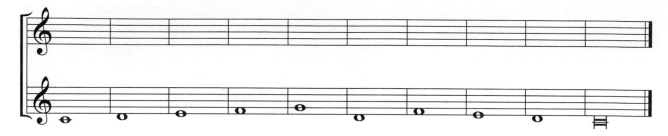

2. Schenker

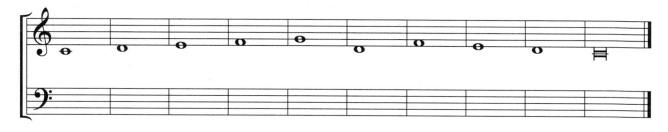

3. Fux

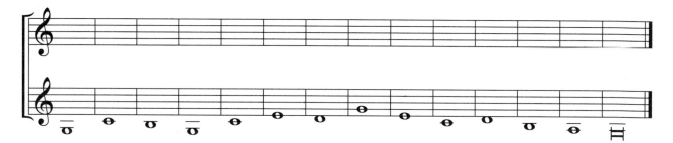

4. Fux

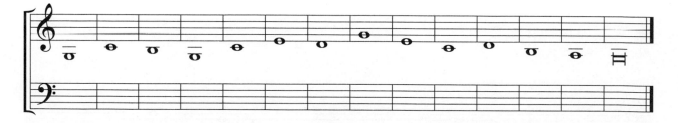

Assignment 8.4

Compose a counterpoint in second species for each cantus firmus that follows.

1. Make sure your counterpoint observes the principles for second species writing.
2. Pay particular attention to the proper beginnings and endings for each example.
3. Analyze all harmonic intervals using numbers.
4. Circle each number representing dissonance. All dissonances should be passing tones.

1. Schenker

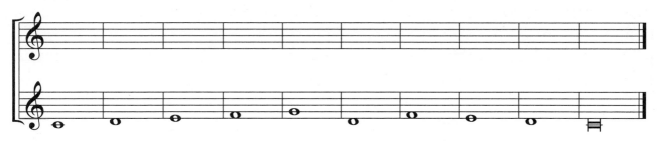

2. Schenker

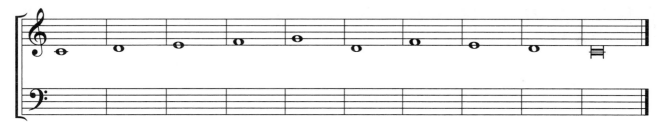

3. Fux

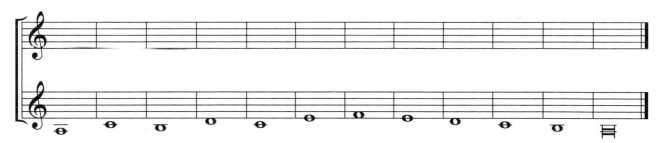

4. Fux

Assignment 8.5

Compose a counterpoint in third species for each cantus firmus that follows.

1. Make sure your counterpoint observes the principles for third species writing.
2. Pay particular attention to the proper beginnings and endings for each example.
3. Analyze all harmonic intervals using numbers.
4. Circle each dissonant number and write the abbreviation for the dissonance name nearby.

1. Schenker

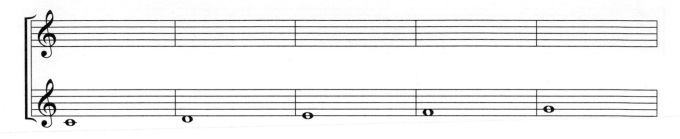

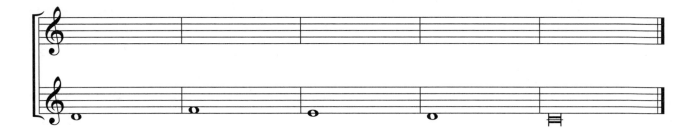

2. Schenker

3. Fux

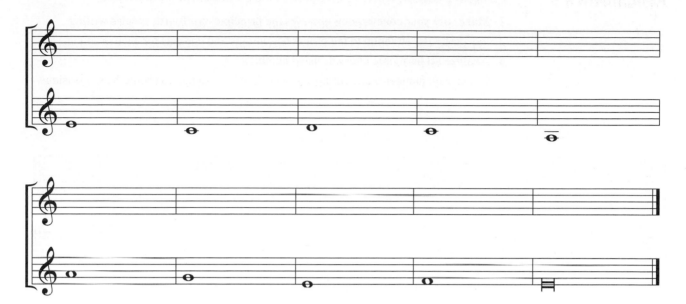

4. Fux

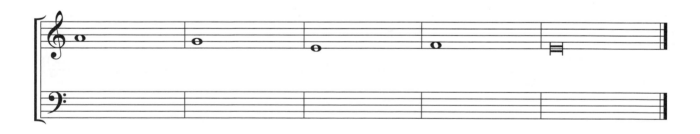

Assignment 8.6

Compose a counterpoint in fourth species for each cantus firmus that follows.

1. Make sure your counterpoint observes the principles for fourth species writing.
2. Pay particular attention to the proper beginnings and endings for each example.
3. Analyze all harmonic intervals using numbers.
4. Circle each number representing dissonance. All dissonances should be suspensions.

1. Schenker

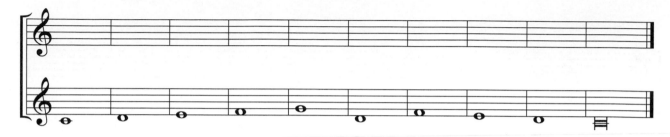

2. Schenker

3. Fux

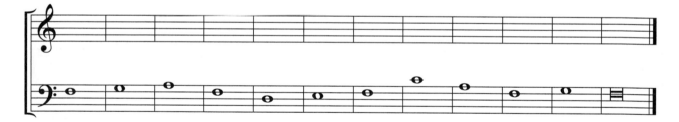

4. Fux

Assignment 8.7

Compose a counterpoint in fifth species for each cantus firmus that follows.

1. Make sure your counterpoint observes the principles for fifth species writing.
2. Pay particular attention to the proper beginnings and endings for each example.
3. Analyze all harmonic intervals using numbers.
4. Circle each dissonant number and write the abbreviation for the dissonance name nearby.

1. Schenker

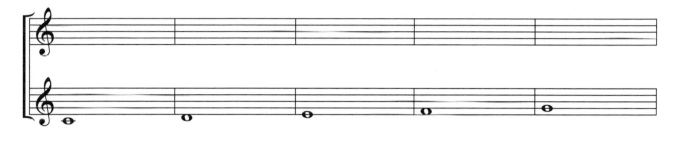

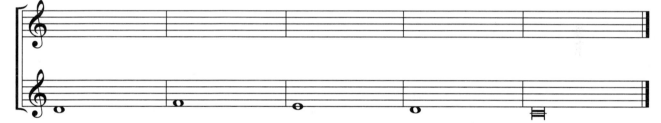

2. Schenker

3. Fux

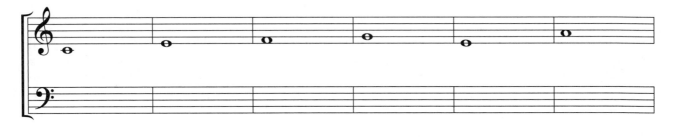

4. Fux

CHAPTER 9

Voice Leading in Four-Part Chorale Writing

TOPICS	Four-Voice Texture	Pedal Bass $^6_4$	Soprano
	Chorale	Parallel P5ths	Alto
	Stylistic Practice	Parallel P8ths	Tenor
	Common Tone	Parallel Unisons	Bass
	Doubling	Crossed Voices	Close Position
	Cadential $^6_4$	Spacing	Open Position
	Passing Bass $^6_4$	Overlap	
	Arpeggiated Bass $^6_4$	Unequal Fifths	

IMPORTANT CONCEPTS

Beginning with this chapter and continuing through volume 1 and much of volume 2, we will place considerable emphasis on the voice-leading practices of the eighteenth- and nineteenth-century composers. Four-part writing demonstrates in an uncomplicated fashion the principles that are the basis of compositions from this time period.

Four-Voice Texture

In *four-voice textures,* the interaction of harmony and melody and their equal importance become clear. The four individual melodic lines come together, generating a chord, while maintaining smooth melodic connections from pitch to pitch. We can observe clearly many of the voice-leading conventions that dominate common-practice-period tonal music in eighteenth-century four-voice compositions.

Figure 9.1

Genevan Psalter: Old 124th, mm. 1–4.

F: I   V   I   IV   I   V   vi   IV   V   I

The chord symbols show that each melody tone is harmonized with a triad in the key of F major.

The cadence is perfect authentic.

Notice the melodic contour of the bass voice. It consists mostly of leaps because the bass voice sings the root factor of each of the chords in the phrase. In four-voice textures the bass is usually a harmonic voice that is controlled more by the chords than by melodic considerations. (We will see later how the use of inversions can help smooth out the bass voice.) In contrast to the bass voice, the soprano, alto, and tenor voices move mostly in conjunct motion.

History

Chorale harmonizations reveal many of the basic idioms of four-part writing in the baroque style. The principles that govern chord progression and voice leading are inherent in chorales, and we can view these practices in their simplest forms without the confusion resulting from the study of large-scale works.

Chorales in the Music of Bach

The *chorale* was the congregational hymn in the German Protestant church at the time of J. S. Bach (1685–1750). Chorale melodies of the eighteenth century were derived from a variety of sources: (1) Latin hymns of the Catholic church, (2) pre-Reformation popular hymns, (3) popular songs of the period, and (4) some original hymn tunes composed by Protestant church musicians. Martin Luther (1483–1546), the founder of the German Protestant movement, was a strong believer in the value of congregational singing during church services. Thus, the chorales became the foundation of liturgical music in the Protestant church. J. S. Bach, who spent the majority of his life as a Protestant church musician, employed chorale melodies in many of his compositions. This body of music is generally regarded as the apex of artistic development of chorale-based liturgical music. Many of Bach's cantatas are climaxed by a four-part setting of a chorale tune. Thus, the chorale settings, which we will examine throughout this book, form an important part of the artistic output of Bach and are worthy models for study.

APPLICATIONS

The best way to understand the practices of eighteenth-century voice leading is to examine works by composers of the period. The following phrases from chorale harmonizations by J. S. Bach have furnished models of good voice leading to generations of students. The excerpts from these chorales in Figure 9.2 will be examined in detail to illustrate typical voice-leading practice. The numbers labeled "stylistic practices" will be explained following the initial presentation of the excerpts.

Figure 9.2

1. Bach: "Lobt Gott, ihr Christen, allzugleich" ("Praise God, Ye Christians, All Together"), BWV 376, mm. 1–2 (transposed).

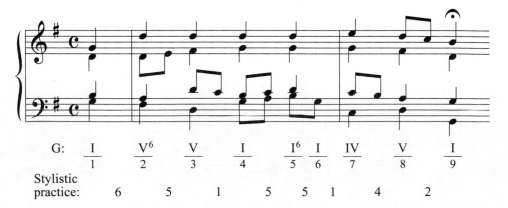

PART B   The Structural Elements of Music

2. Bach: "Ach Gott, vom Himmel sieh' darein" ("Oh God, Look Down from Heaven"),
   BWV 2, mm. 1–2.

$$g: \quad \frac{V}{10} \quad \frac{i}{11} \quad \frac{vii^{\circ 6}}{12} \quad \frac{i^6}{13} \quad \frac{i}{14} \quad \frac{V^6}{15} \quad \frac{i}{16} \quad \frac{V}{17}$$

Stylistic
practice: 1   7   6   5   6   6   1

3. Bach: "Wer weiss, wie nahe mir mein Ende" ("Who Knows How Near My End May
   Be"), BWV 166, mm. 1–3.

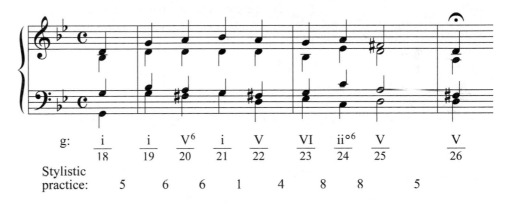

$$g: \quad \frac{i}{18} \quad \frac{i}{19} \quad \frac{V^6}{20} \quad \frac{i}{21} \quad \frac{V}{22} \quad \frac{VI}{23} \quad \frac{ii^{\circ 6}}{24} \quad \frac{V}{25} \quad \frac{V}{26}$$

Stylistic
practice: 5   6   6   1   4   8   8   5

4. Bach: "Der Tag, der ist so freudenreich" ("This Day Is So Joyful"), BWV 294,
   mm. 1–2 (modified).

$$G: \quad \frac{I}{27} \quad \frac{vi}{28} \quad \frac{IV}{29} \quad \frac{ii}{30} \quad \frac{I}{31} \quad \frac{IV}{32} \quad \frac{V}{33} \quad \frac{I}{34}$$

Stylistic
practice: 3   3   3   4   1   4   2

5. Bach: "Nun danket alle Gott" ("Now Let Us All Thank God"), BWV 386, mm. 1–2 (transposed).

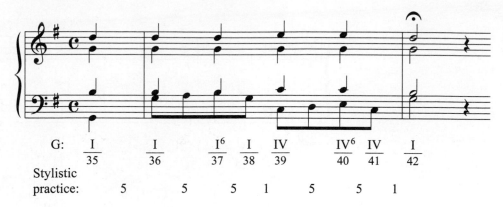

G:	I	I	I⁶	I	IV		IV⁶	IV	I
	35	36	37	38	39		40	41	42

Stylistic practice: 5   5   5   1   5   5   1

Analysis of the Chorale Phrases

Although the 42 chords contained in the five phrases in Figure 9.2 do not by any means constitute a sample large enough for a thorough and valid study, they do illustrate some of the important and recurring patterns in voice leading that have become established procedures. A thorough analysis of the five phrases is well worth the effort.

Rather than examining the phrases on a chord-by-chord basis, we can save time by searching through adjacent triads for voice-leading patterns that are repeated regularly. Also, a better understanding results if we search in an organized manner—by classification of root movement.

Stylistic Practices

A *stylistic practice* is a common method for part writing a particular progression. For example, stylistic practices 1 and 2 below refer to chords whose roots are a P5th or P4th apart. There are no fewer than eight examples of stylistic practice 1 in the five phrases. They connect the following root position chords: 3–4, 6–7, 10–11, 16–17, 21–22, 31–32, 38–39, and 41–42.

Figure 9.3

Bach: Excerpts Illustrating Stylistic Practice 1.

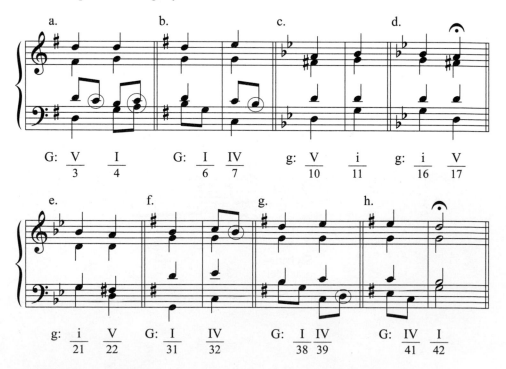

G:	V	I	G:	I	IV	g:	V	i	g:	i	V
	3	4		6	7		10	11		16	17

g:	i	V	G:	I	IV	G:	I	IV	G:	IV	I
	21	22		31	32		38	39		41	42

Two examples of stylistic practice 2 can be observed in the five phrases. They occur between chord numbers 8–9 and 33–34.

Figure 9.4

Bach: Excerpts Illustrating Stylistic Practice 2.

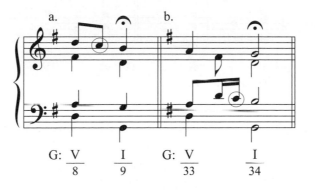

G: V I   G: V I
  8 9   33 34

Root Position

When both chords are in root position, and the two roots lie a perfect 5th or 4th apart:

1. Keep the *common tone* (the tone shared by both triads) and move the remaining two upper voices stepwise to the chord tones of the next triad. If handled correctly, the roots of the chords will be *doubled*.
2. If you cannot keep the common tone, especially when the soprano voice descends scale degrees $\hat{2}$ to $\hat{1}$, move all three upper voices in similar motion to the nearest chord tone. If handled correctly, the roots will be doubled.

Figure 9.5

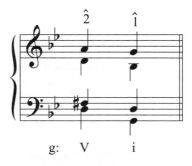

g: V i   g: V i

1. Keep common tone; move other voices by step to nearest chord tone.

2. Do not keep common tone; move all three upper voices in similar motion to nearest chord tone.

The excerpts contain three examples of chord roots that lie a third apart. These connect the chords in Figure 9.2 numbered 27–28, 28–29, and 29–30.

Figure 9.6

Bach: Excerpts Illustrating Stylistic Practice 3.

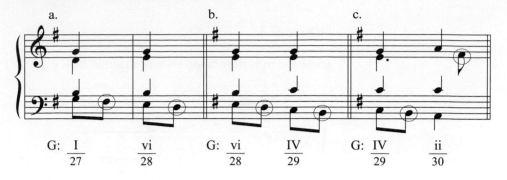

G: I̲   vi̲   G: vi̲   IV̲   G: IV̲   ii̲
   27   28   28   29   29   30

All adhere to the stylistic practice that is followed when roots lie a third (major or minor) apart:

3. Keep both common tones and move the remaining upper voice stepwise. If handled properly, the roots of the two chords will be doubled.

Figure 9.7

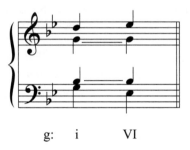

g: i   VI

Keep both common tones.

For adjacent chord roots that lie a major or minor second apart, four examples, all following stylistic practice 4 explained in the following paragraph, can be cited. These occur in Figure 9.2 between chords 7–8, 22–23, 30–31, and 32–33.

Figure 9.8

Bach: Excerpts Illustrating Stylistic Practice 4.

G: IV̲   V̲   g: V̲   VI̲   G: ii̲   I̲   G: IV̲   V̲
   7   8   22   23   30   31   32   33

When roots lie a second apart:

4. Move the three upper voices in contrary motion to the bass, making sure that each voice moves to the nearest chord tone of the next chord. If handled correctly, the roots of the two chords will be doubled. An exception is the progression V to vi or VI. In this case, double the third factor of the vi or VI triad. Only two upper voices will move in opposite direction to the bass.

Figure 9.9

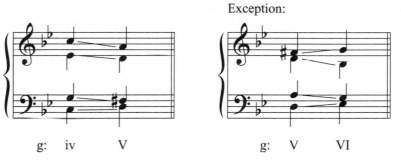

Exception:

g: iv   V

Upper voices in contrary motion to bass.

g: V   VI

Double third of VI triad.

Often in the five chorale phrases, two adjacent chords are the same (example: I followed by another I). The second chord is simply a continuation of the first, and the two are not considered a chord progression. Much flexibility is available to you and only two general warnings are necessary. In the five chorale phrases in Figure 9.2, there are 11 examples of repeated triads: 2–3, 4–5, 5–6, 13–14, 18–19, 25–26, 35–36, 36–37, 37–38, 39–40, and 40–41.

Figure 9.10

Bach: Excerpts Illustrating Stylistic Practice 5.

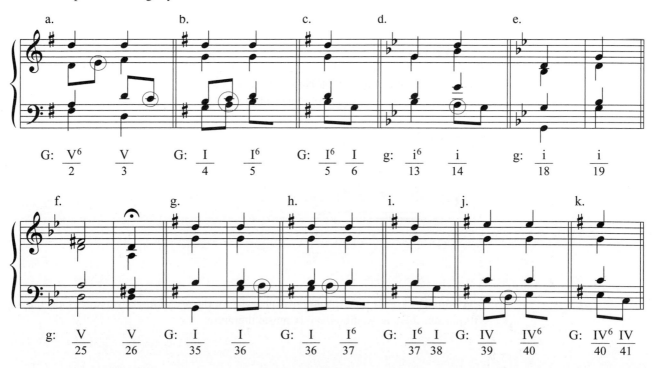

When chords are repeated:

5. Maintain proper doubling and range of voices, and keep the usual order of voices (soprano, alto, tenor, and bass). Otherwise, you are quite free to exchange chord factors among voices. Sometimes a change of position takes place (example: I to I⁶).

First-Inversion Triads

First-inversion triads are used for a number of purposes, including to smooth bass lines and to provide melodic motion in repeated chords.

First-Inversion Triads for Smooth Bass Melodies

Triads in root position establish stability in the chorale and are considered anchor positions, but if all chorales or hymns were composed only of root positions, bass lines would be disjointed. Stepwise movement would be possible only with adjacent chords that are a step apart (IV to V, V to vi, etc.). One of the reasons first inversions are employed is to provide smooth bass lines with a musical balance of steps and skips.

Figure 9.11

Bach: "Wer weiss, wie nahe mir mein Ende" ("Who Knows How Near My End May Be"), BWV 166, m. 1.

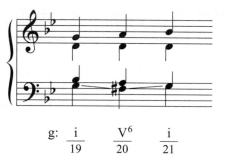

First-Inversion Triads to Provide Melodic Motion

Not only do first-inversion triads diminish the angularity of a bass line, but they may also add another ingredient not available to root positions—they provide an opportunity to incorporate melodic motion in the bass melody.

Figure 9.12

Bach: "Nun danket alle Gott" ("Now Let Us All Thank God"), BWV 386, m. 1 (transposed).

A number of other fundamental reasons exist for the use of first-inversion triads, but we will discuss them as we find them in music literature.

Voice Leading in First-Inversion Triads

The five chorale phrases that Bach harmonized (Figure 9.2) contain nine first-inversion triads. Careful examination of all of these examples indicates that you must treat each first-inversion triad in relation to surrounding chords. Therefore, they do not form preferred patterns of voice leading as in the case of root-position triads. First-inversion involvement occurs in the following groups of chords: 1–3, 4–6, 11–14, 14–16, 19–21, 23–25, 36–38, 39–41.

Figure 9.13

Bach: Excerpts Illustrating Stylistic Practices 6, 7, and 8.

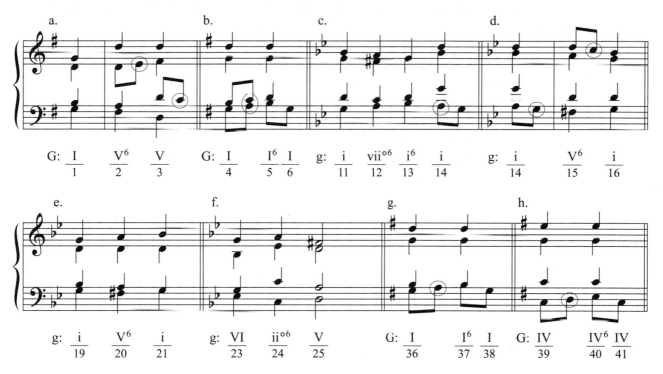

One general stylistic practice statement suffices for voice leading in first-inversion major and minor triads as they occur in chorales or hymns:

6. Double any triad factor that facilitates smooth voice leading. Favored notes are the soprano (found often) and bass (slightly less common). Never double the leading tone (seventh scale degree). Observe general recommendations regarding voice ranges, order of voices, and spacing.

The vii°⁶ Triad

The leading-tone triad is nearly always found in first inversion and progresses most often to the tonic. You should think of it as having a dominant function because the two (V and vii°⁶) have two pitches in common (in C major: G–B–D and B–D–F).

Voice leading for the vii°⁶ triad:

7. Double the third (bass note) or fifth factor. The bass note is preferred. Move all voices with as much stepwise movement as possible. Avoid melodic skips of a tritone.

Chord 12, shown in both Figures 9.2 and 9.14, represents typical voice leading for the vii°⁶ triad—the bass note (the third of the triad) is doubled.

Figure 9.14

Bach: "Ach Gott, vom Himmel sieh' darein" ("Oh God, Look Down from Heaven"), BWV 2, m. 1.

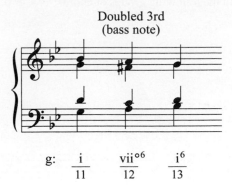

Doubled 3rd
(bass note)

g: i vii°⁶ i⁶
  11   12   13

The ii°⁶ Triad

One final detail remains. Chord 24 of the five chorale phrases (Figure 9. 2) is a ii°⁶ triad that has not yet been discussed. Both vii°⁶ and ii°⁶ are diminished triads, but they do not function in a similar manner: vii°⁶ is related to dominant function and usually progresses to the tonic; ii°⁶ has pre-dominant function and precedes the dominant.

Voice leading for the ii°⁶ triad in minor keys:

8. Double the third (bass note) or the root, which will be in an upper voice. When approaching or leaving the ii°⁶ triad, make voice leading stepwise whenever possible and avoid melodic tritones.

Chord 24, shown in both Figures 9.2 and 9.15, represents typical voice leading for the ii°⁶ triad—the bass note (the third of the triad) is doubled.

Figure 9.15

Bach: "Wer weiss, wie nahe mir mein Ende" ("Who Knows How Near My End May Be"), BWV 166, m. 2.

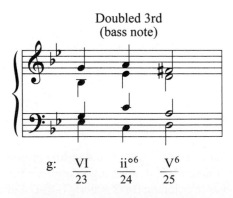

Doubled 3rd
(bass note)

g: VI ii°⁶ V⁶
  23   24   25

Second-Inversion Triads

You should use the second inversion of any triad with extreme caution because of its unstable nature. The chord contains the interval of a fourth and cannot be used in the functional way that typifies both root position and first-inversion triads. The second-inversion position of the tonic chord is common, but that of other triads is found only occasionally.

You should employ second-inversion triads (⁶₄ chords) *only* in one of the following ways:

Cadential—The tonic $^6_4$ chord resolves to the V chord at the cadence. Used in this manner, the $^6_4$ chord is a decoration of the V chord. The bass note is doubled (Figure 9.16a).

Passing Bass—The bass note (5th factor) of the $^6_4$ acts as a passing tone. The passing bass may be found as a tonic $^6_4$ between the IV and IV^6 chords (Figure 9.16b) or as a dominant $^6_4$ between the I and I$^6_4$ chords (Figure 9.16c). The bass note is doubled.

Arpeggiated Bass—The bass note (5th factor) participates in an arpeggiation of the same chord (Figure 9.16d). This usage of $^6_4$ chords occurs occasionally with triads other than the tonic. The bass note is doubled.

Pedal Bass—Also known as *stationary bass* or neighboring tone chords, the bass note (5th factor) is preceded and followed by the same tone and is placed between two root positions of the same triad. This type also occurs occasionally with the IV$^6_4$ (Figure 9.16e) as well as the tonic (figure 9.16f). The bass note is doubled.

Figure 9.16

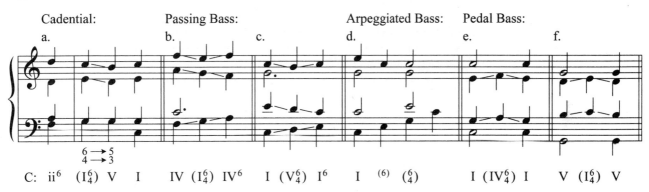

Cadential: Passing Bass: Arpeggiated Bass: Pedal Bass:

a.   b.   c.   d.   e.   f.

C: ii^6 (I$^6_4$)   V   I   IV   (I$^6_4$)   IV^6 I   (V$^6_4$)   I^6 I $^{(6)}$ $\binom{6}{4}$ I   (IV$^6_4$)   I   V   (I$^6_4$)   V

Summary of Stylistic Practices for $^6_4$ Chords

9. a. Except under unusual circumstances, double the bass note (5th of the chord).
   b. Approach and depart from $^6_4$ chords with as few skips as possible.
   c. Only in the arpeggiated $^6_4$ chord is the bass note approached or left by skip.
   d. Use only the four types of $^6_4$ chords described in this chapter: cadential, passing bass, arpeggiated bass, and pedal bass.

Exceptions to Stylistic Practices

As long as you follow stylistic practices 1 through 9, you need not worry about the following guidelines. But occasionally, voice-leading conditions make it impossible to apply stylistic practices. So, although stylistic practices are the norm, they must not be considered unbreakable laws. When you cannot complete a phrase with conventional part writing, you will need further guidelines to prevent you from making unstylistic or unmusical mistakes.

Unstylistic Departures

Inviolate

There are no exceptions to these practices under any conditions:

1. Avoid *parallel perfect octaves* (P8ths), *parallel perfect fifths* (P5ths), and *parallel unisons* (P1s). Successive perfect intervals containing the same pitches are not considered parallel.
2. Never double the leading tone of the scale.
3. Do not write pitches outside the range of a particular voice. Keep all four voices within their ranges at all times.
4. Avoid the melodic augmented second (A2) and fourth (A4) in all voices.

Figure 9.17 shows examples of the inviolate unstylistic departures.

Figure 9.17

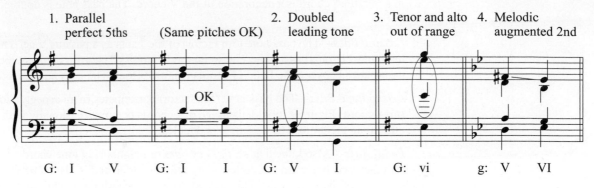

1. Parallel perfect 5ths   (Same pitches OK)   2. Doubled leading tone   3. Tenor and alto out of range   4. Melodic augmented 2nd

G: I   V   G: I   I   G: V   I   G: vi   g: V   VI

Occasionally Broken

Observe these practices carefully unless particular situations permit no other alternative:

5. Avoid *crossing voices.* Keep voices in proper order (from highest to lowest): soprano, alto, tenor, bass. On rare occasions, crossing of voices is justified if it improves voice leading.

6. *Spacing* between adjacent voices should not exceed an octave in the three upper voices. The spacing between bass and tenor voices can be of any reasonable interval (never greater than two octaves).

7. Do not *overlap* two adjacent voices more than a whole step. An overlap occurs between two chords when one voice moves above or below the previous pitch of an adjacent voice. You may employ overlaps of a half or whole step if it improves voice leading.

8. Do not move in the same direction to perfect intervals in the two outer voices (soprano and bass). Some theorists think that such motion, especially in outer voices, creates the effect of parallel perfect intervals.

9. *Unequal fifths,* P5ths to d5ths or vice versa, are found in chorale harmonizations and may be used sparingly. The progression vii°6 to I, under certain circumstances, requires the use of unequal fifths.

10. Melodic augmented seconds and fourths are almost never found in choral literature of the eighteenth century.
    a. The melodic descending d5th appears sometimes in bass voices, but rarely in the soprano.
    b. The d4th is a diatonic interval in the harmonic minor scale (from the third down to seventh scale degrees) and may be written in isolated situations.

11. The leading tone should progress upward to the tonic when it is in an outer voice (soprano or bass).

Figure 9.18 shows examples of the preceding occasionally broken unstylistic departures.

Figure 9.18

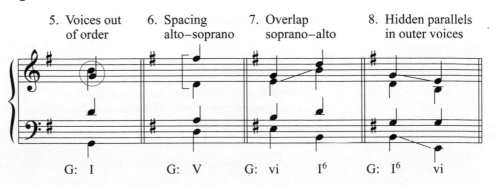

5. Voices out of order   6. Spacing alto–soprano   7. Overlap soprano–alto   8. Hidden parallels in outer voices

G: I   G: V   G: vi   I6   G: I6   vi

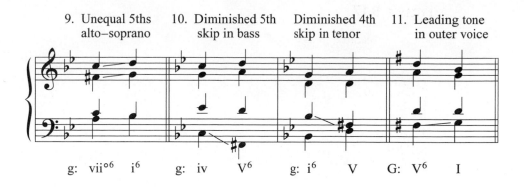

9. Unequal 5ths
alto–soprano

10. Diminished 5th
skip in bass

Diminished 4th
skip in tenor

11. Leading tone
in outer voice

g: vii°⁶   i⁶   g: iv   V⁶   g: i⁶   V   G: V⁶   I

In chorale writing, the voices are divided into four general categories: *soprano, alto, tenor,* and *bass*. In Figure 9.19, whole notes indicate the best usable ranges. Black notes represent pitch ranges that should be used sparingly.

Figure 9.19

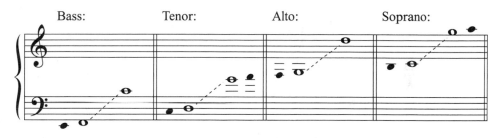

Bass: Tenor: Alto: Soprano:

Voice Spacing

The voice spacing of individual chords in four-voice textures is said to be either close or open. Chords in *close position* have less than an octave between the soprano and tenor (Figure 9.20a), whereas chords in open position have an octave or more between the soprano and tenor (Figure 9.20b).

Figure 9.20

a. Close position: b. Open position:

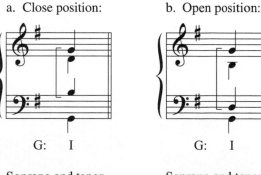

G: I   G: I

Soprano and tenor   Soprano and tenor
less than octave apart   octave or more apart

You can find a summary of stylistic practices and voice-leading guidelines in Appendix A.

Assignment 9.1

Each exercise is a chorale phrase with the tenor and alto omitted. You are to complete a four-voice setting in chorale style using the principles for four-voice writing.

As a keyboard assignment:

If your instructor requests that this be a keyboard harmony assignment, you may do it at the piano. Play the soprano, alto, and tenor with the right hand and the bass with the left hand. This arrangement is not only more comfortable if piano is not your major instrument, but it also maintains voice-leading integrity. The following illustration represents correct procedure.

Keyboard Style Example.

As a written assignment:

Even if you complete this assignment at the keyboard, doing it on paper also has its advantages. Your instructor may request it.

1. You are to add the alto and tenor voices to each phrase according to the first five stylistic practices listed in this chapter on pp. 194–198.
2. All chords are in root position.
3. Write the alto and tenor voices at the same time. You will need to consider both parts to achieve the appropriate doubling and spacing of chords.
4. Try to double the root of each chord.
5. The sharp signs below some bass notes are figured-bass symbols indicating accidentals to be applied to the third of the chord.
6. Add the Roman numeral analysis for all chords in the blanks provided.

2.

g: ___ ___ ___ ___

3.

G: ___ ___ ___ ___

4.

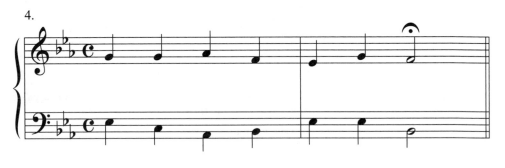

E♭: ___ ___ ___ ___

5.

f♯: ___ ___ ___ ___

6.

D: _____ _____ _____ _____ _____ _____ _____

7.

B♭: _____ _____ _____ _____ _____ _____ _____

8.

b: _____ _____ _____ _____ _____ _____ _____

9.

d: _____ _____ _____ _____ _____ _____ _____

Assignment 9.2

The following chorale phrases contain inverted triads, which are shown by the figured-bass symbols below the bass line (^{6} = first inversion, $^6_4$ = second inversion).

As a keyboard assignment:

If your instructor requests that this be a keyboard harmony assignment, play the exercises on a piano. More detailed information and an illustration are given in assignment 9.1.

As a written assignment:

1. Add the alto and tenor voices to each phrase according to the nine stylistic practices listed in this chapter on pp. 194–201.
2. Add the Roman numeral analysis for all chords in the blanks provided.

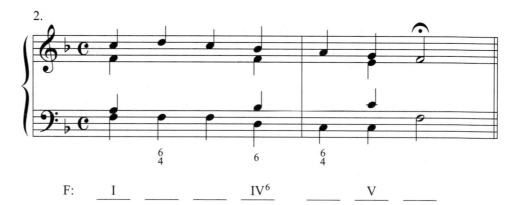

4.

D: I ___ IV ___ ___

5.

c: i ___ i ___ ___

6.

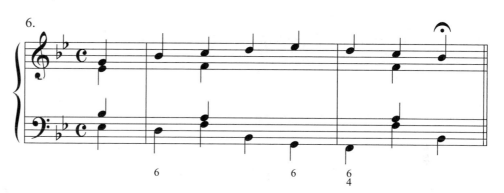

B♭:   IV ___ V ___ ___ V ___

7.

d: V ___ ___ i ___

Assignment 9.3

The following six chorale phrases are similar to those in previous assignments, but they are taken from the chorale settings of J. S. Bach. The directions for completing them are the same as those for assignments 9.1 and 9.2. Be sure to make a complete harmonic analysis of each phrase.

1. "Herzlich lieb hab' ich dich, o Herr" ("Dearly I Love Thee, O Lord"), BWV 174, mm. 18–19 (modified).

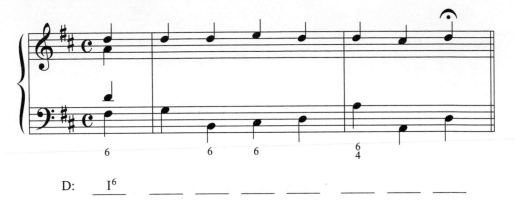

2. "Freu' dich sehr, o meine Seele" ("Rejoice Greatly, O My Soul"), BWV 39, mm. 3–4 (modified).

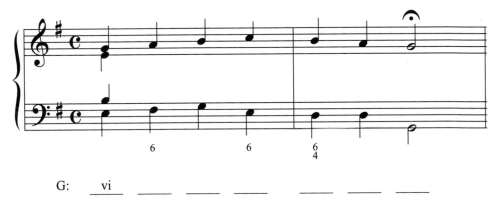

3. "Herr Christ, der ein'ge Gott's-Sohn" ("Lord Christ, the Only Son of God"), BWV 164, mm. 3–4 (modified).

4. "Nicht so traurig, nicht so sehr" ("Not So Sadly, Not So Deeply"), BWV 384, mm. 3–4 (modified).

Eb: vi⁶ ___ ___ ___ ___ ___ ___ ___

*Do not harmonize the passing tone.

5. "Herr Jesu Christ, du höchstes Gut" ("Lord Jesus Christ, Thou Highest Good"), BWV 334, mm. 1–2 (modified).

g: i ___ ___ ___ ___ ___ ___ ___ ___ ___

*The $\frac{3}{3}$ symbol means that the third above the bass note should be doubled.

6. "Erhalt' uns, Herr, bei deinem Wort" ("Preserve Us, Lord, by Thy Word"), BWV 6, mm. 7–8 (modified).

g: V⁶ ___ ___ ___ ___ ___ ___ ___

*The ♯6 symbol means that the sixth above the bass note should be raised one half step.

Assignment 9.4   Each exercise is a figured-bass voice to which you will add soprano, alto, and tenor voices.

As a keyboard assignment:

Play each entire phrase through to become comfortable with the figured bass. When the bass is familiar to you, try to play a good soprano line along with it. When you are satisfied, fill in the inner voices as shown in assignment 9.1.

As a written assignment:

1. On a separate sheet of paper, write out each figured bass, leaving a staff above for the soprano and alto.
2. Write a soprano line to go with the bass line according to the figuration supplied. See Chapter 4 for an explanation of the figured-bass symbols.
3. Fill in the inner voices, checking your voice leading for errors.
4. Make a complete Roman numeral analysis of each exercise.

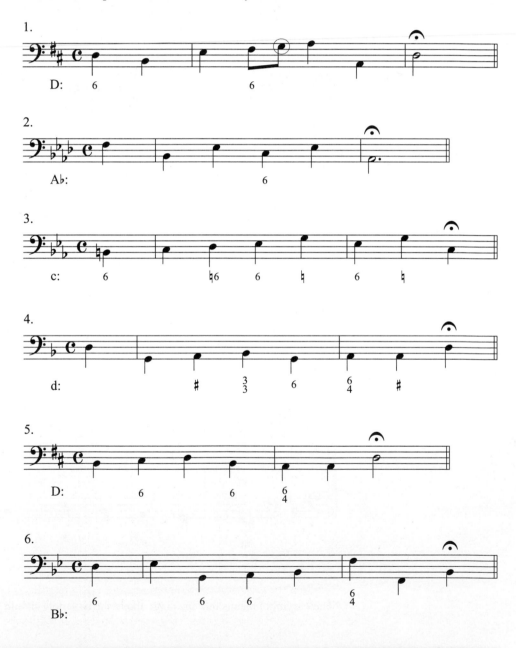

CHAPTER 10

Harmonic Progression and Harmonic Rhythm

TOPICS	Harmonic Progression	Ascending Fifths	Harmonic Rhythm
	Root Relationships	Ascending Seconds	Changes
	Circle Progression	Descending Thirds	Style
	Noncircle Progressions		

IMPORTANT CONCEPTS

In the previous chapters, we have focused attention on voice leading in two-voice and four-voice textures. Now we will concentrate on *harmonic progression*—the way in which chords succeed each other in a piece of music.

Harmonic Progression

From the baroque through the classical and romantic periods, composers employed harmonic progression as a principal organizing force. The movement from one chord to another provides an additional impetus to music and contributes a stimulus not found in melody or rhythm alone. Through all musical styles that involve tonal harmony, the shape of a composition is determined to a great extent by chord progressions. To experience an example, play the two sets of progressions in Figure 10.1 and determine which is the more effective. Both have the same soprano melody.

Figure 10.1

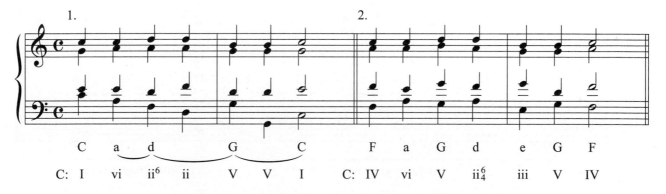

Which progression are you most accustomed to hearing? The chords in the first example seem to progress directly to the final chord, as if it were a predetermined goal. The second example lacks direction and seems to wander aimlessly.

The Relationship of Chords

In tonal music, the tonic chord is the most stable of all. Chords that move away from the tonic tend to create tension. Those that progress toward the tonic give fulfillment and relax the tension caused by the departure. Thus, complete tonal compositions invariably end with the tonic triad and more often than not begin with that same chord.

Root Relationships

Two forces, both involving *root relationships,* govern the relationship of chords in succession. Together they help organize phrases, periods, sections, and other musical units. These two forces are (1) the relationship of the chords to the prevailing tonality and (2) the intervals formed by the roots of adjacent chords. The triads constructed on each of the scale degrees relate to the tonic triad, which is the point of rest and the goal of harmonic progression. We can analyze individual chord progressions in terms of the interval formed between their roots.

Chord Progressions

The best way to study harmonic progression is to consider progressions in groups according to the interval produced by the roots of two adjacent chords. The following general categories will form the basis of our study of harmonic progression.

The Circle Progression

Examples: iii–vi, vi–ii, ii–V, V–I.

Undoubtedly the most common and the strongest of all harmonic progressions is the *circle progression*—adjacent chord roots in ascending fourth or descending fifth relationship. More than any other, this progression has the capability of determining a tonality, giving direction and thrust, and providing order in a section or phrase of music. It is indeed the basis of all harmonic progression.

Circle progressions are often found in succession—for example, ii–V–I, or even vi–ii–V–I. Figure 10.2 illustrates a complete circle from the tonic through all seven diatonic chords to the original tonic. Note that ascending fourths are equivalent to descending fifths (the pitches will be the same in either direction), and that not all of the fourths and fifths are perfect in the diatonic series: ascending augmented fourths and descending diminished fifths are necessary to maintain the diatonic setting. Chords 1, 5, 10, and 11 are seventh chords, but the added factor of a seventh does not affect the root movement or the progression function.

Figure 10.2

Beethoven: Sonata in F Minor, op. 2, no. 1, I: Allegro, mm. 146–152.

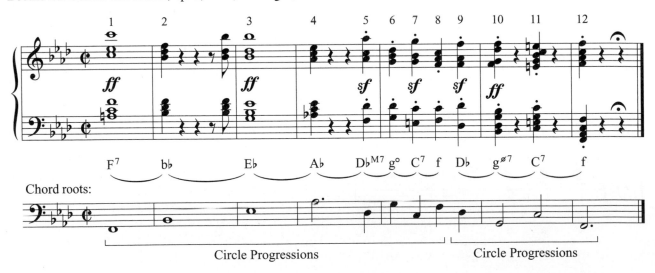

We can derive many harmonic patterns from the progression built of consecutive ascending fourths or descending fifths: I–IV–vii°–iii–vi–ii–V–I. Note that the progression begins and finishes on the tonic.

All of the following common progressions result when specific chords are selected from the I–IV–vii°–iii–vi–ii–V–I series.

I–IV–vii°–iii–vi–ii–V–I

I–   V–I = I–V–I

I–   ii–V–I = I–ii–V–I

I–IV–   V–I = I–IV–V–I

I–   vi–ii–V–I = I–vi–ii–V–I

In macro analysis, you will mark root movement by ascending fourth or descending fifth with a slur to identify circle progression motion. The excerpt in Figure 10.3 illustrates a complete diatonic circle progression. Note the macro analysis slurs indicating the series of circle progression root relationships.

Figure 10.3

Handel: Gigue from Suite (Partita) in G Major, G. 217, mm. 34–35.

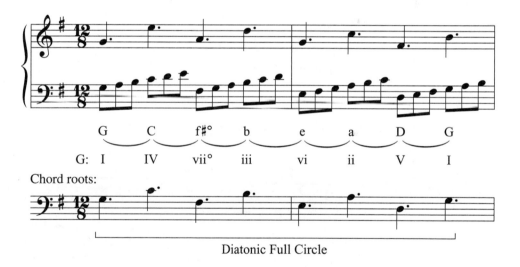

Diatonic Full Circle

Phrases often open with a mixture of circle and noncircle progressions and close with a strong succession of circle progressions. The phrase in Figure 10.4 begins with presentations of both progression types, but then concludes with an extended series of circle progressions (iii–vi–ii–V–I). Chords 4 through 8 illustrate a typical profusion of circle progressions near a cadence. Many phrases end with a ii–V–i circle progression, which results in an authentic cadence.

Figure 10.4

Bach: "Straf' mich nicht in deinem Zorn" ("Punish Me Not in Thy Wrath"), BWV 115, mm. 1–2.

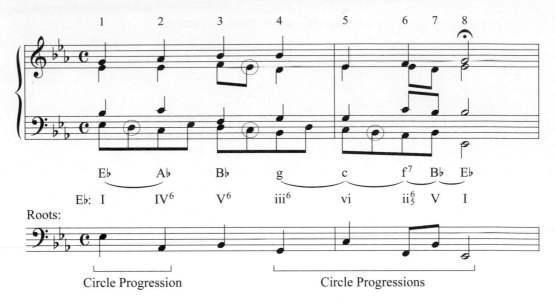

Not all series of circle progressions conclude on the tonic chord. Frequently, phrases will end with the progression ii–V (half cadence), thus leading us to expect that a following phrase will complete the direction toward the tonic.

Figure 10.5

Bach: "Lobt Gott, ihr Christen, allzugleich" ("Praise God, Ye Christians, All Together"), BWV 151, mm. 5–6.

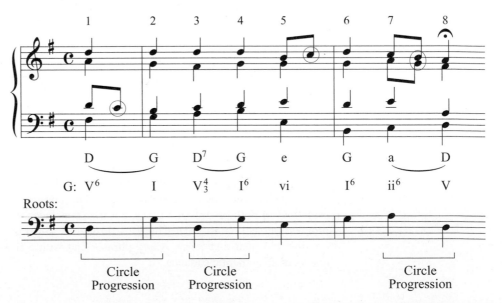

We think of the circle progression as a drive toward the tonic, which, when achieved, is a point of relaxation. In the span of even a very short composition, chord progressions can reach the tonic many times, only to move away and begin another motion toward the goal.

The ebb and flow of music allows for movement away from, as well as toward, the tonic. Composers employ a variety of progression types that include *noncircle progressions*.

Ascending Fifths and Descending Fourths

Examples: I–V, IV–I, V–ii, vi–iii, iii–vii°, and ii–vi.

Compared with the pattern of descending fifths, the *ascending fifth* or descending fourth provides relief from the constant motion toward tonic. The most frequent application is the progression from the tonic to the dominant (I–V), although ascending fifths may occur between chord roots on any scale degrees. The half cadence, which appears often, is an example of this type of movement.

Ascending Seconds

Examples: IV–V, V–vi, I–ii, ii–iii, iii–IV, and vii°–I.

Adjacent chords whose roots lie in the relationship of an *ascending second* perform a most important function even though they are not as abundant as chords related by a descending fifth. The ascending second progression is often used to prepare a shift from the circle progression I–IV to another circle progression, V–I. The resulting progression, I–IV–V–I, is often considered a substitute for I–ii–V–I.

In Figure 10.6 the first two chords (I–V) are a typical example of the ascending fifth progression's departure from tonic. In the middle of the phrase an ascending second progression (I–ii) prepares a change from one circle (V–I in chords 2 and 3) to another (ii–V–I in chords 4 through 6).

Figure 10.6

Tchaikovsky: Symphony no. 5 in E Minor, op. 64, II: Andante cantabile, con alcuna licenza, mm. 8–12.

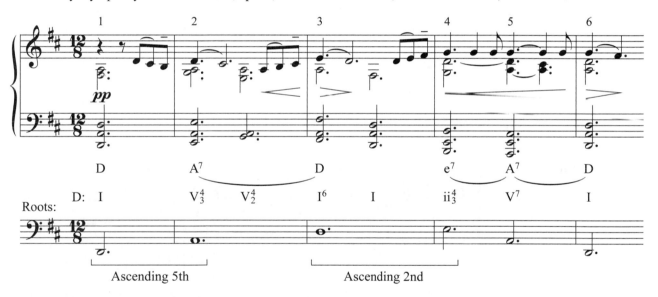

The vii° Triad

The ascending-second root relationship is employed in other capacities, one of which involves the leading-tone triad or seventh chord. Leading-tone harmony is most often considered dominant harmony since the triad contains the third, fifth, and seventh of the dominant seventh chord. For this reason, the leading-tone triad usually progresses to the tonic (vii°–I) in an ascending-second relationship. Thus, the progression vii°6–I, although weaker, functions for all practical purposes as V–I.

In macro analysis, the leading tone to tonic progression is marked with a dotted slur to indicate its similarity to the circle progression. In Figure 10.7, chords 2–3 and 6–7 have been marked with the dotted slur to denote the leading-tone function.

Figure 10.7

Beethoven: Sonata in G Minor, op. 49, no. 1, I: Andante, mm. 1–4.

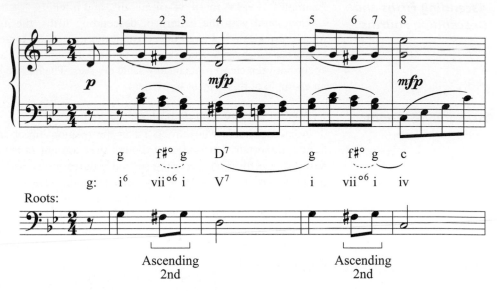

Descending Thirds

Examples: I–vi, vi–IV, IV–ii, iii–I, and V–iii.

Chord roots that lie in a relationship of *descending thirds* serve a definite function in that they provide contrast and facilitate change from one circle progression to another. Descending third progressions are often used in harmonic movement away from the tonic (I–vi) or in a longer chord series (I–vi–IV–ii) as shown in Figure 10.8.

Figure 10.8

Bach: "Der Tag, der ist so freudenreich" ("This Day Is So Joyful"), BWV 294, mm. 1–2.

The Tonic $^6_4$ Triad

The second-inversion tonic triad, especially in the cadence formula I$^6_4$–V–I, reflects little of the stable quality normally associated with the tonic function and should be considered a decoration of the V chord that follows it.

PART B The Structural Elements of Music

Repeated Chords

In instances where the same triad is repeated or recurs in a different position, no progression takes place. In Figure 10.9, the repeated tonic chords at the beginning of the phrase are not considered a progression. Note also that the tonic in second inversion is simply a decoration of the ii–V–I progression that ends the phrase.

Figure 10.9

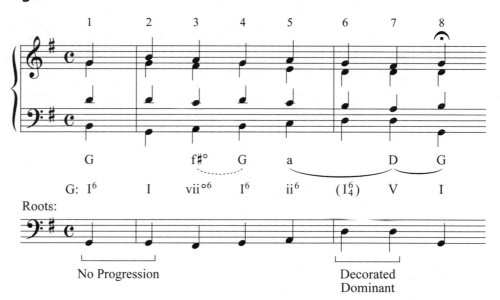

Harmonic Rhythm

Harmonic rhythm is the frequency of harmonic changes in a composition (the rate at which chord progressions change). It is yet another aspect of the rhythmic life of a piece of music. The harmonic rhythm typically has the function of defining or confirming the prevailing meter of a composition. In Figure 10.10, there is one chord per measure.

Figure 10.10

Chopin: Mazurka in B-flat Major, op. 7, no. 1, mm. 1–4.

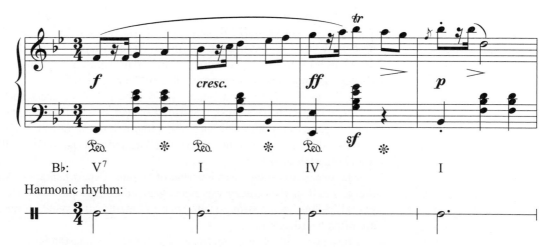

The harmonic rhythm of a composition can consist of slow or fast harmonic changes. Sometimes a single chord will be heard for several measures at a time. Other times, as in chorale settings, each successive melody tone will be harmonized with a different chord. When the harmonic rhythm is slow and extends over many measures, the eventual chord change will occur on a downbeat. Even when the harmonic rhythm is faster than one chord per measure, chord changes will usually coincide with each downbeat.

Figure 10.11

Mozart: Sonata in D Major, K. 284, III: Theme, mm. 1–4.

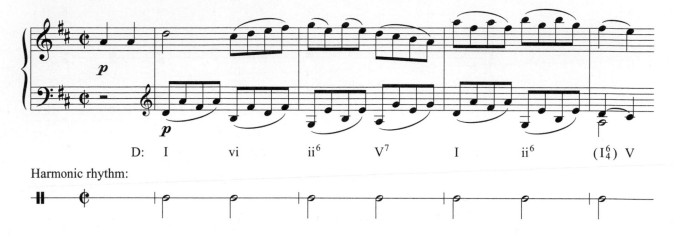

Harmonic rhythm:

History

During the Renaissance period, the emphasis was on melodic lines; chord progressions were only an incidental result. However, a Renaissance composer, Adrian Willaert (1490–1562), produced some early examples of what we now know as circle progressions in some of his works. Although these compositions were probably experimental in nature, the seeds of tonal harmony were apparent.

In the baroque period the tonal system based on the major and minor scales arose, and harmony began to be a stronger factor. Chord progressions, and especially circle progressions, are clearly in evidence in the works of such early baroque composers as Samuel Scheidt (1587–1654) and Claudio Monteverdi (1567–1643). The middle and latter part of the baroque period brought tonal harmony to a high level of sophistication.

The music of the classical period depends heavily for its structure on the standard chord progressions discussed in this chapter. The dominating force of the circle progression is evident in the music of this period, with functional harmony being the mainstay for harmonic relationships.

Whereas the style of the romantic period was marked by increased chromaticism, harmonic progression continued as an important form-creating element of the period. In the last quarter of the century, the use of standard progressions gradually declined as composers became more and more experimental in their approach.

In the post-romantic and impressionistic period, composers such as Maurice Ravel (1875–1937), Richard Strauss (1864–1949), and Gustav Mahler (1860–1911) continued to rely heavily on traditional harmonic progression; but others, such as Claude Debussy (1862–1918), Erik Satie (1866–1925), and Alexander Scriabin (1872–1915), looked for and found other alternatives.

The twentieth century was a period of extreme experimentation. Much of the music of the first half of the century was not organized along tonal lines. However, in the recent past there has been a strong resurgence in tonality, and standard harmonic progressions are often heard again.

Most jazz and popular music is structured around standard harmonic progressions (which jazz musicians refer to as *changes*). The most common of these progressions is the 12-bar blues progression. The table in Figure 10.12 shows common variants of this progression. Notice that the chords are all notated as major triads with a minor seventh (see Chapter 11), which is typical of the blues style.

Figure 10.12

Standard 12-Bar Blues Progressions.

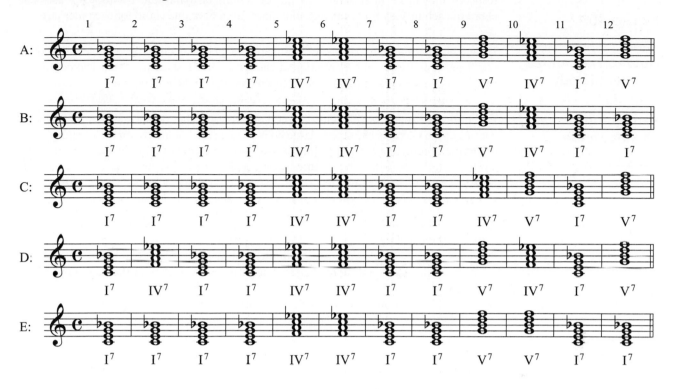

"Sweet Home Chicago," recorded by Robert Johnson in 1936, is a blues song using the first chord progression in Figure 10.12.

Figure 10.13

Johnson: "Sweet Home Chicago."

In this chapter we will concentrate on harmonizing two different kinds of melody: chorales (or hymn tunes) and folk songs. Although the two categories are similar in some respects, they differ in harmonic rhythm. A chorale or hymn tune traditionally uses one chord to each melody note, whereas folk tunes often have one chord for each measure.

How to Harmonize a Tonal Melody

Ultimately, harmonizing a melody is a matter of personal taste. Nevertheless, although you have some leeway in the selection of chords, a certain standard of musical communication, known as *style,* prevents you from exercising complete freedom.

Harmonizing a Chorale Phrase

Earlier in the chapter, we examined several examples of chorale phrases. Bach's harmonizations of the chorales represent a large body of respected literature. In the learning stage, it is quite appropriate for you to imitate the harmonic construction of these magnificent works. After your skills have matured, you can explore individual choice and creativity. However, in this chapter we will try to make our chorale harmonizations as much like those of Bach as possible. The following general principles will guide our choice of chords:

1. You must use half (I–V, IV–V, or ii–V) or authentic (V–I) cadences for the final two notes of each phrase.
2. You should use circle progressions throughout in each phrase. Circle progressions are more often longer and more abundant near the cadence than at the beginning of the phrase.
3. Harmonize each melody note with one chord. It is possible to repeat chords occasionally, but adjacent repeated chords are usually in different positions to provide melodic motion in the bass.
4. Employ first-inversion chords and nonharmonic tones to make a smoother (stepwise) bass melody.
5. Shape the bass line carefully to make it a singable melodic line. Use the principles of species counterpoint as a guide to constructing bass melodies. However, remember that the bass usually has more leaps than the other voices.
6. Avoid overuse of ascending-third and descending-second progressions.

Compare the three harmonizations of a chorale melody shown in Figure 10.14. Only one of the three is by Bach.

Figure 10.14

Version 2:

Version 3:

The following is a set of conclusions about the three examples in Figure 10.14. You must learn to criticize your own work in this way to develop skill in the harmonization of melodies.

1. *Cadence:* No cadence in number 1. Numbers 2 and 3 have authentic cadences.
2. *Circle progressions:* No circle progressions in number 1. Numbers 2 and 3 have three circle progressions each.
3. *Harmonic rhythm:* All three have one chord per melody tone and there is one repeated chord in each harmonization.
4. *Chord positions:* Number 1 has one inverted chord; number 2 has three inverted chords; and number 3 has no inverted chords.
5. *Bass line direction:* Numbers 1 and 2 have a good contour in the bass melody, whereas number 3 is much less acceptable.
6. *Weak progressions:* Number 1 has three descending second progressions and one ascending third progression, whereas numbers 2 and 3 have no weak progressions.

To summarize, the second harmonization is clearly superior to the other harmonizations. This also happens to be Bach's harmonization of the chorale melody "Was Gott tut, das ist wohlgetan" ("What God Does Is Well Done").

Harmonization of Folk and Familiar Melodies

Many of the suggestions for harmonizing a chorale melody also apply to folk and familiar melodies. The most important difference, as stated before, is the harmonic rhythm. The following suggestions for harmonizing a well-known melody are in addition to those given for chorale melodies and are related primarily to harmonic rhythm.

1. Harmonic rhythm is important in establishing a clear meter. For this reason, chords usually change on the first beat of a measure. In $\frac{4}{4}$ and $\frac{6}{8}$ a second chord change often occurs in the middle of the measure. In $\frac{3}{4}$ a second chord change can occur on the third beat.
2. Two melody notes that skip are usually part of a single chord. Look at skips as opportunities to determine the implied chord. If the two notes that skip do not fit into a single chord, or if the harmonic rhythm will be thrown off by harmonizing them with one chord, change the chord.

To test the above general guidelines, *Gaudeamus Igitur* ("Therefore Let Us Rejoice") is shown in Figure 10.15 with four different harmonizations. Play each version and determine which you think is the most acceptable.

Figure 10.15

Gaudeamus Igitur ("Therefore Let Us Rejoice").

Version 1: There is no harmonic cadence at the end of the phrase. Also the harmonic rhythm doesn't support the meter. There is a repeated chord between the third beat of the first measure and the first beat of the second, and the chords change on the second beat of measures 2 and 3.

Version 2: There is an authentic cadence at the end of the phrase. The harmonic rhythm is much too fast for this familiar melody. The harmonic rhythm does not support the meter.

Version 3: The harmonic rhythm is appropriate for this simple melody and there are three circle progressions. A clear authentic cadence completes the phrase.

Version 4: This harmonization attempts to provide a chord change for each melody note, which is not appropriate to the style. There is no cadence at the end of the phrase.

Assignment 10.1

1. The first two chords of each phrase are given. After the first two chords, harmonize each melody in four voices exclusively with descending P5th progressions.

2. Use root position chords exclusively in your harmonization.

3. For maximum benefit, play each phrase on the piano—soprano, alto, and tenor played by the right hand, bass notes played by the left hand. When playing these at a keyboard, the following arrangement is recommended:

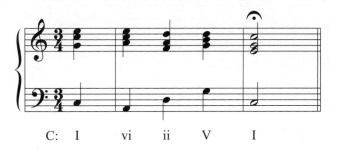

C: I   vi   ii   V   I

4. Harmonize the melodies on paper, in open position whenever possible, with descending P5th progressions.

5. Add the Roman numeral analysis in the blanks provided.

6. If your instructor requests a macro analysis, include chord letter symbols and slurs.

Example:

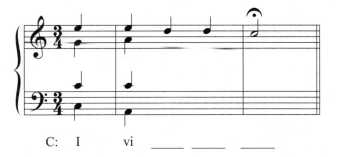

C: I   vi   _____ _____   _____

Completed correctly:

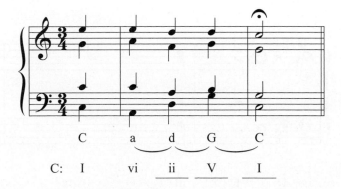

C   a   d   G   C

C: I   vi   ii   V   I

1.

G: I   vi   ____ ____   ____

2.

D: I   iii   ____ ____ ____   ____

3.

A: I   iii   ____ ____ ____   ____

4.

D: I   iii   ____ ____ ____   ____   I

Assignment 10.2

1. Following are five series of Roman numerals taken from Bach's harmonizations of chorale phrases. For each progression indicate the root motion as follows:

as5 = ascending 5th
ds5 = descending 5th
as3 = ascending 3rd
ds3 = descending 3rd
as2 = ascending 2nd
ds2 = descending 2nd

2. Ignore the I_4^6 and leave a blank where there is no chord change.

1. I   ____   I   ____   IV⁶   ____   V⁶   ____   I   ____   ii   ____   V   ____   I

2. I   ____   IV   ____   vii°⁶   ____   I⁶   ____   V⁶   ____   I   ____   ii⁶   ____ I_4^6 ____   V

3. I   ____   ii⁶   ____   V   ____   iii⁶   ____   vi   ____   ii⁶   ____   V   ____   I

4. i   ____   vii°⁶   ____   i⁶   ____   i   ____   iv   ____   V   ____   VI   ____   ii°⁶   ____ i_4^6 ____   V

5. I   ____   vi   ____   IV   ____   ii   ____   V   ____   vi   ____   ii⁶   ____ I_4^6 ____   V

Assignment 10.3

Keyboard assignment:

1. Play the bass notes of each of the five examples in assignment 10.2 on the piano. (For example, the notes of no. 1 in C major are: C C A B C D G C.)

2. Play nos. 1, 2, 3, and 5 in the keys of C major, G major, F major, B-flat major, and D major.

3. Play no. 4 in the keys of A minor, E minor, D minor, G minor, and B minor.

4. Avoid large skips (greater than a P5th), except for the perfect octave.

Assignment 10.4

1. In the following short phrases, the first and occasionally other chords are written out. Harmonize each melody at the piano in four voices (soprano, alto, tenor, bass).

2. Use the progression types listed above each melody.

3. Play all triads in root position, taking the upper three voices with the right hand. Play the bass voice with the left hand.

4. Harmonize the same melodies on paper, using a mixture of open and close positions.

5. Add the Roman numeral analysis in the blanks provided.

6. If your instructor requests a macro analysis, include chord letter symbols and slurs.

1.

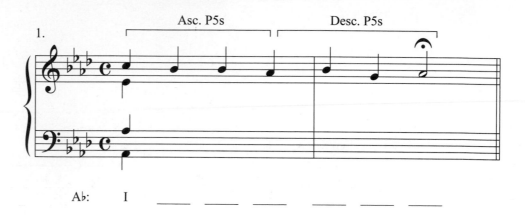

Ab: I   _____   _____   _____   _____   _____   _____

2.

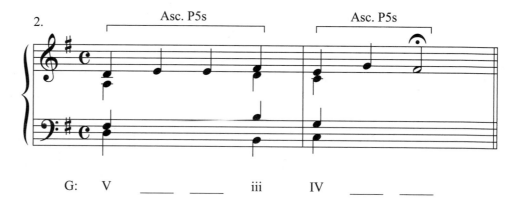

G: V   _____   _____   iii   IV   _____   _____

3.

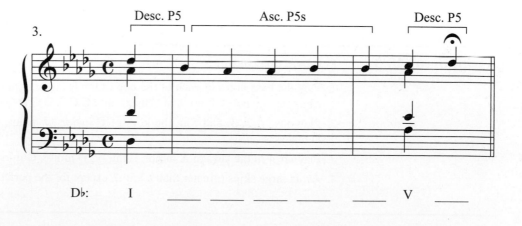

Db: I   _____   _____   _____   _____   _____   V   _____

Assignment 10.5   Using the same directions as in assignment 10.4, harmonize the following melodies:

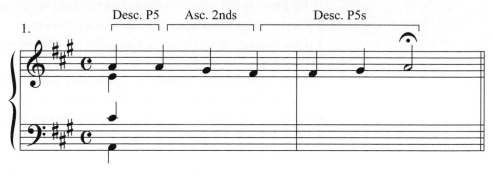

A: I   ___ ___ ___ ___ ___ ___

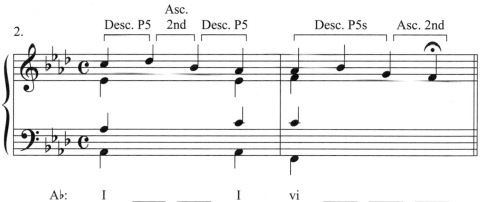

A♭:   I   ___ ___ ___   I   vi   ___ ___ ___

E: I   vi   ___ ___ ___ ___ ___

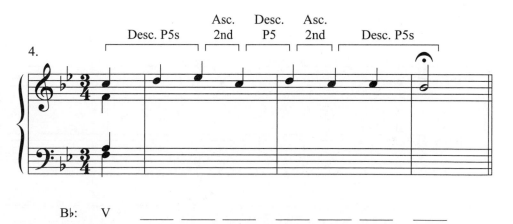

B♭:   V   ___ ___ ___ ___ ___ ___ ___ ___

Assignment 10.6

1. In the following short phrases, the first chord is written out. Harmonize each melody at the piano in four voices (soprano, alto, tenor, bass).

2. Use the progression types listed above each melody.

3. Play all triads in root position, taking the upper three voices with the right hand. Play the bass voice with the left hand.

4. Harmonize the same melodies on paper, using a mixture of open and close positions.

5. Add the Roman numeral analysis in the blanks provided.

6. If your instructor requests a macro analysis, include chord letter symbols and slurs.

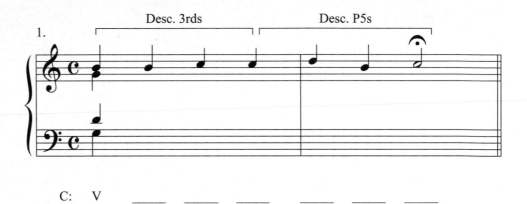

C: V   ____ ____ ____   ____ ____ ____

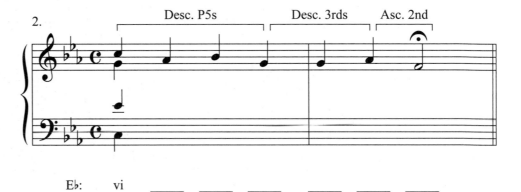

E♭:   vi   ____ ____ ____   ____ ____ ____

3.

Desc. 3rds   Asc. 2nd   Desc. 3rds   Desc. P5   Asc. 2nd   Desc. P5

B♭:   I   ____ ____ ____   ____ ____ ____   ____ ____ ____

Assignment 10.7   The following melodies are folk tunes.

1. Harmonize each melody first with block chords (chords in simple position).

2. When you have arrived at a musically satisfying harmonization, change the block chords to an accompaniment figure or pattern for the piano. Use any of the following patterns if you cannot think of an interesting one yourself. (Use only one pattern consistently throughout a single melody.)

Suggested accompaniment patterns:

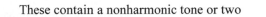

The brackets above the notes in nos. 1 and 2 indicate the harmonic rhythm (one chord per bracket).

1. Folk Song: "The Ash Grove."

2. Folk Song: "Tell Me Why."

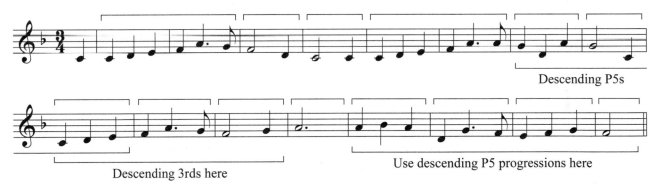

In harmonizing the following melody, use only the I, IV, and V triads. One measure will require three different triads. Which measure is that?

3. Folk Song: "Las Mañanitas."

Assignment 10.8   Following are phrases from chorales.

1. Using principles discussed in this chapter, harmonize each phrase.

2. First, make the basic chord selection. In the first phrase, limit your selection of chords to I, V, IV, and ii, plus those chords in inversion.

3. Place the roots of the chords on the staff.

4. If the bass line seems too angular (too many leaps), consider placing some of the chords in first inversion.

5. When the bass line is satisfactory, add the alto and tenor voices.

6. Include a few nonharmonic tones.

7. Play your harmonizations in class discussing the merits of each.

1. "Herzlich lieb hab' ich dich, o Herr" ("Dearly I Love, O Lord"), mm. 1–2.

2. "Herr Jesu Christ, du höchstes Gut" ("Lord Jesus Christ, Thou Highest Good"), mm. 1–2

Assignment 10.9   Following are five chorale melodies with figured bass as harmonized by Bach.

1. Add the alto and tenor voices according to the figured-bass symbols.

2. Make sure your voice leading conforms to recommended practices.

3. Analyze each chord using Roman numeral analysis.

4. If your instructor requests a macro analysis, include chord letter symbols and slurs.

5. Play your four-part settings in class.

1. "Steh ich bei meinem Gott" ("If I Stand by My God"), BWV 503, mm. 1–2 (modified).

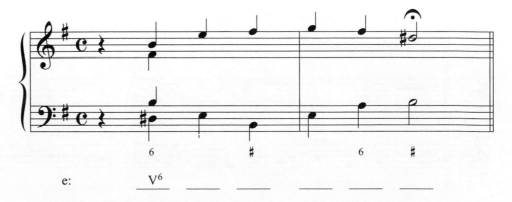

2. "Jesu, meines Herzens Freud'" ("Jesus, Joy of My Heart"), BWV 473, mm. 1–2 (modified).

a: i _____ _____ _____ _____ _____

3. "Befiehl du deine Wege" ("Entrust Thy Ways Unto Him"), BWV 271, mm. 1–2 (modified).

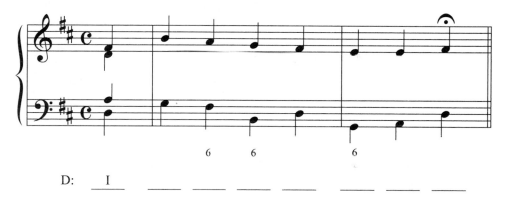

D: I _____ _____ _____ _____ _____

4. "Nun ruhen alle Wälder" ("Now All the Forests Are at Rest"), BWV 44, mm. 1–2 (modified).

B♭:   I _____ _____ _____ _____ _____

5. "Wo Gott der Herr nicht bei uns hält" ("Had God the Lord Not Remained with Us"),
   BWV 258, mm. 1–2 (modified).

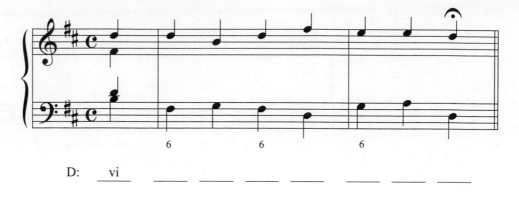

D: vi ___ ___ ___ ___ ___ ___ ___ ___

Assignment 10.10

1. On a separate sheet of paper, write out each figured bass, leaving a staff above for the soprano and alto.

2. Examine the figured bass so you know what possible pitches are available to the soprano voice.

3. Complete the soprano voice first and make sure it is compatible with the bass voice. Play the bass and sing the soprano (or vice versa) to check your results.

   a. Each soprano should contain an ascent and a descent.

   b. The soprano melody should end with scale degrees $\hat{3}$–$\hat{2}$–$\hat{1}$ or, in some cases, $\hat{3}$–$\hat{2}$–$\hat{2}$–$\hat{1}$.

4. When the two outer voices are completed, add alto and tenor voices. Whenever possible, make the inner voices interesting as well.

CHAPTER 11

The Dominant Seventh Chord

TOPICS	Seventh Chord	Dominant Seventh Chord	Major-Minor

IMPORTANT CONCEPTS

The *seventh chord*—a triad with an added note a third degree above the fifth—is so named because in root position it has a characteristic interval of a seventh between the root and the added note. This chapter is devoted to the most common type of seventh chord in tonal music, the dominant seventh.

Dominant Seventh Chord

The *dominant seventh chord* is a diatonic seventh chord built on the fifth scale degree of the major, harmonic minor, and ascending melodic minor scales. The major triad (root, third, fifth) and minor seventh (from root to seventh) create a distinctive sound that is universally linked to the dominant function.

All seventh chords have a particular sound or quality determined by two characteristics—the type of triad (major, minor, diminished, or augmented) and the type of interval from the root to the seventh (m7, M7, or d7). Since the dominant seventh chord consists of a major triad and a minor seventh, its quality is described as *major-minor* (abbreviated as "Mm").

Figure 11.1

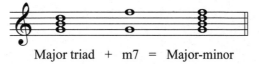

Major triad + m7 = Major-minor

The V^7 is found almost as frequently as the dominant triad. Figure 11.2 is typical of the widespread use of the V^7.

Figure 11.2

Louise Reichardt: "Die Blume der Blumen" ("The Flower of Flowers"), mm. 1–4.

Inversions of the V⁷

The various positions of V^7 are illustrated in Figure 11.3. The numbers you see designate the various positions of the chord and indicate intervals above the bass note. Interpret the first example in the chart as:

7 = Interval of a seventh above the bass.

5 = Interval of a fifth above the bass.

3 = Interval of a third above the bass.

Viewing Figure 11.3, you will see that the 7 (seventh above G) is F, the 5 (fifth above G) is D, and the 3 (third above G) is B.

Baroque period composers often deleted some of the numbers to make manuscript copying less tedious. In Figure 11.3, the column on the right shows the symbols in the simplified form we will use throughout this text.

Figure 11.3

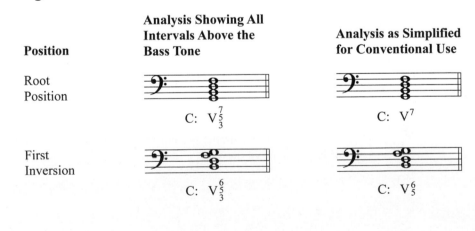

Position	Analysis Showing All Intervals Above the Bass Tone	Analysis as Simplified for Conventional Use
Root Position	C: $V_3^7{}_5$	C: V^7
First Inversion	C: $V_3^6{}_5$	C: V_5^6

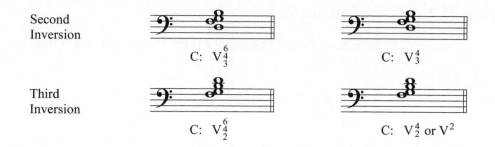

	Second Inversion			
		C: V$^6_4$		C: V$^4_3$

	Third Inversion			
		C: V$^6_4$		C: V$^4_2$ or V^2

Macro Analysis Symbol

In the macro analysis system, dominant seventh chords are handled in the same manner as dominant triads. When labeling dominant seventh chords, include a superscript ^{7} along with the triad letter name (G^7, for example). The purpose of macro analysis is to expose root relationships and harmonic gestures throughout a composition. Therefore, some individual chord details are not emphasized in the system. Do not include inversion indications with your dominant seventh chord labels.

One of the most common circle progressions is the dominant to tonic resolution. The macro analysis system requires you to add the slur symbol to indicate the circle progression when a dominant seventh chord is followed by the tonic (G^7–C, for example).

As mentioned in Chapter 4, macro analysis symbols are typically positioned below the score. When appearing in conjunction with Roman numerals, the macro analysis will occupy the higher level and the Roman numerals will be positioned below.

Figure 11.4

Mozart: Sonata in G Major, K. 283, I: Allegro, mm. 1–4.

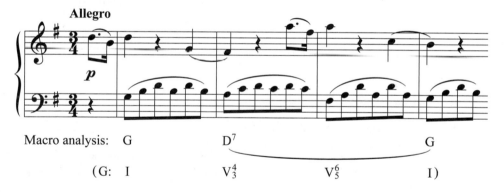

Macro analysis:	G	D^7		G
(G:	I	V$^4_3$	V$^6_5$	I)

History

In music of the Renaissance period, the dominant seventh chord was foreign to the style. The seventh chord developed when nonharmonic tones gradually assumed the importance of a chord tone. In the sixteenth century, the sound, but not the function, of seventh chords came into existence.

Early baroque period composers, such as Monteverdi and Scheidt, introduced the V^7 chord, as well as functional harmony in general. In early seventeenth-century music, examples of dominant seventh chords are scarce and the chords are treated very conservatively. In Figure 11.5, the seventh is prepared and resolved as a suspension, clearly indicating its dissonant status.

Figure 11.5

Monteverdi: "Lasciatemi morire" ("Oh, Let Me Die") from *Lamento d'Arianna,* mm. 6–8.

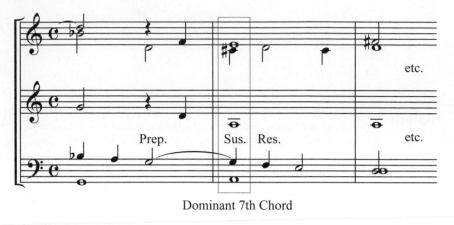

Dominant 7th Chord

Later in the baroque period, V^7 chords were more plentiful and became an integral part of the musical language.

The dominant seventh chord was in constant use throughout the classical period. Its treatment was similar to that of the baroque period.

In the romantic period, dominant seventh chords were plentiful, but freer voice-leading treatment gradually developed. In Figure 11.6, note the descending nature of the bass and the absence of resolution of the seventh factor. In this example tonality is temporarily suspended so no Roman numeral analysis is provided. The seventh factor does not resolve in any of the three major-minor seventh chords, showing that the chord had achieved nearly consonant status.

Figure 11.6

Chopin: Mazurka in F Minor, op. posth. 68, no. 4, mm. 1–4.

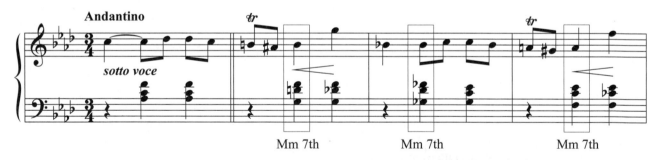

In the post-romantic and impressionistic periods, the functional use of the dominant seventh chord was on the wane. Chords weighted more heavily with dissonance (9ths, 11ths, and 13ths) became common, and as divergent musical styles multiplied during this period, the major-minor seventh chord declined in use as a dominant function.

In most contemporary music written for performance in concert halls or opera houses, the V^7 chord ceases to exist except in those styles that make conscious use of functional harmony. Nonetheless, throughout both Europe and America, popular music continued to use functional harmony. Folk and popular songs, as well as the earlier forms of jazz and blues, were laced with dominant seventh chords. Even into the 1960s, folk and popular songs, mainstream jazz, and blues had changed little in regard to the dominant seventh. Indeed, at the present moment, V^7 is alive and well in the hands of rock and rock-derivative styles.

Figure 11.7, from a jazz composition by Charlie Parker, composed in the early 1950s, illustrates straightforward circle progressions involving V^7. Note that the popular music symbol for the dominant seventh is shown as a capital letter with a superscript $^7(C^7)$.

Figure 11.7

Parker: *Au Privave,* mm. 1–3.

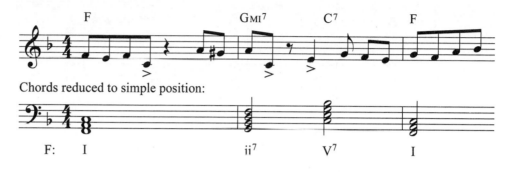

Chords reduced to simple position:

APPLICATIONS

Unlike the dominant triad, the dominant seventh chord contains a dissonance—the seventh factor. Musical style is much affected by the way in which the seventh of the seventh chord is treated.

Resolution of the Dominant Seventh Chord

From the dissonant seventh's emergence in the sixteenth century until the post-romantic and impressionistic periods, composers routinely resolved downward by step in the succeeding chord and followed the V^7 with the tonic triad. The dominant seventh chord can be resolved in a number of ways, but the most common resolution is by a circle progression (V^7–I).

Circle Progression

1. The seventh of the V^7 resolves down one scale step to the third factor of the tonic triad. The seventh factor may be in any voice (soprano, alto, tenor, or bass).
2. When the seventh is the bass note (V_2^4), it must resolve to the third factor of I, and the tonic triad must automatically be in first inversion (I^6).
3. Noting the illustrations in Figure 11.8, you will observe that if you first resolve the seventh down a step, the three remaining voices will move smoothly to notes of the I triad. In the first, second, and third inversion examples, the common tone (G) is retained in the same voice, whereas in the root position example, all three upper voices move in similar motion to the nearest chord tones.
4. In all four examples, all four factors of the V^7 are present. In unusual instances, an incomplete V^7 may be necessary. In such cases omit the fifth factor.

Figure 11.8

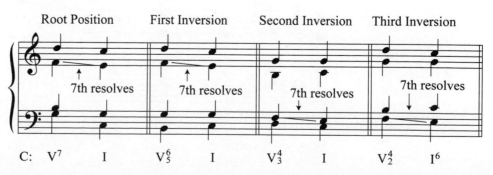

The excerpts in Figure 11.9 show typical V⁷ resolutions in circle progressions. Note that although the chord sevenths resolve downward, the leading tones resolve upward.

Figure 11.9

L. Viola Kinney: *Mother's Sacrifice*, mm. 15–21.

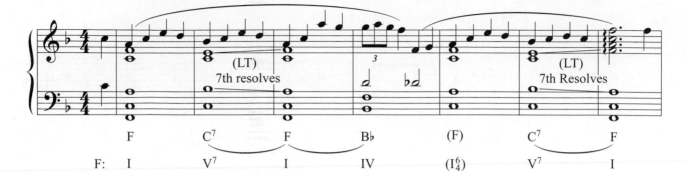

Joplin: *Maple Leaf Rag*, mm. 77–80.

5. In Figure 11.10, the seventh of the chord and the leading tone are both resolved. In such cases omit the fifth factor of the tonic triad and triple the root.

Figure 11.10

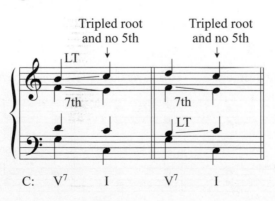

Sometimes a V^7 is diverted temporarily from its normal resolution to I. In these cases root movement will usually progress by second or third (see Figure 11.11). A typical example of this progression type is V^7 to vi (or VI in the minor). Notice the doubling of the third in the vi chord, which avoids parallel perfect fifths.

Figure 11.11

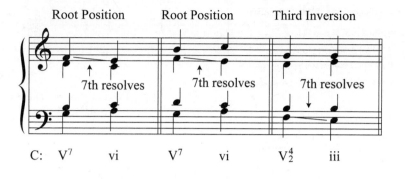

The Bach chorale phrase in Figure 11.12 demonstrates the resolution of the seventh factor in a noncircle progression using common stylistic practice. The seventh resolves one scale degree down to the fifth factor of the vi chord, and the third of the vi chord is doubled.

Figure 11.12

Bach: "O Herre Gott, dein göttlich Wort" ("O God, Our Lord, Thy Holy Word"), BWV 184, mm. 1–2.

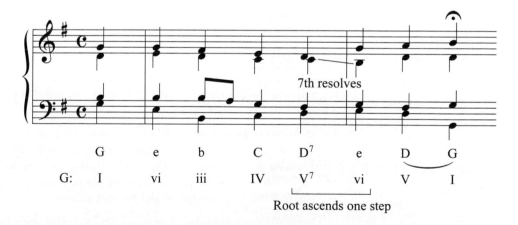

Nonresolution of Seventh Factor

In rare instances the seventh factor of the V^7 chord cannot be resolved in the same voice. This typically occurs when the resolution note is not part of the succeeding chord. In most instances, however, the resolution of the seventh is only delayed and eventually occurs in the appropriate manner after a few intervening chords.

No standard voice-leading pattern has been established for nonresolution of seventh factors. Observe good voice-leading principles and avoid parallel perfect intervals.

Figure 11.13

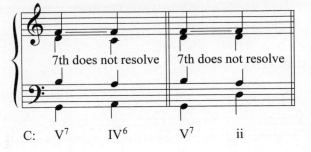

Root movement by step   Roots ascending by P5

7th does not resolve   7th does not resolve

C: V⁷   IV⁶   V⁷   ii

The following illustration by Mozart shows the iv⁶ triad as an embellishment of the V⁷.

Figure 11.14

Mozart: Sonata for Violin and Piano in G Major, K. 379, I, mm. 70–73.

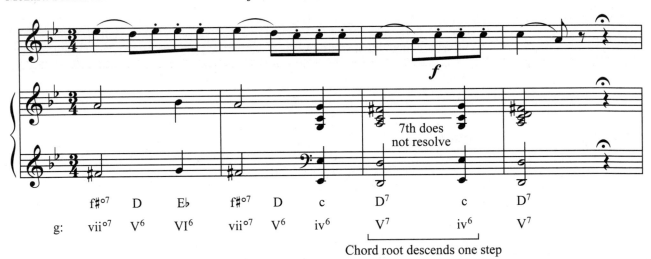

7th does not resolve

	f#°⁷	D	E♭	f#°⁷	D	c	D⁷	c	D⁷
g:	vii°⁷	V⁶	VI⁶	vii°⁷	V⁶	iv⁶	V⁷	iv⁶	V⁷

Chord root descends one step

Stylistic Practices for Voice Leading in V⁷ Chords

We now add the following stylistic practices to the list that begins in Chapter 9 (also see Appendix A):

10. Resolve the seventh of the V⁷ chord down one scale degree in the same voice. In the few instances where the resolution tone is not present, either keep the seventh as a common tone or move it by the smallest melodic interval possible.

11. All four factors of the V⁷ chord are usually present, but for smoothness of voice leading, the fifth may be omitted and the root doubled.

Unstylistic departures, listed on pages 201–203, also apply to V⁷ chords and inversions.

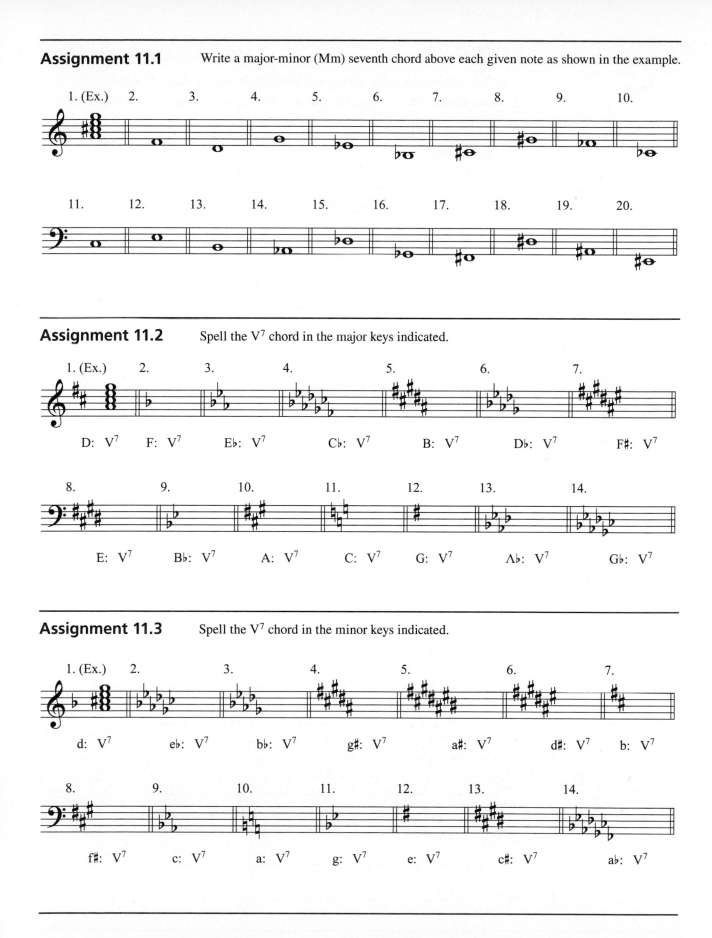

Assignment 11.2   Spell the V⁷ chord in the major keys indicated.

D: V⁷   F: V⁷   Eb: V⁷   Cb: V⁷   B: V⁷   Db: V⁷   F#: V⁷

E: V⁷   Bb: V⁷   A: V⁷   C: V⁷   G: V⁷   Ab: V⁷   Gb: V⁷

Assignment 11.3   Spell the V⁷ chord in the minor keys indicated.

d: V⁷   eb: V⁷   bb: V⁷   g#: V⁷   a#: V⁷   d#: V⁷   b: V⁷

f#: V⁷   c: V⁷   a: V⁷   g: V⁷   e: V⁷   c#: V⁷   ab: V⁷

Assignment 11.4   Each exercise consists of two chords, the first of which is a dominant seventh chord.

1. In the first column, name the key and mode (examples: A minor, C major).
2. In the second column, write the analysis of both chords. Remember that the first is always a dominant seventh.
3. In the third column, write the letter (a, b, or c) that represents the type of progression present in the example:
    a. Circle progression—seventh resolves down one scale step.
    b. Noncircle progression—seventh resolves down one scale step.
    c. Noncircle progression—no resolution of seventh.

	Key	Chord Analysis	Type
1. (Ex.)	G major	V_5^6 I	a
2.	_____	_____	____
3.	_____	_____	____
4.	_____	_____	____
5.	_____	_____	____
6.	_____	_____	____
7.	_____	_____	____
8.	_____	_____	____
9.	_____	_____	____
10.	_____	_____	____

Each exercise consists of two chords, the first of which is a dominant seventh chord.

1. At least one voice-leading error can be found in each example.

2. Find the particular error (or errors) and describe each briefly in the blanks provided.

1. _____

2. _____

3. _____

4. _____

5. _____

6. _____

7. _____

8. _____

9. _____

10. _____

Assignment 11.6   Before completing the following chorale-style harmonizations on paper, play them on the piano using the right hand for the soprano, alto, and tenor and the left hand for the bass voice. The following example shows correct procedure. Note that the V^7 chord has a doubled root, but no fifth. This arrangement is necessary to avoid unstylistic parallels.

D: I   ii^6 V^7 I

After you have completed the keyboard portion of the assignment, write out the harmonizations on paper, using these guidelines:

1. Add the alto and tenor to the following chorale-style harmonizations.
2. Be sure your part writing conforms to recommended practice.
3. Make a complete Roman numeral analysis.

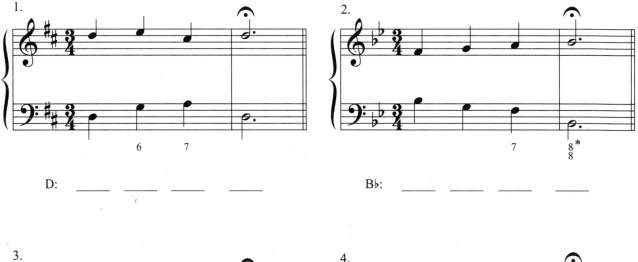

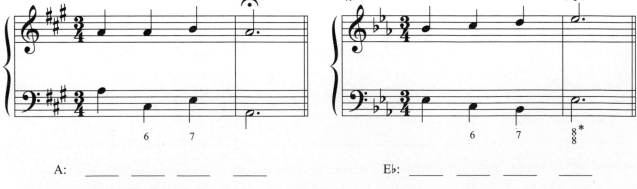

*Double the octave above the bass note.

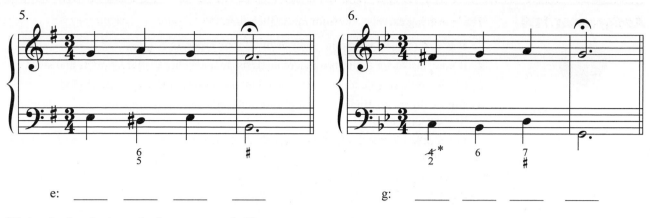

e: _____ _____ _____ _____   g: _____ _____ _____ _____

*Raise the fourth above the bass note one half step.

Assignment 11.7

1. Harmonize the following folk song either at the piano or on paper.

2. Select no more than one chord per measure. In some instances, a single chord will harmonize more than one measure.

3. Use only the following chords: I, V^7, ii or ii^6, vi, and IV.

4. At the piano, play the melody with the right hand and the accompaniment figure with the left hand.

5. Make up your own accompaniment figure or select one from those shown below. Each example shows how the pattern can be fitted into I and V^7. You will have to figure out how the accompaniment pattern can be made to support other chords.

6. All of the arrangements should be played in class, whether written out on paper or improvised at the keyboard.

Accompaniment figures:

Folk Song: "The Sailor."

Assignment 11.8   The following excerpts are from music literature.

1. Make a complete harmonic analysis of all four excerpts.

2. If your instructor requests a macro analysis, include chord letter symbols and slurs.

3. Circle nonharmonic tones and name them, using the standard abbreviations.

4. Above the staves, bracket each phrase and indicate phrase relationships with letters. Review Chapter 6.

5. Label other compositional aspects such as sequences, melodic repetition, and rhythmic repetition.

6. Below the analysis, bracket each cadence and indicate the type (perfect authentic, imperfect authentic, half, deceptive, or plagal).

1. Haydn: Sonata in C Major, Hob. XVI:35, I, mm. 1–16. **CD Track 71**

2. Kuhlau: Sonatina in F Major, op. 55, no. 4, II, mm. 1–27. CD Track 72

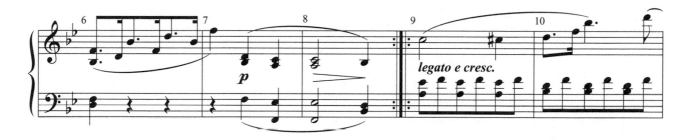

B♭:

3. Beethoven: Sonata in F Minor, op. 57, II: Andante con moto, mm. 9–16. CD Track 73

Db:

4. Haydn: Symphony no. 97 in C Major, I, mm. 76–91 (modified). CD Track 74

G:

Assignment 11.9

Before completing the following chorale phrases on paper, play them on the piano using the right hand for the soprano, alto, and tenor and the left hand for the bass voice. For an example of correct procedure, see assignment 11.6. J. S. Bach harmonized all of these chorales.

After you have completed the keyboard portion of the assignment, write out the harmonizations on paper using these guidelines:

1. Add the alto and tenor to the chorale phrases using good voice-leading procedures.
2. Make a complete Roman numeral analysis.

1. "O wir armen Sünder" ("Oh, We Poor Sinners"), BWV 407, mm. 1–2 (modified).

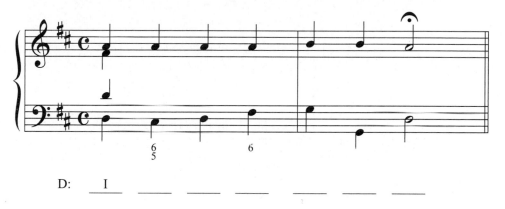

2. "Jesu, deine tiefen Wunden" ("Jesus, Thy Deep Wounds"), BWV 194, mm. 3–4 (modified).

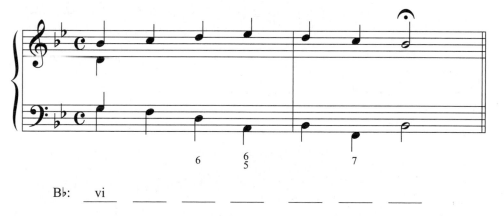

3. "Es spricht der Unweisen Mund wohl" ("The Lips of the Foolish Say"), BWV 308, mm. 5–6 (modified).

4. "Straf' mich nicht in deinem Zorn" ("Punish Me Not in Thy Wrath"), BWV 115, mm. 9–10 (modified).

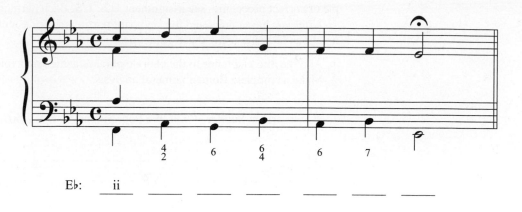

Eb: ii   ___ ___ ___ ___ ___

5. "O Gott, du frommer Gott" ("Oh God, Thou Faithful God"), BWV 45, mm. 3–4 (modified).

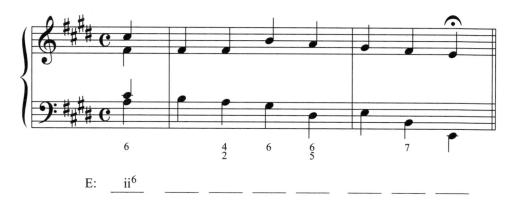

E: ii⁶   ___ ___ ___ ___ ___ ___ ___

6. "Keinen hat Gott verlassen" ("God Has Forsaken No One"), BWV 369, mm. 5–6 (modified).

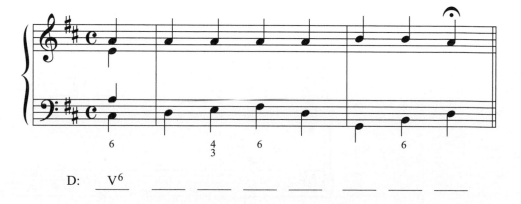

D: V⁶   ___ ___ ___ ___ ___

As a keyboard assignment:

1. If you have difficulty with this type of assignment, become familiar with the figured bass first. Play the bass notes with the thumb of your right hand. Add the other notes of the chord (from figured bass) with the fingers still available. Do not worry about voice leading at this point.
2. After you are familiar with the harmony, play the bass voice with your left hand and begin work on an interesting melodic line. Throughout the study of keyboard harmony, let the right hand take the soprano, alto, and tenor while the left hand plays the bass.

As a written assignment:

1. On a separate sheet of staff paper, write out each figured bass, leaving a staff above for the soprano and alto.
2. Complete the remaining three upper voices according to the figuration supplied.
3. To help you in writing the soprano voice:
   a. On a piece of scratch paper, write out the notes of each chord, including doubled notes.
   b. From this sketch, begin writing the entire soprano melody, giving it a desirable contour—one climax tone and distinct directional movements.
   c. Remember to maintain a majority of steps rather than skips in your melody.
4. When the melody is complete to your satisfaction, add the alto and tenor voices.
5. Make a complete Roman numeral analysis.

The Leading-Tone Seventh Chords

TOPICS	Leading-Tone Seventh Chords	Half Diminished	Fully Diminished
	Diminished-Minor	Diminished-Diminished	Prolongation

IMPORTANT CONCEPTS

Closely related to the dominant seventh chord are the *leading-tone seventh chords*. Like their triad counterpart, these leading-tone seventh chords often function as dominant substitutes but can also appear as harmonic embellishments in linear passages.

Leading-Tone Seventh Chords

Diatonic *leading-tone seventh chords* are built on the seventh scale degree of the major, harmonic minor, and ascending melodic minor scales. In major keys, the quality of the chord is *diminished-minor* (dm). Diminished-minor is also known as *half-diminished*. In minor keys, the quality is *diminished-diminished* (dd), but the name is usually abbreviated to *diminished* or *fully diminished*.

Figure 12.1

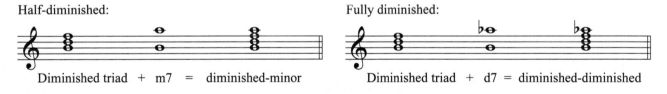

Half-diminished:

Diminished triad + m7 = diminished-minor

Fully diminished:

Diminished triad + d7 = diminished-diminished

Leading-tone seventh chords are represented by vii$^{\varnothing 7}$ and vii$^{\circ 7}$ in Roman numeral analysis. In vii$^{\varnothing 7}$, the vii indicates a chord on the seventh scale step, the $^{\varnothing}$ shows that the quality of the chord is diminished-minor, and the ^{7} means that it is a seventh chord. The $^{\circ}$ in the vii$^{\circ 7}$ designates a diminished-diminished seventh chord. The vii$^{\varnothing 7}$ is used in major keys and the vii$^{\circ 7}$ in minor keys.

Both the vii$^{\varnothing 7}$ and vii$^{\circ 7}$ are associated very closely with the dominant seventh chord because they have three notes in common with the V^{7}.

Figure 12.2

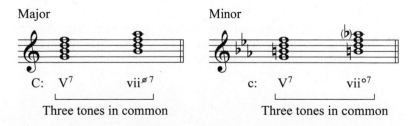

Major

C: V^{7} vii$^{\varnothing 7}$

Three tones in common

Minor

c: V^{7} vii$^{\circ 7}$

Three tones in common

255

Composers frequently substitute leading-tone triads and seventh chords for the dominant in the interest of variety and diversification. In Figure 12.3, Beethoven alternated the vii°$^4_3$, vii°^{6}, and V^6 freely to represent dominant harmony.

Figure 12.3

Beethoven: Sonata in C Minor, op. 10, no. 1, I: Allegro molto e con brio, mm. 13–16.

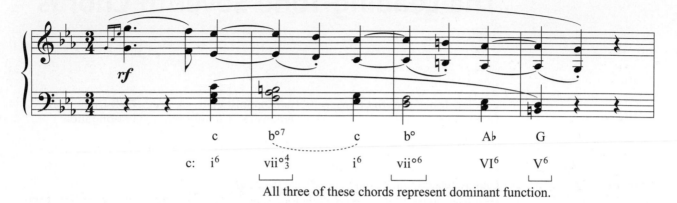

All three of these chords represent dominant function.

Since V^7, vii^{ø7}, and vii°^{7} all represent dominant harmony, composers intermixed them freely. This is particularly true for the subtle half-step fluctuation between vii°^{7} and V^7. In Figure 12.4, the seventh (B-flat) of the vii°^{7} moves down to the root (A) of the V^7 chord. This blended use of vii°^{7} and V^7 results in a reiteration and elongation of the prevailing harmony—also known as a *prolongation*.

Figure 12.4

Mozart: Sonata in G Major, K. 283, III: Presto, mm. 64–69.

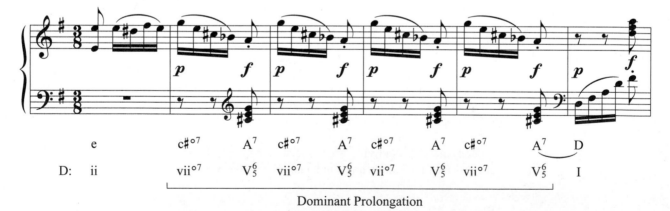

Dominant Prolongation

Progressions from vii^{ø7} and vii°^{7}

Like the dominant seventh, with which they share three common tones, vii^{ø7} and vii°^{7} usually resolve to the tonic (I or i), either directly (Figure 12.5a–b) or through the dominant seventh (Figure 12.5c–d).

Figure 12.5

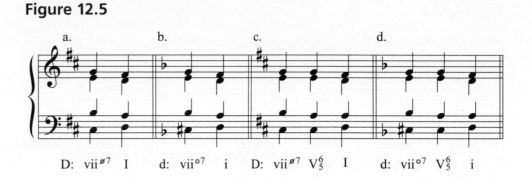

D: vii⁰⁷ I   d: vii°⁷ i   D: vii⁰⁷ V⁶₅ I   d: vii°⁷ V⁶₅ i

Figure 12.6 shows resolutions of the leading-tone seventh chords in all three inversions.

Figure 12.6

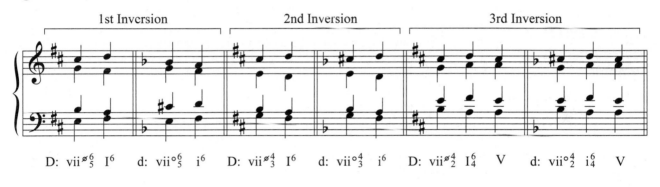

| 1st Inversion | 2nd Inversion | 3rd Inversion |

D: vii⁰⁶₅ I⁶   d: vii°⁶₅ i⁶   D: vii⁰⁴₃ I⁶   d: vii°⁴₃ i⁶   D: vii⁰⁴₂ I⁶₄ V   d: vii°⁴₂ i⁶₄ V

Resolution of Tritone and Seventh Factors

The fully diminished seventh chord (vii°⁷) contains two diminished fifths, which tend to resolve inward. If both are resolved, the result will be a doubled third factor on the tonic chord (Figure 12.7a), but composers often prefer the normal doubling, as shown in Figure 12.7b.

Figure 12.7

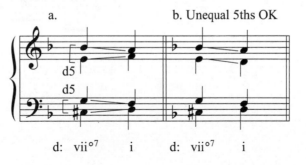

a.   b. Unequal 5ths OK

d: vii°⁷ i   d: vii°⁷ i

The two tones in the leading-tone seventh chords (vii⁰⁷ and vii°⁷) that are nearly always resolved are the root of the chord (the leading tone), which moves upward to the tonic note, and the seventh factor, which resolves downward by step.

Figure 12.8

Mozart: *Don Giovanni,* K. 527, act I, scene XIII, mm. 116–117.

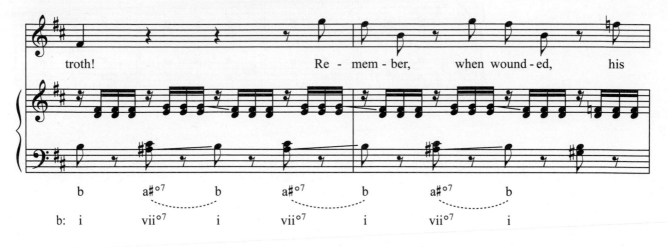

The macro analysis symbols for the leading-tone seventh chords are similar to the vii$^{\o7}$ and vii$^{\circ7}$ of Roman numeral analysis, but the vii is replaced with a lowercase letter representing the root of the chord (b$^{\o7}$ or b$^{\circ7}$, for example). It is not necessary to include inversion indications with your leading-tone seventh chord labels in macro analysis. The purpose is to identify larger harmonic elements.

Because leading-tone seventh chords frequently function as dominant substitutes, macro analysis emphasizes the relationship by adding a dotted slur to progressions exhibiting leading-tone to tonic harmonic motion (b$^{\o7}$–C, for example). Figure 12.9 illustrates the typical application of the dotted slur.

Figure 12.9

Beethoven: Sonata in C Minor, op. 10, no. 1, I: Allegro molto e con brio, mm. 1–8.

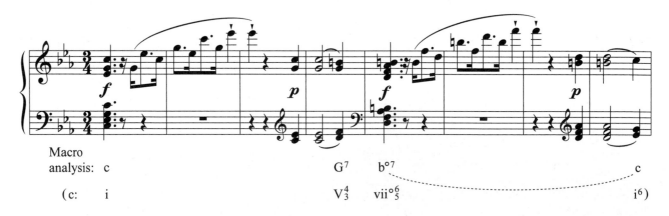

Leading-tone seventh chords were not characteristic of the music of the Renaissance period, but with the ascendancy of the major–minor tonal system in the baroque era, leading-tone seventh chords took their place as part of the harmonic vocabulary. Figure 12.10 shows typical use of the vii$^{\circ7}$ during the baroque period.

Figure 12.10

Elisabeth Jacquet de la Guerre: Sarabande from Suite in D Minor, mm. 21–28.

The classical period continued the use of leading-tone seventh chords with little change in approach from the baroque. The illustration by Mozart in Figure 12.11 is representative of the use of these chords in the classical period.

Figure 12.11

Mozart: Sonata in D Major, K. 284, III: Variation V, mm. 14–17.

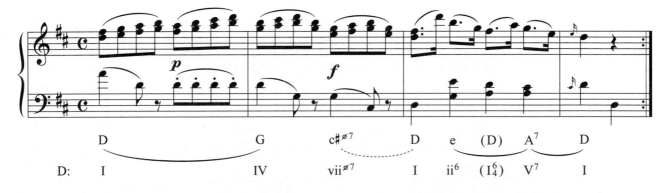

The romantic period saw a more relaxed and somewhat freer use of leading-tone seventh chords. Although more traditional applications continued in the majority, one of the more frequent treatments involves successive diminished seventh chords. Figure 12.12 shows six consecutive diminished seventh chords in descending chromatic motion. Functional harmony is temporarily suspended, but the gradual buildup of tension is a direct result of the series of unresolved diminished seventh chords.

Figure 12.12

Wagner: Overture to *Rienzi,* mm. 346–352.

Harmonic reduction:

With the gradual breakdown of functional harmony, leading-tone seventh chords were used less. Nevertheless, nonfunctional diminished and half-diminished seventh chords were still very much a part of the harmonic vocabulary during the post-romantic and impressionistic period. Figure 12.13 illustrates the use of fully diminished and half-diminished seventh chords in a sequential but nonfunctional pattern.

Figure 12.13

Debussy: *Jardins sous la pluie* (Gardens in the Rain) from *Estampes,* mm. 118–119.

For most concert hall music of the contemporary period, leading-tone seventh chords ceased to exist except for those styles that make a conscious use of functional harmony. Despite this abandonment in the concert hall, popular songwriters and jazz artists consider leading-tone seventh chords an integral part of their style. The popular music symbol for the fully diminished seventh chord is a capital letter with °7 added (C°7); half diminished is represented by a capital letter with MI7(♭5) added (CMI7(♭5)).

Ragtime, an early twentieth-century precursor of jazz, used the leading-tone seventh chords, as shown in Figure 12.14. In this example, the leading-tone seventh chord is a secondary leading-tone chord (see Chapter 14).

Figure 12.14

Johnson: *A Black Smoke Rag,* mm. 77–80.

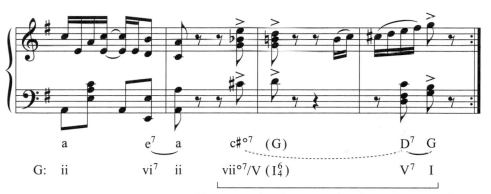

Common chord progression in ragtime music.

APPLICATIONS

Voice leading around half-diminished and fully diminished seventh chords is usually quite smooth. Since diminished intervals naturally resolve inward by half steps, both the vii°7 and vii°7 allow this resolution when followed by the tonic. Such a resolution also permits the seventh to descend one scale degree.

Voice Leading and the vii°7 and vii°7

The following procedures continue the list appearing in Chapters 9 and 11. (See also Appendix A.)

12. Resolve the seventh factor of the vii°7 or vii°7 (and inversions) down one diatonic scale degree.
13. Resolve the root of the vii°7 and vii°7 upward to the tonic note.

Some Pitfalls to Avoid

Avoid parallel P5ths between third and seventh factors in resolving the half-diminished seventh chord (Figure 12.15c and e). Double the third factor of the tonic triad to avoid these parallels (Figure 12.15e and f). In four-part writing, this configuration occurs only when the third is below the seventh.

Although the half-diminished leading-tone seventh chord (vii°7) contains only one tritone, the fully diminished type (vii°7) consists of two (root to fifth and third to seventh). It is possible for both tritones to resolve properly (see Figure 12.15b). Nonetheless, parallel unequal fifths (d5 to P5) are observed in literature and are sometimes written by composers in preference to a tonic triad with a doubled third (Figure 12.15d). When writing an unequal fifth in the vii°7 to i progression, try to resolve at least the root-to-fifth tritone whenever possible.

Figure 12.15

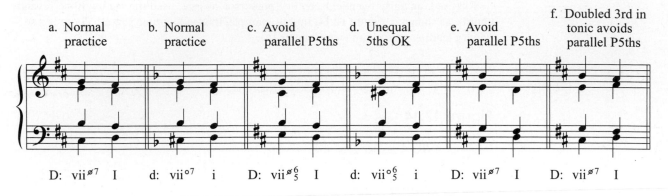

PART B   The Structural Elements of Music

Assignment 12.1   Write a diminished-minor (dm) seventh chord above each given note, as shown in the example.

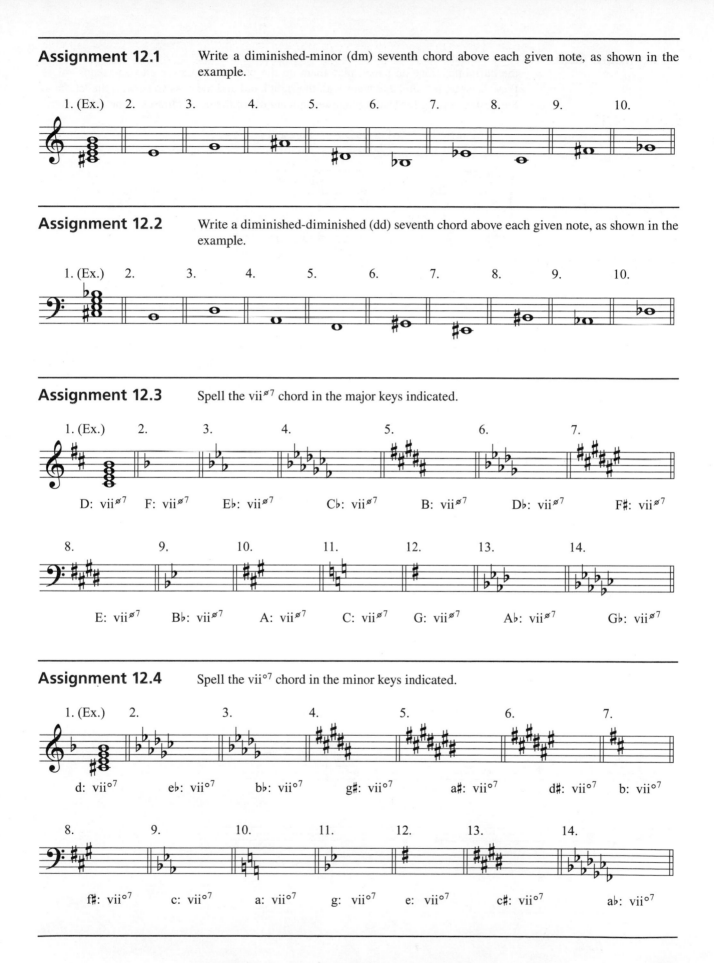

Assignment 12.2   Write a diminished-diminished (dd) seventh chord above each given note, as shown in the example.

Assignment 12.3   Spell the vii^{ø7} chord in the major keys indicated.

Assignment 12.4   Spell the vii^{o7} chord in the minor keys indicated.

Assignment 12.5

Each exercise is a phrase of a chorale melody as harmonized by Bach. Before completing the harmonizations on paper, play them on the piano, adding the alto and tenor voices. Play the soprano, alto, and tenor with the right hand and the bass voice with the left hand. Suggested voicing for leading-tone seventh chords in the three phrases is the following:

Phrase 1
Chord 10:

Phrase 2
Chord 3:

Phrase 3
Chord 6:

After you have completed the keyboard portion of the assignment, write out the harmonizations on paper using these guidelines:

1. Add the alto and tenor to the chorale phrases, using good voice-leading procedures.
2. Make a complete Roman numeral analysis of each chord.
3. If your instructor requests a macro analysis, include chord letter symbols and slurs.
4. Sing the chorale phrases in class.

1. "Herzliebster Jesu, was hast du verbrochen" ("Dearest Jesus, How Hast Thou Transgressed"), BWV 245, mm. 1–3 (modified).

g:

2. "Jesu, meine Freude" ("Jesus, My Joy"), BWV 358, mm. 1–2 (modified).

d:

3. "Hilf, Herr Jesu, lass gelingen" ("Help, Lord Jesus, Send Good Speed"), BWV 344, mm. 9–12.

*Do not harmonize the passing tones.

†These are suspensions—9th to octave above the bass note and 4th to 3rd above the bass note.

As was mentioned previously, Bach harmonized each of these chorale melodies. When you have completed your harmonization, look up the phrases (by title) in any edition of the *371 Bach Chorale Harmonizations*. Compare your results with those of Bach.

Assignment 12.6

The following waltz melodies are typical of those written during the late eighteenth century and much of the nineteenth century. For each melody:

1. Determine the harmonic rhythm.
2. Make a list of possible harmonizations for the melody, using procedures outlined in Chapter 10.
3. Compose a harmonization of the melody, using block chords.
4. From the block chords, fashion an accompaniment that will accentuate the waltz characteristics of the melody.
5. Make an arrangement for piano and/or any group of instruments (or voices) that are played by class members.
6. Be sure to include at least one or two leading-tone seventh chords.
7. Avoid $^6_4$ chords except the cadential $^6_4$ (i$^6_4$ or I$^6_4$).

Assignment 12.7

The following excerpts are from music literature.

1. Make a complete Roman numeral analysis of each excerpt. Indicate seventh chords and inversions with the appropriate symbols.

2. Circle nonharmonic tones and name them, using the standard abbreviations.

3. If your instructor requests a macro analysis, include chord letter symbols and slurs. Label circle progressions with a solid slur and leading-tone progressions with a dotted slur.

1. Legrenzi: "Che fiero costume" ("Disdainful and Ruthless") from *Echi di riverenza,* op. 14, mm. 1–7. **CD Track 75**

2. Haydn: Sonata in B-flat Major, Hob. XVI:2, II, mm. 1–4. CD Track 76

g:

3. Haydn: Sonata in D Major, Hob. XVI:33, II, mm. 1–4. CD Track 77

d:

4. Mozart: "Viennese Sonatina" in C Major, after K. 439b, III, mm. 1–4. CD Track 78

F:

Assignment 12.8   *Write a composition:*

1. Make it 16 measures in length, consisting of four 4-measure phrases.
2. Make the first and third phrases the same.
3. The second and fourth phrases may be of any relationship to the others.
4. Write in $\frac{9}{8}$ meter and B-flat minor.
5. Include at least two or three leading-tone seventh chords.
6. Write for piano or any group of instruments that are played by class members.

CHAPTER 12   The Leading-Tone Seventh Chords

Assignment 12.9 Write an original composition of any form you want and for any combination of instruments you choose. The only restriction is that you demonstrate the conventional use of leading-tone seventh chords.

Assignment 12.10 Each example is a phrase of a chorale melody as harmonized by Bach.

As a keyboard assignment:

If your instructor requests, play each chorale phrase on the piano, adding the alto and tenor voices. Use the suggested voicings for leading-tone seventh chords in assignment 12.5 as models for this assignment.

As a written assignment:

1. Add alto and tenor voices according to the figured-bass symbols. Make sure your voice leading conforms to recommended practice.
2. Make a complete Roman numeral analysis—blanks are provided.
3. Analyze cadence types.

1. "Meines Lebens letzte Zeit" ("The Last Hour of My Life"), BWV 381, mm. 1–2 (modified).

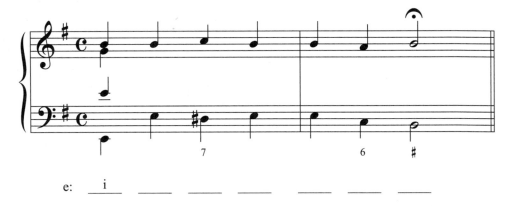

2. "Mach's mit mir, Gott, nach deiner Güt'" ("Do With Me as Thy Goodness Prompts Thee"), BWV 377, mm. 3–4 (modified).

3. "Nun sich der Tag geendet hat" ("When Now the Day Is at an End"), BWV 396, mm. 5–6 (modified).

a: V⁶

4. "Herr Jesu Christ, du hast bereit" ("Lord Jesus Christ, Thou Hast Already"), BWV 333, mm. 3–4 (modified).

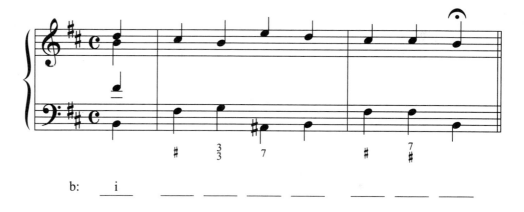

b: i

5. "Herzliebster Jesu, was hast du verbrochen" ("Dearest Jesus, How Hast Thou Transgressed"), BWV 244, mm. 2–3 (modified).

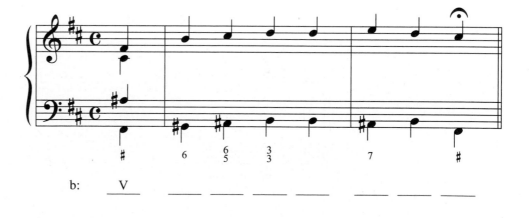

b: V

Assignment 12.11

As a keyboard assignment:

If your instructor requests, play each chorale phrase on the piano, adding soprano, alto, and tenor voices according to the figured-bass symbols. If you have difficulty with this assignment, become familiar with the chords first, then work on a good soprano melody.

As a written assignment:

1. Write out each figured bass on a separate sheet of staff paper, leaving a line above for the soprano and alto.
2. Complete the soprano, alto, and tenor voices.
3. Be sure to observe good voice leading.
4. For help in writing an interesting soprano melody, observe assignments 12.5 and 12.10. Each contains model soprano melodies.
5. Make sure your soprano melody has only one climax tone (highest pitch) and does not wander about aimlessly.
6. Make a complete Roman numeral analysis of each exercise.

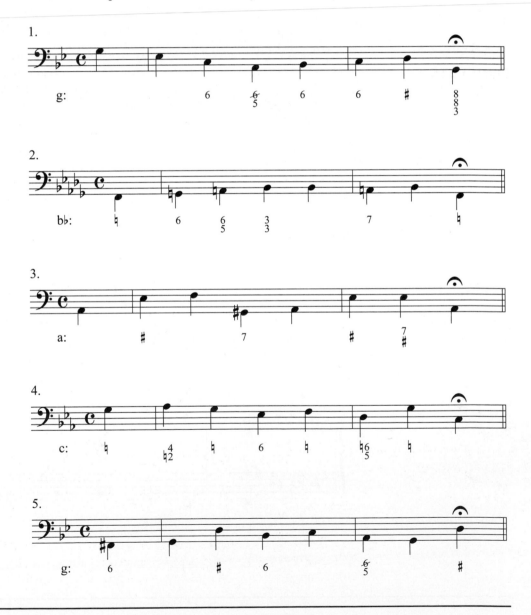

PART B   The Structural Elements of Music

CHAPTER 13

Nondominant Seventh Chords

TOPICS	Nondominant Seventh Chords Minor-Minor Diminished-Minor
	Major-Major

IMPORTANT CONCEPTS

The previous two chapters were devoted to seventh chords possessing dominant function (V^7, $vii^{ø7}$, and vii^{o7}). This chapter addresses the nondominant seventh chords—a collection of chords built on the remaining scale degrees. These seventh chords often serve as preparations for dominant function harmonies.

Nondominant Seventh Chords

Nondominant seventh chords are those diatonic seventh chords that do not possess dominant function. Since only the dominant and leading-tone seventh chords are considered to have dominant function, then all others are nondominant seventh chords. Although the nondominant category encompasses a variety of seventh chord qualities (particularly when we consider the three variants of the minor scale), nondominant seventh chords appear most often in music literature as *major-major* (MM), *minor-minor* (mm), and *diminished-minor* (dm) seventh chords.

Figure 13.1

Major-Major (MM):   Minor-Minor (mm):   Diminished-Minor (dm):

Major triad + M7 = MM   Minor triad + m7 = mm   Diminished triad + m7 = dm

Roman Numeral Symbols

Nondominant seventh chords are represented in Roman numeral analysis with a superscript ^{7} attached to the Roman numeral triad symbols. No additional characters are necessary for the major-major and minor-minor seventh chords, but the diminished-minor chord is accompanied by the half-diminished symbol (^{ø}) positioned between the Roman numeral and the ^{7}:

1. Examples of nondominant *major-major* (MM) symbols: I^7, IV^7, III^7, VI^7.
2. Examples of nondominant *minor-minor* (mm) symbols: i^7, ii^7, iii^7, iv^7, vi^7.
3. Examples of nondominant *diminished-minor* (dm) symbols: $ii^{ø7}$, $vi^{ø7}$.

Illustrated in Figure 13.2 are all of the diatonic seventh chords generated by the major and three minor scales. Although some of these chords do not appear in music literature very often, it is nonetheless important for you to understand that variances in the scales influence the quality of diatonic seventh chords. The double-letter label beneath each chord specifies (1) the quality of the triad and (2) the quality of the seventh:

MM = major-major

Mm = major-minor

mm = minor-minor

dm = diminished-minor

dd = diminished-diminished

mM = minor-major

AM = augmented-major

Note that some of the Roman numeral symbols in Figure 13.2 are accompanied by a subscript M or m beneath the ^{7}. The ^7_M means that the interval between the chord root and seventh is major; ^7_m means that the seventh is minor. This letter has been added as a courtesy symbol to specify the quality of the seventh in the less-common seventh chords.

Figure 13.2

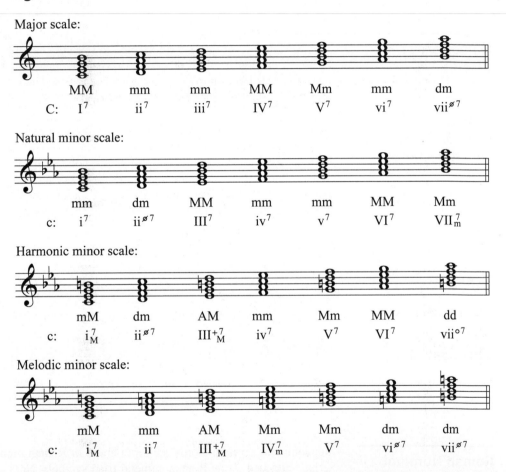

Although the Roman numeral symbols in the preceding figure may seem complicated, some of the symbols are rarely used in analysis. Figure 13.3 lists the diatonic Roman numeral symbols that appear most often in major and minor keys. It is important to note that the chords indicated for minor keys do not use just one form of the minor scale. The mediant seventh chord (III^7) is derived from the natural minor scale, whereas the dominant and leading-tone seventh chords (V^7 and vii$^{\circ7}$) are byproducts of the harmonic and melodic minor scales.

Figure 13.3

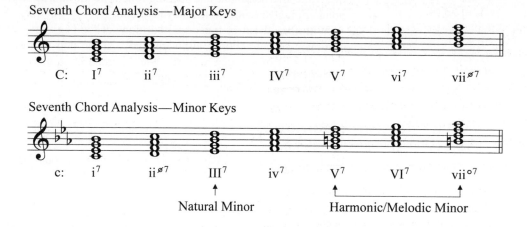

Seventh Chord Analysis—Major Keys

C: I⁷   ii⁷   iii⁷   IV⁷   V⁷   vi⁷   vii°⁷

Seventh Chord Analysis—Minor Keys

c: i⁷   ii°⁷   III⁷   iv⁷   V⁷   VI⁷   vii°⁷

↑ Natural Minor   ↑ Harmonic/Melodic Minor

Macro Analysis Symbols

The macro analysis system also recognizes seventh chords with a superscript ^{7} label. This ^{7} is coupled with root and chord quality symbols that differentiate the various types of seventh chords. The following chart summarizes the macro analysis symbols used to label both dominant and nondominant seventh chords:

Macro Analysis Symbol	Chord Quality	Examples
Capital letter with ^{M7}	major-major (MM)	G^{M7}, $F\sharp^{M7}$, $B\flat^{M7}$
Capital letter with ^{7}	major-minor (Mm)	G^7, $F\sharp^7$, $B\flat^7$
Lowercase letter with ^{7}	minor-minor (mm)	g^7, $f\sharp^7$, $b\flat^7$
Lowercase letter with $^{\varnothing 7}$	diminished-minor (dm)	$g^{\varnothing 7}$, $f\sharp^{\varnothing 7}$, $b\flat^{\varnothing 7}$
Lowercase letter with $^{\circ 7}$	diminished-diminished (dd)	$g^{\circ 7}$, $f\sharp^{\circ 7}$, $b\flat^{\circ 7}$

The addition of a seventh to a triad does not change the application of the macro analysis slur symbols. Solid and dotted slurs are attached to their respective circle and leading-tone progressions whether or not chord sevenths are present. (See Appendix B for a summary of the macro analysis symbols.)

Figure 13.4

Schumann: Novelletten, op. 21, no. 2, mm. 313–317.

Macro analysis: A⁷   D^M7   G^M7   c♯°⁷   f♯⁷   b⁷   e⁷   A⁷   D

(D: V⁷   I⁷   IV⁷   vii°⁷   iii⁷   vi⁷   ii⁷   V⁷   I)

In the Renaissance period, music was not organized in terms of functional harmony. However, like the dominant and leading-tone seventh chords, vertical sonorities resembling nondominant seventh chords may be found.

With the advent of functional harmony at the beginning of the baroque period, nondominant seventh chords, although sparse at the outset, grew in numbers to become an integral part of baroque musical style. Figure 13.5 is a typical example of nondominant seventh chord usage in the baroque period.

Figure 13.5

Bach: "O Ewigkeit, du Donnerwort" ("O Eternity, Thou Word of Thunder"), BWV 20, mm. 3–4.

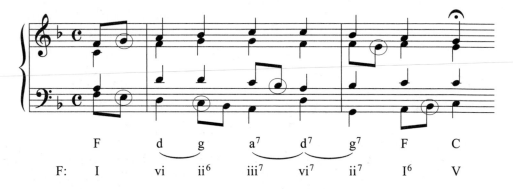

Continuing the trend developed in the baroque period, nondominant seventh chords are found in large numbers in the music of the classical period. Figure 13.6 demonstrates the sequential treatment of a series of seventh chords joined by diatonic circle progressions.

Figure 13.6

Mozart: Sonata in F Major, K. 332, I: Allegro, mm. 196–201.

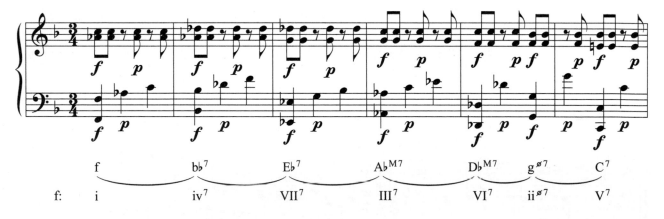

With the increased use of altered chords (chords containing nondiatonic notes), nondominant seventh chords, especially those in circle progressions, became somewhat less common in the romantic period. The following excerpt illustrates a typical use of nondominant seventh chords in this period. Note the organization of chord roots, alternating between an ascending third and a descending fifth. This root movement results in unresolved sevenths for some of the chords.

Figure 13.7

Schumann: "Ich Grolle Nicht" ("I Bear No Grudge") from *Dichterliebe,* op. 48, no. 7, mm. 5–8.

Although functional harmony was on the decline during the post-romantic and impressionistic periods, the chord qualities represented among the nondominant seventh chords were used in large numbers. In Figure 13.8, Debussy includes diminished-minor, minor-minor, and major-major seventh chords, but the setting is the Aeolian mode. Even though Roman numerals can be applied to the individual chords, note that the harmonic movement does not progress in a tonal fashion.

Figure 13.8

Debussy: Sarabande from *Pour le Piano* (For the Piano), mm. 39–40.

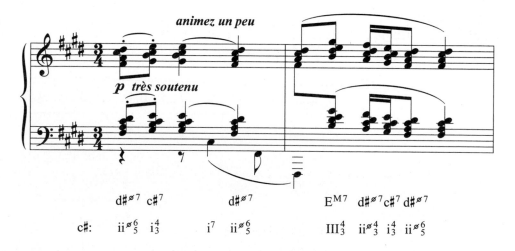

Nondominant seventh chords, as functional harmony, ceased to exist in the contemporary period except for those composers making conscious use of traditional materials.

Even so, the romantic period's legacy of nondominant seventh chords continues to occur in large numbers in jazz and popular music. An example is shown in Figure 13.9.

Figure 13.9

Schmidt: "Try to Remember" from *The Fantasticks,* mm. 17–20.

Nondominant Seventh Chords

Notice the use of popular music symbols in Figure 13.9. The minor-minor quality is indicated by a capital-letter symbol with MI7 added (BMI7–EMI7–AMI7). Popular music symbols for the other nondominant seventh chord qualities (such as major-major = CMA7, major-minor = C7, and diminished-minor = CMI7(♭5)), are listed in Appendix C.

APPLICATIONS

Nondominant seventh chords typically resolve in one of three ways: by circle progression, by noncircle progression and resolution of the seventh, and by noncircle progression with nonresolution of the seventh.

Nondominant Seventh Chords in Circle Progressions

Like the dominant seventh (see Chapter 11), nondominant seventh chords usually progress according to the circle pattern iii–vi–ii–V–I–(IV).

Nondominant Seventh Chord:	Resolves to:
ii⁷ and ii⌀⁷	V or V⁷
vi⁷ and VI⁷	ii or ii°
iii⁷ and III⁷	vi or VI

Resolution of the Seventh Factor

Circle progressions permit the seventh factor of a nondominant seventh chord to resolve down one scale step to the third factor of the following chord.

Figure 13.10

Circle Progressions from Nondominant Seventh Chords.

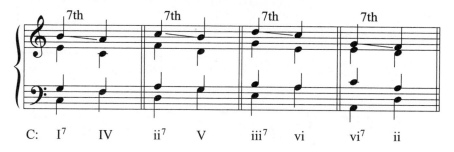

C: I⁷   IV   ii⁷   V   iii⁷   vi   vi⁷   ii

Figure 13.11 shows some typical circle progressions involving nondominant seventh chords in inversion.

Figure 13.11

Circle Progressions from Inverted Nondominant Seventh Chords.

C: ii⁶₅   V   iii⁴₃   vi   vi⁴₂   ii⁶   I⁶₅   IV

<table>
<tr><td>**Noncircle Treatment**</td><td>

Nondominant seventh chords may also resolve in other ways:

1. The IV⁷ (in major) and iv⁷ (in minor) generally move to V.
2. In circle progressions, all nondominant seventh chords eventually resolve to V. However, sometimes the circle is interrupted, allowing vi⁷, for instance, to resolve to IV (and then V) instead of ii (and then V). Some common progressions are shown in Figure 13.12.

</td></tr>
</table>

Figure 13.12

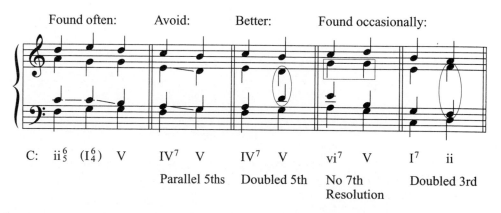

C: ii⁶₅ (I⁶₄) V   IV⁷ V   IV⁷ V   vi⁷ V   I⁷ ii

                        Parallel 5ths   Doubled 5th   No 7th   Doubled 3rd
                                                 Resolution

Figure 13.13 shows a typical example from music literature. Note the series of circle progressions connecting the nondominant seventh chords as well as the resolutions of sevenths down one scale degree.

Figure 13.13

Handel: Allegro from Suite in F-sharp Minor, G. 206, mm. 30–32.

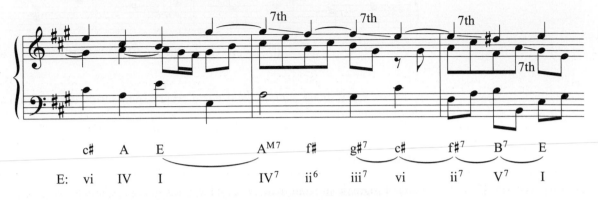

Voice Leading of Nondominant Seventh Chords

This procedure continues the list presented in Chapters 9, 11, and 12. A complete list of all stylistic practices is found in Appendix A.

14. Resolve the seventh factor of nondominant seventh chords one diatonic scale degree down to the third factor of the next chord (in circle progressions). Otherwise, resolve the seventh factor down one step if its resolution is a part of the following chord.

Assignment 13.1 Each note is the root of a seventh chord. Write the requested chord on the staff in simple position as shown in the example.

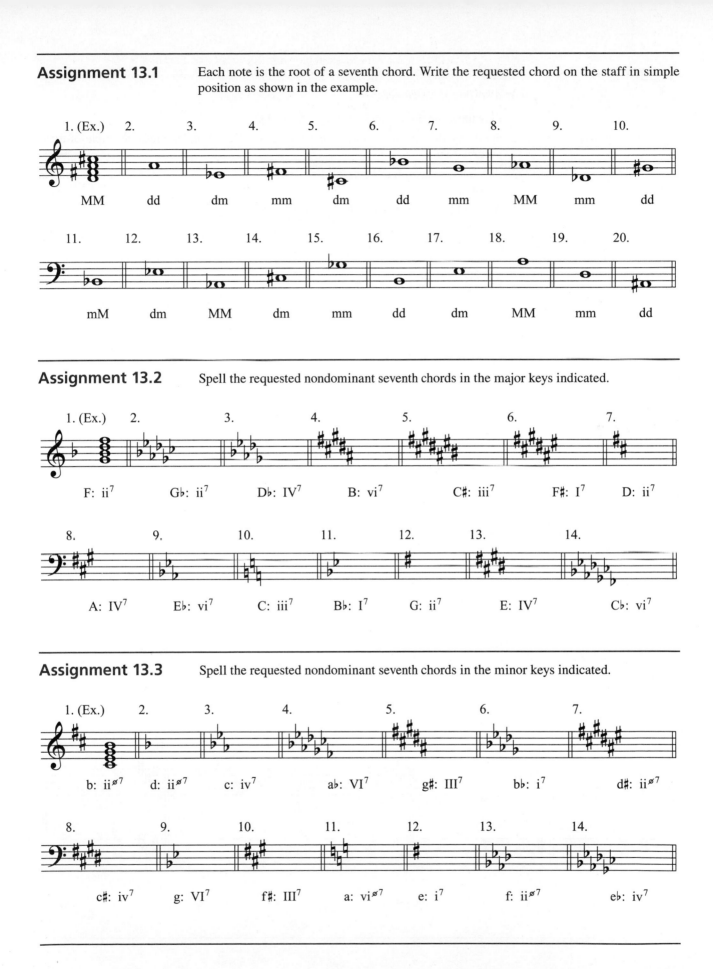

Assignment 13.2 Spell the requested nondominant seventh chords in the major keys indicated.

Assignment 13.3 Spell the requested nondominant seventh chords in the minor keys indicated.

Assignment 13.4

Each given chord is a nondominant seventh chord.

As a keyboard assignment:

1. Play the scale (for example, C major in no. 1).

2. Spell out the resolution chord in your mind. All examples presume circle-of-fifths progressions.

3. Play the nondominant seventh chord and follow it immediately with the resolution chord.

4. As a model for keyboard only, no. 1 is illustrated thus:

1. (Ex.)

C: iii⁷   vi

As a written assignment:

1. Write the circle progression resolution for each given chord on the staff.

2. Check to make sure the root of the second chord is a descending P5th from the root of the given chord. Be sure the seventh factor resolves down one scale degree.

3. Make a complete Roman numeral analysis of each chord.

C: iii⁷   vi   b: ____ ____   A♭: ____ ____   e: ____ ____   E: ____ ____

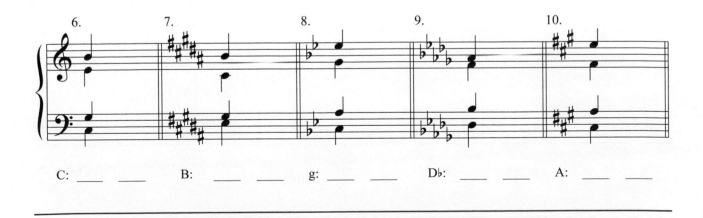

C: ____ ____   B: ____ ____   g: ____ ____   D♭: ____ ____   A: ____ ____

Assignment 13.5 Each example is a phrase of a chorale melody as harmonized by Bach.

As a keyboard assignment:

1. Add alto and tenor as required by the figured bass.

2. Play the examples on the piano—the three upper voices with the right hand, and the bass with the left hand.

As a written assignment:

1. Add alto and tenor as required by the figured bass.

2. Make a complete Roman numeral analysis of each chord.

3. If your instructor requests a macro analysis, include a line of chord letter symbols and slurs.

4. Arrange the chorale phrases for a quartet of instruments played by class members.

1. "Nun komm, der Heiden Heiland" ("Now Come, Savior of the Gentiles"), BWV 36, mm. 1–2 (modified).

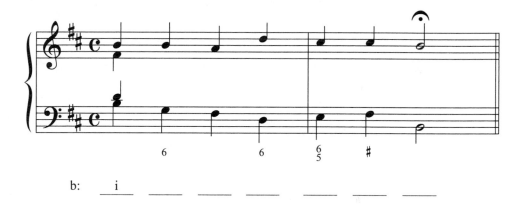

2. "Was willst du dich, o meine Seele, kränken" ("How Now, My Soul, Why Makest Sore Complaining"), BWV 425, mm. 13–14 (modified).

3. "O Ewigkeit, du Donnerwort" ("O Eternity, Thou Word of Thunder"), BWV 20, mm. 3–4 (modified).

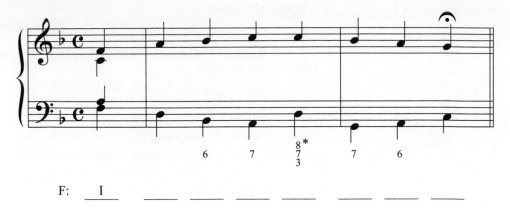

F: I   ____ ____ ____ ____ ____ ____

*Not all chord factors will be present in this chord.

4. "Meines Lebens letzte Zeit" ("The Last Hour of My Life"), BWV 381, mm. 1–2 (modified).

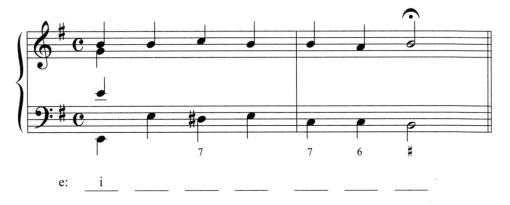

e: i   ____ ____ ____ ____ ____ ____ ____

5. "Jesu Leiden, Pein und Tod" ("Jesus' Suffering, Pain, and Death"), BWV 245, mm. 11–12 (modified).

E: I   ____ ____ ____ ____ ____ ____

Assignment 13.6   Create a four-part chorale-style harmonization of the phrase that follows.

1. Chart the possible harmonizations for the phrase.
2. Include at least one nondominant seventh chord in your harmonization.
3. Use a harmonic rhythm of one chord per quarter note.
4. Follow prescribed four-part writing procedures outlined earlier in this textbook.
5. Make a complete analysis of each chord selected.

"Sei gegrüsset, Jesu gütig" ("Hear My Pleading, Jesu, Treasure"), mm. 1–2.

Here is one possible selection of chords. It leans heavily toward the tonic and dominant and includes one nondominant seventh chord.

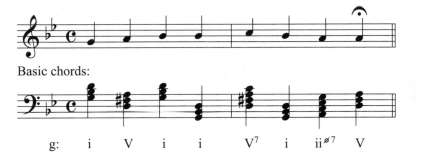

Basic chords:

g: i   V   i   i   V⁷   i   ii°⁷   V

Assignment 13.7   Chart the possible harmonizations of the following chorale phrase, and then answer the questions.

"Herzlich lieb hab ich dich, o Herr" ("Dearly I Love Thee, O Lord"), mm. 1–2 (modified).

1. The cadence tones (the final two tones, A and G) will support an authentic cadence in how many keys?
2. Is a plagal cadence possible at the end of the phrase? A half cadence? A deceptive cadence?
3. Could the entire phrase be harmonized in G major?
4. Could the melody be harmonized entirely with descending P5 progressions?
5. How many of the melody tones could be harmonized as the seventh factor of a seventh chord and also effect either normal or alternate resolution?

Assignment 13.8   Harmonize each of the following chorale phrases:

1. Limit each phrase to one nondominant seventh chord.
2. Use a harmonic rhythm of one chord per quarter note.
3. Follow the prescribed four-part writing procedures outlined earlier in this textbook.
4. Make a complete analysis of each chord selected.
5. Add nonharmonic tones to the harmonization.
6. Divide the class into four sections (soprano, alto, tenor, and bass) and sing one harmonization written by each student.

1. "Wir Christenleut" ("We Christian People"), mm. 1–2.

2. "Wie schön leuchtet der Morgenstern" ("How Brightly Shines the Morning Star"), mm. 1–6.

Assignment 13.9   The following is an example from music literature.

1. Make a complete Roman numeral analysis of the composition.
2. If your instructor requests a macro analysis, include chord letter symbols and slurs.
3. Circle nonharmonic tones and name them, using the standard abbreviations.
4. Above the staves, bracket each phrase and indicate phrase relationships with letters.
5. Label other compositional aspects such as sequences, melodic repetition, and rhythmic repetition.
6. Below the analysis, bracket each cadence and indicate the type (perfect authentic, imperfect authentic, half, deceptive, or plagal).

Schumann: "Volksliedchen" ("Little Folk Song") from *Album for the Young,* op. 68, no. 9. CD Track 79

Assignment 13.10

Each exercise is a figured-bass voice of a chorale phrase.

As a keyboard assignment:

1. Play each exercise, adding the soprano, alto, and tenor voices.

2. If voicing the chords and planning an interesting soprano melody at the same time is too difficult for you, become familiar with the chords first, then work on the soprano melody.

As a written assignment:

1. On a separate sheet of staff paper, write out each figured bass, leaving a staff above for the soprano and alto.

2. Complete the remaining three upper voices according to the figuration supplied.

3. Observe good voice-leading practices.

4. For help in writing the soprano melody, observe the soprano voices in assignment 13.5. Each is a traditional chorale melody and will give you an idea of the style.

PART B   The Structural Elements of Music

Secondary Dominants and Leading-Tone Chords

TOPICS	Secondary Dominants	Tonicized Chord	Nondiatonic Tones
	Altered Chords	Tonicization	Four-Chord Formulas
	Primary Dominants	Secondary Leading-Tone Chords	Tritone Substitution

IMPORTANT CONCEPTS

We have already observed the characteristics of the primary dominant chords (V and V^7) and the primary leading-tone chords (vii°, vii^{ø7}, and vii°^{7}) in their diatonic settings. Similar in function to these chords are the secondary dominants and secondary leading-tone chords. These chords act as dominants and leading tones to scale degrees other than the tonic.

Secondary Dominants

Secondary dominants are chords that are altered to sound like dominants. This means changing triads to make them major and changing seventh chords to make them major-minor. Any major or minor diatonic triad may be preceded by a chord that is, in effect, its dominant or leading tone.

In Figure 14.1a, the vi triad is preceded by iii, but in Figure 14.1aa, vi is preceded by its own dominant. The ii triad (E–G–B) is transformed into a secondary dominant simply by making it major (E–G♯–B). The E major triad sounds like the dominant for A minor even though the A minor triad exists in C major as vi.

Figure 14.1

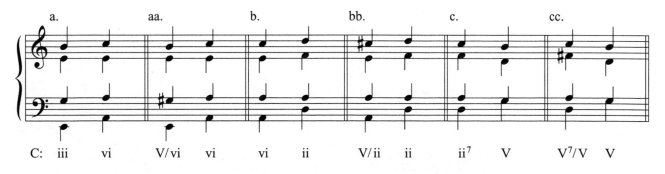

C: iii   vi   V/vi   vi   vi   ii   V/ii   ii   ii^7 V   V^7/V   V

Characteristics of Secondary Dominants

1. To be a secondary dominant, a chord must be either a major triad or a major–minor seventh chord. When you see the slash (/), read it as the word "of." The symbol V/vi means V of vi.

2. Secondary dominants are called *altered chords* because they contain nondiatonic tones—tones that are not found in the prevailing key. Secondary dominants are created out of diatonic chords that have been changed to make them major and major-minor.

Figure 14.2

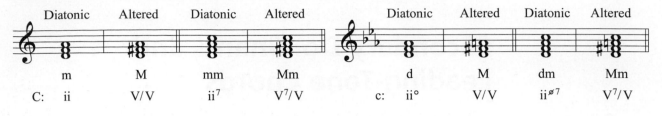

3. Secondary dominants, because they are temporarily raised to the status of dominant, naturally resolve to their temporary tonic, just as *primary dominants* (V) resolve to tonic (I). Thus, most often secondary dominants move in circle progressions V/vi to vi, V/ii to ii, V/iv to iv, and V/V to V.
4. In circle progressions, the chord to which secondary dominants progress is called a *tonicized chord*. When V/ii progresses to ii, the ii triad is the tonicized chord. Notice that only major and minor chords can function as tonicized chords. This process of creating the effect of a temporary tonic is known as *tonicization*.

Figure 14.3

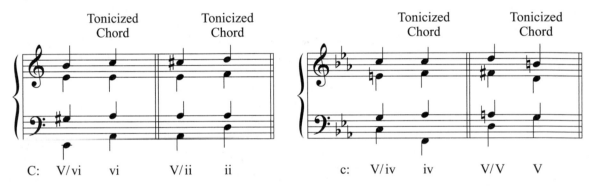

5. Secondary dominants may occasionally follow other secondary dominants. In these cases the progression is frequently based on circle progression root movement (see Figure 14.4).

Figure 14.4

Diatonic circle progressions:

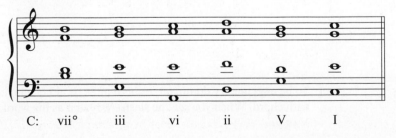

Same chords changed to secondary dominants:

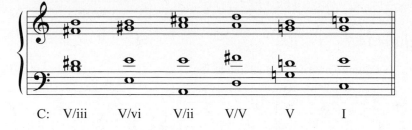

C: V/iii   V/vi   V/ii   V/V   V   I

6. Infrequently, a secondary dominant will resolve unexpectedly to a chord that does not follow circle progression root movement. In Figure 14.5, the secondary dominant (V^7/V) progresses to a triad (iii) whose root is a step above that of the secondary dominant. The effect is similar to that of a deceptive cadence where the dominant sidesteps its natural progression to the tonic.

Figure 14.5

Irregular resolution of a secondary dominant:

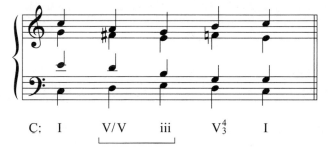

C: I   V/V   iii V_3^4 I

7. Just as primary dominants may be inverted, so also may secondary dominants.

Figure 14.6

Secondary dominants in inversion:

D: I V^6/ii   ii   V   I   I V_5^6/ii   ii   V   I

8. In major keys, the secondary dominant triad of IV is simply the tonic (I), so it is not called a secondary dominant (no altered pitches). However, V^7/IV (in C major, C–E–G–B♭)

does contain an altered note, so it is listed as a secondary dominant. In minor keys, both V/iv and V⁷/iv include altered pitches and are considered secondary dominants.

Figure 14.7

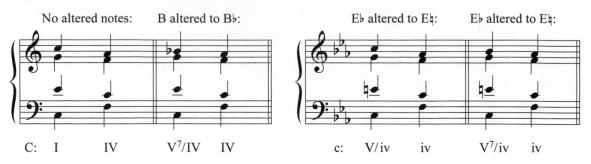

No altered notes: B altered to B♭:   E♭ altered to E♮:   E♭ altered to E♮:

C: I   IV   V⁷/IV   IV   c: V/iv   iv   V⁷/iv   iv

Part Writing Secondary Dominant Chords

The voice leading of secondary dominant chords is the same as for primary dominant chords. Secondary dominant triads require that you carefully maintain recommended doublings because the third of the chord has the function of a leading tone and should not be doubled. All other conventional part-writing practices apply.

Resolve the seventh of the V⁷/ chord down one scale degree in the same voice. It is important to remember that all four factors of the V⁷/ are usually present, but for smoothness of voice leading, the fifth may be omitted and the root doubled.

Figure 14.8

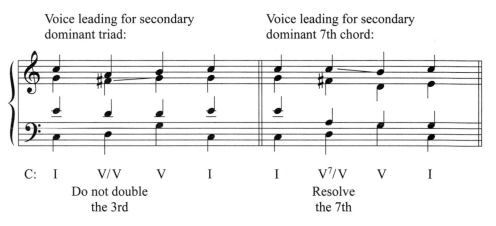

Voice leading for secondary dominant triad: Voice leading for secondary dominant 7th chord:

C: I   V/V   V   I   I   V⁷/V   V   I

Do not double the 3rd   Resolve the 7th

Secondary Leading-Tone Chords

Because leading-tone chords are often used as dominant substitutes (see Chapter 12), they also may function as temporary leading-tone chords—leading-tone-sounding chords in a key other than the prevailing key. The primary leading-tone triad in C major is B–D–F (vii°), but any major or minor triad (ii, iii, IV, V, or vi) in C major may have its own leading-tone triad or seventh chord—called a *secondary leading-tone chord*. In Figure 14.9a, the vi triad is preceded by V⁷, but in Figure 14.9aa, vi is preceded by its own leading-tone seventh chord. The V⁷ is transformed into a secondary leading-tone seventh chord simply by making it a diminished seventh chord (G♯–B–D–F), so it sounds like a leading-tone seventh chord to the A minor triad (the A minor triad is vi in the key of C major).

Figure 14.9

Diatonic progressions:

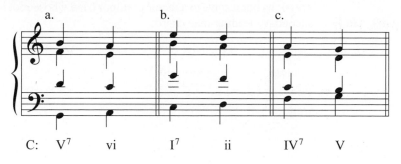

C: V⁷   vi   I⁷   ii   IV⁷   V

Same progressions with secondary leading-tone chords:

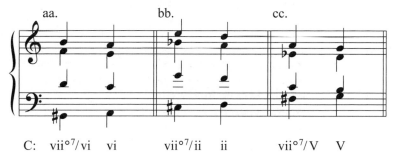

C: vii°⁷/vi vi   vii°⁷/ii ii   vii°⁷/V V

Characteristics of Secondary Leading-Tone Chords

1. Secondary leading-tone chords have only three qualities:

   Diminished triad—vii°/

   Diminished-minor seventh chord—viiø⁷/

   Diminished–diminished seventh chord—vii°⁷/

2. Like secondary dominants, secondary leading-tone chords are called altered chords because they contain *nondiatonic tones*. Secondary leading-tone chords are created out of diatonic chords that have been changed to make them diminished, diminished-minor, or diminished-diminished (Figure 14.10). Notice in Figure 14.10c that a fully diminished seventh chord resolves to a major triad. Fully diminished seventh chords are more common as secondary leading-tone chords than half-diminished seventh chords and may precede either a minor or a major chord.

Figure 14.10

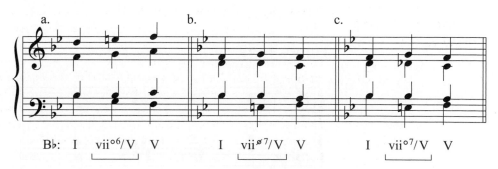

Bb: I vii°⁶/V V   I viiø⁷/V V   I vii°⁷/V V

3. Because they are temporarily raised to the status of leading-tone chords, these chords naturally resolve to their temporary tonic, just as primary leading-tone chords resolve to their tonic. Thus, secondary leading-tone chords do not normally move in circle progressions but resolve to a major or minor triad whose root is a half step above that of the secondary leading-tone chord.

Chord	Resolution
vii°⁷/ii	ii
vii°⁷/iii	iii
vii°⁷/IV	IV
vii°⁷/V	V
vii°⁷/vi	vi

4. Secondary leading-tone chords create a leading-tone relationship with diatonic major and minor triads:

   In major keys: ii, iii, IV, V, vi

   In minor keys: III, iv, V, VI

Figure 14.11

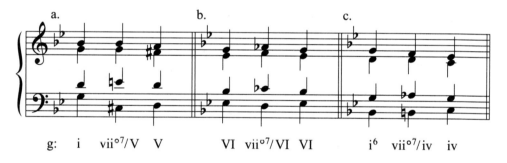

g: i   vii°⁷/V V   VI vii°⁷/VI VI   i⁶ vii°⁷/iv iv

5. When secondary leading-tone chords resolve in a conventional manner, the resolution chord is called a tonicized chord. When vii°⁷/V resolves to V, the V triad is the tonicized chord.
6. Secondary leading-tone chords occasionally follow other leading-tone chords. In Figure 14.12, chord 2 proceeds to another diminished seventh chord. In these cases, conventional resolution is often impossible.

Figure 14.12

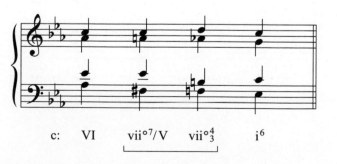

c: VI   vii°⁷/V   vii°⁴₃   i⁶

The voice leading of secondary leading-tone chords is the same as for primary leading-tone chords. For vii°⁶/ there is no established voice-leading pattern, but the bass note should be doubled, avoiding skips of a tritone, and all voices should move with as much stepwise movement as possible. Avoid doubling the root of a secondary leading-tone triad because the root functions as a leading tone and should never be doubled.

For the secondary leading-tone seventh chords, resolve the seventh of the vii°⁷/ or vii°⁷/ (and inversions) down one diatonic scale degree. Resolve the tritone (root to fifth) inward if a d5th and outward if an A4th. However, it is not possible to do so in all situations.

Figure 14.13

Voice leading for secondary leading-tone chords:

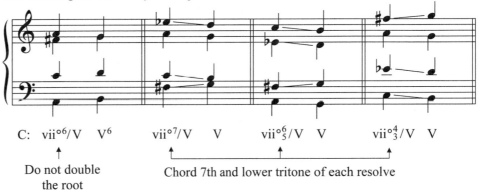

Macro Analysis

Macro analysis can be used to pinpoint secondary dominants and leading-tone chords in tonal compositions. The macro letter symbols draw attention to chords that differ from diatonic harmonies and the circle progression slurs emphasize tonicization. Beyond these fundamental basics, macro analysis can be used as a preparatory step to completing a Roman numeral analysis that includes nondiatonic chords.

To identify secondary dominants and leading-tone chords using macro analysis, follow these steps:

1. Analyze all of the chords using the macro analysis letter symbols. Do not attempt to add circle progression slurs or Roman numeral analysis symbols at this stage.

Figure 14.14

Beethoven: Sonata in G Major, op. 14, no. 2, II: Andante, mm. 17–20.

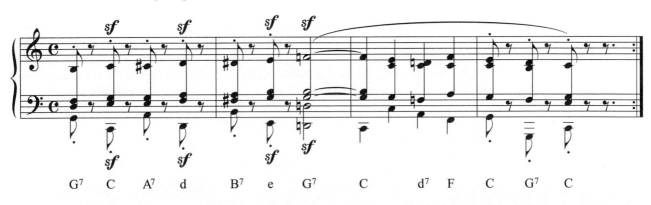

2. Next, identify the macro letter symbols that represent nondiatonic harmonies. This step assumes you are familiar with the diatonic symbols. In Figure 14.14, the key signature and final cadence confirm that the excerpt is in the key of C major. The diatonic triads and seventh chords for the key of C major are listed in Figure 14.15.

Figure 14.15

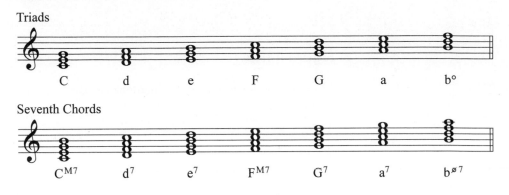

Triads

C   d   e   F   G   a   b°

Seventh Chords

C^{M7} d^7 e^7 F^{M7} G^7 a^7 $b^{\varnothing 7}$

Notice that two chords in the excerpt, A^7 and B^7, are not listed with the diatonic chords for C major. Both A^7 and B^7 are nondiatonic chords in the key of C major.

Figure 14.16

Beethoven: Sonata in G Major, op. 14, no. 2, II: Andante, mm. 17–20.

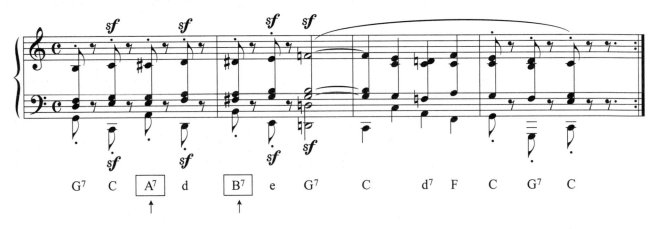

G^7 C A^7 d B^7 e G^7 C d^7 F   C G^7 C

3. The third and final step is to complete the macro analysis with slurs. Roman numerals and inversion labels can also be added at this stage. Remember that nondiatonic chords will require a nondiatonic analysis—in this case, secondary dominants. Notice how the process of tonicization becomes evident with the addition of the circle progression slurs. For just an instant, the harmony moves away from the established key.

Figure 14.17

Beethoven: Sonata in G Major, op. 14, no. 2, II: Andante, mm. 17–20.

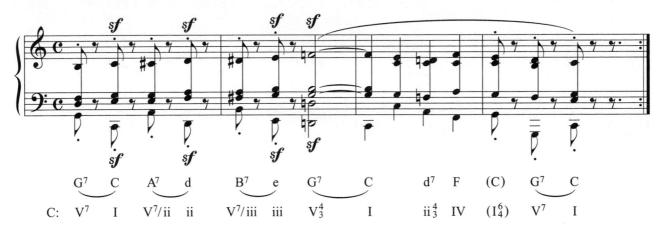

C:	G^7	C	A^7	d	B^7	e	G^7	C	d^7	F	(C)	G^7	C
	V^7	I	V^7/ii	ii	V^7/iii	iii	V^4_3	I	ii^4_3	IV	(I^6_4)	V^7	I

History

The historical use of secondary dominants and leading-tone chords varied in the style periods. Until the baroque period and the development of functional harmony, secondary dominants and leading-tone chords as such were not found, but cautious use and conservative part writing of these chords marked the style of baroque period usage. Illustrated in Figure 14.18 is V^7/V. What would be the analysis of chord 6 without the A-sharp?

Figure 14.18

Bach: "Es ist das Heil uns kommen her" ("Salvation Unto Us Has Come"), BWV 86, mm. 9–10.

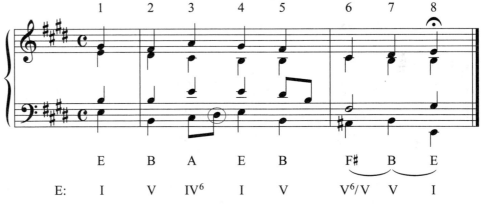

	E	B	A	E	B	F♯	B	E
E:	I	V	IV^6	I	V	V^6/V	V	I

Another baroque period example is provided in Figure 14.19, but this time with a secondary leading-tone triad tonicizing the dominant (vii°⁶/V). How would you analyze the nonharmonic tones labeled 1, 2, and 3 in the excerpt? As (1) unaccented appoggiaturas or (2) upper-neighboring tones?

Figure 14.19

Purcell: Minuet from Suite no. 8 in F Major, Z. 669, mm. 9–13.

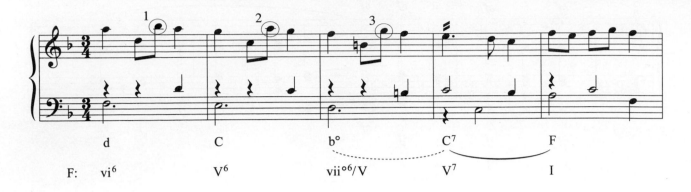

In the classical period, as a natural development of the baroque period, secondary dominant and leading-tone chords are found in somewhat greater frequency. Progression of these chords to their tonicized resolutions constitutes by far the largest number of examples, but occasional nontraditional utilizations begin to appear. Figure 14.20 shows a representative example of secondary dominant and leading-tone chords in the classical period.

Figure 14.20

Mozart: Fantasia in C Minor, K. 475, mm. 91–94.

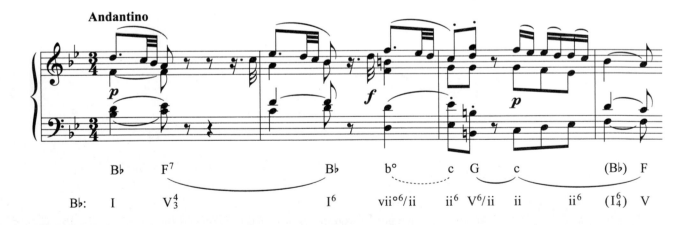

Figure 14.21 shows a secondary dominant and a secondary leading-tone chord decorating the basic diatonic circle progression, vi–ii–V–I, in the final measures of the phrase.

Figure 14.21

Maria Wolowska Szymanowska: Nocturne in B-flat Major, mm. 1–5.

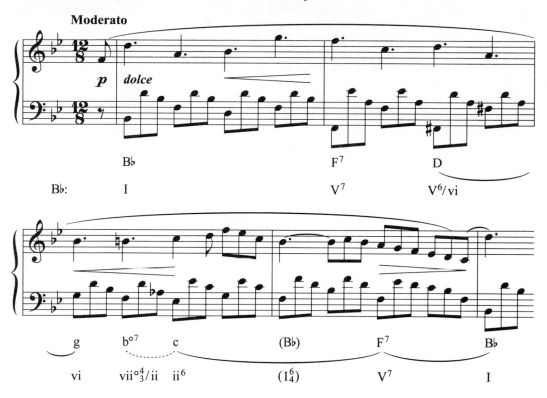

During the romantic period, secondary dominant and leading-tone seventh chords increased in frequency, especially those that are seventh chords. Part writing became more daring with wider skips and seventh factors not always being resolved. Figure 14.22 illustrates successive secondary dominants—a common occurrence in romantic period music.

Figure 14.22

Chopin: Polonaise in C-sharp Minor, op. 26, no. 1, mm. 82–83.

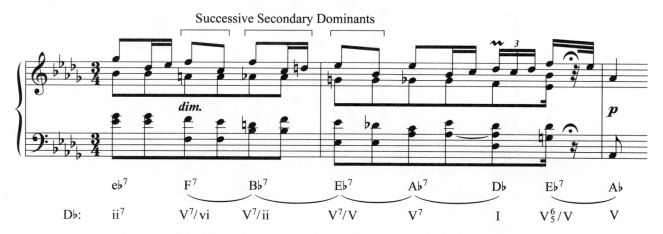

Figure 14.23 illustrates a half-diminished secondary leading-tone chord. This particular chord quality (diminished-minor) is somewhat less familiar than the more common diminished–diminished secondary leading-tone chord. The excerpt shown provides example of a decorated dominant seventh chord. The prevailing V^7 harmony is embellished with I^6_4, ii^{o6}, and $vii^{ø7}/V$.

Figure 14.23

Brahms: Intermezzo in C Major, op. 119, no. 3, m. 49–51.

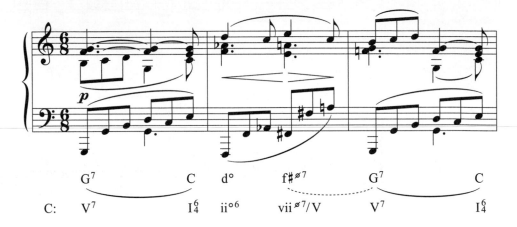

Because the strong dominant-to-tonic relationship began to wane during the post-romantic and impressionistic period, secondary dominant and leading-tone chord function became less and less common. Figure 14.24 illustrates the use of a secondary dominant, which offers a fleeting suggestion of F-sharp major, a key not closely related to G major.

Figure 14.24

Debussy: *Minstrels* from Preludes, Book I, no. 12, mm. 17–20.

One of the cornerstones of popular song accompaniments is the secondary dominant. These chords appear in abundance in modern-day popular songs and may occur singly or in successions of circle progressions.

Figure 14.25

Backer, Davis, Cook, and Greenaway: "I'd Like to Teach the World to Sing," mm. 1–8.

Jazz, excluding some avant-garde styles, likewise makes considerable use of secondary dominants. Secondary leading-tone chords are used only occasionally in popular songs and even less in jazz. A study of four-chord formulas, so common to the jazz and popular style, is in order.

Four-chord formulas (sequence of four chords) are a particular compositional device of jazz and popular music. Groups of four chords, played as a unit, are often used as stylized accompaniments and turnarounds for popular songs and as the basis for jazz improvisations.

Some four-chord formulas consist entirely of secondary-dominant seventh chords (for example: C7–A7–D7–G7), whereas others are a mixture of nondominant and secondary-dominant sevenths. Some of the typical four-chord formulas are:

Typical Chord Formulas								
Analysis Symbols					*Popular Music Symbols (in C major)*			
I7	vi7	ii7	V7	=	Cma7	Ami7	Dmi7	G7
V7/IV	V7/ii	V7/V	V7	=	C7	A7	D7	G7
I	vii°7/ii	ii7	V7	=	C	C#°7	Dmi7	G7
iii7	vi7	ii7	V7	=	Emi7	Ami7	Dmi7	G7

Often the harmonic structure of a phrase consists of a succession of four-chord formulas. When used in this manner, the patterns impart a distinct orderliness and logic to the music that is immediately perceived by the listener.

One innovation relating to the dominant seventh in the popular and jazz styles is the use of a *tritone substitution*. In a circle-of-fifths progression, a major–minor seventh chord can be replaced by the major-minor seventh chord an augmented fourth below.

Figure 14.26 shows a harmonic accompaniment using the circle-of-fifths pattern exclusively.

Figure 14.26

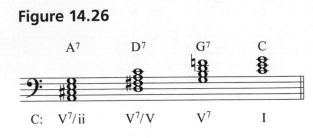

Figure 14.27 shows the same accompaniment pattern except for the substitute chord whose root lies a tritone above or below.

Figure 14.27

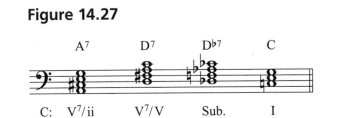

Figures 14.28 and 14.29 demonstrate harmonic substitutions that transform a circle-of-fifths progression into a chromatic-descending progression.

Figure 14.28

Gershwin: "Nice Work If You Can Get It," mm. 1–4.

PART B   The Structural Elements of Music

The same composition with substitutions:

Figure 14.29

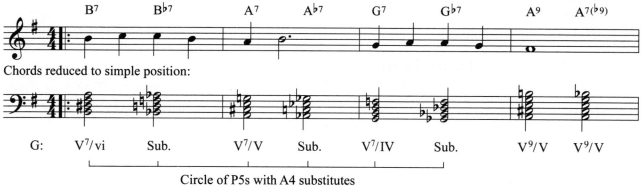

Chords reduced to simple position:

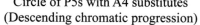

G: V^7/vi   Sub.   V^7/V   Sub.   V^7/IV   Sub.   V^9/V   V^9/V

Circle of P5s with A4 substitutes
(Descending chromatic progression)

Assignment 14.1

Write the following secondary dominant chords in the keys indicated.

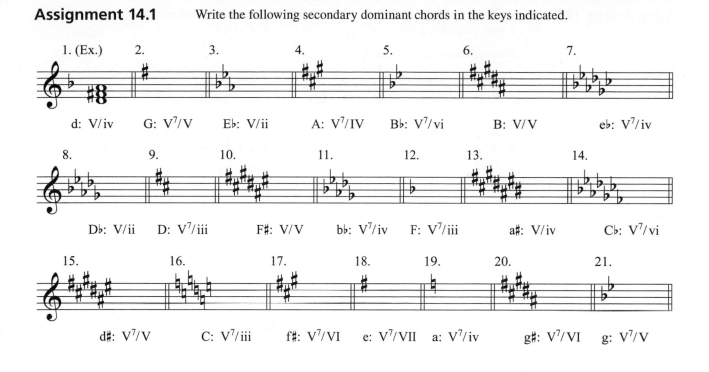

1. (Ex.) d: V/iv
2. G: V⁷/V
3. Eb: V/ii
4. A: V⁷/IV
5. Bb: V⁷/vi
6. B: V/V
7. eb: V⁷/iv

8. Db: V/ii
9. D: V⁷/iii
10. F#: V/V
11. bb: V⁷/iv
12. F: V⁷/iii
13. a#: V/iv
14. Cb: V⁷/vi

15. d#: V⁷/V
16. C: V⁷/iii
17. f#: V⁷/VI
18. e: V⁷/VII
19. a: V⁷/iv
20. g#: V⁷/VI
21. g: V⁷/V

Assignment 14.2

Write each requested secondary dominant and leading-tone chord in simple position. The tonicized chord is given at the end of each staff.

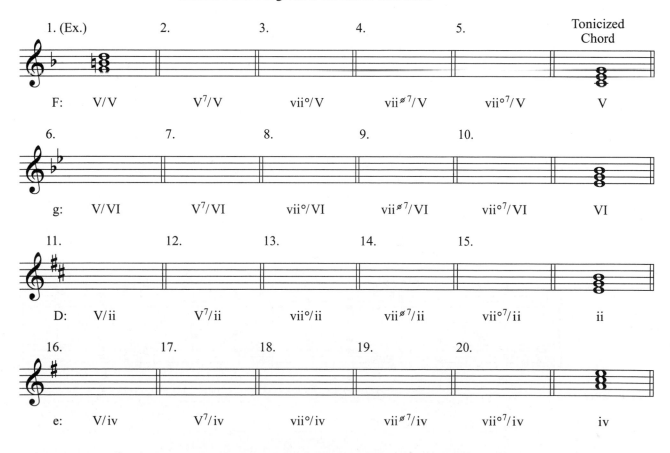

1. (Ex.) F: V/V
2. V⁷/V
3. vii°/V
4. vii⌀⁷/V
5. vii°⁷/V

Tonicized Chord: V

6. g: V/VI
7. V⁷/VI
8. vii°/VI
9. vii⌀⁷/VI
10. vii°⁷/VI

VI

11. D: V/ii
12. V⁷/ii
13. vii°/ii
14. vii⌀⁷/ii
15. vii°⁷/ii

ii

16. e: V/iv
17. V⁷/iv
18. vii°/iv
19. vii⌀⁷/iv
20. vii°⁷/iv

iv

Each exercise contains a potential secondary dominant or leading-tone chord followed by a tonicized chord.

As a keyboard assignment:

1. Play the example first and become accustomed to the procedure.
2. Then play each exercise in the same way—the two chords as printed, then as a secondary dominant or leading-tone chord resolving to its tonicized chord.
3. Do not change the letter name of any pitch—add or subtract accidentals only.
4. While you are playing each exercise, determine the analysis of both chords.
5. If you are playing this for your instructor, call out the analyses as you play.

As a written assignment:

1. Write the analysis of each chord as it appears without accidentals.
2. Then add the necessary accidentals to make the first chord a secondary dominant or leading-tone chord, and write the analysis with alterations.
3. Do not change the letter name of any pitch. Add or subtract accidentals only.

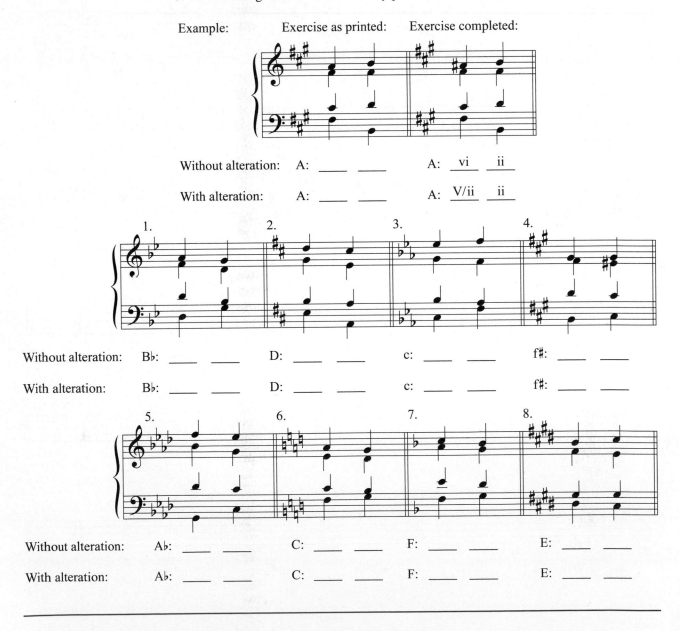

PART B   The Structural Elements of Music

Assignment 14.4
Following are several chorale phrases harmonized by Bach with figured bass.

As a keyboard assignment:

1. Play each phrase at the piano adding the alto and tenor voices.
2. Be sure to observe the figured-bass symbols accurately.
3. Play the soprano, alto, and tenor with the right hand and the bass with the left hand.
4. The circled eighth notes in exercise no. 7 are nonharmonic tones and do not need to be harmonized.

As a written assignment:

1. For practice in voice leading, add the alto and tenor as specified by the figured bass.
2. Supply the harmonic analyses in the blanks provided.
3. Make sure voice leading conforms to recommended practice.
4. Do not harmonize the circled eighth notes in exercise no. 7. They are nonharmonic tones.

1. "Wir Christenleut'" ("We Christian People"), BWV 40, mm. 10–11 (modified).

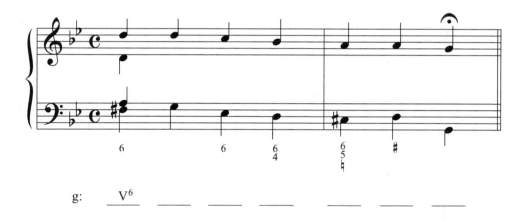

2. "Was betrübst du dich, mein Herze" ("What Makes You Grieve, My Heart"), BWV 423, mm. 15–16 (modified).

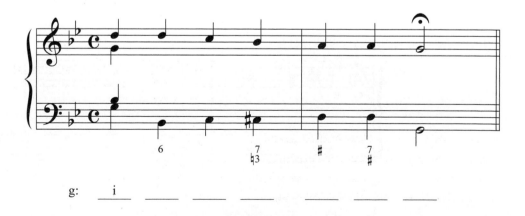

3. "Herr Christ, der ein'ge Gott's-Sohn" ("Lord Christ, the Only Son of God"), BWV 96, mm. 7–8 (modified).

d: VII⁶ _____ _____ _____ _____

4. "Wenn ich in Angst und Not" ("When I in Anxiety and Need"), BWV 427, mm. 1–2 (modified).

E♭:   I _____ _____ _____ _____ _____

5. "Meinen Jesum lass' ich nicht, weil" ("I Will Not Leave My Jesus"), BWV 154, mm. 8–9 (modified).

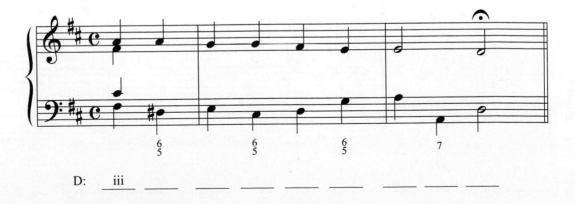

D: iii _____ _____ _____ _____ _____

6. "Puer natus in Bethlehem" ("A Boy Born in Bethlehem"), BWV 65, mm. 5–7 (modified).

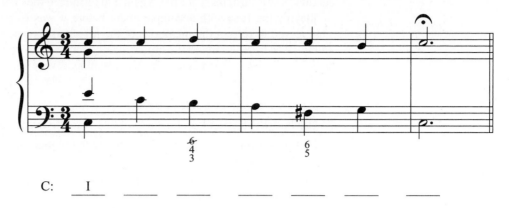

C: I   _____   _____

7. "Was mein Gott will" ("What My God Wills"), BWV 244, mm. 5–6 (modified).

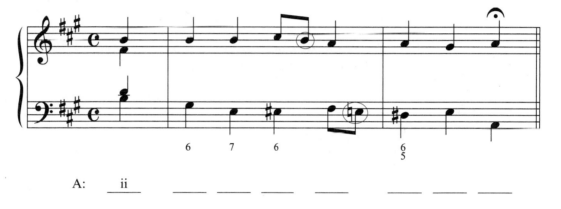

A: ii   _____   _____   _____   _____

Assignment 14.5

1. After completing the figured-bass chorales in assignment 14.4, decorate each with non-harmonic tones. Passing tones, neighboring tones, and suspensions should be the most frequently used nonharmonic tones but others, such as anticipations, changing tones, escape tones, and appoggiaturas, can also be applied effectively.
2. Try to add one nonharmonic tone per beat, although sometimes it is not possible. Do not put all the nonharmonic tones in one voice.
3. As an illustration, chorale phrase 2 from assignment 14.4 (page 305) is shown with nonharmonic decorations by Bach.

Bach: "Was betrübst du dich, mein Herz" ("What Makes You Grieve, My Heart"), BWV 423, mm. 15–16 (modified). **CD Track 80**

Assignment 14.6   A chorale prelude is a type of composition based on the chorale itself. In the seventeenth century, it was customary for the organist to introduce the chorale in the Protestant church by playing the tune with accompaniment before it was to be sung by the congregation. This served to refresh the memories of the members in case they had forgotten the tune. At the same time, it offered the organist an opportunity to elaborate on the melody and/or harmony. As time progressed, organists developed very sophisticated contrapuntal compositions using chorale melodies, and these came to be called chorale preludes.

1. Write a very short chorale prelude.

2. Use both the harmony and melody of one of the four-part exercises in assignment 14.4.

3. Compose a very short melodic or rhythmic figure that can be used to decorate each note of the soprano voice.

4. Apply this figure successively to each tone of the melody and keep at least part of the harmony tones beneath it.

5. Two possible beginnings of a phrase are shown here as illustrations. In both, the melody appears in the soprano voice and is simply an arpeggiation of the original harmony. Each chord of the four-part phrase is given an entire measure in this illustration.

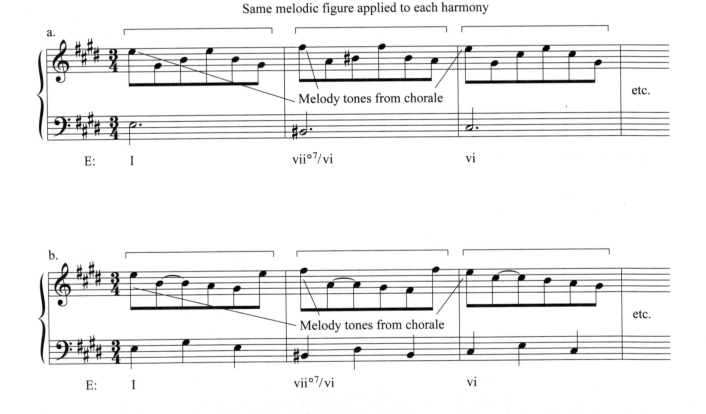

6. The figure you select should be different from either of the preceding ones. With each different melody tone, it may be necessary to deviate slightly from the figure as you first present it. Thus, if your figure is designed for a triad in root position, it will probably have to be altered to fit a first-inversion triad or a seventh chord.

Assignment 14.7   Each exercise is a soprano melody to be harmonized.

As a keyboard assignment:

1. Harmonize each melody at a keyboard, experimenting with a variety of chords to obtain the best possible result.
2. Play the soprano, alto, and tenor voices with the right hand and the bass voice with the left hand.
3. Use at least one secondary dominant or leading-tone chord in each exercise.

As a written assignment:

1. Experiment with many chord combinations by writing them on staff paper in block style (no part writing yet).
2. When you arrive at a basic harmonization you like, place it in four-voice writing.
3. Use at least one secondary dominant or leading-tone chord in each exercise.

1. "Werde munter, mein Gemüte" ("Be Glad, My Soul"), mm. 1–4.

2. "Jesu Leiden, Pein und Tod" ("Jesus' Suffering, Pain and Death"), mm. 1–4.

Assignment 14.8   The following excerpt is a folk song with chord symbols for which you will create a keyboard accompaniment.

1. Sing or play the melody several times.
2. Sing the melody and accompany it with block chords, based on the chord symbols.
3. Using the basic structure provided by the given chords, do a harmonization that includes at least one secondary dominant. Experiment with several possibilities and do not write new chords above the staff until you have tried them with the melody. (Measure 6 is one possible place for a secondary dominant.)
4. Prepare an accompaniment pattern and use it with each chord.
5. In class, sing the melody and accompany it at the keyboard.
6. Improvise a short composition based on the printed melody.

Folk Song: "Billy the Kid."

Following are three excerpts that include secondary dominants and leading-tone chords.

1. Make a complete Roman numeral analysis of each excerpt.
2. Circle nonharmonic tones and name them, using the standard abbreviations.
3. If your instructor requests a macro analysis, include chord letter symbols and slurs.

1. Bach: "Für deinen Thron tret' ich hiermit" ("Before Thy Throne I Herewith Come"), BWV 327, mm. 1–8.
   CD Track 81

2. Beethoven: Sonatina in G Major, Anh. 5, no. 1, II: Romanza, mm. 1–8. CD Track 82

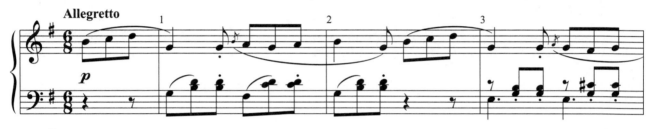

3. Clara Wieck Schumann: Prelude II in B-flat Major, op. 16, mm. 48–52. CD Track 83

Assignment 14.10

This assignment is based on an excerpt from a Mozart piano sonata.

1. Make a complete harmonic analysis of the excerpt.
2. If your instructor requests a macro analysis, include chord letter symbols and slurs.
3. In class, after you have prepared the analysis, discuss the following:
   a. Phrase lengths.
   b. The presence or absence of musical periods.
   c. Cadences.
   d. Circle progressions (especially examples of successive roots a descending fifth or ascending 4th apart).
   e. Climax tones, melodic ascent and descent.
   f. Resolution of secondary dominant and leading-tone chords.
   g. Modulations.

Mozart: Sonata in D Major, K. 311, II, mm. 1–39. CD Track 84

CHAPTER 14   Secondary Dominants and Leading-Tone Chords

311

Assignment 14.11   The following song with figured-bass accompaniment is by G. P. Telemann. The figured bass was intended to be realized (played at sight) by a harpsichordist.

1. (Optional.) If you would like to realize this figured bass at a keyboard, please do so.
2. Write the chords requested by the figured bass on the blank staff by arranging them in a keyboard idiom for piano or harpsichord. Since the figured-bass line will serve as the left-hand part for the realization, arrange the remaining chord notes for the right hand.
3. The figured-bass line in measures 9–12 is ornamented with nonharmonic tones. Realize the chords according to the figures (or lack thereof) appearing on the beats.
4. Ask a fellow class member to prepare the vocal part (or play it on an instrument or keyboard) and accompany her/him with your realization.
5. Make a complete harmonic analysis of the composition.

Telemann: "Geld" ("Money") from *Singe-, Spiel- und Generalbass-Übungen*, TWV 25:40.

Assignment 14.12

Each exercise represents a figured-bass voice.

As a keyboard assignment:

Complete the figured-bass portion of the assignment before preparing a soprano melody.

As a written assignment:

1. On a separate sheet of staff paper, write out each figured bass, leaving a staff above for the soprano and alto.
2. Write the remaining three upper voices according to the figuration supplied.
3. Write the entire soprano voice first—making sure, of course, that the pitches you select are a part of the supporting harmony.
4. Make a complete harmonic analysis.

Modulation

IMPORTANT CONCEPTS

Compositions from the common practice period frequently include more than one tonal center. The change from one tonic to another is often accompanied by the appearance of nondiatonic accidentals and harmonic movement emphasizing the new tonal area.

Modulation

Modulation is a process that results in a shift of tonal center. The term applies to those occasions in music when one established tonal center gives way to another.

Closely Related Keys

Most modulations occur between *closely related keys,* which are those keys that differ by no more than one accidental in the key signature. If the original key is C major, the closely related keys are G major and F major, and the relative minors of each of the three keys, A minor, E minor, and D minor. If the original key is A minor, the closely related keys are E minor and D minor, and C major, G major, and F major (Figure 15.1).

Figure 15.1

Keys Closely Related to A Minor:

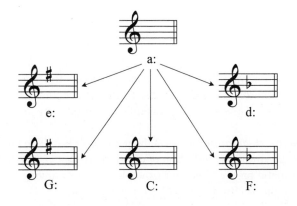

An easy way to understand modulation is to observe the ebb and flow of circle progressions. Up to this chapter, circle progressions have consistently remained diatonic; that is, they have remained within the limits of a single tonal center. In Figure 15.2, the first progressions move through a circle: vi–ii–V–I, then repeat the ii and V all in D major. However, both sets of circle progressions in the second phrase conclude with the A major triad, the chord preceding it is an E chord and acts as a dominant seventh, and G-sharp is found exclusively from measure 6 on. All of this evidence points toward a modulation from D major to A major—a fact that will be quite evident when the excerpt is heard.

Figure 15.2

Mozart: Sonata in D Major, K. 284, III: Theme, mm. 1–8.

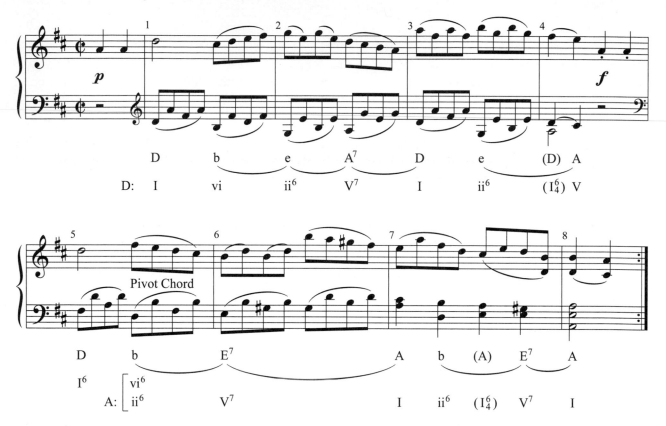

<table>
<tr><td>Common-Chord
Modulation</td><td>A common chord, meaning a chord that is common to each of two keys, offers a smooth introduction to the new key, since it is diatonic to both the old and the new key. This common chord is often called a pivot chord because it becomes a sort of middle ground between the two keys. Common-chord modulation is the name given to a modulation where a common chord (or chords) exists. Figure 15.2 contains a common chord—labeled in measure 5 as the pivot chord between D major and A major.</td></tr>
<tr><td>Chromatic
Modulation</td><td>A chromatic modulation occurs at the point of a chromatic progression (a progression that involves the chromatic inflection of one or more tones). The letter name remains the same in a chromatic progression—for example, in the following Bach chorale. At chord 2, the tenor is D, but in chord 3, the D becomes D-sharp.</td></tr>
</table>

Figure 15.3

Bach: "Du grosser Schmerzensmann" ("Thou Great Man of Sorrow"), BWV 300, mm. 5–6.

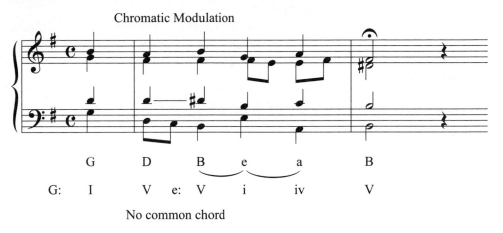

Chromatic Modulation

G   D   B   e   a   B

G: I   V   e: V   i   iv   V

No common chord

Chromatic modulations often occur in passages where the two keys involved are not closely related. They are somewhat less smooth than the common chord modulation and, on occasion, can call attention to the modulation.

Phrase Modulation

Phrase modulation, also known as *direct modulation,* occurs between phrases, periods, or larger sections where a phrase cadences in one key, and the next phrase begins immediately in a different key. In Figure 15.4, a phrase modulation occurs between phrases, the first of which is in E minor, and the second of which begins immediately in C major.

Figure 15.4

Mozart: Sonata in A Major, K. 331, III: "Alla Turca" Allegretto, mm. 6–12.

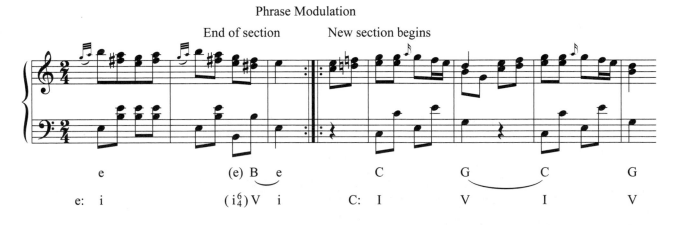

Phrase Modulation

End of section   New section begins

e   (e) B   e   C   G   C   G

e: i   (i_4^6) V   i   C: I   V   I   V

Other Modulation Types

There are a number of other modulation types in tonal music, which will be discussed in the second volume of this book. These modulations often include enharmonic chord spellings to facilitate the modulation to foreign keys (keys that are not closely related).

Modulations in Period Construction

Chapter 6 sets the parameters for identifying phrases and periods in music. With the introduction of modulation, some further information may be helpful. In two-phrase periods:

1. Either phrase may contain a modulation.
2. Either phrase may cadence in a key different from the key at the beginning of the period.
3. The basic definition of a period remains: the cadence at the end of the second phrase must be stronger than the cadence at the end of the first phrase.

The following parallel period (Figure 15.5) begins in D major but ends in A major. Only the first measure of each phrase is the same.

Figure 15.5

Mozart: Sonata in D Major, K. 284, III: Variation XII, mm. 1–8.

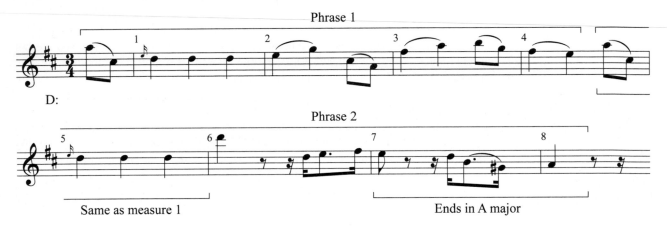

In Figure 15.6, the second phrase is a sequence of the first phrase, transposed up a step.

Figure 15.6

Grieg: *The Last Spring,* op. 34, no. 2, mm. 3–10.

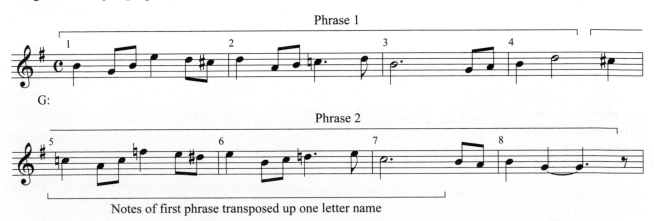

Figure 15.7 illustrates a contrasting period where the second phrase is in the key of the dominant.

Figure 15.7

Haydn: Sonata in C-sharp Minor, Hob. XVI:36, II: Scherzando, mm. 1–8.

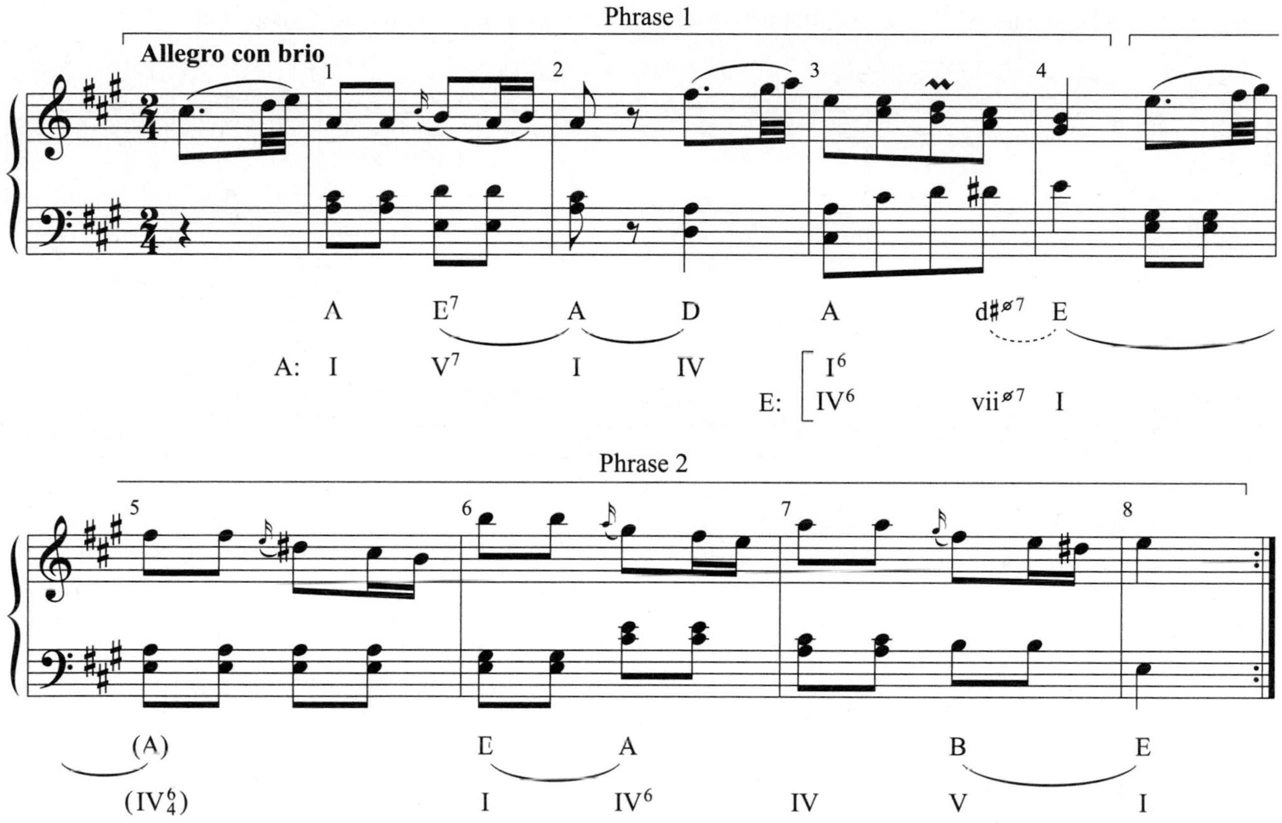

Analysis

Measure	Phrase	Cadence	Key	Symbol	Form
1–4	1	Half	A major	a	Contrasting Period
5–8	2	Perfect Authentic	E major	b	

Analytical Symbols for Modulations

Use the following symbols to analyze modulations:

1. Common chord—select the common chord and analyze it in both keys:

   C: I ii⁶ V I ⌈vi⁶
   G: ⌊ii⁶ V I

2. Other types of modulation—name the new key and adjust chord analysis accordingly:

   G: I V I a: V⁶ I V i

Macro analysis is a helpful tool for identifying modulation and can be used as a preparatory step to Roman numeral analysis. By using the following strategy it may simplify the process to determining if a modulation exists:

1. Analyze an entire section with the macro analysis letter symbols. Do this before considering key centers or Roman numerals.

Figure 15.8

Schumann: "Soldatenmarsch" ("Soldiers' March") from *Album for the Young,* op. 68, no. 2, mm. 1–8.

2. After completing the macro letter names, go back and read through the analysis. Pay particular attention to the symbols that change from the pattern established at the beginning of the excerpt. Changes in symbols frequently occur at the ends of phrases and often point to a modulation. In this example, the C symbol appearing in measures 2 and 6 changes to c♯° in measure 7. This change from C to c♯° indicates a modulation has occurred.

Figure 15.9

Schumann: "Soldatenmarsch" ("Soldiers' March") from *Album for the Young,* op. 68, no. 2, mm. 1–8.

3. After the differing symbols are identified, scan the area containing the new symbol to determine where the modulation begins and ends. Be sure to study the score both before and after the symbol change. When music modulates to a closely related key, the modulation may not be readily apparent until a cadence appears in the new key. To determine where the modulation begins, work backward from the cadence.
4. Complete the macro analysis with slurs. The circle progression and leading-tone slurs often help to verify the new key of the modulation.
5. When the macro analysis is completed, add key indications, Roman numerals, and inversion symbols.

Figure 15.10

Schumann: "Soldatenmarsch" ("Soldiers' March") from *Album for the Young,* op. 68, no. 2, mm. 1–8.

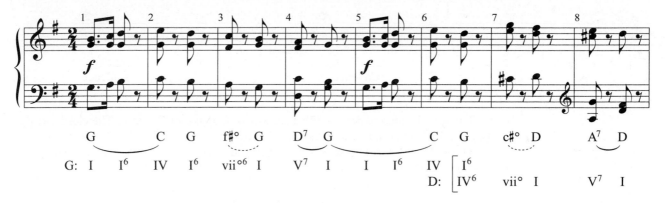

History

Most compositions of the Renaissance period are modal and did not contain modulations in the tonal sense, but simple modulations to closely related keys began to develop in the early baroque period. Joachim Burmeister (1564–1629), in his treatise *Musica poetica* (*The Poetics of Music*), was one of the first theorists to distinguish between major and minor modes. Composers were reluctant to wander far from the original tonic of a composition because the prevailing system of tuning caused serious intonation problems. By 1700, with the changes in the tuning system, modulation became an integral part of the musical style.

Modulation became somewhat more venturesome during the classical period. During the last 25 years (1800–1825) of the period, composers, such as Beethoven (1770–1827) and Haydn (1732–1809), explored modulation to distant keys.

It was during the romantic period that composers carried modulation to the limits. Composers such as Wagner (1813–1883), Franck (1822–1890), and Liszt (1811–1886) developed highly chromatic styles in which frequent and unusual modulations were featured.

During the post-romantic and impressionistic periods, a number of composers expanded their tonal language beyond the bounds of traditional tonality. With the demise of major-minor tonality, modulation became a much less important factor in music.

Much of the music written in the twentieth century goes beyond the tonal system based on major and minor keys. Except for some forms of jazz that incorporate atonality and free tonality, both jazz and popular music are essentially tonal. Consequently, modulation still plays an important role in this music.

APPLICATIONS

Melodies can be harmonized to include modulation, and often, several options are possible when creating a harmonization. The following suggestions will be helpful in harmonizing melodies that modulate.

Harmonizing Melodies That Modulate

The same procedure should be followed for melodies that modulate as for those that do not. This procedure is described in Chapter 10. To illustrate the technique, two phrases of the chorale tune, "Keinen hat Gott verlassen" ("God Has Forsaken No One"), are harmonized to show each step of the process.

Figure 15.11

"Keinen hat Gott verlassen" ("God Has Forsaken No One"), mm. 1–4.

The key signature indicates either the key of G major or E minor. The closely related keys are D major, C major, B minor, and A minor.

The end of the first phrase would support cadences in G major or C major. Three possibilities for the first cadence are shown in Figure 15.12.

Figure 15.12

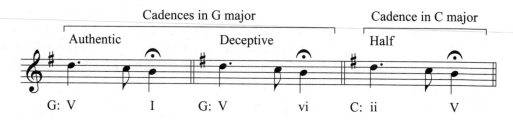

Figure 15.13 shows these same cadences in four-part harmony.

Figure 15.13

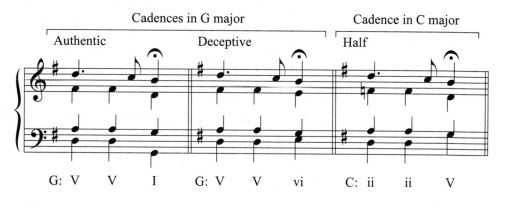

Five possibilities for the second cadence are shown in Figure 15.14.

Figure 15.14

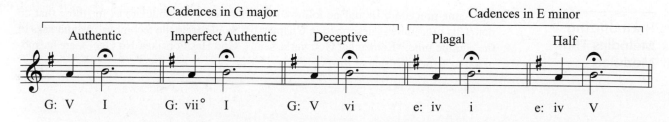

Figure 15.15 shows these same cadences in four-part harmony.

Figure 15.15

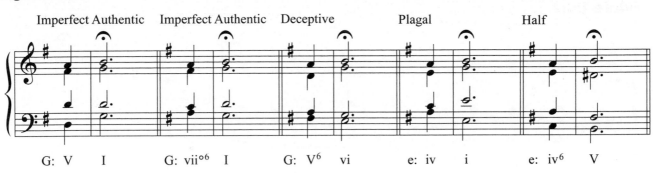

We will choose the key of G major and the key of E minor to illustrate the process of modulation. The two phrases are shown in Figure 15.16 with possible harmonizations. We have indicated circle progressions by drawing a line between chords.

Figure 15.16

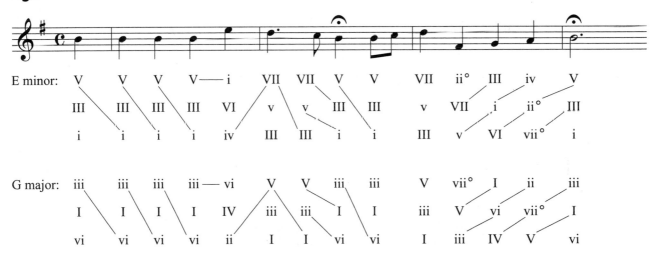

Play the chorale melody on the piano and accompany it (using block chords) with several combinations from the preceding possibilities. When a selection has been made, follow the procedures described in Chapter 10, fashioning a compatible bass line, adding the remaining voices, and finally inserting appropriate nonharmonic tones. The following suggestions will assist you in making good choices:

1. Remember that the descending P5 progression involving dominant and tonic harmony is important in establishing a key. Be sure you include such progressions to clarify the key, particularly after a modulation.
2. For the present, it is desirable to include at least one common chord just before the new key is to be initiated.
3. Start your selection of chords with the cadence and work backward to establish a smooth set of progressions.

From the previous information, two students made harmonizations. The first (Figure 15.17) conceives the entire melody in G major, whereas the second (Figure 15.18) begins in E minor, modulates to G major, then returns to E minor.

Figure 15.17

Figure 15.18

Finally, the harmonization of these two phrases by J. S. Bach is presented in Figure 15.19 for comparison.

Figure 15.19

Bach: "Keinen hat Gott verlassen" ("God Has Forsaken No One"), BWV 369, mm. 1–4.

Assignment 15.1   Name the five closely related keys to the given key.

1. (Ex.)	G major	(G)	C	D	e	a	b
2.	F minor	(f)	___	___	___	___	___
3.	E♭ major	(E♭)	___	___	___	___	___
4.	E minor	(e)	___	___	___	___	___
5.	A major	(A)	___	___	___	___	___
6.	C♯ minor	(c♯)	___	___	___	___	___
7.	G♭ major	(G♭)	___	___	___	___	___
8.	B♭ minor	(b♭)	___	___	___	___	___
9.	B major	(B)	___	___	___	___	___
10.	D♯ minor	(d♯)	___	___	___	___	___

Assignment 15.2   The following phrases in four-part harmony illustrate two types of modulation.

1. Analyze each chord.
2. Since each set modulates, indicate the following:
   a. The type of modulation
      (1) Common chord
      (2) Chromatic
   b. If the modulation is of the common-chord type, circle the common (pivot) chord, and be sure to analyze it in both keys.
   c. If it is a chromatic modulation, indicate the new key and continue analyzing in the new key.
3. Circle and label each nonharmonic tone.

For common chord modulations:

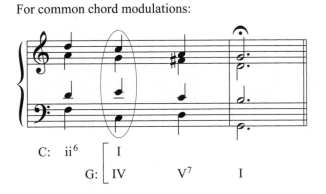

For chromatic modulations:

4. How to spot a modulation:

    a. By all means, play the music you are analyzing. Sometimes this is sufficient in itself to recognize modulation.

    b. Look for accidentals or pitches that are not part of the established key.

    c. Look for a cadence in a new key. If it can be analyzed as V–I, I–V, IV–V, or some other recognized cadence in a different key, then trace back to the point of modulation and analyze in the new key from that point on.

    d. After you have found enough evidence to support a new key, look back to the first occurrence of a nondiatonic note (one that is not a scale tone in the established key) and determine whether the chord preceding it could be analyzed in both keys (the established and the new key). If so, you have discovered a common-chord modulation.

    e. If the first nondiatonic note is taken chromatically (has the same letter name but different pitch in the preceding chord), the modulation is chromatic.

1. Modulation type? _____ 2. Modulation type? _____

3. Modulation type? _____ 4. Modulation type? _____

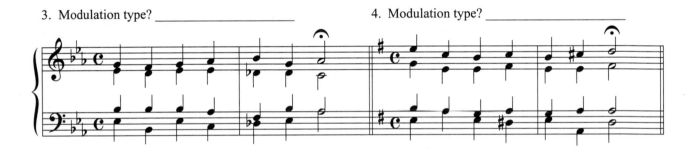

5. Modulation type? _____ 6. Modulation type? _____

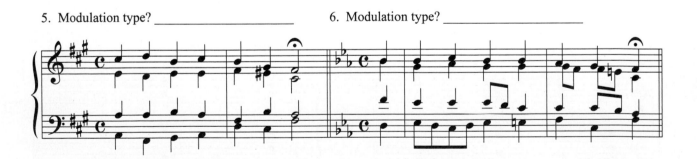

Assignment 15.3   Each exercise is a chorale phrase as harmonized by Bach. Before completing the harmonizations on paper, play them on the piano, adding the alto and tenor voices. Be sure to read the figured-bass symbols accurately.

   After you have completed the keyboard portion of the assignment, write out the harmonizations on paper:

1. Add the alto and tenor using voice leading that conforms to recommended practice.

2. Analyze each chord and indicate the point of modulation with the new key name.

1. "Freu' dich sehr, o meine Seele" ("Rejoice Greatly, O My Soul"), BWV 194, mm. 1–2 (modified).

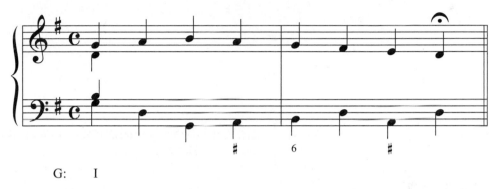

G: I

2. "Wenn mein Stündlein vorhanden ist" ("When My Brief Hour Is Come"), BWV 429, mm. 1–2 (modified).

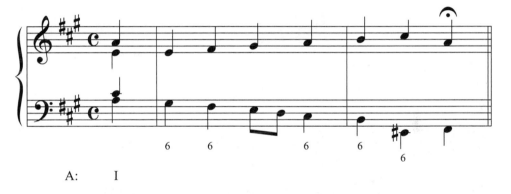

A: I

3. "Keinen hat Gott verlassen" ("God Hath Forsaken No One"), BWV 369, mm. 1–2 (modified).

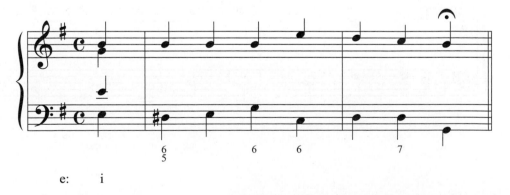

e: i

CHAPTER 15   Modulation   **327**

4. "Wer weiss, wie nahe mir mein Ende" ("Who Knows How Near My End May Be"),
BWV 166, mm. 6–7 (modified).

g: V

5. "Wie schön leuchtet der Morgenstern" ("How Brightly Shines the Morning Star"),
BWV 36, mm. 1–2 (modified).

D: I

6. "Des heil'gen Geistes reiche Gnad'" ("The Holy Ghost's Abundant Mercy"), BWV 295, mm. 1–4 (modified).

d: i

Assignment 15.4

Following are three short excerpts from music literature.

1. Analyze each chord and indicate the modulations as described in this chapter.
2. See assignment 15.2 for suggestions about analyzing modulations.
3. Have a class member play each excerpt.
4. Discuss in class the harmonic rhythm and the relationship of the phrases.

1. Schubert: Variations on a Theme by Hüttenbrenner, D. 576, Variation XIII, mm. 1–8. **CD Track 85**

A:

2. Schubert: Impromptu, op. 90, no. 1, D. 899, mm. 14–17. **CD Track 86**

E♭:

3. Schubert: Écossaise no. 8, D. 977, mm. 1–8. **CD Track 87**

d:

CHAPTER 15   Modulation

Assignment 15.5

Following is a complete chorale harmonization by Bach. It contains modulations.

1. A fermata marks the end of each phrase.
2. Sing the chorale in class and have a class member direct the performance.
3. Make a complete harmonic analysis of the chorale, circling and labeling each nonharmonic tone.
4. Discuss the key relationships present. Are all keys closely related? Closely related keys are: C, D, a, e, b. We found 20 circle progressions. How many did you find?

Bach: "Nun preiset alle Gottes Barmherzigkeit" ("Now Let Us All Praise God's Mercy"), BWV 391. CD Track 88

Assignment 15.6

Following are five excerpts from Protestant chorale melodies that were harmonized by J. S. Bach, as well as other composers of the baroque period.

1. Using the procedures outlined in this chapter, prepare two harmonizations for each of the excerpts. Make one modulation in each melody.

2. Complete these harmonizations in four voices (soprano given, add alto, tenor, and bass).

3. Select as your primary harmonic rhythm one chord per beat (quarter note).

4. Play the harmonizations in class. Select the most appropriate setting.

5. Arrange a few of the harmonizations for a quartet of instruments that are played by class members. Perform these in class.

1. "Gelobet seist du, Jesu Christ" ("Praise Be to You, Jesus Christ"), mm. 1–2.

2. "Wo Gott der Herr nicht bei uns hält" ("Had God the Lord Not Remained with Us"), mm. 1–2 (modified).

3. "Mit Fried' und Freud' ich fahr' dahin" ("With Peace and Joy I Journey Thither"), mm. 1–2.

4. "Beschränkt, ihr Weisen dieser Welt" ("Confine, Ye Wise Men of This World"), mm. 29–32 (modified).

5. "Brunnquell aller Güter" ("Fountainhead of All Virtues"), mm. 1–4 (modified).

Assignment 15.7   Following are four excerpts from instrumental music of the classical period.

1. Using the procedures outlined in this chapter, prepare two harmonizations for each of the exercises.

2. These may be completed in any texture and for any media you want. If you are a pianist, write for the piano idiom. If you are an instrumentalist, use the given melody as your solo part and write a piano (or instrumental) accompaniment.

3. Play the melody several times and select the harmonic rhythm that seems most appropriate.

4. Play your completed work in class.

5. Be sure to add all interpretation marks, phrasings, tempo indications, etc., to your harmonization.

Assignment 15.8   Each exercise is a figured-bass voice.

1. On a separate sheet of staff paper, write out each figured bass, leaving a line above for the soprano and alto.

2. Be sure to analyze the figured bass so you know what notes are possible in the soprano.

3. Complete the soprano first, then the two inner voices (alto and tenor).

4. Be sure to observe acceptable voice-leading practices described in previous chapters.

5. To help in writing the soprano melody:

   a. Sketch in the entire soprano melody, making sure that the pitches you select are part of the supporting harmony.

   b. Write one soprano note for each bass note. These are to be chorale melodies.

   c. As you write, continually check to see whether your melody has a recognizable contour—usually with two or three definite directions. If you find you have four or more, you should make some revisions.

   d. Look at the soprano melodies in assignment 15.6. Use them as models.

1. Begins in F major:

2. Begins in E minor:

3. Begins in E minor:

4. Begins in G major:

5. Begins in F major:

Assignment 15.9

Following is a complete chorale melody harmonization by Bach.

1. Analyze each chord below the staff.
2. Discuss modulations and the form of this composition.
3. Divide the class into four sections (soprano, alto, tenor, and bass) and sing the chorale in class. Ask a class member to conduct the performance.

Bach: "Jesu, du mein liebstes Leben" ("Jesus, Thou My Dearest Life"), BWV 356. **CD Track 89**

Assignment 15.10

Following is a complete composition by Bach.

1. This work is divided into two major sections by the repeats. In each section, identify the number of phrases and determine the key at the end of each phrase.

2. If the key at the end of the phrase is different from the beginning, identify the point of modulation.

3. Make a harmonic analysis of the work that accounts for each modulation. What modulation type predominates in this work?

4. If your instructor requests a macro analysis, include letter symbols and slurs. It will be helpful to complete the letter symbols before the Roman numeral analysis.

Bach: Gavotte from French Suite no. 5, BWV 816. CD Track 90

G:

Assignment 15.11

The following waltz melody is typical of those written during the romantic period.

1. Determine the harmonic rhythm.

2. Make a list of possible harmonizations for the melody.

3. Fashion an accompaniment that accentuates the waltz characteristics of the melody.

4. Make an arrangement for piano and/or any group of instruments (or voices) that are played by members of the class.

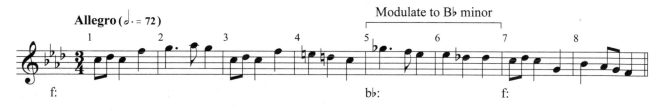

Assignment 15.12

1. Compose a short composition in the following form:

Measures	Key	Phrase Relationship	Cadence
1–4	A major	a	Half in A major
5–8	Modulate to E major	a′	Authentic in E major
9–12	Modulate to A major	b	Half in A major
13–16	A major	a″	Authentic in A major

2. Employ a homophonic style (one melody with accompaniment).

3. Use a number of nondominant seventh chords.

4. Write for any instrument (or voice) or combination that interests you.

5. Perform the compositions in class.

CHAPTER 16

Two-Part (Binary) Form

TOPICS	Formal Divisions	Simple Forms	Compound Forms
	Closed Formal Divisions	Two-Part Form	Bar Form
	Open Formal Divisions	Binary Form	

IMPORTANT CONCEPTS

Form in music is the result of the interaction of all the structural elements. You are already familiar with the smaller elements of form—phrases and periods—but in this chapter we will begin to consider the organization of complete compositions.

Formal Divisions

A piece of music can generally be divided into two or more major sections, and the boundaries between these sections are called *formal divisions.* Formal divisions are the result of strong harmonic and melodic cadences and rhythmic factors, such as rests, fermatas, longer note values and so on. The formal divisions define the sections of a composition, and these sections are labeled with capital letters: A, B, C, etc. If a section of music is repeated, the same letter is used: A, A, B, B, etc., and if it contains similar material, this is designated by adding primes to the previous letter: A, A′, A″, etc.

Open versus Closed Formal Divisions

A section is designated as *closed* if it cadences on the tonic of the composition (the original tonic) and *open* if it cadences elsewhere. Open formal divisions commonly conclude with half cadences, or they may modulate to related keys, which requires a following section or sections to complete the tonal direction.

Simple versus Compound Forms

Smaller compositions are generally in one of the two *simple forms:* two-part (binary) form or three-part (ternary) form. Larger works are generally in *compound form* in which the sections may themselves be complete binary or ternary forms. In volume 1, we will concentrate on the simple forms, reserving our treatment of compound forms for volume 2.

Two-Part Form

Two-part form, also called *binary form,* consists of two main sections. In many binary forms the first section is open, concluding with a half cadence or moving to a related key, whereas the second section, which is often longer than the first section, concludes with a perfect authentic cadence on the tonic. The antecedent–consequent period is a microcosm of the typical binary form.

Figure 16.1

Similar material in both parts:

Part I: A

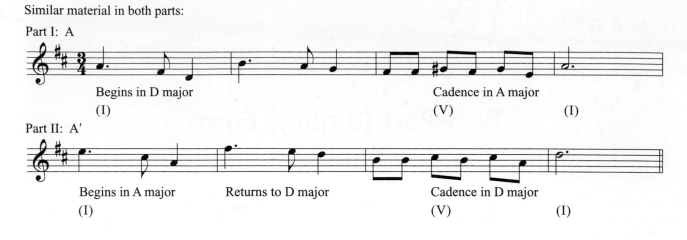

Begins in D major
(I)

Cadence in A major
(V)

(I)

Part II: A′

Begins in A major
(I)

Returns to D major

Cadence in D major
(V)

(I)

The two sections of a binary form are often repeated, as Figure 16.2 illustrates. Notice the open form of this example.

Figure 16.2

Bach: Menuet II from Partita no. 1 in B-flat Major, BWV 825.

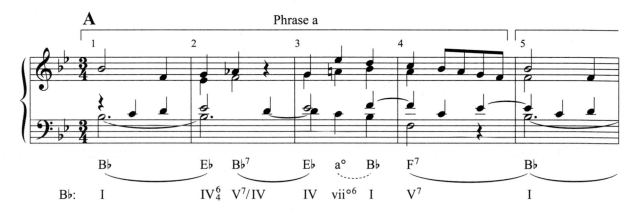

B♭   E♭ B♭⁷   E♭ a° B♭ F⁷   B♭

B♭:   I   IV⁶₄ V⁷/IV   IV vii°⁶ I V⁷   I

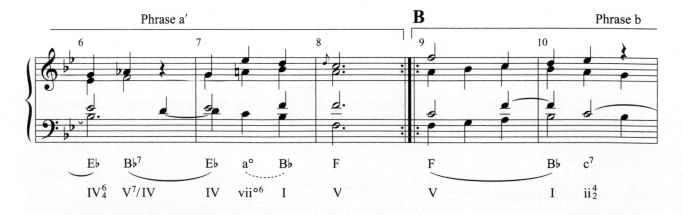

E♭ B♭⁷   E♭ a° B♭ F   F   B♭ c⁷

IV⁶₄ V⁷/IV   IV vii°⁶ I V   V   I ii⁴₂

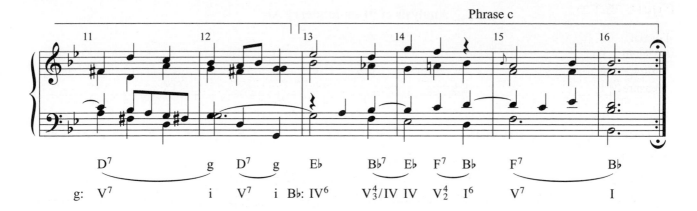

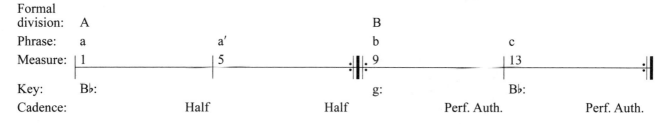

Analysis of Menuet II from Partita no. 1 by Bach

Formal division:	A			B	
Phrase:	a	a′		b	c
Measure:	1	5	9		13	
Key:	B♭:		g:		B♭:	
Cadence:		Half	Half	Perf. Auth.		Perf. Auth.

Figure 16.3 is an example of a binary form without repeated sections in which both sections are closed. The material of the second section is quite contrasting with the material of the first section.

Figure 16.3

Folk Song: "Londonderry Air."

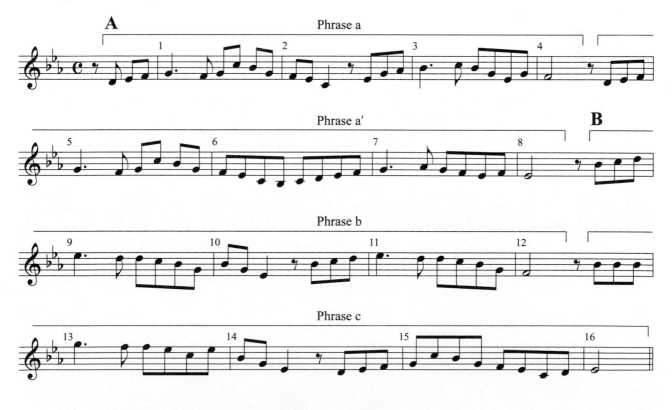

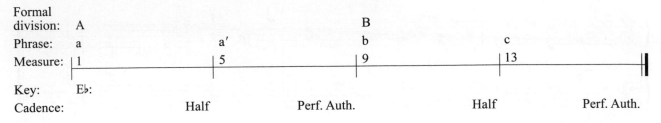

Analysis of "Londonderry Air"

Formal division:	A		B		
Phrase:	a	a'	b	c	
Measure:	1	5	9	13	
Key:	E♭:				
Cadence:		Half	Perf. Auth.	Half	Perf. Auth.

A type of two-part form very popular in the baroque and classical periods consists of motivic material common to both the A and the B sections. Figure 16.4 typifies this treatment in the classical period. It is essentially in homophonic texture (a single melody line with supporting accompaniment).

Figure 16.4

Haydn: Sonata in A Major, Hob. XVI:5, II: Menuet.

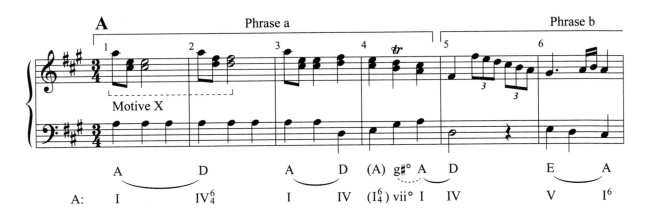

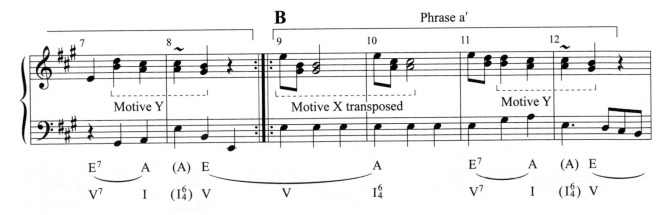

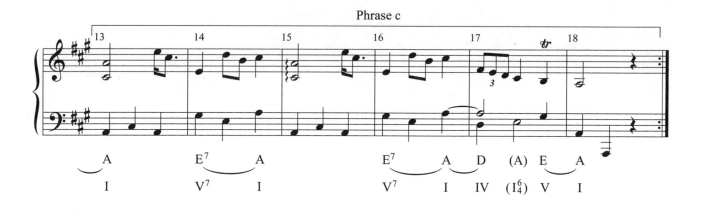

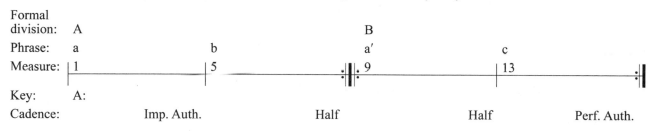

Analysis of Sonata in A Major Menuet by Haydn

Formal division:	A			B		
Phrase:	a		b	a′		c
Measure:	1		5	9		13
Key:	A:					
Cadence:		Imp. Auth.		Half		Half	Perf. Auth.

Note:

1. Phrase **a′** is related to phrase **a** in that it contains the same motive transposed.
2. The only perfect authentic cadence occurs at the end of the composition.
3. There is an absence of sequences.

The majority of baroque dance movements are in binary form, and Figure 16.5 is a good illustration of the thematic unity so characteristic of the genre.

Figure 16.5

Bach: Gavotte I from English Suite no. 3 in G Minor, BWV 808.

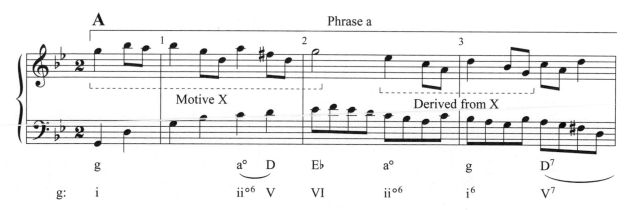

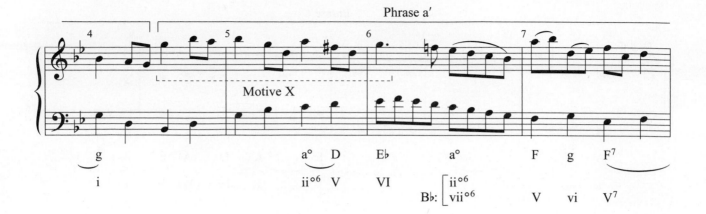

Phrase a'

Motive X

g a° D E♭ a°   F g F⁷

i ii°⁶ V VI   F g V⁷

B♭: ⎡ ii°⁶
     ⎣ vii°⁶   V vi V⁷

B

Phrase b

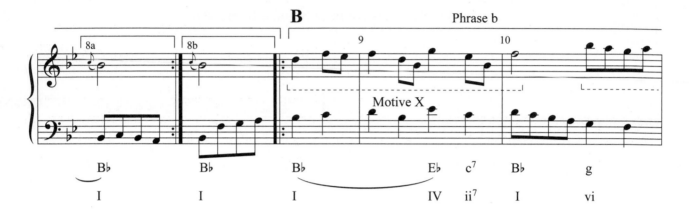

Motive X

B♭   B♭   B♭   E♭ c⁷ B♭ g

I   I   I   IV ii⁷ I vi

Phrase b (continued)

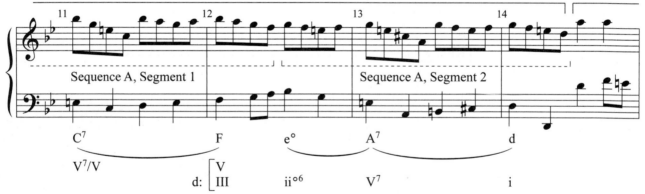

Sequence A, Segment 1   Sequence A, Segment 2

C⁷   F e° A⁷   d

V⁷/V

d: ⎡ V
   ⎣ III   ii°⁶ V⁷   i

Phrase b'

Secondary Sequence

A d g   A⁷ d g⁷

V i iv   V⁷ i iv⁷

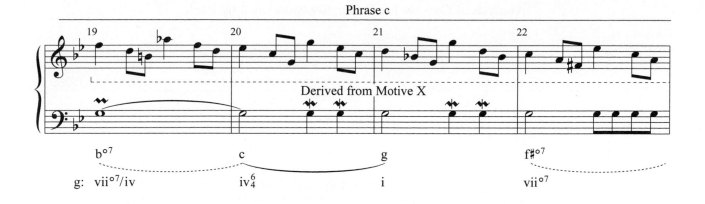

Phrase c

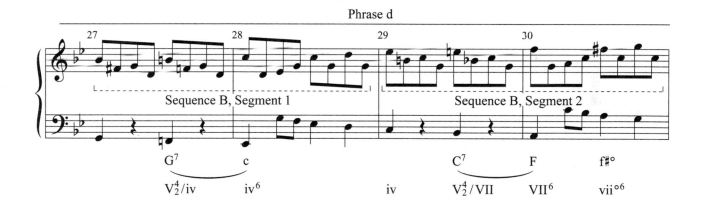

Phrase c (continued)

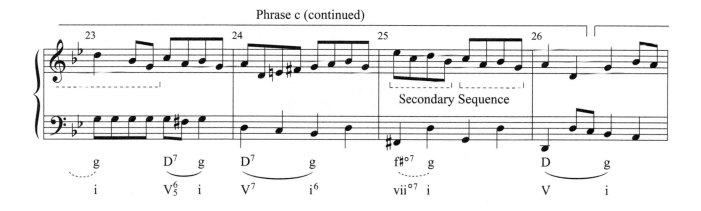

Phrase d

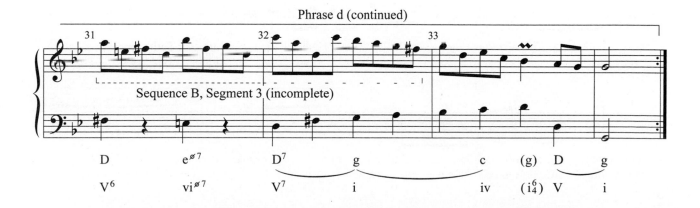

Phrase d (continued)

Analysis of Gavotte I from English Suite no. 3 by Bach

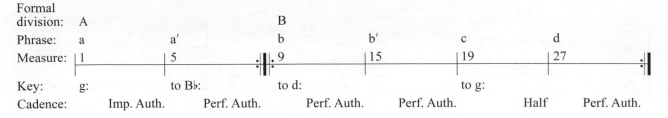

Formal division:	A			B				
Phrase:	a	a′		b	b′		c	d
Measure:	1	5	9		15	19		27
Key:	g:	to B♭:	to d:			to g:		
Cadence:	Imp. Auth.	Perf. Auth.	Perf. Auth.		Perf. Auth.		Half	Perf. Auth.

Notice that the first section of the Bach Gavotte is in the usual open form. Either motive X or derivatives of it appear frequently in part A and in part B. This is a compelling force for unification of the two parts and ensures organization in the composition. The motive appears only once in the lower voice (in measures 14–16). The lower voice, for the most part, simply provides supporting counterpoint for the upper voice, which contributes most of the melodic interest.

Two important sequences occur, one in measures 10–14 (sequence A) and the other in measures 27–33 (sequence B). Secondary sequences (sequences of less structural significance) are also found in measures 17 and 25.

The cadences in measures 4 and 26 are considered weak because the melodic line has only a brief pause at those moments and immediately continues to the next phrase.

History

The forerunner of binary two-part form was a structure from the medieval period known as *bar form*. This is a name given to a song form used by the Minnesingers (aristocratic poet–musicians from the twelfth to fourteenth centuries) and Meistersingers (middle-class poet–musicians from the fourteenth to sixteenth centuries). Bar form consists of an A part (called *Stollen*) that is repeated and a B part (*Abgesang*) that is not repeated. As bar form developed, the B part began to contain either a section or all of the A part and thus has a rounded binary character (see Chapter 17). Figure 16.6 is an example of the *canzo*, which resembles the bar form. The composition shown in Figure 16.6 was written toward the end of the twelfth century and may have been performed as an unaccompanied solo song.

Figure 16.6

Ventadorn: "Be m'an perdut" ("Indeed All My Friends"), mm. 1–13.

Part A (*Stollen*)

Be m'an___ per - dut lay en - ves Ven - ta - dorn___ Tuih mei___ a -
Non ay___ ra - zon que ieu___ ia___ mays lai___ torn___ Tant es ___ vas

mic pos ma___ do - na_____ no m'a - ma.
mi bra - va___ e___ nos_____ re - cla - ma.___

Part B (*Abgesang*)

Tot iorn me fai sem - blan____ i - rat____ e morn Car en s'a - mor mi de - lieg

Repetition of the last section of Part A

em so - jorn E de____ res als nos ran - cu - ra____ nis cla - ma.

The bar form continued into the Renaissance, although its use was not extensive. The two-part concept found its way into a variety of compositions of this period, among them the German part song and the German lied.

It was during the baroque period that the use of two-part form became most extensive. Suite movements of extended length (allemande, courante, sarabande, gigue, minuet, bourree, gavotte, etc.) were written using this construction, and only the basic elements of the older bar form remained.

The classical period, especially the early part, saw considerable use of the two-part form. From the concise shape of the baroque suite movements, the classical composers began to evolve embryonic development sections at the beginning of the second section, the theme (or themes) from the first section were repeated at the end of the second section in the original key, and the result was the sonata form (see volume 2).

The use of the binary form continued through the romantic period, although in greatly diminished numbers. Much greater freedom was taken in adapting the construction to nineteenth-century musical thought. Examples of binary form can be found in the works of Schubert, Berlioz, Mendelssohn, Bizet, and Schumann.

Although examples of binary form can be found during the post-romantic and impressionistic period, it was not an essential element in this era. This is also true of later style periods. Although works by Bartók, Villa-Lobos, Britten, and other composers, employ two-part form, the binary form is not a common practice of contemporary composers. Two-part forms are seldom found in jazz and popular music.

Assignment 16.1

The following works are compositions for analysis.

1. Become familiar with the compositions by playing them on the piano or listening to recordings.
2. Make a complete harmonic analysis of each composition.
3. On a separate sheet, address each of the following:
   a. Phrase relationships.
   b. Formal outline.
   c. Key schemes.
   d. Compositional devices such as imitation, sequence, phrase extension, and so on.
   e. Harmonic vocabulary such as circle progressions, noncircle progressions, secondary dominants, leading-tone chords, and so on.
   f. Cadence types.
   g. Open or closed formal construction.

1. Handel: Air from Suite in E Major, G. 148, mm. 1–7. **CD Track 91**

2. C. P .E. Bach: March from the *Notebook for Anna Magdalena Bach*, BWV Anh. 122. CD Track 92

3. Scarlatti: Sonata in G Major, K. 431, L. 83. CD Track 93

4. Bach: Menuet from French Suite no. 3, BWV 814. CD Track 94

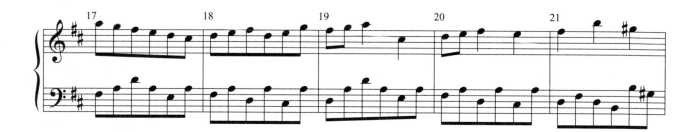

PART B   The Structural Elements of Music

Assignment 16.2

Following is the first section (A) of a two-part baroque-style suite movement.

1. Compose the second section (B).

2. Carefully analyze the first section.

3. Begin the B section in the same key as the final cadence of the A section.

4. Adapt some material from A for use in B.

5. B may be somewhat longer than A.

6. End B in the same key as the first phrase of A.

7. When the composition is completed, arrange it as an oboe solo with accompaniment. If the class has no student of oboe, arrange the solo for another appropriate instrument.

8. Have each student play his or her completed composition while the others provide an oral analysis.

CD Track 95

Assignment 16.3   Write a composition in two-part (binary) form.

1. Begin in E-flat major.

2. Make the A section about 8 to 16 measures long.

3. Let the A section modulate to B-flat major.

4. Start the B section in B-flat major and return to E-flat major.

5. The B section should be somewhat longer than the A section.

6. Have each student play his or her composition in class while the others provide an oral analysis.

Assignment 16.4   Additional examples of binary form are listed at the end of this assignment. Selections from this list may be chosen for listening, either in live performance or in recordings, for aural analysis. Aural recognition of form is an important analytical skill.

Bach: "Goldberg Variations" (the theme and/or any variation)

English Suite no. IV (Sarabande)

English Suite no. Vl (Courante)

English Suite no. III (Courante)

(Nearly all of the dances in the English Suites are in two-part form. The particular movements listed here are somewhat shorter and require less-advanced piano technique than the others in the collection.)

Handel: Suite no. 4 for Klavier (Sarabande)

Suite no. 7 for Klavier (Andante)

Scarlatti: Sonata in E Major, K. 380, L. 23

Chopin: Prelude, op. 28, no. 20

Prelude, op. 28, no. 10

CHAPTER 17

Three-Part (Ternary) Form

TOPICS

Three-Part Form
Ternary Form
Repetitions
Expanded Ternary Form

Auxilliary Members
Rounded Binary Form
Incipient Three-Part Form
Refrain

Bridge
Release
Quaternary Form

IMPORTANT CONCEPTS

This chapter presents one of the most prevalent small homophonic forms in music. Although the two-part examples presented in Chapter 16 were based on similar materials that united the two sections (a characteristic that typifies the form), you will notice that the works in this chapter contain sections with differing, and often contrasting, elements.

Three-Part Form

Three-part form, also called *ternary form,* is a sectional form consisting of three principal parts (A B A) in which each section is a complete musical statement.

Part I	Part II	Part III
A	B	A
Statement	Contrast	Restatement

The A sections of three-part forms are typically closed in formal design (they cadence on the tonic). Three-part forms are found in a wide variety of sizes, from as short as three phrases to movements lasting many minutes. In this chapter, we will concentrate on the smaller examples of this form, but in volume 2, you will discover several larger versions of the ternary design.

An independent, or complete, three-part form at the very lowest level (three-phrase) is somewhat rare. Figure 17.1 is an example of this construction.

Figure 17.1

Schumann: *Kinder-Sonate* no. 1, op. 118, mm. 1–14.

Notice that the first phrase has a cadence on the tonic, which is typical of the closed A section in three-part form.

The three-part form is one of the most prevalent small homophonic forms in the nineteenth century. In the usual pattern, both A sections are at least a period in length. The B as well is usually at least a period in length, although it may sometimes be only a single phrase. Figure 17.2 is a typical example.

Figure 17.2

Chopin: Mazurka in C Major, op. 33, no. 3.

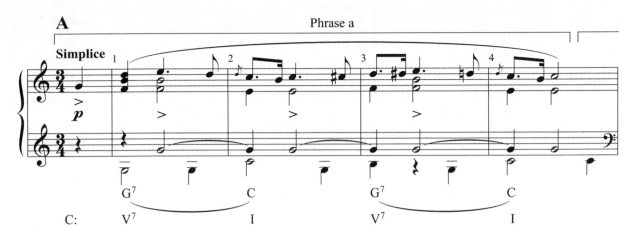

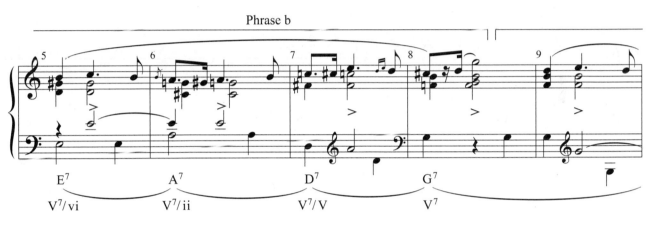

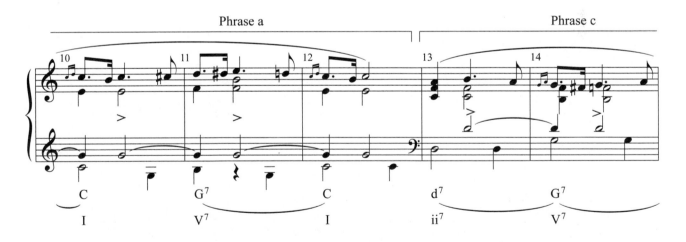

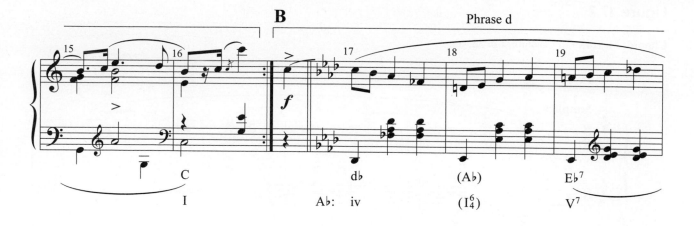

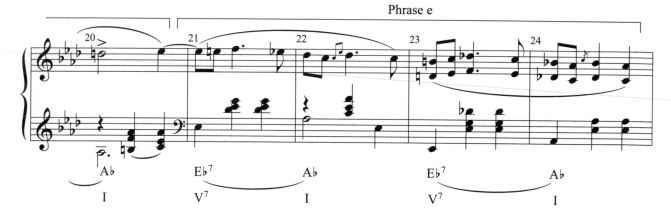

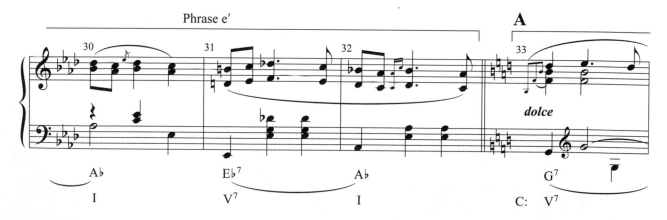

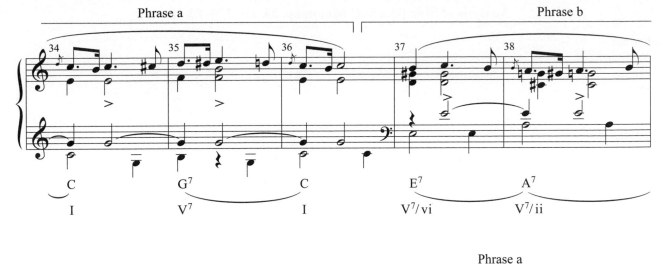

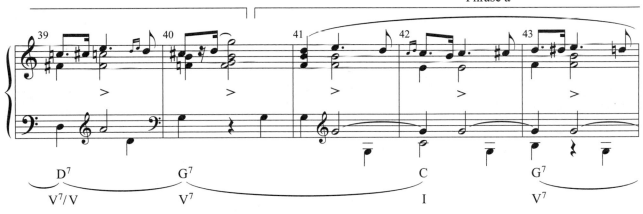

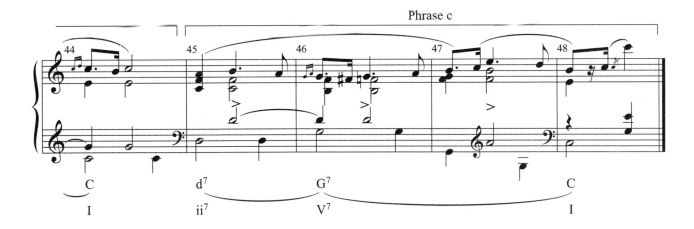

Formal division:	A			
Phrase:	a	b	a	c
Measure:	1	5	9	13
Key:	C:			
Cadence:		Perf. Auth.	Half	Perf. Auth.	Perf. Auth.

Formal division:	B			
Phrase:	d	e	d'	e'
Measure:	17	21	25	29
Key:	A♭:			
Cadence:		Imp. Auth.	Imp. Auth.	Imp. Auth.	Perf. Auth.

Formal division:	A			
Phrase:	a	b	a	c
Measure:	33	37	41	45
Key:	C:			
Cadence:		Perf. Auth.	Half	Perf. Auth.	Perf. Auth.

Figure 17.2 clearly illustrates the function of the B part in this form: to provide contrast with the A part and to create a need to return to the A part to complete the pattern. The degree of contrast between the A and B parts varies considerably from composition to composition. In some examples, the thematic material of B may be derived from that of A, resulting in a slight degree of contrast. In other examples, such as the Chopin Mazurka quoted previously, the B may provide a sharp contrast with A.

Expanded Ternary Form

Repetition

The ternary form may be expanded by the use of *repetitions* of any section. The repeats may be made with double bars and repeat signs, or they may be written out if the composer wants to provide a different setting of the music when repeated. Such compositions are said to be in *expanded ternary form.*

Auxiliary Members

The three-part form may be expanded by the use of *auxiliary members,* such as an introduction to precede the first A, a transition between the sections, or a coda after the final A part that serves to bring the composition to a close.

The following is a list of suggested examples of the expanded three-part form:

Chopin: Mazurka in A Minor, op. 17, no. 4.
Chopin: Waltz in D-flat Major, op. 64, no. 1.
Prokofiev: *Classical Symphony* in D Major, op. 25, III: Gavotte.
Mendelssohn: *Songs Without Words,* op. 19, no. 3; op. 30, no. 2; op. 30, no. 4; op. 38, no. 4; op. 53, no. 1; op. 53, no. 3; op. 53, no. 5.

Rounded Binary Form

Many short compositions exhibit characteristics of both binary and ternary forms. These works are said to be in *rounded binary* or *incipient three-part form.*

The rounded binary form differs from true binary form in that the first section (A) is repeated (sometimes in part) at the end of the second section, as you can see in Figure 17.3. The rounded binary form differs from true ternary form in that the B section is not a complete section in itself, but is connected with the returning A material.

The rounded binary form was an important precursor of sonata form that prevailed during the classical and romantic periods. Sonata form will be discussed in the second volume of this text.

Figure 17.3

Mozart: Sonata in D Major, K. 284, III: Theme, mm. 1–17.

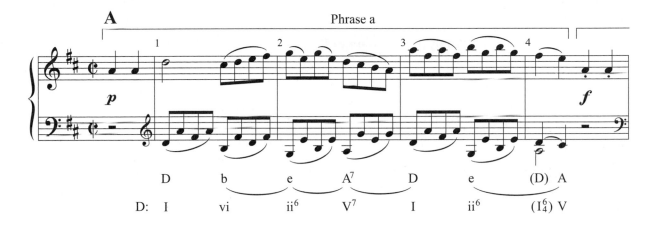

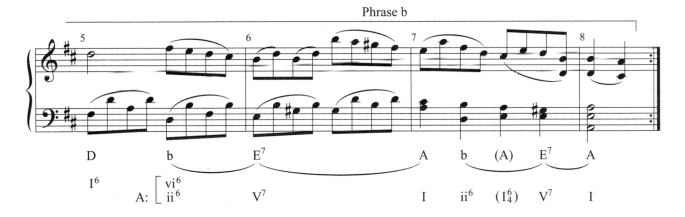

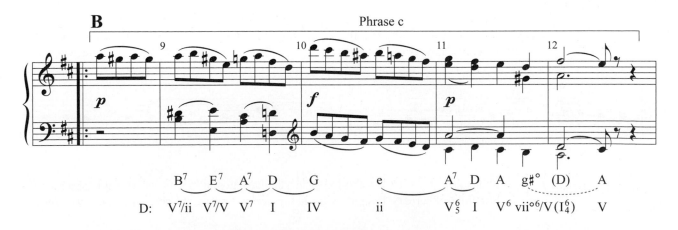

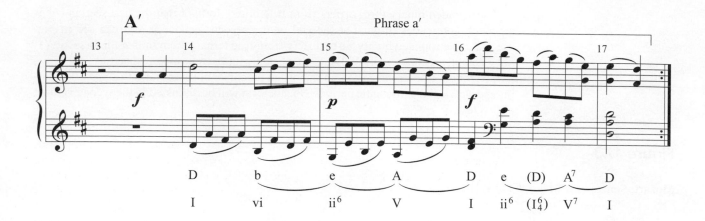

Analysis of Sonata in D Major Theme by Mozart

Formal division:	A			B	A'	
Phrase:	a	b		c	a'	
Measure:	1	5		9	13	
Key:	D:	to A:		D:		
Cadence:		Half	Perf. Auth.		Half	Perf. Auth.

History

The history of ternary design in Western music can be traced back to the liturgical chants of the early Christian church of the medieval period. The principle is present in chant settings of the *Kyrie eleison* (Lord Have Mercy) and the *Agnus Dei* (Lamb of God). It also appears in the structure of medieval secular song.

Figure 17.4

Kyrie eleison (in modern notation).

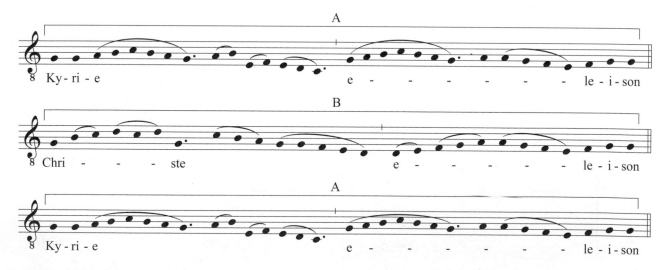

Josquin des Prez (1440?–1521), in "Faulte d'argent" (Lack of Money), observes the principle of ternary design, as do many composers of the sixteenth-century *chansons*

(songs). The arias found in seventeenth-century and early eighteenth-century operas, oratorios, and chamber cantatas utilize the principle in the form of the *da capo* (A B A) aria. In the baroque suite, the ternary design is achieved by alternating two dances, repeating the first after the second—for example, bourrée I, II, I, or minuet I, II, I, resulting in an A B A sequence.

The minuet and trio in the symphonies and chamber music of the classical period are an outgrowth of the baroque dance suite. The minuet and trio, and sonata forms (to be described in volume 2), are the most important examples of ternary design in instrumental music of the classical period. The da capo aria, which was established in the baroque period, continued as the best representative of ternary design in vocal music in the classical period.

The basic ternary design persisted through the nineteenth century in the character pieces of Schubert, Schumann, Mendelssohn, Chopin, Brahms, and other composers. It made its way into the twentieth century, notably in the shorter works of Debussy and Bartók.

Many popular songs, particularly from early in the twentieth century, are in a verse and a chorus (*refrain*) form. Most popular songs from the mid-twentieth century consist only of a chorus. The chorus was generally in ternary form with repeated first phrase (a a b a). Typically, it was 32 measures long, divided into four 8-measure phrases. In the following illustrations, each letter indicates an 8-measure phrase.

Common Popular Chorus Forms

a a b a   a a′ b a   a a b a′   a a′ b a″

The b section of the popular song chorus is often called the *bridge* or *release*. The popular chorus form is often referred to as a *quaternary form,* because it usually consists of four phrases.

The 32-bar chorus in ternary design was more prevalent in the popular music of the first half of the twentieth century, and contemporary examples that follow the form in every detail are relatively rare. Many contemporary songs, however, show some similarity to the form. Figure 17.5 is a good example of a contemporary song that is an expanded 32-bar design with the B and A sections repeated in new keys.

Figure 17.5

Webber and Nunn: "Memory" from *Cats*.

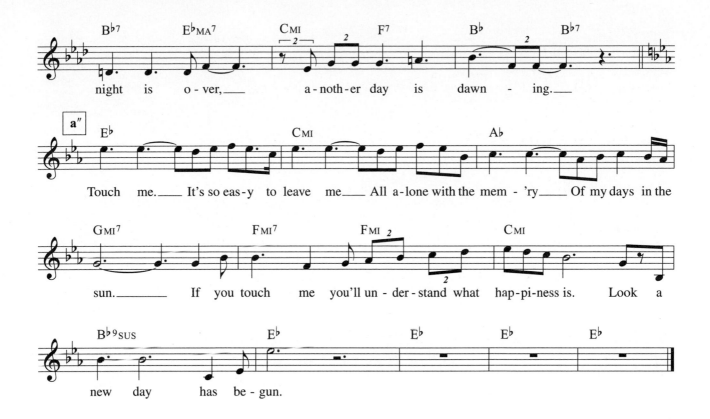

night is o - ver,____ a - noth-er day is dawn - ing.____

a″

Touch me.____ It's so eas-y to leave me____ All a-lone with the mem - 'ry____ Of my days in the

sun._____ If you touch me you'll un - der-stand what hap-pi-ness is. Look a

new day has be - gun.

Assignment 17.1

The following compositions are to be analyzed:

1. Become familiar with the work by listening to a recording or playing it on the piano.
2. Make a complete harmonic analysis.
3. On a separate sheet, address the following:
   a. Phrase relationships.
   b. Formal outline.
   c. Key schemes.
   d. Compositional devices such as imitation, sequence, phrase extension, and so on.
   e. Harmonic vocabulary.
   f. Cadence types.

1. Schumann: "Trällerliedchen" (Humming Song) from *Album for the Young,* op. 68, no. 3. **CD Track 96**

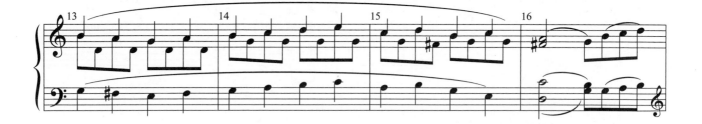

2. Mendelssohn: *Songs Without Words,* op. 30, no. 3. CD Track 97

3. Haydn: Sonata in A Major, Hob. XVI:12, II: Menuet. **CD Track 98**

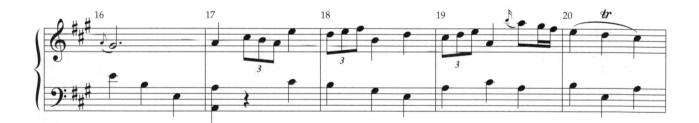

Assignment 17.2

Analyze the menuetto and trio from Mozart's *Eine Kleine Nachtmusik*. The menuetto is a good example of a rounded binary form with partial restatement of the A section. The trio is an example of the complete restatement of the A section within the B section.

1. Become familiar with the work by listening to a recording or playing it on the piano.
2. Make a complete harmonic analysis.
3. On a separate sheet, address the following:
   a. Phrase relationships.
   b. Formal outline.
   c. Key schemes.
   d. Compositional devices such as imitation, sequence, phrase extension, and so on.
   e. Harmonic vocabulary.
   f. Cadence types.
4. Now consider the form of the complete movement (including the *Menuetto da capo* indicated at the end of the trio). What form do you see in the complete movement?

Mozart: *Eine kleine Nachtmusik,* K. 525, III: Menuetto and Trio (modified). CD Track 99

Menuetto da capo

Assignment 17.3   Choose one or more of the following compositions for analysis, as you did with the compositions in assignment 17.1. These compositions are also excellent for aural analysis.

Brahms: Four Piano Pieces, op. 119, nos. 1, 2, 3.
Chopin: Prelude in F-sharp Major, op. 28, no. 13.
Chopin: Mazurka no. 16 in A-flat Major, op. 24, no. 3.
Chopin: Etude in C Minor ("Revolutionary"), op. 10, no. 12.
Schumann: "An Important Event" from *Scenes from Childhood,* op. 15, no. 6.
Schumann: *Papillons,* op. 2, nos. 4 and 5.

Assignment 17.4   Write a composition using the following guidelines:

1. Key of A major
2. $\frac{6}{8}$ meter
3. Form: three-part according to the following outline:

Measures	Key	Cadence	Overall Form
1–4	A major	Half	A
5–8	A major	Authentic	
9–12	E major	Half	B
13–16	E major	Authentic	
17–20	A major	Half	A
21–24	A major	Authentic	

4. Incorporate at least two secondary dominants in the composition.

5. Write for whatever instrument or instruments you want.

6. Write in a homophonic style (single melody with accompaniment).

Summary of Part-Writing Practices

Triads

These refer to special part-writing situations that occur often.

1. **Root Position.** When two roots lie a P5th or P4th apart, keep the common tone and move the remaining two upper voices stepwise to the chord tones of the next triad. If handled correctly, the roots of the chords will be doubled.

2. **Root Position.** When two roots lie a P5th or P4th apart, especially when the soprano voice descends scale degrees $\hat{2}$ to $\hat{1}$, move all three upper voices in similar motion to the nearest chord tone. If handled correctly, the roots of the chords will be doubled.

3. **Root Position.** When roots lie a third apart, keep both common tones and move the remaining voice stepwise. If handled correctly, the roots of the chords will be doubled.

4. **Root Position.** When roots lie a second apart, move the three upper voices in contrary motion to the bass, and make sure that each voice moves to the nearest chord tone of the next chord. If handled correctly, the roots of the two chords will be doubled. An exception is the progression V to vi or VI. In this case, double the third factor of the vi or VI triad. Only two upper voices will move in opposite direction to the bass.

5. **Any Position—Repeated Chords.** Maintain proper doubling and range of voices, and keep the usual order of voices (soprano, alto, tenor, and bass). Otherwise, you are quite free to exchange chord factors among voices. Sometimes a change of position takes place (example: I to I⁶).

6. **First Inversion.** Double any triad factor that facilitates smooth voice leading. Favored notes are the soprano (found often) and bass (slightly less common). Never double the leading tone (seventh scale degree). Observe general recommendations regarding voice ranges, order of voices, and spacing.

7. **First-Inversion (vii°⁶).** Double the third (bass note) or fifth factor. The bass note is preferred. Move all voices with as much stepwise movement as possible. Avoid melodic skips of a tritone.

8. **First-Inversion (ii°⁶).** Double the third (bass note) or the root, which will be in an upper voice. When approaching or leaving the ii°⁶ triad, make voice leading stepwise whenever possible and avoid melodic tritones.

9. **Second Inversion.** No established voice-leading pattern, but double bass note and use only the four types of ⁶₄ chords described in Chapter 9.

**Dominant Seventh
Chords**

10. Resolve the seventh of the V⁷ chord down one scale degree in the same voice. In the few instances where the resolution tone is not present, either keep the seventh as a common tone or move it by the smallest melodic interval possible.

11. All four factors of the V⁷ chord are usually present, but for smoothness of voice leading, the fifth may be omitted and the root doubled.

12. Resolve the seventh factor of the vii^{ø7} or vii^{o7} (and inversions) down one diatonic scale degree.
13. Resolve the root of the vii^{ø7} and vii^{o7} upward to the tonic note.

14. Resolve the seventh factor of nondominant seventh chords one diatonic scale degree down to the third factor of the next chord (in circle progressions). Otherwise, resolve the seventh factor down one step if its resolution is a part of the following chord.

UNSTYLISTIC DEPARTURES

Inviolate

There are no exceptions to these practices under any conditions:

1. Avoid parallel perfect octaves (P8ths), parallel perfect fifths (P5ths), and parallel unisons (P1s).
2. Never double the leading tone of the scale.
3. Do not write pitches outside the range of a particular voice.
4. Avoid the melodic augmented second (A2) and fourth (A4) in all voices.

Occasionally Broken

Observe these practices carefully unless particular situations permit no other alternative:

5. Avoid crossing voices.
6. Spacing between adjacent voices should not exceed an octave in the three upper voices.
7. Do not overlap two adjacent voices more than a whole step.
8. Do not move in the same direction to perfect intervals in the two outer voices (soprano and bass).
9. Unequal fifths, P5ths to d5ths or vice versa, should be used sparingly.
10. The melodic descending d5th appears sometimes in bass voices, but rarely in the soprano. The d4th may be written in isolated situations.
11. The leading tone should progress upward to the tonic when it is in an outer voice (soprano or bass).

Summary of Triad Doubling Practices

Position	Chord Type	Double
Root position	Major and minor triads	Root
First inversion	Major and minor triads	Soprano or Bass*
First inversion	Diminished triads	Bass Note
Second inversion	Major and minor triads	Bass Note

*Never double the bass note of V^6.

Macro Analysis Symbols

Macro analysis is a flexible, elective analytical technique. It may be used by itself or in conjunction with Roman numerals. For the purpose of this textbook, Roman numerals usually accompany the macro analysis. This appendix provides a summary of the analytical technique's symbols.

Macro Analysis Symbol	Illustration	Symbol Meaning	Examples
Capital letter	C	Major triad	G F# Eb
Capital letter with $^+$	C$^+$	Augmented triad	G$^+$ F#$^+$ Eb$^+$
Capital letter with ^{7}	C^7	Major-minor 7th chord	G^7 F#^{7} Eb^7
Capital letter with ^{M7}	C^{M7}	Major-major 7th chord	G^{M7} F#^{M7} Eb^{M7}
Lowercase letter	c	Minor triad	g f# eb
Lowercase letter with $^\circ$	c$^\circ$	Diminished triad	g$^\circ$ f#$^\circ$ eb$^\circ$
Lowercase letter with ^{7}	c^7	Minor-minor 7th chord	g^7 f#^{7} eb^7

Macro Analysis Symbol	Illustration	Symbol Meaning	Examples
Lowercase letter with $^{\circ 7}$	$c^{\circ 7}$	Diminished-diminished 7th chord	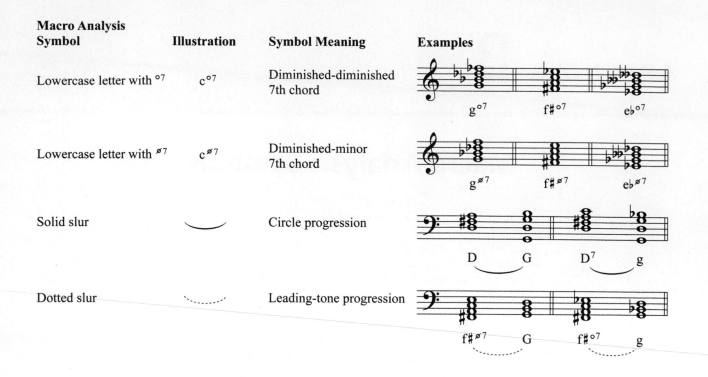
Lowercase letter with $^{\varnothing 7}$	$c^{\varnothing 7}$	Diminished-minor 7th chord	
Solid slur	⌣	Circle progression	
Dotted slur	⌣	Leading-tone progression	

The following phrase is provided to demonstrate the application of macro analysis symbols.

Mozart: Fantasia in C Minor, K. 475, mm. 91–94.

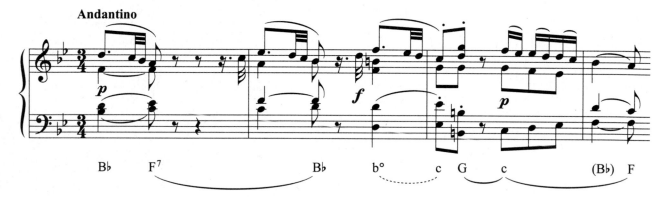

Popular Music Chord Symbols

Following is a comprehensive list of chords found in jazz and popular song accompaniments. All are based on C but may be transposed to any other tone. This chart is a synthesis of the symbols presented in *The New Real Book* series (Sher Music Co.) and represents adaptations of the recommendations made by Carl Brandt and Clinton Roemer in *Standardized Chord Symbol Notation*.

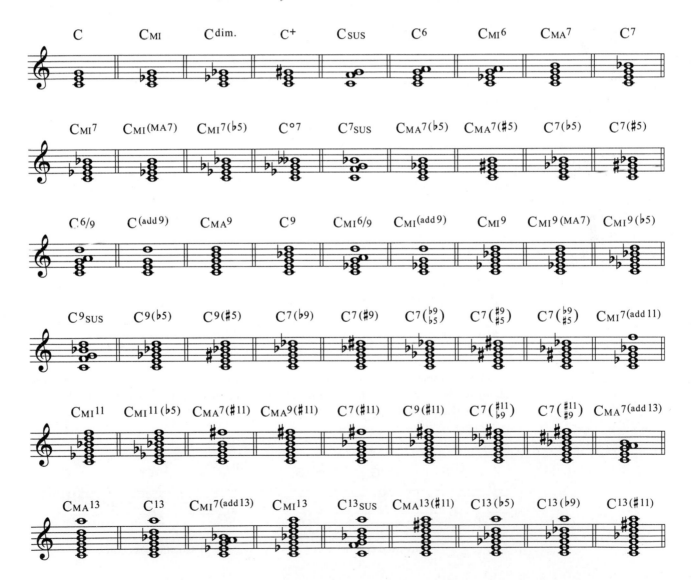

Alternative chord symbols for some common chords:

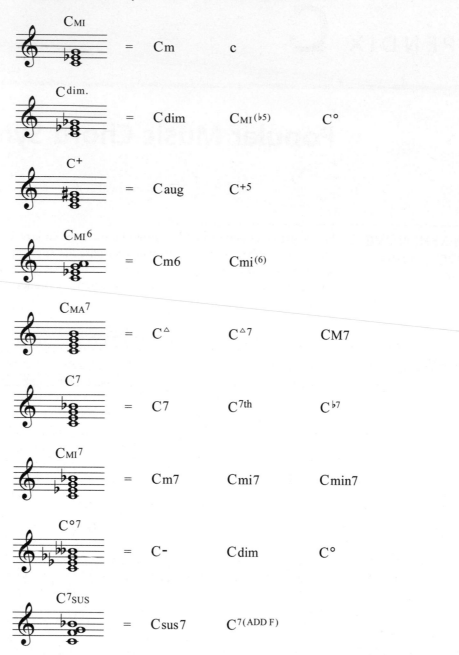

C MI	=	Cm	c
C dim.	=	Cdim	CMI(♭5)	C°
C+	=	Caug	C+5
CMI 6	=	Cm6	Cmi(6)
CMA 7	=	C△	C△7	CM7
C7	=	C7	C7th	C♭7
CMI 7	=	Cm7	Cmi7	Cmin7
C°7	=	C-	Cdim	C°
C7SUS	=	Csus7	C7(ADD F)

Chord inversions are shown by the addition of a diagonal line to the right of the basic chord symbol, followed by the letter denoting the bass note for the inversion. The diagonal line can also be used to indicate a bass note that is dissonant with the chord above.

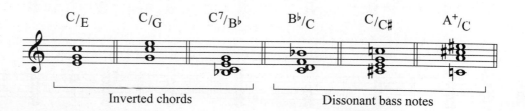

C/E   C/G   C7/B♭   B♭/C   C/C♯   A+/C

Inverted chords   Dissonant bass notes

History

For purposes of style identification, the history of music is divided into style periods. The music within a particular style period is thought to share certain common traits, although there is a great deal of variety in the music within each style period. The following brief summary will introduce the style periods and place them in the context of European and American history.

Medieval Period (500–1450)

The medieval period or "Middle Ages" encompasses the time following the fall of the Roman Empire to the Italian Renaissance. The early part of this period was characterized by invasion after invasion by the Huns, the Visigoths, the Vandals, and the Ostrogoths, who took control of large areas of Europe. Furthermore, Europe was ravaged by the bubonic plague around 542. The Christian church and a few strong landowners, who exchanged protection from the invaders for near slavery on the part of the peasants who worked their land, dominated the society that emerged from these chaotic times. Walled cities and castles were built all over Europe as further protection.

As society became more secure from outside invaders, interest in the arts flourished. The greatest patron of the arts in this time was the church, and most of the medieval music we know is religious in nature. The church preferred vocal music. Instruments were used, for the most part, to supplement the singers, and there was no distinction drawn between vocal and instrumental music. The earliest music notation developed around 900.

The feudal courts also encouraged the arts. Little is known of the secular music of the time, except for the body of music composed by the troubadours of southern France, the trouvères of northern France, and the minnesingers of Germany, Bavaria, and Austria. This music generally deals with the theme of courtly love, the adoration of an unattainable woman from afar.

Renaissance Period (1450–1600)

The term "Renaissance" refers historically to the era of the rebirth of culture and intellectual curiosity that followed the Middle Ages. It began (1450) at the time of Christopher Columbus (1446–1506), and its middle period saw the rise of the Protestant Reformation movement spurred by Martin Luther. It reached its zenith at about the time of Shakespeare (1564–1616). The overriding function of music in the Renaissance period was sacred; that is, to contribute to worship, although secular works did exist and were an important part of the literature.

Vocal music was far more common than instrumental music during the Renaissance, and it was during this period that choral music became fully established. Choruses of the time were usually small groups of perhaps 12 to 15 singers, whereas today a chorus may include several hundred. Through much of history, the choral group has been divided into four parts—the familiar soprano, alto, tenor, and bass—and referred to as a "mixed" chorus. Late Renaissance music often required a fifth part, either a second soprano or a second tenor. Works for 6-, 8-, and even 16-part choruses were not exceptional. Choruses were frequently accompanied by instrumental groups that usually doubled the voice parts. Most often in chapels, however, the groups sang a cappella, or unaccompanied.

Baroque Period (1600–1750)

The baroque was a period of many changes. Baroque composers arranged for the words of sung texts to be more easily heard. They preferred new tonality systems to the modality of the Renaissance. Instrumental music came of age and began to assume more importance than vocal music for the first time. Improvisation of music was a common practice, particularly in the performance of accompaniments (see figured bass in Chapter 4) and in the performance of opera singers, who were expected to improvise embellishments at certain points in their arias.

Rameau, in his *Traite de L'Harmonie* (1722), sought to prove the invertibility of chords and designed an entire system of harmony that recognized the progression of triads and other sonorities. The older systems of tuning (just and meantone) found a new competitor in equal temperament, a system that allowed more freedom for modulation and a method of tuning that would eventually supersede all others in the ensuing century.

The baroque period paralleled the rise of the European colonies in the Western hemisphere. Shakespeare was still alive at the period's beginning, and George Washington (1732–1799) was a young man at its close.

Classical Period (1750–1825)

This period encompassed the lives of many of our best-known composers, whose works are still performed regularly in concert halls throughout the world. Haydn, Mozart, and Beethoven were included in this artistically wealthy period. The balance shifted even more in favor of instrumental music, although operas and sacred and secular vocal music continued to be written. Chamber music, orchestral, and other instrumental works gained the ascendancy. The sonata and the symphony developed during the classical period, and the string quartet took the place of the older trio sonata. The pianoforte (our modern piano), invented about 1710 by Christofori, became a popular household instrument. The improvisatory attitude toward performance died out, except in a few instances like the cadenzas in concertos. In the classical period the orchestral literature grew in size and importance, and the orchestra itself acquired more color and flexibility. Clarinets became permanent fixtures along with flutes, oboes, and bassoons.

The early classical period saw the American Revolution and the formation of the United States.

Romantic Period (1825–1900)

In the United States, the romantic period began with the presidency of Andrew Jackson and ended with that of McKinley. A wrenching civil war tore at the basic fibers of the country, most of the states west of the Mississippi were admitted to the union, railroads spanned the country, and big business became a dominant force in our country for the first time.

Music of this period was dominated by a wider range of emotional expression, more personal and individual styles, and more subjectivity. Musical forms, such as the sonata and symphony, became longer and more involved, but shorter forms, especially piano compositions, were also numerous. Harmony and orchestration expanded and the level of dissonance in music increased.

As against the classic ideals of organization, symmetry, control, and perfection within acknowledged limits, romanticism sought independence, movement, and passion, and pursued the mysterious or exotic because its ideals could not be obtained. Romantic art was characterized by the spirit of longing and seeking after an unattainable goal.

Post-Romantic and Impressionistic Period (1875–1920)

This period in the United States began with the Reconstruction days after the Civil War and ended at about the time of World War I. The Spanish-American War (1898) was fought, and Theodore Roosevelt (1901–1909) and Woodrow Wilson (1913–1921) were presidents.

As a movement among French painters, impressionism sought to eliminate the heroic subjects, the obsession with realistic detail, and the representational quality of romantic painting. In essence, the impressionist painter hoped to capture the impression a subject or object made on him or her rather than to paint its literal representation. So too, in music, composers such as Debussy aspired to renounce the clear phrase structure and goal-oriented harmonic idiom of the past and replace them with a purposeful understatement and ambiguity that was evocative, but very different in effect from the romantic style. The impressionist composers abandoned traditional thematic development and became more concerned with the color or mood of a particular moment.

Contemporary Period (1920–Present)

The period from 1920 to the present has seen the development of great diversity of musical styles and techniques. Much of this development can be traced back to the upheavals caused by World War I (1914–1918) and World War II (1939–1945), which caused disruption of the established cultural institutions in Europe and, at the same time, brought peoples of diverse cultural backgrounds together. The development of recording technology, radio and television transmission, and rapid transportation created a sense of world community in which all manifestations of human culture could freely intermingle. In more recent times, technological advances have made possible the development of electronic and computer instruments for the composition and synthesis of music.

Jazz and Popular Music (1900–Present)

Popular song as now found in the United States evolved near the beginning of the twentieth century. Some notable composers of popular song are George Gershwin, Cole Porter, Richard Rodgers, Irving Berlin, Vernon Duke, and Burt Bacharach. Popular songs by these and other composers were the dominant music with mass appeal until rock music became firmly entrenched in the 1960s.

African American music is among the most notable expressions of religious, folk, and art music in the United States. The blues refers to an African American song of sorrow. The blues, which arose from the gospel and country music of the deep South, has not only been perpetuated as a unique style of its own but has infused and inspired nearly all types of African American music, some twentieth-century classical music, and the popular songs and rock music of the present day. Jazz, the general term for various music of African American creation, has undergone many changes from its beginning and interpretations in its brief history, and its acceptance as a substantive art form has at last been accomplished.

Since the 1960s, rock music, which developed out of the traditions of the blues, jazz, and popular music, has become the dominant form of music with mass appeal.

Expression Marks

Expression marks represent a composer's attempt to convey aspects of interpretation to a prospective performer. The most frequently used expression marks include tempo marks and dynamics symbols. Tempo marks are concerned with setting the pace of a given work, whereas dynamics symbols focus on relative degrees of intensity.

Representative Tempo Marks

presto	very fast (with a sense of haste)
allegro	fast (with a sense of cheerfulness)
allegretto	moderately fast (literally, a "little" or small allegro)
moderato	moderate (neither fast nor slow)
andante	an easy walking pace
lento	slow (with a sense of laziness)
adagio	quite slow (in a quiet, easy manner)
largo	very slow (with a sense of breadth and expansiveness)
grave	very slow (with a sense of solemnity, sternness, and seriousness)

Representative Dynamic Marks

pp	*pianissimo*	very soft
p	*piano*	soft
mp	*mezzo piano*	moderately soft (literally, "half" soft)
mf	*mezzo forte*	moderately loud
f	*forte*	loud (literally, "strong")
ff	*fortissimo*	very loud
sfz	*sforzato*	with a forced accent (literally, "excessive" or "coerced")
sf	*sforzando*	synonymous with *sforzato* for musical purposes

Representative Character and Mood Marks

A third category of expression marks consists of terms and phrases (usually in Italian) intended to suggest the character and/or mood of a given work or smaller sections within a larger work. For example:

accelerando	becoming faster (literally, "accelerating")
animato	animated
con brio	with energy, spirited
calando	becoming softer (with a sense of waning or sinking)
cantabile	in a singing style (literally, "singable")
crescendo	increasing in intensity (literally, "growing")
diminuendo	becoming softer (with a gradual sense of lessening or reducing)
giocoso	in a playful or joking manner
legato	to be performed smoothly (literally, "bound" or "linked" together)
marcato	marked or stressed (emphasizing each note)
morendo	fading, becoming softer (literally, "dying")
rallentando	gradually slowing down (literally, to "relax" or "slacken")

ritardando	gradually slowing down (literally, to "delay" or "defer")
scherzando	joking, whimsical
smorzando	dying away (literally, "becoming extinguished")
sperdendosi	fading away (literally, "disappearing" or "becoming dispersed")
staccato	detached (literally, "separated")
vivace	lively (literally, "full of life, flourishing")

Although some of these musical terms seem to be synonymous, the serious composer is sensitive to subtle shades of meaning and will often prefer one over another. The equally serious and responsible performer must also be sensitive to the composer's choices.

Instrument Ranges, Transpositions, and Foreign Names

In the charts on the following pages, the instruments are of two types.

Nontransposing Instruments

Nontransposing instruments produce a pitch that is the same as the written pitch. In the chart, the nontransposing instruments are those whose actual sound is "as written."

Transposing Instruments

Transposing instruments produce a pitch other than the written pitch. In the following chart, the actual transposition is given for instruments of this type. Most transposing instruments developed from traditions of the past, and to convert these instruments to nontransposing instruments would not be feasible since it would require rewriting a large part of the literature of music and retraining performers on the transposing instruments.

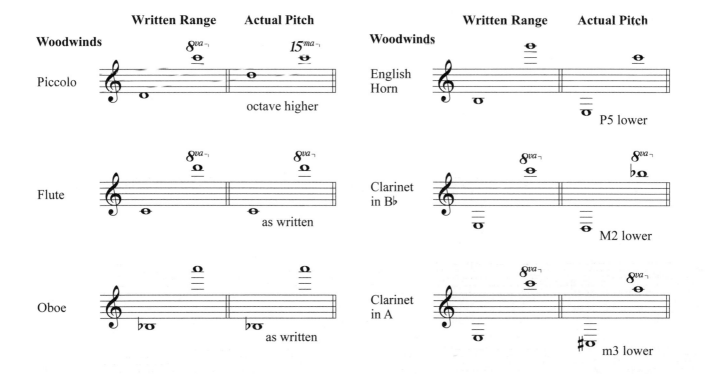

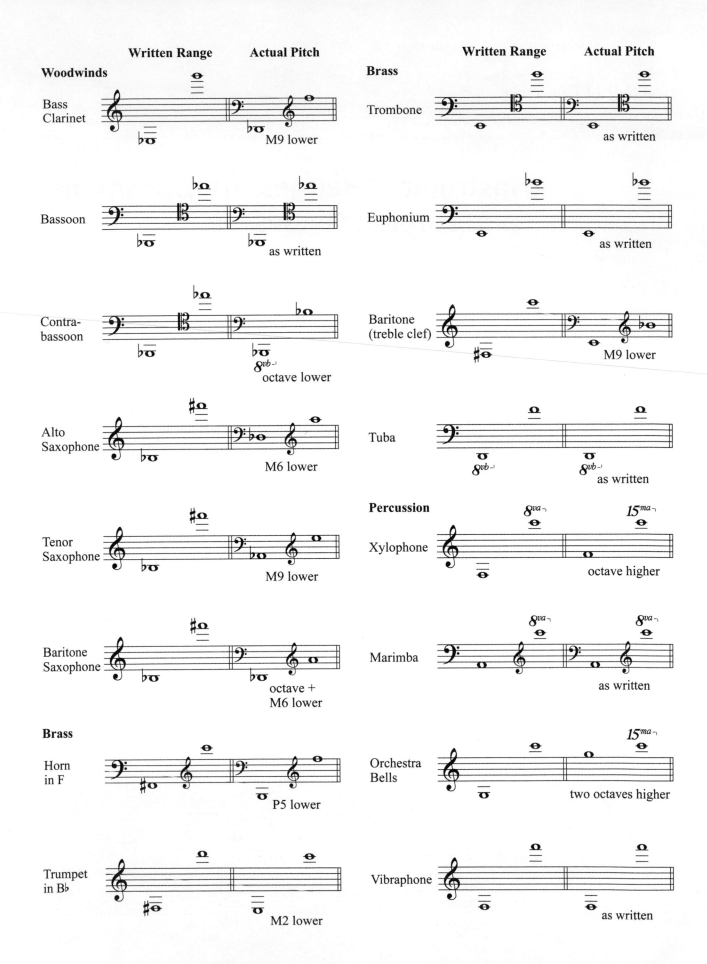

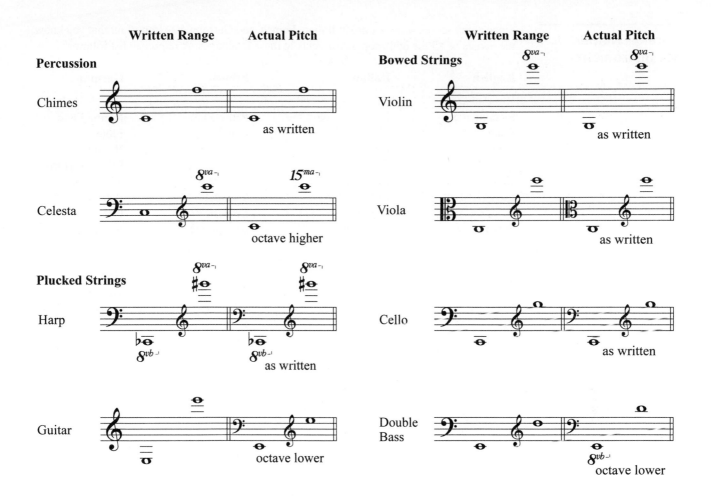

In earlier periods, before the mid-nineteenth century, the trumpet and horn had not yet been fitted with valves and only a few notes (those in the natural harmonic series) were available. For this reason, it was necessary to pitch these instruments in different keys depending on the key of the composition. The changes were accomplished by adding short lengths of tubing (called crooks) to the instrument. An illustration of the common transpositions for the natural horn and trumpet follows. This information becomes important when studying classical period orchestral scores.

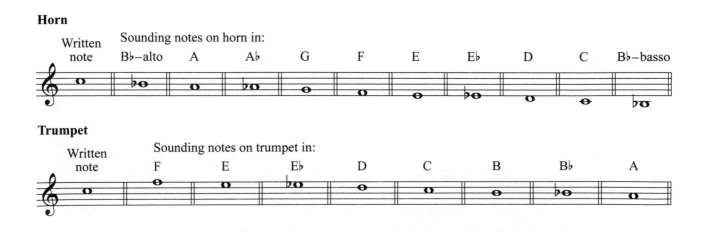

Since many scores we study are in Italian, French, and German, it is important that you know the names of all the common instruments in these languages. A reference list follows.

English	Italian	French	German
Woodwinds:			
Piccolo	Flauto Piccolo	Petite Flute	Kleine Flöte
Flute	Flauto	Flute	Flöte
Oboe	Oboe	Hautbois	Hoboe
English Horn	Corno Inglese	Cor Anglais	Englisch Horn
Clarinet	Clarinetto	Clarinette	Klarinette
Bass Clarinet	Clarinetto Basso	Clarinette Basse	Bassklarinette
Bassoon	Faggoto	Basson	Fagott
Saxophone	Sassofono	Saxophone	Saxophon
Brass:			
Horn	Corno	Cor	Horn
Trumpet	Tromba	Trompette	Trompete
Trombone	Trombone	Trombone	Posaune
Euphonium	Eufonio	Basse à Pistons	Baryton
Tuba	Tuba	Tuba	Basstuba
Percussion:			
Timpani	Timpani	Timbales	Pauken
Xylophone	Silofono (Xilofono)	Xylophonc	Xylophon
Marimba	Marimba	Marimba	Marimba
Orchestra Bells	Campanelli	Jeu de Timbres	Glockenspiel
Vibraphone	Vibrafono	Vibraphone	Vibraphon
Tubular Chimes	Campane	Cloches	Glocken
Celesta	Celesta	Celesta	Celesta
Snare Drum	Tamburo	Tambour	Kleine Trommel
Bass Drum	Gran Cassa	Grosse Caisse	Grosse Trommel
Cymbals	Piatti	Cymbales	Becken
Triangle	Triangolo	Triangle	Triangel
Tam-tam	Tam-tam	Tam-tam	Tam-tam
Bowed Strings:			
Violin	Violino	Violon	Violine
Viola	Viola	Alto	Bratsche
Cello	Violoncello	Violoncelle	Violoncell
Bass	Contrabasso	Contre Basse	Kontrabass
Plucked Strings:			
Harp	Arpa	Harpe	Harfe
Guitar	Chitarra	Guitare	Gitarre

Glossary

Accent   Emphasis on one note. Accents are of three types: dynamic, agogic, and tonic.

Accidental   Any of the symbols such as sharps, flats, and naturals, which are used to raise or lower the pitch of a note.

Adagio   A slow tempo.

Agogic accent   An accent created when one note is longer than surrounding notes.

Allegro   A fast tempo (It., lively or merry).

Andante   A moderately slow tempo (It., walking).

Arpeggiation   Playing the notes of a chord one after another. The horizontalization of a chord.

Bar line   A vertical line drawn across the staff to indicate measures in a musical composition.

Beam   A broad, straight line connecting two or more eighth notes.

Beat   The steady pulse of music. Beats form the basis of the sense of musical time.

Blue tone   Blue tones (or "worried" notes) are tones that are between the diatonic and flatted thirds and sevenths, which characterize the blues scale.

Blues   A type of popular music coming from black American vocal music, which developed in the United States in the early twentieth century, characterized by repeated chord progressions, blues progression, and the blues scale.

Blues progression   Any of the repeated chord progressions that characterize the blues. A typical blues progression consists of 12 measures of tonic, subdominant, and dominant triads with minor sevenths. (See Twelve-bar blues—standard.)

Blues scale   A major scale with a flat third and seventh. It must be remembered that the flat third and seventh were sometimes "worried" notes, thus their pitches did not always correspond to equal-tempered tuning.

Blues scale with added flat fifth   A classic blues scale (flat third and seventh), but with an additional flat fifth. This scale is a somewhat later development in blues. Flat ninths are also included on occasion.

Boogie-woogie   A modern blues style created for instrumental application. Boogie-woogie is characterized by an adaptation of the ground bass principle—a repetitious bass figure that suggests the blues chord progression.

Cadence—authentic   A cadence consisting of the dominant-to-tonic harmonic progression.

Cadence—deceptive   A cadence made up of a harmonic progression from the dominant to a chord other than the tonic. V to VI is the one most often found.

Cadence—half   A cadence consisting of a harmonic progression ending on the dominant. Most half cadences conform with one of the following: IV to V, I to V, or II to V.

Cadence—harmonic   A formula consisting of two chords that bring a phrase, section, or composition to a conclusion.

Cadence—plagal   A cadence made up of a harmonic progression from subdominant to tonic. The Amen cadence (IV to I) is a typical example.

Canon   A melody that can be sung against itself in imitation.

Chorale   Lutheran melodies that are the counterparts of English hymn tunes. These melodies were adapted from (1) well-known popular songs of the period, (2) Catholic hymn tunes, and (3) German hymn melodies predating the Reformation.

Chord   A combination of three or more pitches sounding at the same time.

Chordal texture   A texture in which the musical material is concentrated into chords with relatively little melodic activity.

Chromaticism   The introduction of some pitches of the chromatic scale into music that is basically diatonic in orientation, or music that is based on the chromatic scale instead of the diatonic scales.

Circle of fifths   A clockface arrangement of the 12 pitches in the order of the number of accidentals in the key signature.

Circle progression   A common chord progression that provides a structural basis for most tonal music, consisting of a series of chords with descending fifth root relationships.

Clef—alto 𝄡 A C clef or "movable" clef. The indentation in the signature signifies that middle C is on the middle line of the staff.

Clef—bass 𝄢 Called the F clef because dots are placed on the fourth line of the staff to indicate the F below middle C.

Clef—soprano 𝄡 A C clef or movable clef. The indentation signifies that middle C is on the bottom line of the staff.

Clef—tenor 𝄡 A C or movable clef. The indentation in the sign signifies that middle C is on the fourth line of the staff.

Clef—treble 𝄞 Called the G clef because the curved line of the signature terminates on the second line of the staff to establish G above middle C.

Closely related keys The keys that differ from the tonic key by no more than one accidental. In major: IV, V, ii, iii, and vi; in minor: iv, v, VI, VII, and III.

Common chord In a modulation a common chord is one that is diatonic to both keys (the original and the new).

Common time C Another name for a $\frac{4}{4}$ meter signature. This meter is often indicated with a large capital C as a meter signature.

Compound division The division of the beat into three equal parts.

Compound meter A meter in which the beats have a compound division.

Consonance A combination of sounds producing a feeling of repose, or little desire for resolution. Consonances in tonal music are: P1, P5, P8, M3, m6, m3, M6.

Conventional four-chord formula In popular music, a harmonic progression pattern containing four chords. Most four-chord patterns occupy two measures, for example, I vi⁷ ii⁷ V⁷. Such formulas occur so often in popular songs as to be critical components of style.

Cross relation A conflict, produced by a tone in one voice, followed in another voice by the same tone (same letter name) altered a half step; for example, D-sharp in one voice followed immediately by D-natural in another voice.

Cut time ¢ Another name for the $\frac{2}{2}$ meter signature. This meter is indicated with a large capital C with a vertical line drawn through it. (See Common time.)

Degree One of the notes in a scale. Degrees are usually numbered starting with the tonic (the lowest tone of the scale).

Diatonic Any one of the common scales made of whole steps and half steps in a particular pattern. The white keys on a keyboard instrument form a diatonic scale.

Dissonance A combination of sounds that produce harsh or discordant results, or that increase the desire for resolution. Dissonances in tonal music are: M2, m2, M7, m7, P4, and all diminished and augmented intervals.

Divisive rhythm A rhythmic system in which regularly recurring pulses of equal duration are divided in various ways. Most Western music is characterized by divisive rhythm.

Dominant The fifth scale degree of a diatonic scale.

Double flat ♭♭ A symbol written to the left of a note head, which lowers the pitch by a whole step.

Double period A succession of four phrases in which each of the first three is punctuated by a half cadence and the fourth is terminated by an authentic cadence.

Double sharp 𝄪 A symbol written to the left of a note, which raises the pitch by a whole step.

Duple meter A meter that consists of two beats.

Dynamic accent An accent created when one note is louder than surrounding notes. Often indicated with the accent sign.

Elision A musical situation in which the end of one pattern overlaps or coincides with the beginning of the next pattern.

Embellishing tone Melodic decorations and ornaments to structural and secondary tones.

Enharmonic Two tones having the same pitch but different spelling; for example, F-sharp and G-flat are enharmonic.

Expanded monophonic texture A monophonic texture in which a single melody is doubled at various intervals, often in octaves.

Figured bass A bass melody with numbers and musical symbols beneath it to indicate the chords to be played. Known also as basso continuo and thorough bass. A device of the seventeenth to mid-eighteenth centuries.

Flag ♪ The curved shaded line extending from the end of a stem used to indicate an eighth or shorter note.

Grand staff A combination of the treble and bass clefs that is commonly used to notate keyboard music.

Half step The smallest interval on the standard keyboard. The interval between two adjacent keys (including both black and white keys) is a half step.

Harmonic progression Movement from one chord to the next; a succession of chords or a chord progression.

Harmonic rhythm The frequency of harmonic changes in a composition; the rate of chord change.

Harmonic support The harmonic aspect of the accompaniment in a homophonic texture.

Harmony The study of simultaneously sounding tones or concern with the chordal structure of a musical composition.

Homophonic (texture) A single, clearly defined melody with chordal accompaniment; for example, a popular song, a Mozart minuet, a Johann Strauss waltz, and nearly all music of the nineteenth century.

Imitation The repetition of a melody or melodic group in close succession, but in a different voice; the repetition of a melody at a different pitch level in a polyphonic texture.

Imitation—real An imitation with no modifications except for the usual diatonic adjustment of half and whole steps. The exact transposition of a melody at different pitch levels.

Improvise To extemporize; to play on the spur of the moment. To perform without a prepared text or composed material.

Incipient three-part form See Three-part form—incipient.

Interval The relationship between two tones.

Interval—compound Any interval greater than an octave. Usually compound intervals are expressed as simple equivalents (the octave is subtracted; for example, a major tenth interval—a compound major third.

Inversion (of intervals) Occurs when the lower tone forming the interval becomes the upper tone (or vice versa); for example, a major third becomes a minor sixth when inverted at the octave.

Inversion (of a melody) A procedure for deriving another form of a given melody. An ascending interval in a melody becomes a descending interval (and vice versa) of the same size in the inversion of the melody.

Jazz A popular music influenced by the blues, popular song, and other musical genre. Jazz is characterized by highly sophisticated improvised melodic lines over chord progressions (changes) with a steady beat and considerable syncopation.

Key Music that is based on a major or minor scale is said to be in a key. Keys are identified by their tonic.

Key signature An arrangement of accidentals at the beginning of a staff which indicates the pitches that will be most common in a piece of music. Key signatures are associated with particular major and minor scales.

Keynote See Tonic.

Largetto A tempo slightly faster than largo.

Largo A very slow tempo (It., broad).

Ledger line A small line written above or below the staff to extend its range.

Major scale A diatonic scale with half steps between the third and fourth and the seventh and eighth scale degrees.

Measure One unit of meter, consisting of a number of accented and unaccented beats. A measure is indicated in music notation by bar lines.

Melody An organized succession of pitches.

Meter The system of regularly recurring pulses most often grouped by periodic accents; for example, $\frac{3}{4}$ meter indicates that the beats are grouped by threes with the quarter note representing one beat or pulse.

Meter—asymmetrical Those meters in which the pulse cannot be divided into equal groupings of two, three, or four in the measure; for example, $\frac{7}{4}$, $\frac{5}{4}$, $\frac{11}{8}$.

Meter—compound Meter in which the basic pulse may be subdivided into groups of three; for example, $\frac{6}{8}$, $\frac{9}{8}$, $\frac{12}{8}$.

Meter—simple Meter signatures whose upper numbers are 1, 2, 3, or 4. The basic subdivision of the pulse is in duplets.

Meter signature A symbol placed at the beginning of a composition to indicate the meter of the piece. Meter signatures usually consist of two numbers, the lower of which indicates a note value (i.e., 2, 4, 8) and the upper the number of these notes per measure.

Middle C The C nearest to the middle of the piano keyboard. This note is an important point of reference because it is on the ledger line between the treble and bass staves on the grand staff.

Mode—Aeolian A system of seven tones with the same arrangement as the natural minor key (A to A on the white keys of the piano). Not one of the original church modes; developed with the advent of polyphony.

Mode—Dorian A system of seven tones with the same arrangement as from D to D on the white keys of the piano.

Mode—Ionian   A system of seven tones with the same arrangement as our major key scale (C to C on the white keys of the piano). Not one of the original church modes; developed with the advent of polyphony.

Mode—Locrian   A system of seven tones with the same arrangement as from B to B on the white keys of the piano. Seldom found in music literature because of tritone relationships.

Mode—Lydian   A system of seven tones with the same arrangement as from F to F on the white keys of the piano.

Mode—Mixolydian   A system of seven tones with the same arrangement as from G to G on the white keys of the piano.

Mode—Phrygian   A system of seven tones with the same arrangement as from E to E on the white keys of the piano.

Modes—authentic   Associated with Gregorian chants. The octave ranges of the Dorian, Phrygian, Lydian, and Mixolydian modes coincide with each modal scale, each with the final as first note.

Modes—church (or medieval or ecclesiastical)   Classified at the time of Pope Gregory I (about A.D. 600). The church modes consist of a system of eight scales derived from the codification of liturgical chants. These ecclesiastical scales served as the basis for musical composition until the sixteenth century.

Modes—Plagal   Associated with Gregorian chants. The octave ranges of Hypodorian, Hypophrygian, Hypolydian, and Hypomixolydian modes begin a P4th below and extend to the P5th above the final.

Modified 12-bar jazz blues   Variants of the standard 12-bar blues and 12-bar jazz blues progressions. Most variants incorporate progressions found in the popular songs of the period. In some variants the harmonic rhythm is increased to more than one chord per measure.

Monophonic texture   A musical texture consisting of a single melodic idea, that can be doubled in various ways. (See Expanded monophonic texture.)

Natural   A symbol written to the left of a note head, which cancels a previous sharp or flat.

Natural minor scale   The basic form of a minor scale with half steps between the following scale degrees: 2–3 and 5–6.

Neume   A symbol used in the early notation of music (circa A.D. 650 to A.D. 1350).

Nondominant seventh chord   A diatonic seventh chord that does not have dominant function. Since dominant and leading-tone seventh chords are considered to have dominant function, then all others are nondominant seventh chords.

Nonharmonic tone   A tone that does not fit into the surrounding harmony. (See anticipation, appoggiatura, changing tone, escape tone, neighboring tone, passing tone, pedal tone, retardation, suspension, below.)

Nonharmonic tone—anticipation   A nonharmonic tone that anticipates a chord tone in the following chord. Anticipations are normally approached by step and the anticipated tone is repeated in the following chord.

Nonharmonic tone—appoggiatura   A nonharmonic tone preceded by a leap and resolved by step.

Nonharmonic tone—changing tone   Two successive nonharmonic tones. Leads from a chord tone by step, leaps to another nonharmonic tone, then leads to a chord tone by step.

Nonharmonic tone—escape tone   A nonharmonic tone that is approached by step and resolved by leap.

Nonharmonic tone—neighboring tone   A nonharmonic tone that is approached by step and left by step in the opposite direction.

Nonharmonic tone—passing tone   A nonharmonic tone that is approached by step and left by step in the same direction.

Nonharmonic tone—pedal tone (pedal point)   A held or repeated note, usually the lowest-sounding voice, which alternates between consonant and dissonant relationships with the chords above it.

Nonharmonic tone—retardation   A nonharmonic tone similar to a suspension except that the resolution is upward instead of downward.

Nonharmonic tone—suspension   A nonharmonic tone that is held over from a previous chord tone and resolves downward by step. The three phases of suspension are preparation, suspension, and resolution.

Nontransposing instruments   Instruments in which the produced pitch is the same as the written pitch.

Notation—mensural   Measured notation. First drawn up by Franco of Cologne in the thirteenth century. Bar lines did not appear until the seventeenth century.

Notation—tablature   Notation using letters, numbers, or a diagram. In the case of the vihuela, lute, and guitar, the diagrams frequently represented the strings of the instruments.

Ostinato   A short musical pattern which is repeated throughout a given passage. Ostinatos generally are a part of the supporting or accompanying material in a piece of music.

Parallel supporting melody   A melodic idea that moves essentially in parallel with either a primary or a secondary melody (PSM).

Pitch class   All notes of the same name on the keyboard.

Polyphonic texture   A musical texture consisting of more than one melodic line.

Prestissimo   As fast as possible. Faster than presto.

Presto   A very fast tempo. Faster than allegro.

Primary melody   The most significant melodic idea in a given musical texture (PM).

Quadruple meter   A meter consisting of four beats.

Rhythm   The movement of music in time. A pattern of uneven duration over the steady background of the beat.

Rhythmic support   The rhythmic aspect of the accompaniment in a homophonic texture.

Round   A canon at the unison. One singer begins the round and, upon reaching a certain point, is joined by a second singer who begins at the beginning. Rounds are usually in three or four parts.

Scale   A summary of the pitch material of a piece of music arranged in order from the lowest to the highest pitches.

Secondary melody   A melodic idea of lesser prominence in a musical texture (SM).

Sequence—modulating   A sequence that leads from one tonal center to the next. In some sequences of this type each segment is technically in a different key.

Seventh chord   A triad with an added factor a third above the fifth (seventh above the root).

Simple division   The division of the beat into two equal parts.

Simple meter   A meter that has a simple division of the beat.

Solfeggio   A system used to help singers remember the pitches of the various scale degrees in a diatonic scale.

Sonority   A group of pitches sounding at the same time. A simultaneity.

Spacing   The interval distance between voices or factors of a chord.

Staff   A group of five horizontal lines on which music is notated.

Standard 12-bar blues   Twelve-bar units repeated as many times as lyrics dictate. Accompanying each 12-bar unit is a routine harmonic progression (with several variants): I, IV, I, V, IV, I, V.

Static support   An unchanging element in a musical texture. Static supporting (SS) parts may be pedal tones or ostinatos.

Step progression   Selected tones from a melody that give it direction. Certain tones (usually not adjacent) proceed by stepwise motion either up or down to provide direction to the melody.

Subdivision   The division of the beat in simple meter into four equal parts or in compound meter into six equal parts.

Swing   The rhythmic style of most jazz, in which the division of the beats is uneven and there is considerable stress on the notes between beats.

Syncopation   A rhythm in which normally unaccented beats are stressed either through agogic or dynamic accent.

Tactus   The name given to the pulse in medieval and Renaissance music. The tactus was said to be equal to the heart rate of a person breathing normally (in the range of 60 to 70 beats per minute).

Temperament—equal   A system of tuning in which an octave is divided in 12 equal half steps. This leaves no pure intervals except the octave but makes possible the use of all 12 keys.

Temperament—just   A system of tuning in which both the fifths and thirds are pure (according to the natural overtone series).

Temperament—mean-tone   A system of tuning in which the pure fifths are compromised in favor of pure thirds.

Temperament—Pythagorean   A system of tuning in which the tones of the scale are arrived at by selecting a series of 12 pure fifths. This, of course, does not provide 2:1 octaves.

Tempo   The speed of the beat in music, which may be expressed in general terms or in beats per minute.

Tempus imperfectum   A rhythmic system of the medieval and Renaissance periods in which rhythmic values were divided in two parts.

Tempus perfectum   A rhythmic system of the medieval and Renaissance periods in which rhythmic values were divided in three parts.

Ternary form   See Three-part form.

Tessitura   The average range of a particular voice or instrument in a composition. If a tessitura is "high," the notes tend to be in the higher extreme of the total range of that voice or instrument.

Texture   A term that refers to the way the melodic, rhythmic, and harmonic materials are woven together in a piece of music.

Theme   A melodic figure or phrase that is the basis for a composition or section of a composition.

Three-part form   A form most often found in homophonic music, but existing as well in three-part polyphony, the first and third parts of which are either the same or nearly so. Usually designated by the letters A B A, three-part form is also known as ternary form.

Three-part form—incipient   Related both to two- and three-part form. Consists of three sections with the first and third similar, but with a middle section that is often shorter than the other two and that is frequently repeated along with the third section.

Tie   A curved line connecting two notes, which indicates that they are to be played as a single note.

Tonality   A system of tones (e.g., the tones of a major scale) used in such a way that one tone becomes central and the remaining tones assume a hierarchy that is based on their intervallic relationship to the central tone or tonal center.

Tone   A musical sound of definite pitch.

Tonic   The keynote of a piece of music. The tone that is felt to be a point of rest, where the music can logically conclude.

Tonic accent   An accent created when one note is higher in pitch than surrounding notes.

Tonicized chord   A chord that functions temporarily as a tonic (having been preceded by a secondary dominant).

Transposing instruments   Instruments that produce a pitch other than that written.

Transposition   The process of rewriting a piece of music or a scale so that it sounds higher or lower in pitch. This involves raising or lowering each pitch by the same interval.

Triad   Strictly speaking, a triad is any three-tone chord. In tertian harmony, a triad is a chord built in superposed thirds. The four types of triads are major, minor, diminished, and augmented.

Triad—augmented   A triad consisting of a major third and an augmented fifth above the root.

Triad—diminished   A triad consisting of a minor third and a diminished fifth above the root.

Triad—first inversion   The position of a chord in which the third factor is the lowest-sounding tone.

Triad—major   A triad consisting of a major third and a perfect fifth above the root.

Triad—minor   A triad consisting of a minor third and a perfect fifth above the root.

Triad—root position   The position of a chord in which the root is the lowest-sounding tone.

Triad—second inversion   The position of a chord in which the fifth factor is the lowest-sounding tone.

Triple meter   A meter consisting of three beats.

Turnaround (turnback)   A term used in popular song to denote four-chord formulas that signal the repetition of a period or return to a previous period. Typical turnabout: $I–vii°^7–ii^7–V^7$ (in popular music chord symbols in C major: $C—B°^7—D_M^7—G^7$).

Twelve-bar blues—standard   See Standard 12-bar blues.

Twelve-bar jazz blues   A variant of the 12-bar blues harmony characterized by ii^7 to V^7 progression in the ninth and tenth bars.

Twelve-bar jazz blues—modified   See Modified 12-bar jazz blues.

Two-part (binary) form   A form, often found in homophonic as well as polyphonic compositions, consisting of two organically related parts. Frequently the two parts are bound together by the same thematic material, but this is not always the case.

Unison   Two pitches that are the same. Several singers singing a melody together.

Whole step   An interval consisting of two half steps.

Credits

Figure 1.30: *Au Privave* by Charlie Parker. © 1956 Atlantic Music Corporation, Hollywood, CA.

Figure 1.31: *Our Musical Heritage: A Short History of Music,* 2nd ed., by Curt Sachs. Copyright © 1955, Prentice Hall, Englewood Cliffs, NJ.

Figure 1.32: An antiphon in Gregorian chant from *The Liber Usualis,* no. 801, ed. by the Benedictines of Solesmes. Copyright © 1952, Desclée & Co. Publishers, Belgium.

Assignment 1.7: "Bulgarian Rhythm" from *Mikrokosmos,* vol. IV, no. 115, by Béla Bartók. Copyright © 1940 by Hawkes & Sons (London) Ltd. Rencwed 1967. Boosey & Hawkes, Inc.

Figure 4.28: *Mr. P.C.* by John Coltrane. © 1977 Jowcol Music, Woodland Hills, CA.

Figure 6.2: "My Way" by J. Revaux and C. François. Words by Paul Anka. Original French Lyric by Gilles Thibault. Music by J. Revaux and C. Francois. © Copyright 1967 by Societe des nouvelles editions Eddie Barclay, Paris, France. © 1969 for U.S. and Canada by Spanka Music Corporation, 445 Park Avenue, New York, NY 10022. All Rights Reserved.

Figure 6.2: *Appalachian Spring* by Aaron Copland. © Copyright 1945 by The Aaron Copland Fund for Music, Inc. Copyright Renewed.

Figure 6.5: Symphony no. 5 in E-flat Major, op. 82, by Jean Sibelius. © Copyright 1915 by Wilhelm Hansen Musik-Forlag. Copyright renewed, Edition Wilhelm Hansen, AS, Copenhagen.

Figure 6.30: "I Walk the Line" by John R. Cash. © 1956 (Renewed 1984) House of Cash, Inc. (BMI)/Administered by Bug Music. All Rights Reserved.

Figure 7.2: *Taylor Made Piano* by Billy Taylor. From Billy Taylor's *Taylor Made Piano,* 1982, Wm. C. Brown Communications, Inc., Dubuque, Iowa.

Figure 7.4: Eight Etudes and a Fantasy for Woodwind Quartet by Elliott Carter. Copyright © 1955 (Renewed) by Associated Music Publishers, Inc. (BMI). International Copyright Secured. All Rights Reserved.

Figure 7.15: "Freely, Freely" by Carol Owens. Copyright © 1972 Bud John Songs, Inc. (ASCAP). EMI Christian Music Publishing.

Assignment 7.1: "Try to Remember." Words by Tom Jones. Music by Harvey Schmidt. Copyright © 1960 by Tom Jones & Harvey Schmidt. Copyright Renewed. Chappell & Co. owner of publication and allied rights throughout the world. International Copyright Secured. All Rights Reserved.

Figure 10.13: "Sweet Home Chicago" from Robert Johnson, composer. Horoscope Music Publishing Co., Jamaica, NY.

Figure 11.7: *Au Privave* by Charlie Parker. © 1956 Atlantic Music Corporation, Hollywood, CA.

Figure 13.9: "Try to Remember" from *The Fantasticks,* Words by Tom Jones. Music by Harvey Schmidt. Copyright © 1960 by Tom Jones & Harvey Schmidt. Copyright Renewed. Chappell & Co. owner of publication and allied rights throughout the world. International Copyright Secured. All Rights Reserved.

Figure 14.25: "I'd Like to Teach the World to Sing." Words and music by Bill Backer, Billy Davis, Roger Cook, Roger Greenaway. © 1971 Shada Music Co., Inc. Original record and commercial produced by Billy Davis.

Figures 14.28 and 14.29: "Nice Work If You Can Get It." Music and Lyrics by George Gershwin and Ira Gershwin. © 1937 (Renewed) George Gershwin Music and Ira Gershwin Music. All Rights administered by WB Music Corp. All Rights Reserved. Warner Bros. Publications U.S. Inc., Miami, FL 33014.

Figure 17.5: "Memory" from *Cats* by Andrew Lloyd Webber. Text by Trevor Nunn after T. S. Eliot. Music Copyright © 1981. The Really Useful Group Ltd. Text Copyright © 1981 Trevor Nunn and Set Copyrights Ltd. All Rights for The Really Useful Group Ltd. for the United States and Canada administered by Songs of PolyGram International, Inc. All Rights in the text controlled by Faber and Faber Ltd. and administered for the United States and Canada by R&H Music Co. International Copyright Secured. All Rights Reserved.

Musical Example Index

Minuet in G Minor, G. 242, 104
Te Deum (Chandos), 69
Harrison, Annie (1851–1944)
"In the Gloaming," 143
Hatton John (d. 1793)
"Duke Street," 30
Haydn, Franz Joseph (1732–1809)
Piano Sonatas
Sonata in A Major, Hob. XVI:5, 340–341
Sonata in A Major, Hob. XVI:12, 368
Sonata in A Major, Hob. XVI:30, 109
Sonata in B-flat Major, Hob. XVI:2, 267
Sonata in C Major, Hob. XVI:3, 142
Sonata in C Major, Hob. XVI:35, 248
Sonata in C-sharp Minor, Hob. XVI:36, 319
Sonata in D Major, Hob XVI:4, 143
Sonata in D Major, Hob XVI:33, 143
Sonata in E-flat Major, Hob. XVI:49, 127
Sonata in E Major, Hob XVI:13, 143
Sonata in F Major, Hob. XVI:9, 143
Sonata in G Major, Hob. XVI:11, 145
Sonata in G Major, Hob. XVI:40, 136
String Quartet in E-flat Major, op. 76, no. 6, Hob III:80, 158
Symphonies
Symphony no. 28 in A Major, 53
Symphony no. 94 in G Major ("Surprise"), 27
Symphony no. 95 in C Minor, 131
Symphony no. 97 in C Major, 250
Symphony no. 101 in D Minor ("Clock"), 130
Symphony no. 102 in B-flat Major, 123
Symphony no. 104 in D Major, 130
Trio no. 1 in G Major for Piano, Violin, and Cello, Hob. XV:25, 124
Herbert, Victor (1859–1924)
"Gypsy Love Song" from *The Fortune Teller,* 129
Hymn to Saint John *(Ut queant laxis),* 46

I

"I've Been Working on the Railroad," 142
Ives, Charles (1874–1954)
Three Places in New England, II: Putnam's Camp, Redding, Connecticut, 23

J

Jacquet de la Guerre, Elisabeth (ca. 1666–1729)
Sarabande from Suite in D Minor, 259

Johnson, Charles Leslie (1876–1950)
A Black Smoke Rag, 261
Johnson, Robert (1912–1938)
"Sweet Home Chicago," 221
Jones, Tom (1928)
"Try to Remember" from *The Fantasticks,* 159
Joplin, Scott (1868–1917)
Maple Leaf Rag, 240
Josquin des Prez (ca. 1440–1521), 148
"Faulte d'argent," 360
Tu Solus Qui Facis Mirabilia, 148

K

Kinney, L. Viola (ca. 1890–?)
Mother's Sacrifice, 240
Kirnberger, Johann Philipp (1721–1783)
Les Carillons, 54
Kulhau, Friedrich (1786–1832)
Sonatina in F Major, op. 55, no. 4, 249
Kyrie eleison, 360

L

Lalo, Victor A. (1823–1892)
Concerto Russe, op. 29, I, 120
"Las Mañanitas," 231
Legrenzi, Giovanni (1626–1690)
"Che fiero costume" from *Echi di riverenza,* 266
Liszt, Franz (1811–1886)
Au lac de Wallenstadt, no. 2 from *Années de pèlerinate, première annee, Suisse,* 160
"Londonderry Air," 339–340
"Long, Long Ago," 142

M

Mahler, Gustav (1860–1911)
"Urlicht" from Des Knaben Wunderhorn, 131
Mendelssohn, Felix (1809–1911)
Songs Without Words
Songs Without Words op. 19, no. 6, 160
Songs Without Words op. 30, no. 3, 366–367
Songs Without Words op. 30, no. 6, 149, 151
Songs Without Words op. 53, no. 3, 161
Songs Without Words op. 62, no. 1, 121
Songs Without Words op. 85, no. 6, 130
Monteverdi, Claudio (1567–1643)
"Lasciatemi morire" from *Lamento d'Arianna,* 238
Morley, Thomas (1557–1643)
"Nancie" from *The Fitzwilliam Virginal Book,* 133
Mozart, Wolfgang Amadeus (1756–1791)
Bastien und Bastienne, K. 50, no.1, 161
Don Giovanni, K. 527, act I, scene XIII, 258

Eine kleine Nachtmusik, K. 525, 53, 369–370
Fantasia in C Minor, K. 475, 296, 376
Piano Sonatas
Sonata in A Major, K. 331, 138, 317
Sonata in A Minor, K. 310, 34
Sonata in C Major, K. 309, 124, 128
Sonata in C Major, K. 545
Sonata in D Major, K. 284, 124, 143, 220, 259, 316, 318, 359–360
Sonata in D Major, K. 311, 311–312
Sonata in E-flat Major, K. 282, 143
Sonata in F Major, K. 332, 274
Sonata in G Major, K. 283, 256
Recordare from Requiem in D Minor, K. 626, 152
Sonata for Violin and Piano in G Major, K. 379, 242
String Quartet in A Major, K. 454, II, 72
Symphony no. 40 in G Minor, K. 550, 150, 155
"Viennese Sonatina" in C Major, after K. 439b, 267
Mussorgsky, Modeste (1839–1881)
"The Great Gate of Kiev" from *Pictures at an Exhibition,* 92

N

Nunn, Trevor (b. 1940)
"Memory" from *Cats,* 361–363

O

Owens, Carol (b. 1931)
"Freely, Freely," 150

P

Palestrina, Giovanni Pierluigi da (ca. 1525–1594)
In Festo Transfigurationis Domini, 157
Parker Charlie (1920–1955)
Au Privave, 14, 239
Purcell, Henry (1659–1695)
"Chaconne" from *King Arthur,* Z. 628, 133
Minuet from Suite no. 8 in F Major, Z. 669, 296
"Thy Hand Belinda" from *Dido and Aeneas,* Z. 626, 42

R

Rameau, Jean Philippe (1683–1764)
"Guerriers, suivez l'Amour" from *Dardanus,* 120
Ravel, Maurice (1875–1937)
"Laideronnette Imperatrice des Pagodes" from *Ma mère l'Oye,* 40–41
Reichardt, Louise (1779–1826)
"Die Blume der Blumen," 236
Revaux, J. (b. 1940)
"My Way," 120
Rimsky-Korsakoff, Nicholas (1844–1908)
Scheherazade, op. 35, 119

Subject Index

Neighboring tone, 102, 176, 181, 201
Neoclassicism, 151
Neumatic notation, 15–16
Neumes, 15, 392
The New Real Book series, 85, 377
Ninth chord, 77
Noncircle progression, 215, 276, 277–278
    with resolution, 241
Nondiatonic scale, 41–44
Nondiatonic tones, 274, 288, 291
Nondominant seventh chord, 271–286,
        374, 392
    in circle progressions, 276
    noncircle treatment, 277–278
    voice leading of, 278
Nongapped pentatonic scales, 41
Nonharmonic tone, 97, 102–103, 156,
        392
    accented neighboring tone, 105
    accented nonharmonic tone, 103,
        104–109
    accented passing tone, 104–105
    accented versus unaccented non-
        harmonic tones, 109
    anticipation, 102, 104, 111, 392
    appoggiatura, 102, 108–109, 111, 392
    changing tone, 109, 110, 111, 392
    double neighboring tones, 110
    escape tone, 102, 103–104, 111, 392
    inverted pedal tone, 110
    involving more than three pitches,
        109–111
    neighbor group, 110
    neighboring tone, 111, 392
    passing tone, 102, 111, 392
    pedal tone (pedal point), 109, 110, 111,
        153, 392
    preparation, 106, 107
    resolution, 106, 107
    retardation, 102, 108–109, 111, 392
    successive passing tones, 109, 110
    suspension, 102, 106–109, 111, 392
    unaccented neighboring tone, 103
    unaccented nonharmonic tone, 103
    unaccented passing tone, 103
Nonperiod construction, 129
Nontonal transposition, 66
Nontraditional scale, 44, 46
Nontransposing instruments, 385, 392
Non-Western scales, 43
Nota cambiata, 176
Notation
    beam, 17–18
    directions for, 16–20
    duration, 8–9
    dynamic, 14–15, 20, 390
    flag, 18, 390
    head, 16
    history, 15–16
    instrumental notation, 20
    intensity, xiv
    mensural notation, 16, 392
    neumatic notation, 15–16
    piano notation, 20
    pitch, 3
    present notation, 16
    staff, 3, 4–5, 393

stem, 16
tablature, 392
vocal notation, 18
Notehead, 16

O

Oblique motion, 170, 171
Oboe, 380
Octatonic scale, 43
Octave, 56
Octave doubling, 147
Octave identification, 6–7
Open formal divisions, 337
Orchestra, 380
Organum, 77
Ostinato, 153, 392
Outer voices, 80, 202, 203
Overlap, 202

P

Palestrina, Giovanni Pierluigi da, 165
Parallelism, 147
Parallel motion, 171
Parallel perfect fifths, 201, 202, 241
Parallel perfect octaves, 201
Parallel period, 125
Parallel relationship, 38–39
Parallel supporting melody, 153, 392
Parallel unisons, 201
Partials, xv–xvi
Part song, 345
Part writing, 297–298
Passing bass six-four, 201
Passing tone, 102, 111, 173
Pedal bass six-four, 201
Pedal point, 110
Pedal tone, 109, 110, 111, 153
Pentatonic scale, 40–41
Percussion, 387, 388
Perfect authentic cadence, 98, 101, 129,
        191, 337
Perfect consonance, 170, 171, 172, 173,
        175
Perfect fifth, 31, 75, 176
Perfect interval, 56, 57–58
Period, 125–129
    antecedent-consequent period, 125,
        127, 337
    contrasting period, 126–127
    double period (four-phase period),
        128–129, 390
    extended phrase, 130–131
    modulations in period construction,
        318–319
    parallel period, 125, 318
    phrase member, 124
    three-phrase period, 127–128
Phrase, 97, 123–124
    antecedent phrase, 125, 127
    chorale phrase, 194, 222–223
    consequent phrase, 125, 127
    extended phrase, 130–131
    four-bar phrase, 133, 134
    modification of a phrase, 129–131
    parallel period, 125, 318
    period, 125–129

repeated phrase, 129
three-phrase period, 127–128
Phrase member, 124
Phrase modulation, 317
Phrygian half cadence, 98
Phrygian mode, 44, 166, 169, 392
Pianissimo, xiv, 15, 383
Piano, xiv, 15, 383
Piano (instrument), 3–4, 6, 29, 32, 40, 380
Piano notation, 20
Pitch, xiv
    notation, 3
    octave identification, 6–7
Pitch class, 27, 393
Pitch inventory, 47
Pivot chord, 316
Plagal cadence, 99, 100, 389
Plagal mode, 44–45, 392
Plainsong, 16
Plucked strings, 387, 388
Polyphonic texture, 148, 392
Popular music, 381
    chord symbols, 83, 85–86, 239, 261,
        276, 377–378
    dominant seventh chord, 238
    harmonic progression, 220
    homophonic texture, 151
    leading-tone seventh chords, 261
    modulations, 321
    nondominant seventh chord, 276
    phrase construction, 134
    secondary dominant and leading-tone
        chords, 298–301
    seventh chords, 86
    ternary design, 361
    tritone substitution, 300–301
    two-part form, 345
Post-romantic and impressionistic period,
        380–381
    cadence types, 101
    dominant seventh chord, 238, 239
    harmonic progression, 220
    leading-tone seventh chords, 260
    modulations, 321
    nondominant seventh chords, 275
    phrase and period construction, 134
    secondary dominant, 298
    texture, 151
    two-part form, 345
Preparation, 106, 107
Present notation, 16
Prestissimo, 393
Presto, 383, 393
Primary dominant, 288, 289
Primary melody, 151–152, 393
Primary triads, 75
Prolongation, 256
Protestant Reformation, 379
Pulse, 10, 12
Pure fifth, 61
Pythagorean temperament, 393
Pythagorean tuning, 61

Q

Quadruple meter, 392
Quarternary form, 361